MEMORIES
for
TOMORROW

The Memoirs of
Jean-Louis Barrault

MEMORIES
for
TOMORROW

translated by
Jonathan Griffin

LONDON
THAMES AND HUDSON

for Madeleine

Acknowledgments
The photographs are from the archives of Jean-Louis Barrault except the
following: Service de documentation photographique Paris, 11; Cliché S. N.
Pathé Cinema, 18; National Film Archive, 19; Roger Viollet, 35, 46, 54;
Photo Pic, 39–45; The National Theatre, 48; Camera Press, 50.

First published in the United Kingdom in 1974 by
Thames and Hudson Ltd, London
Souvenirs pour demain © 1972 Jean-Louis Barrault
English translation © 1974 Jonathan Griffin

ISBN 0 500 01086 2

Printed in Great Britain by
Hazell Watson and Viney Ltd,
Aylesbury, Bucks

Contents

The status of actors
was the lowest of the low among the Romans
and an honourable one among the Greeks:
which is it with us?
We think of them like the Romans,
we live with them like the Greeks

(La Bruyère)

To the reader

While my inner orchestra is tuning up.

IT IS SCRUPLE that has made me treat this autobiography in the form of 'stories'. Though I have worked conscientiously to avoid romancing, I cannot guarantee the historical, or even police-court, exactitude of the facts I have remembered.

Clever indeed the man who can say what exactly his life has been! And clever indeed the man who could tell me what my life has been! I have my own impression, you have yours.

Also, there can be no question of my analysing myself or judging myself: either I would be presenting myself to my own advantage; or else, craftily, exaggerating my faults.

At each moment of our existence we are living on at least three planes:
- we are
- we think we are
- we want to appear.

What we are – we do not know. What we think we are – we imagine. What we want to appear – we get wrong.

Added to which, a man is not *one*, but three. And indeed *many more*. We are one in three persons: head, heart and belly.[1] And on the top of the tetrahedron there appears 'the Double', while in the most remote recesses of our Being there are, moving about, yet other 'Presences'.

In reality, each of us is in himself a society, a realm, a world – a universe at the bottom of a well: an inner population, a mob, in the midst of which one feels, in the last resort, alone. There lies the torment.

Gods, deliver me from my sterile torment. (Æschylus)

Torment, sister of my solitude . . . because, at the end of the road, there is Death. And yet, up to this day, I have been cheerful and happy. For this I thank my star.

I happened once to be lunching with a young woman who had everything in her favour: beauty, birth, wit, wealth. But as we talked of this and that, I began to discover in her what seemed like a caged animal, suffering, unhappy. I was intrigued. Our conversation grew more and more intimate and serious, affectionate, close. I questioned her with real concern. At one point she said to me:

'And you – tell me!'

I was not expecting my life to interest her, and I said so.

'No,' she said, 'tell *Me*!'

[1] Plato.

7

She wanted me to describe *her*. I refused, pointing out that she would not recognize herself.

What we are, what we have lived . . . God alone knows, 'and I know him, he'll not tell us' (Feydeau).

I notice that the first two writers I quote from are Æschylus and Feydeau. Life lies between the two. In Æschylus's time a poet was expected to treat a subject in the form of a tragic trilogy plus a fourth play, a comic one, on the same subject, treated from the angle of 'the absurd'. Each event in life has in fact its absurd aspect.

Third writer, Kafka: 'Don't take things too seriously.'

In the seething broth of those 'farces' which animate us, there are abysses, unknown lands that appear all of a sudden. There are eyes in that 'broth', they are the surprise sides of our Being, like those 'windows' in mountainous country through which one catches sight of new horizons: the points of mystery.

My mother was apt to be considered by other people as a charming, feckless and superficial woman; at the moment of her death she appeared to us as a grave and strong patriarch. She had become another person.

At each moment of existence we are Other to ourselves and to the Others. A human being is unforeseeable. And lastly, we think we are whole, when we are only one half of a worm in search of its other half: our need of love. To join together again the whole worm, the androgyne, is the first of all our instincts. We are halves of unity. The Creature joined together again is the couple.

Mesa, I am Ysé, it's I. (Claudel, *Partage de Midi*)

That instant when the two halves come to a standstill facing each other. A strange silence falls, and the subterranean dialogue is joined. There is no longer either time or space, it is the lightning-flash discharge of the Present. The minute of Truth, when bullfighter and bull have just met.

Ysé, I am Mesa, it's I.

We actors, when we come on stage, must in theory concentrate on the following three questions:
   – Where do I come from?
   – What state am I in?
   – What am I here to do?

I shall try to answer the first question correctly. You will imagine the second. As for the third, my suggestion is: try to understand. This is my aim in life. It is why I love this phrase of Lenin's:

Learn, learn so as to act and understand.

It is not by inclination that I am setting out on this walk – the past lacerates me. It is to obey a command: it is salutary sometimes to obey.

From the confusion of my memories I have chosen – for the sake of the unity of the subject which I am – those that have struck me, struck as a medal is struck; out of brotherhood towards the reader, those that could be generalized and become adopted by all; and finally, from a sense of their usefulness, those that might have some importance for my conduct today and tomorrow. 'Memories for tomorrow' – why not?

In the theatre, as I shall show in detail, we pursue a personal dream and, at the same time, we have the secret desire that our individual sensations may be shared by as many people as possible. We want for ourselves a collective heart. May it happen like that in the present case.

One last word: a walker stops sometimes. He pauses. He changes his objective. He was looking at the view – now he contemplates a blade of grass, or he withdraws into himself. I shall now and then do the same, suddenly, for no apparent reason. I invite you at those times to sit down with me, side by side, for the sake of the grass-blade, or the view, or ourselves.

ONE

I was not born to share hatred, but love.
                    (Antigone)

The Wild Sapling

MY MOTHER brought me into the world on 8 September 1910 at ten in the morning, according to the register in the *mairie*. This happened at 11, rue de l'Eglise, Le Vésinet – a residential suburb of Paris, seventeen kilometres from Notre Dame.

My father, Jules Barrault, was a young chemist there. His dispensary was a modest one, and he made both ends meet by working at the lunatic asylum in the neighbourhood. His real love was politics: he was a socialist, one of the first Leninists, out of idealism. Deep down in him he felt as a poet, which made him faint at the sight of blood when an injured man was brought into his shop. He was thirty-four, and had only eight more years to live.

My mother, Marcelle Hélène, née Valette, must have been barely twenty-five. As regards the 'happy event', let us recall that 1910 is a year remembered for the floods in Paris, that 8 September is the birthday of the Virgin, to whom I was naturally dedicated – and still gladly dedicate myself, as I do to the colour blue which goes with her. Also that 8 September is the birthday of Alfred Jarry. The Virgin, Jarry and myself: I like this company.

September eighth! I have often imagined how, round about the eighth of the preceding December, in a time of winter frost, two young people had drawn close, lain down, embraced and made love, to become, by the light of their mutual spark, my father and my mother.

I was not the first to come and disturb the peace of that home. For four years already a little boy had been reigning there. He was 'the image of his father': dark, delicate-featured, on the tall side, with an ice-blue gaze and an enchanting face in a halo of long black locks. He answered to the name of Max-Henry. Max, my brother!

My parents had warned him of my coming. He had accepted the 'good fortune', elegantly and generously. All the same, a week later, when the maternal tenderness was busy with powdering my buttocks, he asked: 'Is my little brother going to stay long?'

In point of fact my mother, after managing a boy, had wanted a girl. As I was emerging from my boat of placenta, the doctor cried out: 'What a fine little boy!'

My mother then moaned, half smiling, half wincing: 'Ah, *merde*!'

That is the first word I heard on earth. In France it has the reputation of bringing luck.[1] My life, up to now, supports that. And it is doubtless from

[1] *Merde*, meaning 'shit', is used, for instance, by students just before an exam, to wish each other luck. (*Translator's note.*)

11

Marcelle Barrault, with her outspoken language, that I get mine. My mother
had done her job well: I weighed nine pounds. Out of scientific curiosity the
doctor weighed the lot – baby, placenta and the rest: fifteen pounds in all.

I must have been very ugly: screwed-up eyes, mouth a gash from ear to ear,
not a single hair on the skull, an enormous head lolling in all directions over
a body all rolls of fat. Apparently I took eighteen months to find any sort of
way of moving, well or ill: bandy legs, body bloated from all that pap. Ugly,
but probably of a happy disposition, since my sweetest delight was to sit on
the warm and springy cushion of nappies which I had just not merely soiled
but filled. There was something of the baby Gargantua in my case. Too bad
if this reflection should seem pretentious. Anyhow, these things are only
stories. I was not worried about any of that. I had been given life, I was living.

I have always had what a doctor friend of mine has diagnosed as a
'leisure complex'. I am ready to lose anything you like except one thing:
time. This is because, as far back as my memories go, I have always found
myself in the company of Death. The joy of living is so great that none of
it must be lost; but at the same time life seems so unsure. It is so beautiful
that it can't last. Well, last is what it must, and to make it last it must be
kept filled. Art is long, life is short, there must be no missing the art of
living.

Recently, driving my car, I had become lost in my thoughts. My double,
who never leaves me and with whom I chat constantly, muttered: 'What
are you looking for? Have you lost something?' 'Yes,' I answered, 'a
minute.' That minute of which, one day, death will rob me.

So there is no reason why I should not have been caught, as early as my
first breath, by this panic frenzy.

There is one thing I must state as a fact, for it continued for a very long
time: my mother, wanting a daughter, always considered me as one. She used
to call me her 'little girl', and my brother used to call me 'ma Nénette'. The
word caught on during the 1914 war: two little woollen dolls which people
sent to the soldiers to protect them were called Nénette and Rintintin. Max
took possession of Rintintin, so I was Nénette.

I can see from here the psychoanalysts screwing up their noses, stalking
a neurosis. 'That child who sits laughing out loud among his excretions,
who wipes his bottom with the window curtains [another of the family
stories] and whom his mother – note that: his mother – calls her little
girl – is sure to come our way!'

I have nothing against Freud, whom I regard as a genius. A few months
ago I re-read the story of his life. He is the hero of the id, the ego and the
super-ego. He suffered, for us, all the cruelties of the unconscious – but,
with all the respect, admiration and affection I bear him, I have the impression that what he suffered from his own temperament made him
unable to resist his longing to make us believe we were all afflicted as he
was.

For the moment let us return to that child, less than two years old, who had been christened Jean-Louis. O yes, with a very lukewarm Christianity! My father, as a free-thinker, would have preferred us to choose our religion at the age of eighteen. He had his scruples. And indeed, why at eighteen? The family must have said to him: 'None of that nonsense!' And he being courteous, the boys were baptized. In those days he contented himself with attending, as first assistant to the mayor of Le Vésinet, the republican ceremonies of 14 July. The family savoured the story of the mayor's famous speech when, in front of the unfurled flag (there were not yet all those monuments to the dead, clearly a recent invention), he had celebrated the virtues of the three colours of France in these terms:

'Red,' he proclaimed, 'symbol of the blood shed for the Fatherland; white, symbol of the purity of the French soul, Joan of Arc. . . .' When he came to blue, after a short hesitation, he plunged: 'And as for blue – if it were green, it would be hope!' (Thunderous applause.)

Le Vésinet had an amateur dramatic society, called 'L'Essor'. My youthful father and mother were members of it, and acted in comedy. My father, it seems, was excellent in François Coppée's *Le Luthier de Crémone*. My mother had a pretty voice, a ravishing monkey-face and a catlike gaze. This cat had also *du chien* – could charm the birds off the trees. Life at Le Vésinet must have been very pleasant and carefree. Unfortunately the Barrault couple's theatrical career was cut short, for when I was two my parents presented me with Paris.

My father had taken a chemist's shop in the Avenue Wagram. We lived at 142, rue de Courcelles. This elegant quarter, the Plaine Monceau, was gripped between the Place des Ternes – its bachelor rooms, its kept girls coming downstairs in their fur coats to fetch their milk – and the Batignolles quarter: a real village, of which there are so many in Paris. I have in mind especially the village of Passy, where unknown to me a little girl called Madeleine Renaud was playing with her little cousin, Christian Bérard.

Away beyond, far and wide over Paris from Maxim's to the Moulin-Rouge, with Feydeau at the head, the gay life was in full swing. A real before-the-war life. But of this too I knew nothing – and indeed, what could I have done about it?

So much for the 'legendary' part, about my birth. While waiting for real memories, let us examine my ancestral inheritance: my atavism – 'the situation', according to Sartre – the genetic code, according to the biologists – 'your pedigree', whispers my double, as usual mockingly.

MEMORY FROM BEFORE MY BIRTH

I believe deeply in memory before birth.

Our imagination exists only if it can play with our memory, with the store, the great bazaar of everything we have registered. If what we had at our disposal, to recompose according to our fancy, were merely the materials we accumulate after our birth, imagination would be a late and poor faculty and might even be possible only at the moment when we have lost the strength and desire to play.

Luckily our genetic past holds itself in reserve deep down in us, and it looks as if, from the first post-umbilical cry onwards, we are already capable of inventing all sorts of stories whose source lies in what we get from our ancestors.

Imagination, play of memory. This idea is a favourite with present-day biologists, who because of it join up again with mythology. For myself, I feel a physical satisfaction every time Science turns out to be in agreement with Poetry. Ever since Antiquity the nine Muses, symbol of human imagination, have been the daughters of Mnemosyne, of Memory.

So it was not mere literature, it was true, concrete, real? Deciphering reality is what I delight in.

The concrete! What one holds in one's hand, what one can touch, sniff, eat, grip, salivate, sweat. Being! It already smells of a stage, it seems to me.

For the moment, let us observe the individuals out of whom the cells of my organism were made.

Paternal branch

The Barraults are pure Burgundians from Tournus. A small Gallo-Roman, chiefly romanesque town, famous for its rose-pink stone church: the Abbey of Saint Philibert, in the pure romanesque style.

The first Barrault recorded at the Town Hall was a *maître chamoiseur* (master leather dresser) – his job was tanning chamois skins. In 1698 he had acquired a piece of land at the spot called 'Beauregard', in the hamlet of La Croix-Léonard: a vineyard overlooking the town, with a view that extends two hundred kilometres eastwards. The old house has been replaced: one stone bit, bearing the date 1623, has been preserved and cemented into the new house, which dates from 1850.

From the foot of the house the rows of vines flowed away. We have the house still. To us it is sacred, even though there are now only fields there. The vines have been pulled up, killed by the wines of the Midi, by the spirit of speculation and political deals. This made a lifelong impression on me. It is a major factor in my conduct till now, and to come. I know properties that have been bought by people who were reimbursed on condition that they destroyed everything. That was called *la prime à l'arrachage* – premium for uprooting: it could be as truly called a premium for murder. Never could the anarchists, in the conventional sense of the word, have done as much. The State: a murderer. The politicians: criminals. Birth of my rebellion.

From the terrace in front of the house, in clear weather (which is a sign of rain next day), you can see the range of the Jura, the Alps and the massif of Mont-Blanc. At our feet: Tournus – its romanesque belfries, the broad ribbon of the Saône, and then the vast plain of Bresse, garnering maize and chickens.

One of the Barraults, François, was mayor of Tournus; he was, they say, a hatter. But all of them were 'owner-winegrowers' down to my grandfather Henri-Philibert, whose vineyards were his only trade.

The men used to choose their wives, by preference, from Mâcon. One of these seems to have brought to one of my forefathers, as part of her dowry, a house of which M. de Lamartine was a tenant. He never paid his rent. My ancestor, inflamed to white heat, to crime heat, by his wife the owner, went off to Mâcon. Lamartine defeated him. When he got back to Tournus, he had to confess to his wife that the poet not only had still not paid, but had borrowed money from him.

The blood of the Barraults, then, comes of pure Burgundian juice. For three centuries wine has flowed in our veins. I feel I am a peasant. In point of fact my hands are more like great paws.

'Old Barrault' was an odd fellow: a practical joker, a rowdy and sometimes cruel. A true child of the region.

His last wishes sketch a good likeness of him. In his will he had stipulated that his coffin should be placed in his vat room. One of his casks, a small quarter-cask of white wine (25 litres) was reserved for this ceremony. It was to be placed at the foot of the catafalque, together with two glasses. The first glass was to be set, filled, on his coffin. Each of his friends in turn was to fill the other glass at the tap and drink Old Barrault's health. This rite done, his own glass was to be taken and offered to the first passer-by on the road. Winegrowers are artists.

He had two sons, Adolphe and Jules; I don't know which was the elder. For them their father had planted a lime tree at each end of the terrace. Adolphe, when a twenty-year-old sailor, was murdered in a brawl at Toulon. Jules vanished in 1918. Old Father Barrault did not recover from the blow. The weatherbeaten stone of our vault at Tournus is raised on four hefty lion-claws. It is simple, leprous and beautiful. There they all rest in peace. On the terrace, the two lime trees are still there. They are now a hundred years old. I love their bark like my own skin.

What made my father choose a chemist's shop – he, a man who was constantly homesick for the house where he was born? A man who dreamed only of Lamartine, Samain, Verlaine and universal brotherhood?

Maternal branch

My mother was born in the heart of Paris, in the rue Rambuteau. I would like to be able to say that this maternal branch of the family was Parisian, for there are few places as harmonious as the *quais* of the Seine. I love Paris boundlessly and suffer from all the things that are done to her, the jealousies she arouses. This conglomeration of villages will never feel provincial. The spirit of Paris is unique, it is to be found nowhere else. Besides, Madeleine Renaud was born in Paris, her ancestors go no further afield than the Ile-de-France, and her mother, apparently by chance, was also born in the rue Rambuteau.

With her broad forehead and small chin, Madeleine has the Reims smile.

When we travel about the world with our company, we bring with us not only France, but particularly Paris. *The pride of Paris* – the phrase was up in lights on the front of the Winter Garden, New York – on Broadway. Were we proud! Paris made us, to Paris we belong.

But on the plane of ancestral inheritance let us remain objective. This maternal branch was formed by the convergence of two spearheads. One, from my grandmother's side, comes from Lorraine; where, I don't know, but from the east of France. The other, from my grandfather's side, comes from the centre, from the Bourbonnais. Mind, I did not say Auvergne! My grandfather would have exploded. Although, from his village, it would have taken only a few metres to pass from the one province into the other, he would not have it that he was an Auvergnat. In fact he possessed the qualities and defects of one. But he would not admit it.

My maternal grandfather? A fantastic specimen! We fought a great deal, but I admired him and still do. He must have influenced me at many points by winning me over as well as by hardening my position. Monsieur Valette, a real character out of a novel, worthy of Balzac.

He was called Louis-Charles-Camille-Napoléon-Eugène. Born on the same day as Prince Eugène (1856) he counted as the Emperor's godson and received his *louis d'or* every year. He was therefore a Bonapartist, sported a moustache and small pointed beard in the style of Napoléon III, and had even pushed imperial zeal so far as to have the same stature as Napoléon I.

He was possessed of an overwhelming vitality and a health that would stand anything. In the comedy of my life, grandfather Valette is a major role, in theatre language a plum. Something between Labiche and Henri Becque. Balzac, did I say? Let us keep him for the actual memories.

He was worthy of his mother. I did not know her, but from all accounts she was worth knowing. She had come in clogs all the way from the gorges of Chouvigny (Auvergne or Bourbonnais?) to do domestic service in Paris. She had set her choice on a working mason, and married him; she had accumulated a small fortune by buying town houses in disrepair and doing them up with the help of her mason husband, whom she made sweat for it – houses which she sold as soon as they were put to rights, in order to buy another house in disrepair, do it up, sell it and so on. How odd that I never knew that woman and yet, faithful to her destiny, have done the same thing with theatres through which I have passed – the Marigny, the Odéon, etc.; only I did not sell them, I was driven out of them.

This great-grandmother of mine had a funny temperament. When she had eaten and drunk too much, she would leave the table at the dessert stage, go into the kitchen, pull away the gas pipe, attach one end of it to the tap in the sink and dig the other end into her backside and there! – she had a self-service cold water enema. Relieved in this way, she could return to her place at the family table and finish her meal with appetite.

One day she got it into her head that the reason why the cat and the parrot were not on good terms was that they had never been introduced to each other, so she put the cat into the parrot's cage. Feather and fur flew and the screeches were terrible. Slightly disappointed by this 'unexpected' reaction, she separated them.

She died of bronchial pneumonia at the age of eighty-nine. The doctor, as he listened to her chest, muttered : 'I can hear noises !'

'Bloody idiot !' she answered. 'Those are street noises.' And she expired.

Her man must, I imagine, have dreamed only of emancipation. He was a *communard*; but I am much afraid he may never have been allowed to speak a word.

Louis Valette was a worthy son of his mother. As a young man he worked in a factory making liqueur boxes – those old inlaid boxes now so sought after by the antique dealers. In that factory there were three marriageable daughters : Cécile, Hermance and Berthe. With a view to becoming one day the owner, he entrusted an old friend of his mother's with the task of going and choosing one of these daughters for him. A tea party was arranged. The old friend arrived. Cécile brought in tea, Hermance the sugar, Berthe the little cakes. The old 'Célestine' appraised each of the fillies and, on her return, told the young man : 'Ask for Hermance.' That is how my grandmother was chosen. A gentle and distinguished woman, she was less resigned than she appeared, but possessed a mysterious tactfulness.

Sensing that the luxury craft of making liqueur boxes was going to suffer from competition with more fashionable gadgets, Louis Valette abandoned it and set up as a chandler at 55, rue de Lévis. This was a small shopping street, a real market at the centre of a very high class quarter – aristocracy and private houses. My grandfather had two principles :

a) To sell perishable goods, otherwise one has soon exhausted the valuable customers. (For this reason he had no use for liqueur boxes, or for antique dealers.)

b) To make your fortune, there are two methods :

    1. make money,

    2. cut down overheads.

This seems beyond criticism : it is what is called French common sense.

My grandmother, who was the cashier, never spoke of her husband except as 'Monsieur Valette'. At table she would call him '*mon petit Jésus*'. They loved each other deeply, and celebrated their golden wedding. I suspect them, however, of having each arranged a life of their own, to satisfy certain recesses of the soul which the other might neglect. . . .

A lusty man, a quick worker and with no time to lose, my grandfather got her with child five times : three miscarriages, a girl, a boy. The boy, Robert, was known as Bob. My uncle played a very important part in my life : let us put him aside for the moment.

Families go through periods of ascendance, and it must be clear by now that my grandfather corresponds to one of these. His education had been rudimentary, but he was an excellent autodidact and never stopped teaching himself, chiefly with the help of the *Dictionnaire Larousse*, and especially of its pink pages, from which one could learn by heart a lot of Latin quotations; at that time, it was useful to slip these into conversations in order to appear cultivated. A perfect specimen of the Parisian small shopkeeper, thrifty and ambitious, he would have bled himself white for his family. Indeed he did so. But his family had to pay the price. At table what a formidable moralist! One would have liked to hit him over the head with a rifle butt.

To satisfy his pride, he sent his children to the smartest schools. My mother was sent to the Convent which brought up the aristocratic hussies whose parents – or rather their chauffeurs – were customers of this naïf chandler. There my mother, poor thing, had to learn, the hard way, what are called class distinctions. The daughter of this small *bourgeois gentilhomme* was made to suffer the worst humiliations at the hands of the nobility, and this marked her for life.

She found human warmth again in the person of a splendid aunt, a typical large-hearted anarcho-populist. Aunt Adèle, with her usual plain speaking, would console her by saying: 'We are descended from the Crusaders . . . down the back stairs!'

Still, my mother did receive a particularly refined education (although, having suffered so much from it, she became the opposite of stuck-up). For example, it would not have entered her head to open a boiled egg with anything but the edge of a fork, certainly not a knife, nor even a spoon. She knew that salad is served in reverse order, the host helping himself first, for with salad 'politeness is at the bottom of the dish' (because of the dressing). Of course she used to cut all the cheeses before having them passed round, etc. With her, service at table could be reduced to the utmost simplicity, but never would a fault of that kind have been committed. She had, above all, an obsession about not leaving a mark on her glass when she drank. And in fact, how many people dirty the edge of their glass with the grease from their lips, when these are still shiny with food; it is enough to make one sick. I have retained the same disgust, to the point of obsession, and I know why. It is because my life is exactly like a dirty glass.

My mother was engaged. The date of the marriage had been fixed. There was a meal. Her fiancé dirtied his glass outrageously. My mother broke off the engagement. But for that dirty glass, she would never have known my father and I would not be there. Chance and necessity.

But I am there. At the moment I am about four. At this age one can enter into the reality of existence. The memories are immediate.

Setting. In Burgundy: Beauregard, the Saône and Saint-Philibert de Tournus. In Paris: the Plaine Monceau, the Batignolles. Our home: rue de Courcelles. Grandfather's: rue de Lévis. (He has now retired from business and is living on his income. And from number 55 he has moved to number 43. Not complicated.)

The cast. A family composed, on the father's side, of refined middle-class peasants in love with poetry; on the mother's side, of well-to-do shopkeepers, essentially common, but sensitive to matters of art.

We shall now, as on television, interrupt the explanations that were meant for those unable to view the preceding episodes – myself the first, because not yet in the world – and shall at last allow the actors to come on the stage.

FIRST STEPS

When I was four, I was convinced that during the night before my birthday I would grow enormously, like Alice in Wonderland. Actually my horizon was scarcely higher than the top of a table; and when, on 2 August 1914, my father was called to the colours, all I perceived was a pair of red breeches. The rest was lost in shadow. This is my first memory of my father. Were there many others? A meagre, sad stipple! One night, the raspy touch of a trench beard, kissing me in my little bed. A visit on leaving – he had come to see his 'cat': she must have been enchanting.

Ah yes, 1915. A terrific expedition, to the wars. The 'cat' left for the front, taking her litter with her. It was in the North, at Saint-Mihiel. The guns rumbling. In the distance machine-gun fire. It is easy to imagine what went on in the heads of two little boys, aged nine and five, in the midst of all those soldiers: this was real as real could be. Our mother had managed to overcome all the difficulties, raise all the prohibitions, pass all the barriers. She wanted to see her man – her husband – she could not help it. We stayed with a marvellous lady who made us enormous slices of bread and quince jam. An indelible memory, which even today makes my mouth water. I adore quince jam. Memories are valid only if they crop up again in the present – le temps retrouvé.

Twenty-five years later, in '40, Madeleine would unwittingly repeat for me exactly the same exploit.

When I was six, tragedy came. The sense of misfortune makes itself felt like a pasty mouth, a taste of soap, a kind of sick feeling. We were at Beauregard, and the meal was coming to an end. Our parents were talking to each other harshly. They were quarrelling, it was clear. Max and I were asked to go and and play outside. It was summer, the windows were open. We made a pretence of running round the house, but we stopped 'out of breath' under the window to catch some words. Our parents were going to separate. . . . Why? I could not understand, but I felt as if the walls of our house were crumbling. My heart split in two. I ran off to hide in the box thicket, to cry. Did I understand why I was crying? Sometimes tears come before pain.

> The 'cat' must have made a blunder. And feelings, to my father, were no joking matter.

He went off again. The war continued.

He was a front line stretcher-bearer. My mother ran the chemist's shop, and there I played with the labels, with the powders like unleavened bread, with the small swing doors that divided the customers' area from the dispensary.

The smell of chemists' shops! It is my whole childhood. Here too the memory is actual. Other memories of smells: the oil-cloth in the kitchen of a small house at Poissy, rented by my grandfather; the smell of the great cabbage fields on the plain of Poissy, where men went out to shoot partridge. Those smells are associated with the rows between men already old, who threw chairs at each other's heads because of the Dreyfus case. The women would protect the children with their skirts, and we all took refuge upstairs while the beards shouted insults at each other.

> *Too young to have seen Sedan and too old for the Marne,*

my grandfather had become an exasperating patriot.

At a private school where I was sent to learn to read, I lost myself in the rusty hair of a little girl at the next desk. I loved the smell of her hair; so I loved her. I felt tenderness, I was six.

One day, apparently, I said: 'In my heart it is crowded, like in the métro.' My mother melted with tenderness at 'her little girl', the tomboy. Cat and kitten became thick as thieves, always exchanging endearments. Max grew serious: he played at taking the father's place. He was twelve. I learned to play by myself, under the tables. I acquired the taste for 'little huts'.

Spring '18 – my father now inoculated us with premonitions. He had been transferred to Le Havre Hospital, in the Kléber barracks. He felt death approaching and wanted to see his children again. We were sent to live out. I stayed with a lady called Mme Cauvin. I slept in her room. She was a widow. At nightfall, under the alarming light of the petrol lamp, she would climb on to her bed in her nightdress and talk to her husband – a portrait of him in uniform hung on the wall. Hallucinations! I hid under the bedclothes. Not far from me there was a parrot: he was covered with a rug, but in the morning, when daylight was restored to him, he would start crying:

'Jean-Louis, go to school. Quick, quick, quick!'

Then he would play parades, balancing on one foot, then on the other:

'Left, left, left right left, left, left . . .'

I was frightened and at the same time fascinated by the strangeness.

A nurse came regularly to fetch us to the barracks. A gigantic double iron gate, and now, in the opening, there appears a thin silhouette in sky blue, still young but with white hair. My father. We played with the soldiers. We waited for hours in the long rooms with their rows of white beds (like sand dunes, Jarry wrote).[1] Gloomy, mortuary scenes, from which my father's affection seemed to trickle, drop by drop.

Summer came; he took us, on leave, to Beauregard. Mother was not there. He talked to me – I think for the first time – as a little man. I hope I too took him seriously. He brought out fine bottles from the cellar. He taught us the taste for wine. We visited the vineyards. We took part in the vintage. When night came, we would lie, snuggling against him, on the wall of that terrace where I still never lie down without a shiver. He talked to us about the stars,

---

[1] 'Sengle' in *Les Jours et les Nuits*.

life, love, his approaching death, and our mother, whom he loved. There are two lines by him which stay in my memory:

> *My heart's an old man sitting on a hill*
> *Looking down at the road by which he came....*

That is himself at that moment: he was forty-two. Those nights at Beauregard when I was eight!

We returned to Paris. A reconciliation between Marcelle and him began. Alas, we would not see him any more.

He went back as a stretcher-bearer, to look after the wounded, but especially the soldiers with Spanish influenza. In fact it was typhus. He caught it and was carried off in forty-eight hours. By an irony of fate, when he collapsed he was on twenty-four hours' leave. Therefore, administratively, my mother was never a war widow. She had no right to a pension.

> This, without any doubt, was the starting-point of my taste for the absurd, my veneration for Kafka and my contempt for bureaucracy.

Jules Barrault died on 16 October 1918. At that time I was attending the communal school in the rue Ampère: my mother remembered her convent for rich people, my father was a socialist and my grandfather was thrifty.

Three weeks later the deliverance of the Armistice burst upon us. On that 11 November we were in class, and the general joy was all the greater because the master was an ex-service man, discharged on account of a severe wound. He walked with a stick.

Great was his surprise at discovering, in the midst of the general rejoicing and the shindy authorized in the name of the Victory of God's Justice, a child weeping in a corner. It was followed by a fit of righteous indignation, which made him give me such a thrashing that he broke his stick on my back. I returned home with my body all swollen. The 'cat' put out her claws. Next day we all met in the headmaster's study. The teacher denied nothing. The consequence was that my mother administered a couple of formidable blows to the ex-service man decorated with the *croix de guerre*. Had he not, after all, by beating me, insulted the dead?

> In so far as it is true that what we live through in childhood forges our character for ever, this event is surely one of the sources of the unpleasant-nesses I later had with the military – not forgetting the business of Jean Genet's *The Screens*.

Every time, in the great world, living people organize a war, for me they are insulting the dead and my father. Every time the ex-service men make a song and dance around their trophies, they seem to me ready to break their sticks on my back, and I have a vision of my mother boxing their ears in the very heaven of glory, to a noise of flags flapping. A dog that has been beaten never forgets.

Two years later my mother had decided to get married again: to a childhood friend, Louis Martin, a young officer in the Reserve, still hot from all his battles as a leader of tanks. He was elegant, of good family, an interior-designer and painter in watercolours, and, I suppose, not negligible as a male insect. He was about thirty. She teased the piano, he stroked the violin. Their idyll fed greedily on melodies by Saint-Saëns, Chopin and Massenet. Max was jealous: he had become more and more 'the father'. Every time the two lovers wanted to go out he would be laid low by a sudden pain. My mother would take off her hat and spend the evening fussing with the thermometer. Louis would bite his lips. And I would take refuge under the table, imagining that I was under a tent, out in the Sahara in conversation with some Bedouin chieftain. I had seen the film with Rudolph Valentino: *The Son of the Sheik*.

Max refused to go to the wedding. I gave them my benediction. The mere fact that my mother was basking in love made me happy. Nonetheless, a child who loses his father when he is eight is in danger of being an orphan till he dies. I have spent my life searching for the father figure: in Dullin, in Claudel, in Rabelais, and now in my juniors.

> An orphan does not manage to become a real adult. As regards the well-known theory of the war between father and son and the conflict of generations, I myself – and again may Freud forgive me – shall have experienced only the bitterness of frustration. On our first visit to the United States, as we came out from a lecture given at one of the Universities (Princeton, I believe), a student came up and said to me point-blank:
>
> 'I hate my father, what am I to do?'
> 'You hate your father?'
> 'Yes ...'
> 'Truly?'
> 'Yes.'
> 'Then kill him!'
> The conversation ended there.
>
> 'Not everyone can be an orphan,' Jules Renard used to say. I take this phrase to mean: 'Not everyone can have the homesickness for a father.' A corner of our being will suffer loneliness for life, and be nervous and fear-ridden.

My mother, Louis Martin, my brother (tamed at last) and myself quickly formed a team of four excellent comrades. Some evenings we played poker. When I had a good hand, the blood would rise to my forehead and even to my ears. When I had not, I would grow pale, and my eyes would dull. They, seeing so clearly what my hand was like, laughed themselves silly, and I, not understanding how they knew, became furious.

I have always been a bad player. When all is going well, I rush to shout it from the rooftops, and I awaken jealousy. When it is going badly I turn nasty.

On other evenings we were taken to the cinema. I was terrified by the silent films, which showed only robbers running over the roofs or climbing in through windows after crawling along the gutters. Fear entered into me and has never left me. Even today I have a child's fear of the dark. My vagabond imagination constructs a terrifying universe. When I go swimming, the water is filled with monsters. When I walk at night, they are watching me from behind every object. I get gooseflesh. My spinal column freezes with terror. If, crossing a road, it occurs to me that the bus might have run over me, the scene immediately becomes real, my legs tremble from emotion and I have to lean against a wall or something to recover my balance. Often a cry escapes me, because my mind has automatically imagined some horror. For some time I was a sleepwalker. Puberty, they said. It was chiefly fear of death : I used to stop myself from sleeping for fear of never waking.

Sunday morning was the morning for lying in bed late, in my mother's enormous bed. My brother Max would tease me. I was his scapegoat. He would stifle me under the bedclothes. This has made me a claustrophobe for life, and for me going in a lift is a martyrdom.[1] Max was also my protector; not a hair of my head must be touched. I was his own, his plaything, his 'nénette'.

Yes, charming comrades, but not very sure of themselves. Louis, who had gone away for four years of war when he was very young, had practically never worked. He had had a golden youth, riding and going to many parties. He was more at ease in gloves than with a hammer. Mother was weak and in love. This nice little set was short of money, or let it seep away. My brother, who was very sensitive, was unhappy at school. An authority was needed. Then began the reign of my grandfather (1920–1928).

CHILDHOOD, ADOLESCENCE

After the cruel disappearance of my father life had changed. The chemist's shop was liquidated, the rue de Courcelles abandoned. Like magnetized iron filings, the family clustered round Old Valette. He held the purse-strings. He had a house at the corner of the rue de Lévis (his fief) and the rue de la Terrasse. There he installed his daughter, her children and her second husband – cursing as he did so, inflicting sermons on us all, while supporting us all. We found him unbearable, but we were all very glad to eat at his table.

In my opinion, he was only once unforgivable. Bob, his son, had been severely wounded in August 1918, by a bullet which passed through both his thighs. Three months in hospital, then the Armistice. He returned to the paternal nest on crutches. He had just been through four years as an infantry-man in the trenches, 'among the vermin, in the urine and mud'.

His father's welcome to him was : 'Young man, that's not everything. You're a man now, you must earn your living. I give you a week to find a job, in a week's time you will not be living here any more.'

[1] *Newspaper item invented by my double:* A man, told that one day he would be shut in a box and the lid nailed down, has died of shock.

Bob answered: 'No, not a week, at once!'

Right about turn on his crutches, and he was gone.

For the first time in history the civilians had been frightened. Because of the aircraft and Big Bertha. They were taking vengeance.

War memorials were being unveiled. The Unknown Soldier was invented. Endless talk. Processions. Big speeches. Victory euphoria. And Clemenceau was sent home. It was because of my uncle and of the many others in his his situation that I learned by heart at a very early age these lines by Georges Chennevières:

> Hobbling old men! merciless, bloody killers!
> You, who take vengeance for your age on us
> And, dreading Death and cringing to her face,
> Point out to her where to find handsomer victims . . .
> I loathe you, not for having been plain cowards
> Or said nothing when it was time to speak,
> But for your speech when you ought to have said nothing:
> For having spattered those whom you owed silence
> With your orations, your condolences –
> With words that murdered them a second time.

Bob forgave his father; he was a splendid person. But he never completely recovered from the sacrifice of his youth. People are always talking about the ones who were killed, and those who were physically wounded (he was one of them). They mention too seldom those whose vitality was sapped by that horrible war, those who during a very slow agony retained the gaze of ship-wrecked men, those who became bores about Verdun and Les Eparges, those whose enthusiasm and curiosity about life had given place to cynicism and bitterness, and who slowly died of these things.

Barbusse, in *Le Feu*, tried to serve Justice. Hats were doffed to him and politeness was satisfied. Human animality was busy throwing itself into the good life. Gay evenings, bawdy talk, tales of war and of moppers-up of trenches, sensuality. There was a confusion between sexual power and fire power. 'You will not be a man, my boy, until you have had your first ejaculation!' I listened to it all, wide-eyed; it marked me, but in the opposite way.

And progress was galloping on: cars with differentials, Hertzian waves, the first crystal sets, broadcasting, negro art, the coming of Jazz, ragtime. At fifteen I was a champion at the Charleston. Lindbergh the flying fool. But also Nungesser and Coli.

> What is a dead man and who is there to remember us? (Claudel, *Tête d'Or*).

I was present at the post-war whirlwind.

Bob had found work in Les Halles, as a wholesaler in flowers imported from England and Holland. He started work at five in the morning. He was always exhausted. After his father's injustice he had been consoled by a young Montmartre model, who had become his mistress. It took two years to make my grandfather accept the idea that one could marry one's mistress (you would think we were back in the Dark Ages). And so Adrienne, who had the attractiveness of Frans Hals' *La Bohémienne* (in the Louvre), entered the family, digging a trench between modernism and tradition.

Every year, after raking in the rents that fell due on 15 January, my grandfather and grandmother, as respectable property owners, went off to Nice. A huge black leather trunk was loaded on to a taxi – one of those taxis which had won the battle of the Marne. They did not return till three months later, to rake in the rents due on 15 April.

In the interval we would receive a letter telling us that 'Mémée' had lit a cigarette from the rays of the sun, by using a magnifying glass; and then a parcel of sweets at the moment of the Carnival. They were perfect specimens of the small *rentier*, such as are still to be met with on the Promenade des Anglais.

I had passed through the six forms at the communal school in three years, for I was an excellent pupil, and I was now sent to the Collège Chaptal. Not to a *lycée*, especially not the Lycée Carnot. That would have been too *chic*, too snobbish, not for the likes of us.

My mother had a tough memory. Chaptal was a lay college, for the 'people', and the sciences and modern languages were taught there. Having no doubt exhausted the pink pages of the *Petit Larousse*, my grandfather, with dreams of putting me into some trade, now held that Greek and Latin were completely useless. I was content to fall in with whatever was thought best. As soon as I went to school I began gobbling up everything that was put before me. Indeed I possessed an unshakable credulity. I believed, for instance, that Napoleon III had won the battle of 'Plebiscite', a battle like Austerlitz or Marengo. The grown-ups laughed at me. But after all, it was not as stupid as all that.

Another blow from fate: Louis Martin fell ill. He had to have fresh air. Beauregard came to mind, and so all three – he, mother and Max – went off to the paternal house. Back to the soil! Five hectares of vineyards, one or two cows, a horse and the goat – enough to live on.

Bob was given possession of the flat in the rue de la Terrasse (which suited him since business was difficult), on condition that he gave me a bed and my dinner. I was to lunch with my grandparents. All this, of course by fiat of King Valette. So my mother was far away. And there was I, between my uncle and my grandfather. Between the cat and the parrot, now in the same cage. I was fourteen.

While my mother, unknown to me, had dreamed of the stage (she had a veneration for Réjane, whom she thought she resembled), Bob thought only of painting: he had a real talent for pastel. I was from now on, secretly, at grips with two vocations.

Let us now take the opportunity of painting a few pictures, including some portraits: it will make a change from a chronological account, which could become boring.

Education

To me school was the best of games. When I felt ill I concealed it, not to miss
going there. I have never understood why people who go blue in the face over
a bridge table, spend hours squinnying over crosswords, concentrate on a chess-
board as if their lives depended on it – why these people suddenly adopt an
expression of disgust, superiority and contempt when one mentions grammat-
ical analyses, problems of geometry, logarithms or questions of history : the
game is the same one, and is not any more tiring.

Suggest going and exploring a forest, or fishing for crayfish and kissing the
girls – that's fine; but to what are usually called 'games' I prefer school.

My brother attached too much importance to the personality of the teacher.
And it was because he would come up against a particular one in the following
year that he chose to cut short his studies. To me the teachers were, on the
whole, a huge joke. One had an enormous beard, another a beetroot where the
nose should be; this one had a lisp, that one, in the maths class, made us go
through gymnastics in an attempt to teach us 'common factors' and 'common
denominators'.

The 'profs' ! In my eyes, no more responsible than the insects that transport
the pollen. Some of them were intelligent, others real cretins. Just as everywhere, especially among pupils. You need very few people in order to have
before you the various samples of humanity. It can be seen at once in their
eyes.

No, the teacher has no importance. Just as in night-clubs, where the customer
is asked to bring with him his gaiety, the value of studies lies in the student.
Just as the value of the master lies in the disciple. This for the benefit of
present-day youth, who, as they too recognize, are sometimes – not always,
but sometimes – looking for an alibi, a way of escape.

I had a particular passion for maths, and more than once I have found the
solution to a problem in a dream. Above all, I loved solid geometry. To recon-
stitute in three dimensions an object of which one has only the projection in
one plane, to pass from the shadow which is cast to the 'thing' turning in the
light, is – oh yes ! – it is exactly like taking a text printed on paper and making
of it a show. This poetry of space was leading me on. But I was not yet aware
that that is what theatre is.

Education? It is, as Valéry said, to 'dabble in the unknown by means of
what one knows', and he adds : 'It is divine !' I agree with him.

Not that I think I was an out-and-out model student. Very much the
opposite. I was so happy at going to class that I was as jumpy as a flea. I was
noisy, I kept imitating, I made the others laugh. I was electric. Sometimes I
missed winning a prize because of my behaviour. I spent hours in the passage
because the teacher had turned me out; and my delight was to go and steal the
cleaner's broom, arrange it against the door and then make a noise, until the
exasperated teacher would rush to the door, open it and receive the broom on
his head. As for the ushers, those 'poor, seedy creatures' whose business was to
keep us under discipline between classes, we maltreated them as mischievously

as squirrel-monkeys. Little did I think that one day – but let us not anticipate. When I see my small poodle shaking my slipper in a pretence of hysterical rage, it reminds me of that time.

I was slightly ahead of the others and, more important, I was not growing very fast (I had adenoids, so I was the smallest in the class). The big ones bullied me and I fought back furiously like a devil – as I did with my brother.

I had worked out a method for learning my lessons. I played the teacher :

'You, so-and-so, stand up and say your lesson. Why are you blushing?'

'I haven't learnt it, sir !'

'Very well, nought for you.' (Of course I had chosen the classmate I liked least.)

Then I learnt two lines.

'So-and-so, say your lesson. . . . Is that all you know? Two lines?'

'Sir, I didn't have time; my mother. . . .'

'That's enough. Copy out three times. . . .'

Another two lines, and so on. When I knew the lesson perfectly :

'Barrault, my boy, say your lesson.'

I said it to myself out loud.

'Excellent, Barrault, ten marks.'

I had invented a philosophy : harmonism, according to which 'the drawing of the trajectory of one's life must make, on the day of one's death, a pretty curve.' Even today I have nothing against such an aesthetic wake.

Grandfather

At lunch I sat on his left and he watched me closely. Above us, in the centre, a large hanging lamp. Never any butter on the table. Once a year oysters (*portuguaises*) for Christmas, after the Midnight Mass. Chicken very very rarely. My grandmother, when she had finished her dish, would push the remains to the edge of her dirty plate, choose a fresh bit, put it on the same plate and ring. The maid arrived.

'Here's for you, girl.'

'Thank you, madam.'

And the maid would carry away the plate, the remains and her portion. I found that terrible. Was that, then, life between human beings? And yet my grandmother was kindness itself. I could not understand. The customs of civilization, no doubt.

Each Thursday my grandfather gave me ten francs.

'What are you going to do with them?'

'Don't know. Spend them, I suppose.'

'You little fool ! At your age, when my mother gave me twenty sous, I would bring back forty at the end of the week. I had bought sweets and sold them again. You'll never get anywhere in life.'

And so, one fine day, after having handed me the usual ten francs :

'What are you going to do with them? Don't know, as usual?'

'Yes, I know.'

'At last!'

'I'm going to give them back, because you get on my nerves!'

That was the first time I was called an anarchist. It was not to be the last.

For all that, when our back was turned, he never tired of praising us. We were paragons, the *nec plus ultra*, etc. Everything he did and said was *for our good*. And I think, when all is said and done, he was right. Nowadays parents dare not budge an inch. So many dreadful things have been said about them, poor wretches, they get complexes. And so the children come up against nothing but emptiness. Try playing squash without a wall.

When my grandfather had scolded us too much, a gentle voice could be heard:

'*Mon petit Jésus*, your friends are waiting for you.'

He would get up, go and clean his teeth, sprinkle himself with strong scent and depart to join some friends for a game of cards.

He thought he had found a way of making himself useful by committee work for the children of men killed on active service. This sometimes kept him out until two in the morning. My grandmother was not deceived. It was said in the family that one day he had been thrown out into the street in his briefs . . . by the husband. He was then nearly eighty. Either these are old wives' tales, or the future belongs to us.

Sometimes also he would sing at table. It was he who taught me all the tunes from Offenbach's *La Vie Parisienne*. He used to go to the Théâtre Moncey because there one could smoke and read one's paper. Ah, what a customer he was! He would travel kilometres to bring back a kilo of apples because they were two sous cheaper. One day he brought back a couple of dozen collars which he was never able to wear – too small! But they were so cheap. . . . Towards the end of his life he used to spend his afternoons at the Père Lachaise cemetery. When someone expressed surprise, he answered with a beaming smile: 'That's where all my friends are now!'

In the midst of this whirlwind my grandmother had constructed her own domain. After the meal she would withdraw into her room, don an apron, put two glove-fingers on her thumb and forefinger, place her feet on a small stool, take an ashtray, which she stood lightly on her chest, and smoke three cigarettes in succession, like a small locomotive. Almost as soon as she had sucked the smoke in, she would puff it out, making rings. What silence, what calm, what affectionate gentleness there was in that room! One was at the eye of the hurricane.

When my grandmother died, I was present at a memorable scene: my grandfather, stunned by grief, fainted. He was brought round. Half-mad, he talked to his wife as if she was still alive. The dear woman was now reposing among flowers in the next room. The undertakers arrived. Old Valette's conditioned reflexes functioned.

'Come in, gentlemen, come in. Welcome.'

'We've come about the coffin.'

'Ah! the coffin. My dear wife. . . .'

He fainted and was brought round.

'What's it cost, your coffin?'

'Oak?'

'No. Pine. And the handles? The screws are included in the price? . . . No? Yes, screws included.'

'Very well, sir, screws included. And what about the name?'

'Her name? My darling baby! Ah!'

He fainted and was brought round.

'Don't engrave Valette, it's too long, put Briy, her maiden name, that will be three letters fewer. . . . Yes, Briy, Briy, my little wife! Ah!'

He fainted and was brought round.

'Tell me, that's the plate and the screws – but the stand is naturally included, isn't it?'

'Oh, no, sir!'

'Well, either you put down stand included, or I'll go elsewhere.'

'All right, sir!'

Everything was put through a fine sieve. At the end he accompanied them to the door:

'Au revoir, gentlemen. Don't bother, I'll shut it.'

They were gone. He turned to me and said, rubbing his hands:

'See, little fool? Today I've saved 1500 francs.'

And he went over and fainted again on the stiffened body of his wife.

Later, when I presented Madeleine to him (that she was a sociétaire of the Comédie Française made no difference, she was all the same an actress), I was nervous about his reaction. He looked her up and down intently, evaluated her, and then told me to follow him into the next room. Decidedly anxious, I did so. He lowered his voice so as not to be heard outside and said to me:

'Never do any harm to that woman, do you understand? You've won the jackpot!'

He was a good coper of human beings.

He had never been ill, never been to the dentist. His teeth were like two necklaces of perfectly rounded pearls – a little yellow, that was all.

He used to take cold-water tubs, wash with kitchen soap and then sprinkle himself with sugary perfume. He had no dealings with a thermometer until shortly before his death, and then took it as an outrage. He was so conscious of his health that not long before giving up the ghost he asked:

'Do you know anyone who would be interested in my carcass? There are so many sick people. It's a wicked waste to let such a machine rot.'

That is enough about him for the moment. I shall meet him again on my way. Sometimes, when I am tetchy or when I am going through the accounts of the Company in my little book, my double whispers to me: 'Stop imitating Old Valette!' My grandfather will never be wholly expunged.

Uncle Bob

At my uncle's, in the evenings, I was at the antipodes. There everything was happy-go-lucky, uncontrolled, 'artistic', more or less bohemian. My uncle was not living the life he would have liked to be his – which indeed applies to so many people. This made a deep impression on me. It is why I have lived the life I wanted. My grandfather was what he was; he accepted himself as he was. Not so my uncle: he lived in a state of homesickness for a different way of life. He had indeed resigned himself, smilingly and philosophically; he never whined to anyone; on the contrary he was kindly, charming and cheerful.

Deeply damaged by the war which had smashed his youth, he lived one life and dreamed of the other. By five in the morning he was gone to sell his flowers on the floor of Les Halles; he would come back exhausted and then talk only of painting. He had to be carried to bed, dropping with sleep. 'Adrienne take the arms and Jean-Louis the feet,' he would mutter with a smile, his eyes half-closed.

Adrienne, his wife, had a perfect model's figure; she was composed; and she looked rather like a Creole, with a mat complexion, thick eyelids, abandoned mouth, and a heavy gaze that seemed to speak of bed. Her bodice, left negligently open, revealed glimpses of two fine breasts, delicate skinned, neither too pink nor too dark – 'mouche au rosier'.[1] The curves of her thighs were good, her legs were long – and there was always one of them trailing behind her. She would sprawl in armchairs, inhaling the smoke from her cigarette of black tobacco with the same withdrawal, the same inner dialogue that would have been hers had she smoked hashish, while her left arm, open and dangling, held at its end a glass of red wine. She was not trying to provoke desire; she was simply there, where chance had set her down.

At the end of dinner, if my uncle felt strong enough, we would open the dictionary and, for half an hour, pick words at random, finding out their real meaning and their etymology – and this would send us on to other words. It was a fascinating game, this game of the mot juste, and I play it still.

My uncle bought me books. He taught me to love the masters of the Louvre, the Impressionists and the Cubists. He is the one who opened me to painting and to poetry, the whole range from Apollo to Dionysus. His father was bringing me Reality, and he Dream. It was left for me to discover that art is the dream in which one must not dream, and that everything is real, even the dream-world.

Bob sometimes treated me as a joke. On Thursdays, the school holiday, he would look for me in the evening and stare with his dark eyes into mine:

'What have you done today?'

'I went and played football in the Bois de Boulogne.'

'Are you quite sure?'

His gaze would take on an inquisitorial intensity. I would begin to blush.

'Er ... yes!'

'And yet someone saw you at four o'clock in the Place Pigalle. Don't deny it!'

I would go purple in the face. My forehead was covered with sweat. I no

[1] Rimbaud, Comédie en trois baisers.

longer knew how to answer. I no longer even knew who I was. Everything
began to swim. A mist covered my eyes. And then a great burst of laughter
readjusted life within its real outlines, and as my eyes cleared a bit I saw my
uncle's face coming close to kiss me.

'Well, don't you see I was making fun of you?'

> Such games are dangerous to a child : from them I contracted a guilt
> complex. A policeman or a customs officer has only to come in sight, and
> immediately I look guilty. And those gentlemen are infallible. If I argue,
> I always believe it is the other who is right. I have to wait until I reach a
> point of indignation and rebellion before I give a jump and say : 'But in
> God's name, no, no ! He's the one who is wrong !' How often I have been
> bluffed.
>
> Unknowingly, my uncle was enlarging for me the world of Kafka.

Needless to say, I was completely given over to myself : I escaped from
my grandfather's control, and Bob could not bear to control me. What luck it
was that study was my passion.

At mid-day 'order within repression'. In the evening 'a life adrift'. On the
one hand a paternal dictatorship, on the other a belated childhood. Meanwhile,
out there at Tournus in the house of my ancestors, my three Parisian zebras
lived, playing at being farmers, galloping in all directions like a flock without
a shepherd.

On Sundays we used to go by train to the valley of the Chevreuse, where Bob
had bought a cottage. From the station where we got out a two-decker *diligence*
took us to a hamlet called Les Mousseaux. It was a place frequented by artists,
actors, painters, writers. I had struck up an acquaintance with a man who had
a sharp gaze and a bloated face like a trapper. He intrigued me, and used to tell
me fantastic stories. He had only one arm. The two of us would climb to the
top deck, I would sit on his knee and, while the horses trotted under the vary-
ing Ile-de-France sky, he would transport me by his stories to the forests of the
Orinoco or to the Far Far West. This man was the poet Blaise Cendrars. He
would disappear all of a sudden, then be seen again, a couple of months later,
going by like a whirlwind, at the wheel of an enormous Hispano-Suiza, steering
with a hook in place of his missing arm. Another time the two of us would
meet again soberly on the upper deck. To make a fortune and get through the
lot was the breath of life to him. It was Cendrars who gave me the taste for
adventure, the joy of knocking about the world.

'In everything you do,' he said to me one day, 'I wish you a pencil point in
your eye.' (I was beginning to draw.)

He was in love with Raymone, a delicious actress in Jouvet's company. Painting, theatre : the two temptations which hovered over my studies. . . .

At that time I made another astonishing acquaintance : frank, innocent, a
'buddy', straightforward, no flattery, no beating about the bush, exacting,
loyal, racy, comic, playful, tender, warm and devoted : *the dog* – that human
being with a long muzzle ! She was called Malines, and was a superb Belgian

sheepdog bitch, a prize Malinoise. Tawny coat, black velvet face, perpendicular ears, elegant paws – she never barked but made a detour and leapt at the neck. She could do what she liked with me. Did not Beaumarchais have engraved on his dog's collar: 'Monsieur de Beaumarchais is mine'? Nothing could have been truer. From that time on I have been a dog's man. I cannot live without a dog at my side.

And when bedtime came, there alone in my bed, never taking a corner of my eye off the imaginary death that was trailing me like a policeman, I would keep asking myself: 'Shall I be a painter? or an actor? or. . . .' I had a third temptation. This one I had contracted at Tournus.

Beauregard

Every summer, during the holidays, we all regrouped at Beauregard. The house was large enough. Besides, the family was short of money. There were even paying guests.

The more people there were, the more pleased I was. My nervous nature has need of company, and I can never recover solitude except among people.

> The man who is unable to people his solitude is also unable to be alone in a busy crowd. (Baudelaire)

I was very soon attracted by the daily life of the peasant, especially the wine-grower. My delight was to go out with the shepherds and herdsmen. I was dirty and had lice (I still have an itching head) – a real little clodhopper. And while my brother, who was more refined than me, was improving his tennis and running after his first girls, while parents and friends were conversing politely on the terrace, I was sloping off to rejoin my little friends among their herds.

I loved milking the cows. I used to fight with the young goats – they had all the beauty of relief sculptures. We played among the bushes, rolling one another over in the grass and cow dung. One day I experienced a strange phenomenon. We were playing cops and robbers, and I had hidden in a hedge with a girl. She had a cold and held in her hand a soaked handkerchief. The cop was approaching. I took fright. I clutched her hand and the handkerchief, and suddenly I received a discharge in my belly. Why had the unctuous damp-ness of the handkerchief caused me to 'vomit' between my legs? At the time it seemed to me more odd than anything else, and then I forgot about it. Later on, I realized that adults call it the sexual instinct – the thing the psycho-analysts delight in sniffing at.

Inevitably it was the winegrowers' life that captivated me most. To love is to become the other person. The phenomenon of love is, in my opinion, at the very heart of a profession. The guide becomes the mountain, the sailor becomes the sea, the winegrower becomes his vineyard. Let us call it the *sixth sense* which belongs to the artisan or the artist – it is the same thing. That sense which puts you into communication with the incommunicable, that sense which no rule can rival. That sense which makes us say: 'That is the way, not any other', without being able to explain why.

I have seen gardeners, with the secateurs, literally carving a tree – and the tree, as it grew, has kept that beauty ever since. Today, when I observe a nurseryman busy on one of his pear-trees, I see how his secateurs run, stop, hesitate, sniff and make a choice, while at the other end an eye lights up, closes, skims and becomes intent, and not far from it a mouth is uttering little murmurs, gasps, moans. It is the *sixth sense* sputtering. The winegrower has it all the year round, for every stage the vineyard goes through: the pruning, the suckers, the spraying, the vintage, the blending and – always in harmony with the moon – the slow, patiently attentive alchemist's work, down in the cellars swathed in cobwebs.

At fifteen I was capable of doing my day's work as a winegrower. I learned to prune, to dig, to cut back, to tie up. One year, when I had worked well at the Collège, I was asked what I wanted as a reward:

'To do a course of training on a farm.'

Rather surprised and not exactly delighted, my parents found a farmer near Cluny who would take me on. I took the cows to the bull. I groomed the horses, cleaned out the stables. I was woken at dawn with a glass of *marc*. We did the harvesting. I would kill myself climbing the ladder with a two-hundred-pound sack on my back. It was much too heavy for me, and the hefty peasants laughed. But I was too proud to give in, and I would foul my breeches from exhaustion.

I came home for the vintage. I would have hated to miss that. It was the sacred moment of the year. The first time I went into a vat – stark naked – I was five.

The vintage takes place at the end of September, three months, as they say, after the lilies bloom. In September it is no longer summer and not yet autumn. I love the moments of ambiguity in the rhythm of life. This surely comes from the co-existence with death, the *co-naissance*, which I have mentioned. I love estuaries, I love the twilight hour, when day has just gone and it is still not night, when night is at its end and it is still not day. Hamlet's hour, and Romeo's. Shakespeare's hour. The poet's hour. Life is an estuary that flows into death: the communion of saints.

September is a marvellous month. True, the days are already shortening, the first touches of cold make themselves felt, long trails of mist wander in the bemused valleys. But the stones are still warm with summer, men's skin is still bronzed, their lungs are rejuvenated, the fruit is golden, the grapes are ripe. Nature is answering the sun, returning his courtesy. Out of the energy of his rays she has cooked the harvests.

Among these, slightly excelling the grain harvest, a divinity is enthroned – the vintage. It is the vintage that initiated me into the sensuality of life.

It must have rained last night. Everything is soaked. You squelch through the mud, each step sucks you back. The vineleaves are pearled and, covered with pink dew, the clusters gleam like velvet, your fingers tingle. The vintagers move from puddle to puddle, bent double, because in Burgundy the vines are short and cruelly hard on one's thighs. A small rose-pink sun pierces the mist.

Broken tones, as the painters say. At intervals you straighten up, relax and chat for a little; bits of gossip circulate across the rows.

'I want to see your bums!' Old Barrault used to shout, as he watched his vintagers. Everyone would plunge back among the vines. Now this touch of the galleys is there no longer; just a few dogs playing at shepherds. Some of them get drunk gobbling up fallen grapes. Nothing is more amusing than making a chicken or a dog drunk and watching their precarious leaps.

During the vintage season the young people from the plain come up to be taken on. Boys and girls, they sleep in the barns; there is an atmosphere of adventure, escapade, freedom, making free.

The mud on one's shoes, the hot blood kindled at one's fingertips by the first frosts, the smell of fermentation from the hods of grapes beginning to work, the singing around the fire at nightfall, the sheep being roasted – all this transfigures labour into festivity and life into desire. Then there are mandolines, there is dancing, people fight with knives. In the huge vats the clusters are macerating. For five or six days on end, the men take off their clothes and go in, to tread the grapes.

I can see myself again as a child, dancing from one vat to the other while clinging to the rim of the enormous oak barrel, set up like an altar. My mother kept watch over me with a pilot candle: the gases emanating from the fermentation are asphyxiants, and there were deaths every year; if the layer of carbonic gas rises, the candle goes out. They drive the gas away by flapping sheets.

Later on, when I was a young man, my mother no longer kept watch over me – and I plunged deeper into the treacle of the vintage. It scratches your ankles, then your knees; then your belly is being scraped, the warm mixture of clusters and pips rakes you from your private parts to your chest, a wet and yet rough belt. At the bottom, your feet are swimming in the juice, in the blood. You come out sticky and drunk with the ethyl vapours. You feel virile, full, sensual, ready for anything. Not a thought in your head.

While the harvest is fermenting, the door of the cellar is forbidden to women – because of the menstrual flows which are, it seems, disastrous to the secret working of the wine. At the end of the fifth day the master winegrower tastes the vat every hour – the *sixth sense* is functioning. And suddenly the bell rings. The moment has come for drawing off the new wine. There it flows with its froth, and the smell of it pricks one's nose and one's imagination.

What is left behind goes to the press, and everyone converges on that, around the *cadenche* (a long iron bar used for turning around the big oily screw, to the rhythm of its clack). It grows stiffer and stiffer; the man who, at the end, manages to move the *cadenche* unaided will have the right to choose his girl.

Later on, I again came upon that warm, sticky and intoxicating feeling one gets from the vat – but I was in a bed. Still, the vintage is what first revealed to me the mystery of Bacchus. I remained faithful to that pagan rite until I was twenty-four. But even today, when the end of September comes, I feel the call of the vintage vibrating in me, as others hear the call of the forest.

That young man of seventeen, who had just passed his *bachots* in science, modern languages, maths and philosophy, where exactly did he stand? He had grown in all directions, like a wild plant that has not been trimmed. Who would act as his gardener? Was he aware of what he wanted? What were his secret desires?

Around me – or better, in me – three claims: nature, painting, theatre.

I loved life in the country, work on the land and the magic elixir of wine. I loved Beauregard, its terrace, its lime trees, its life, and its loft in which I had made so many voyages among the old odds and ends, the family portraits, the gaps in the tiles – places where the stars appeared. I loved the customs, the traditions which form the ceremonial of life. I loved the animals, though some of them frightened me. Horses, for instance, which attract me but alarm me and are alarmed in my company. A bit nervy and fragile for a horseman. I have a holy horror of snakes, above all. More than that – in their presence I behave like a bird. Even before I have seen them they fascinate me. And yet the air of the fields tempted me, along with the familiar rites of the table, the customs of the countryside, the fusion with sun, rain and wind.

Since I loved maths and the physical sciences, I might go through the Agro (Institut agronomique), to become a forester, or Maisons-Alfort, to become a vet. I thought of that. Yes, to be an '*ingénieur des Eaux et Forêts*' would suit me pretty well, for, while inspecting the woods, I could paint watercolours on the edge of some clearing: I loved painting. Louis Martin painted, and so, above all, did my uncle. I tried my hand at it sometimes, with good results. We worked from life. I succeeded best with portraiture, and even caricature. I had a feeling for the essential line, 'the pencil point in the eye'. My drawings remind one of Sem. I was fond of Forain, with his biting captions. Daumier above all. Already observation of human beings – what a landscape a face is!

'But you must earn your living!'

'Why shouldn't he become a drawing teacher?'

My mother had an answer for everything.

I loved Van Gogh, his tragic life; when I thought of him, I would touch my ear. It was still there, but I would have gladly cut it off if that would have made me a hero like him. I loved heroes. Above all, above all I loved the theatre. I was always making up, disguising myself. I learned soliloquies. I thought up subjects. I played whole scenes, with myself as audience.

While I was at Chaptal and in Paris, my mother, at Tournus, to make her winter evenings rather more cheerful, joined a society that got up shows. Jacques Jacquier, an old actor who had acted with Sylvain, was the moving spirit of these. Marcelle had found once more the atmosphere of the amateur dramatic society at Le Vésinet. She acted in comedies and was happy. Louis accompanied her. Max also joined in. He was excellent, had a pleasant tenor voice and could act with subtlety. To my mother the theatre was like a pregnant woman's fantasy. Which of us would inherit it, Max or I? For the moment, Max, without question. Of us two, he was the artist.

With my farmers, my vintages and my maths prizes, it was hard to imagine me becoming a barnstormer. And over this, anyway, my grandfather intervened with a categorical 'no', without exceptions. To have a pimp, a tramp, a layabout in the family – no, never should he set foot in this house again ! If this acting business were kept on the level of a social amusement, well and good, by way of a little fun; but life must still be taken seriously.

Painters are beggars, actors ne'er-do-wells.

Theatre very soon became a secret, which I associated with the underworld. I began to have a passion for François Villon. Nonetheless I put on some shows for my parents and their friends, but all children do that.

My first success was Athalie's Dream. Jacques Jacquier, the old pro, encouraged me: I 'should persevere'. I learned Act V of *Le Roi s'amuse* (Victor Hugo), in which Triboulet, the court fool, thinks he has assassinated the King when it was really his daughter, if I remember rightly. The body is in a sack. I had no sack, but I had my dog, Culot, Malines' son. A superb Malinois, who was the darling of the neighbourhood. While I was spouting my alexandrines, he lay on his back, I pulled one of his paws, then another, and patted him on his chest, and he licked his chops with pleasure : we acted together. Culot, my brother with the pricked-up ears.

When I was nearly sixteen, Raymone, Cendrars' wife, wanted to introduce me to Jouvet. I refused. Jouvet frightened me, I didn't dare. Besides, the stage was a scorching thing, like hell. It was too sober for a scamp. And at the same time the stage tempted me. There was also the cinema. Ah, to change one's skin, become Another Person !

What is more, I had a vague impression that my tastes had changed. Rhetoric and philo had marked me. I now had a passion for poetry, literature, the play of ideas. I was aware that Paul Valéry, the great man at that moment, loved number as well as letters, but I was beginning to be sorry I had not done Latin. I have been sorry about that for the rest of my life, and the war that people wage against the so-called dead languages seems to me ridiculous – for one thing, because they bring knowledge of the roots which have formed most of our words. If the schools provided no more than a class for teaching Greek, Latin, Germanic, Arabic and other roots on which our mother tongue is organized, that would already be something; it would help us to understand what we read and to express ourselves with more precision. And the game would be fascinating.

In short, between these aspirations I remained hesitant and timid. I shall never lose that defect. It should be said in my defence that a family council was held, that Grandfather Valette pronounced, that the decision was in his hands alone, that he was the one who was paying for my education and my keep. It was already splendid that he should have given up the idea of putting me into some trade in perishable goods, and that he should have authorized me to go back to Chaptal for another year, to do advanced mathematics.

That hesitant and timid disposition is something I recognize as a defect, and I do compensate for it : I am obstinate, and I like to gather the fruit when it is ripe. I like to obey, perhaps from weakness of character, but I am marvellously passionate and obstinate when it comes to the choice of what commands I am to accept. The rest is a matter of indifference, and then I become pliable.

I like Polonius's advice: 'Take each man's censure, but reserve thy judgment.' I like also, and consider as vitally important, the sense of Destiny as Æschylus conceived it. Our Destiny is the resultant of three forces:

The moral heritage of the *past* (genetic code);

The curve of the *future* (theoretical consequence of that genetic code encountering the events that are in store for us);

The opportunity offered by chance in the *present*, or, in other words, the faculty of choosing between several solutions available at the given instant, but choosing rapidly, with the help of the sixth sense.

This possibility of CHOICE is what I call *liberty*. Our life does not follow one road, but is at every moment at a crossroads where we must choose. We are a long way from 'fate' as Sophocles saw it. And so, up to a point, we can steer our Destiny. We partly make our Destiny and are responsible for it.

This is why, in spite of the opinion of the greatest thinkers, I am stubborn in my love of liberty. It is also why I am on the lookout for the unexpected. I have a passion for observing chance.

It is, lastly, why I have often come to attach interest to something or other that apparently was not worthwhile, wondering whether there might not be, underneath, some little spark that would be quite useless for other people but, for me, a revelation. All is sign. But one can only make a sign to someone else. If one is significant, it is for another person. To be, one must be two. And for these two to communicate by signs, both of them must open themselves. This is complicated and difficult, it retards decisions.

It is only limited people who know what they want – reactionaries or propagandists. They obey themselves, but they do not know how to listen. Fear and hesitation are not so much defects as inconveniences. I was to find them again in Hamlet, in Mesa, in Ionesco's Béranger. There are also those Shakespearean heroes, Henry VI, Macbeth, Richard II: the heroes of hesitation.

Once again I left Beauregard for Paris, parting from my mother. She grew more and more bohemian. As long as Louis continued to satisfy her as a lover, nothing else mattered. Always with a cigarette between her lips, she presided over the life of the house. Cats, chickens, rabbits, dogs and goats lived communally. She made a single dish for the lot: a tubful, in the kitchen. She had succeeded where my great-grandmother had failed: birds and cats lived in harmony. I can still see that confusion of pecking beaks, lapping tongues, twitching rabbit nostrils, and snuffling goats, under the supervision of Culot, the police dog, controlling the traffic. When he judged that one of them had had his share, he would show his fangs and scare the glutton away. Then, when they had all withdrawn, he would absorb what was left in three gulps. A real pelican.

Since no confession is complete without a sexual couplet – it was at the age of sixteen and a half that I first had a woman. The very first time I fainted with emotion at the sight of the naked breasts and the offered belly. I made up for it next day. In accordance with tradition, she was a friend of my mother's. That aspect seems to me quite normal. One point is worth remarking, I remained faithful during four years, for I loved her.

Back at Chaptal for the first 'année d'X' (year of preparation for the Polytechnique – the Collège had a good reputation for preparing boys for the Polytechnique and the Grandes Ecoles), I was thrilled to learn that two and two no longer made four, and I understood Valéry better.

Mathematics flow into poetry, as much as literature does. But my demons were at me. My grandfather lost patience and would not feed me for another year. He cut me off at the end of the second term, telling me that I must now earn my living. I was eighteen. I am grateful to him: it enabled me to cut adrift, to take flight from the nest and try out my wings.

And he has gone, leaving the family faces. (Claudel, *Tête d'Or*)

THE DUCK FLIES OFF

Birds that are about to migrate make big circles in the sky before choosing their direction. I described three of these, still without knowing what I was doing, before setting out for the Théâtre de l'Atelier: as an apprentice bookkeeper, as a flower-salesman in Les Halles, and as a junior master, or usher, at Chaptal.

Each of these experiences was an enriching one and marked me for ever. Let us review them quickly.

Bookkeeper
What is a young man who dreams of Van Gogh, and whose grandfather has been a chandler, likely to think of doing? Get a job with a paint manufacturer! And so something that might seem absurdly crazy on the part of a boy preparing with ease for entrance to a grande école was imbued, in fact, with a strict logic, leaving nothing to chance – in short, with a true French cartesianism.

I was engaged as an apprentice bookkeeper by the firm of Lefranc, in the rue de la Ville-l'Evêque, close to the Madeleine (I mean the theatre of that name, where Sacha Guitry was showing his wares). And thanks to the head of my section I was given another chance of penetrating very early into the world of Kafka. At the centre of the room, two desks stood face to face. The door would open violently. The head of section came in with a rush. If the window was open, he went quickly and closed it. If it was closed, he opened it with the precipitation of one who is stifling. Then he sat down in front of me. The telephone would ring, the head of section would pick it up, would stand to greet the customer at the other end of the wire, would go through a series of little bows and ingratiating smiles. It was an order. He signed to me to take notes from his dictation.

'Certainly, sir, nothing easier. . . .'

(His hand was held out towards me.)

'Oh yes, in a week's time, certainly. Have you got that down?'

(I did not know what to answer . . . he had not said anything!)

'It will be done, sir!'

(He clicked his heels.)

'*Merci, monsieur! Au revoir, monsieur! A votre service, monsieur!* You can rely on me.'

(At last he put down the receiver.)

'You've noted all that down?'

'But you didn't give me anything.'

Which brought down his wrath on my head. After that, the head of section made me stand behind him, so as to jump to it more quickly if he should need my services. For hours, up behind his shoulder, I watched him scratching away at his papers while I stood, emptied of my substance, behind him. After several days of this, I pulled out an English book from my pocket. While waiting for him to require of me my very soul, at least I would not be wasting my time. Suddenly he turned round. He had sensed something odd in the air.

'What are you doing?'

'Learning English, while I wait for you to give me something to do.'

'I have not your full attention. It is your duty to be at my dis-po-si-tion. Put that book away!'

By the end of three months spent like that, I was ready to have recourse to Æschylus's 'opportunity offered by chance'. He had sent me to the Boulevard Magenta to have a new film put in his camera. His holiday was approaching. I carried out the commission, but I then asked the photographer:

'May I telephone?'

'Certainly.'

I rang up my head of section. I imagine that, for me, he did not stand to attention, but remained comfortably in his chair, which did not prevent him from hearing the following:

'Monsieur, your camera is loaded, but you will please come and collect it yourself, for I shall not be returning to your office. Let the director know. And *merde.* . . .'

And I took to the road, without even going to collect my pay. To me the road is a great refuge. Every time I get into a serious conflict, instead of clinging I escape. Is this cowardice? Perhaps. But I find a deeper explanation for it. If one wants both to respect the point of view of other people and to remain in harmony with oneself, what else is there to do?

I got this from another great-grandparent – the one from Lorraine – who, when an argument arose at the family table, would wipe his mouth, roll up his napkin, push back his chair and go out without a word, to the stupefaction of the family.

Besides, there is in the act of going away a rather significant physical position: one shows one's bum.

Today I say thank you to that head of section for having enriched my documentation about that inexhaustible and inextricable world called bureaucracy – that 'eternal rump', as Michelet said.

Les Halles

I was longing to get back to my studies, but I wanted to earn my living, if only out of pride, as a defiance to my grandfather. I could not see myself going to him with my tail between my legs.

'Tomorrow morning you come with me to Les Halles, to sell flowers,' my uncle suggested. 'You will keep the books, and in the evening you will telephone the customers. The rest of the time you'll have off for painting and study.'

I said yes without pausing to think. I loved the atmosphere surrounding my uncle. I accepted the job in the market and enrolled myself at the Ecole du Louvre.

During the whole season, I was out on the floor of Les Halles before daybreak, and I sold my flowers in between the cheese halls and the fish hall. At noon, the despatch of flowers to the provinces, and the accounts. The afternoon was free, the evening spent at the telephone until ten or later, to get the next day's orders. Up at four in the morning. In spite of the shortage of sleep, the air of Les Halles did me good. I grew stronger and, above all, learned to sleep anywhere – a habit I have kept.

The life in Les Halles gave me the taste for overwork. For the first time I was rubbing up against human beings. One piece of advice: never go to sleep standing on the platform of a bus. Instead of receiving sympathetic looks, you will be riddled with hostile glances and vicious observations:

'Just look at that! He's drunk, must be – either drunk or drugged.'

'That's right, I am — both; but with fatigue.'

The bastards!

Life in the market was indeed marvellous. There I found my first artists. I found again the sixth sense. For example, that of a salesman. There is a real art in ripening a recalcitrant customer. At café bars, going up and down the pavements, picking my way between the crates, I had plenty of chance to witness vivid jousts between the need to sell and the adventure of buying – real revue sketches. Les Halles, my first theatre.

The belly of Paris: all sorts of human beings swarmed there, from the tramps who swallowed broken eggs they found in the gutters, to gay dogs rounding off a night out with a plate of onion soup. The market porters: protectors of the weak and rescuers of revolutions. The middle-men making their entry. I can still see Mme Valentin, the florist from the avenue Victor-Hugo, getting down from her limousine: her chauffeur, hat in hand; herself in clogs and a little pleated satinette dress. In the afternoon, their free time, those people would go off to bet on the races, alongside the grandest families of the Turf.

Paris, Les Halles! My youth. The church of Saint-Eustache, where Molière was baptized and Marivaux buried. The Fontaine des Innocents. Historic Paris. For three hours already we had been in the middle of it, among the shouts, the mud, the entangled vehicles, the confusion of smells, the rats hanging on by their teeth to the carcasses of beef, and now the constellation of the street lamps was paling, for the night sky was gradually whitening; our feet were cold, our noses running. Two florists were arguing over a single dozen roses, the only ones of exceptional quality left on the market. I held my bunch like a lance.

I was happy living, learning . . . in order to act and understand.

The usher

Much as I delighted in the strange life of the market, so agreeably out of the ordinary, and in the special enjoyment produced by the intoxication of over-work, my studies were suffering from it. I could feel I was working badly, rather as one does when dreaming. When sleep is insufficient, dreams spill over into the waking state. It is not unpleasant, but it is hazy and does not stay put. There had to be a change.

Chaptal, at my request, received me back within its walls – as an usher. I had lived there for eight years as a pupil; here I was back again, on the other side of the barrier. Another lesson in human nature: the whole of cruelty and promiscuity in miniature.

One child alone is enchanting; in a group, there is no knowing which to lay hold of without missing another. At the start, what I really wanted was to play with them – it was natural, I was only nineteen. But how they took advantage of this, the little monsters! I had no authority. Either I treated them as young brothers, or else I was cursing them.

In this, indeed, I have not changed. I have never managed to make myself feared. For that, you must keep your distance, and this bores me. The women – secretaries, stage staff or actresses – move me: I cajole them, I embrace them. I treat men as comrades, joke with them, tell funny stories, student stories, bawdy stories. All of them are my comrades. They all call me by my Christian name. I am delighted.

When I am angry, I revert to my grandfather's tetchiness. The rage of men who feel they are small. I call them every name under the sun, ending with: 'No, do what you like, you'll not make me a martinet! The one thing you like is authority, the big stick, really you're natural slaves, you don't deserve to be given a living.' Irritated at first, they end by falling about laughing and consoling me.

But the children drove me crazy. I was being well and truly punished for my schoolboy ragging. One of my colleagues, Max Lejeune, did have authority. Not a word, ever, louder than any other; no one would have dared to stir. He became a member of Parliament, then a Minister. He was already a Socialist; we became friends, and I accompanied him to the political meetings at which he was training for the fight, roaring himself purple in the face on the platform while I drew caricatures of him and of his friends and adversaries.

On holidays there were always a few kids mooching about in the yards, deserted by their parents, like dogs abandoned on the roads. One father asked to see me, one day, to tell me of the bad things he thought of his child. The kid was perhaps twelve years old.

'Beat him, sir! Beat him!' were the man's last words as he left the two of us.

There were also children who were incorrigible.

It is evening, during prep. A child is whimpering on his bench. I call him out and question him.

'I can't do my problem.'

'Show me.'

I read the piece of paper.

'But it's impossible, your problem!'

'Think so? That's what I thought.' And he goes back to his place snuffling.

Next day I am summoned by the head usher and brought face to face with the teacher. The child is there. There is an argument. I am treated roughly.

'From the paper which I read, the problem was impossible.'

We look into it. We are on the point of realizing that the child had faked the paper on purpose when, in a wicked tone, he breaks in :

'How do you expect us to do our problems when you don't even agree among yourselves!'

Off he goes, shouting with joy.

The dormitory – I have just put out the lights. All the kids are excited. Giggles, mumbles, muffled blows, patter of bare feet in the dark. An atmosphere of hysteria. Angrily I put on the lights again. Two of the children are together. Age about fourteen. They are twins.

'What are you doing there?'

'We like sleeping together.'

'Right! But in that case, silence everyone!'

I go back to lie down. I put out the lights and the lot of us, myself first, like so many 'innocents', go off to sleep, lulled by the moans from the twins caressing one another. . . . Bottom of the gulf!

I was *au pair*, which meant that I received board and lodging but no salary. Sometimes I would be three weeks on end with only five sous. You could buy nothing with that except a stamp. It did not destroy our enjoyment. The corridor of our rooms was as noisy as the yard where the pupils had their recreation. Were not we ourselves kids? I painted portraits of my companions. I acted for them, made up, disguised myself, imitated the masters.

We had made a ball out of old newspapers and we used to play on the boulevard. If one of us had earned a little money, we would go out as far as the rue Notre-Dame-des-Champs and drink Samos wine. I found some nice companions, and even made a real friend, Guy Tosi, who was preparing for an exam in Italian. A few years later we achieved that perfect feeling which, I think, belongs only to men : pure and total friendship. I shall come back to this.

I used to go to the Louvre, always on foot. One day, touched by the sight of a little boy moping all by himself on a Thursday, when all the others were with their parents, I took him to the Museum, and while I was studying the pictures he slid on the polished floors. On the way back I gave him an ice on the terrace of the Brasserie de l'Univers. I did not know that at the Théâtre Français, opposite, there was a young laureate of the Conservatoire making her début, by name Madeleine Renaud. Sixth sense indeed! We would need a seventh, an eighth, an infinity of others. We are poor creatures.

Someone had seen me with the child. Next day I was nearly expelled. The powers-that-were had taken me for a satyr. Ever since then, suspicion has disgusted me. People attribute to you their own thoughts; it is as though they glue their sticky skin on your skin.

I was doing well at the Ecole du Louvre. As regards the History of Art, I soon made the distinction between the two words. One of the teachers stuck to the History and taught us about Velasquez's troubles with his landlord, without ever looking at one of his pictures. I sheered off. Another, on the contrary, initiated us into the alchemy of Art. Robert Rey took us right into the world of the Impressionists. It was thrilling. I was to come across Robert Rey again.

All my efforts to become a painter failed: at the competition held by the Galerie des Beaux-Arts, four were accepted and I was fifth. I obtained an interview with a famous teacher: Devambez. He scarcely glanced at my portraits, for I had not previously done three years at an academy. In that direction, life was resisting me.

I was about to start preparing for the exam in architecture when, on a sudden impulse, I sent a letter to Charles Dullin, the famous Volpone whom I had admired at the Théâtre de l'Atelier. This time life snatched me up.

When I look back on those moments of my life, there comes to mind this magnificent phrase of Claudel's:

> That enormous Past pushing us forwards with
>   an irresistible power
> And in front of us all that enormous Future
>   breathing us in with an irresistible power
>   (Partage de Midi)

All my attempts in the field of painting came up against difficulties; the first and only time that I made a movement in the direction of the theatre, I was literally 'breathed in'.

Was my destiny waiting for me at the street corner? What had happened inside me? Was I more knowledgeable about the theatre? Certainly not. I had gone there perhaps ten times in my life.

In 1915 I had been taken to the Châtelet, to see a patriotic piece called Les Exploits d'une petite Française, acted by a child: Gaby Morlay. I had been twice to the Comédie Française: Hernani, with Albert Lambert and Madeleine Roch. I had found them ridiculous. When they fell they raised a cloud of dust, and for a long time afterwards, as a joke, I used to yell: 'You are my lion, superb and generous', followed by the gnash of teeth representing 'tragic feeling'. On the other hand, I had been moved to enthusiasm by De Feraudy and Fresnay in Géraldy's *Les Grands Garçons*; also by the modern style, and the presence of two irresistible creatures – Marie Bell and Madeleine Renaud (here again, no presentiment – what a savage I was!) – in A *quoi rêvent les jeunes filles*. The production was by Charles Granval – this I realized only later. *Le Gland et la Citrouille*, spoken by a certain Pierre Bertin, had pleased me considerably.

Then I had fallen in love with Valentine Tessier in *Siegfried* and in *Amphytrion 38*, with Jouvet's company at the Champs-Elysées.

Oh yes, before that, my mother, who worshipped Gémier, had taken me to see 29° *à l'Ombre* and *L'Avare*. But in the part of Harpagon that evening, Gémier had been replaced by a young hopeful called Charles Dullin. Lastly, *L'Acheteuse*, at the Œuvre, by Mme Simone. That was about all my theatrical luggage.

Not exactly ground, there, for the imperatives of a vocation. These, therefore, could only come from inside me. The desire to change skin, to feel what other people felt. To become the Other Person. Is that not how I defined Love? But was I really conscious of this? Certainly not. Of all that I had received up to that point, especially during those three years of complete liberty, what I loved most was having had the chance to mingle with the rest of humanity.

> In a studio, at grips with myself, would I not have panicked? In my case we must not forget the fear I have mentioned. Fear of the unknown. Fear of the dark. Fear of death. Fear of that solitude which I can bear only when among other people. When I am alone, my solitude is peopled with nightmares.
>
> Here I willingly hand over to the analysts: let them extrapolate.

Little by little my passion for the stage had grown stronger. In vain some people warned me against that dangerous, ungoverned, abnormal life; some even predicted for me a life of immorality; I was more and more prepared to run the risk of becoming 'a bad lot'.

Opposite Chaptal, at the Théâtre des Arts, I had also seen the Pitoëffs: *Les Criminels* and *La Charrette de Pommes*. I liked those artists too, I could feel they were poets.

I had even walked on in a thriller, which featured one of the stars of the Grand-Guignol: Maxa. You can imagine the effect when the usher was discovered posturing on the stage of the theatre opposite. Once again I was threatened with dismissal.

I prefer to give up trying to understand. What is certain, clear and decisive is that I wanted more and more to go on the stage. I wanted it frantically. Whether nice or a bad lot, a saint or a ne'er-do-well, hardly mattered – it had become a blind and deaf need. I wanted the theatre desperately. All through my life, indeed, I have acted like that, 'desperately'. When one has turned all the questions over and over, examined all the excellent reasons for not doing something, and still, in spite of all the arguments of prudence, wants all the same to do that thing, then one acts 'desperately'. André Gide had an interesting definition of sin : 'Sin is the one thing one cannot not do'.

I desired the theatre like a sin.

The difference between an intellectual nature and an artist's nature is that the latter acts first from need – it is only later that it tries to understand its action; whereas the intellectual thinks first and then, on the basis of his conclusions, decides on his conduct.

Often since then I have been asked what the theatre represented for me at that time. My explanations are inexhaustible. At the time I could only have answered : I wanted it.

A vocation is simply desire. I had therefore 'desperately' sent a letter to Dullin. A very ordinary letter :

21 January 1931

Monsieur,

I am a student, aged 20, a pupil at the Ecole du Louvre and for painting, I am an usher at the Collège Chaptal where I did my secondary studies.

But on the generally repeated advice of the people I know and following the strong inclination I have had for a long time now deep down in me for the theatre (or the cinema), I would be happy to have the opinion, if that were possible, of an eminently competent person. . . . With this in mind, may I ask you to grant me a short interview? Hoping very much for a favourable reply, though only if it is not too much to ask of you, please accept, Monsieur, the expression of my deep and respectful admiration !

A few days later I received from his office a summons. He was proposing to give me an audition. In certain circumstances the Present, by a kind of premonition, fixes in one's memory for ever each instant that is lived through.

Though I loved painting very much, I remember nothing about my visit to Devambez. On the contrary, I remember all the details of my journey from the Batignolles to the Théâtre de l'Atelier. No doubt my subconscious was taking in this 'something' that was happening, and engraving it carefully for me to remember in future. I had borrowed from among my companions a frock coat, gloves and hat. Dullin would certainly have preferred to see me as I really was. But I had had the automatic reaction of a young man who is engaged and is on the way to ask for his fiancée's hand.

I had rehearsed two scenes : from *Britannicus* (Narcisse and Néron) and from *Les Femmes Savantes* (the scene with Chrysale), and while I threaded my way through the crowd in the Place Clichy, then in the Places Blanche and Pigalle, I told the beads of my alexandrines.

The rue Dancourt is steep, you get out of breath. Evening was approaching. The Atelier, in the middle of its trees, with its wooden doorway, courtyard and eaves, suggests a farm in the country.

Mme Vernie, the doorkeeper, asked me to wait a moment. By now I did not know where my heart had gone – somewhere in the direction of the ears, for they were throbbing and humming. I could go up : a staircase that might lead to a hay-loft – and there I was, face to face with 'Him'.

Dullin, with his stoop, looked up at me, but his eye was piercing. Attentive? An understatement. He scrutinized me with a curiosity that was avid, yet affable. His thin voice had a smile in it, but his lips were drawn back, rather like when my dog showed his fangs.

'What have you brought me?'

'Néron and *Les Femmes Savantes*.'

'Have you brought someone with you? I mean, someone who can act as your feed?'

'No, I didn't know . . . I have learned it all.'

He smiled. My ignorance must have touched him.

'Well, let's have it all.'

He squatted down in an armchair that stood against the wall in which the window opened, in the corner. I was acting, therefore, mainly at the window. The lines came flowing, and whenever I changed character I gave a leap like a goat and addressed the shade I had just left. By turns the 'budding monster' and the 'treacherous adviser', and then by turns each of the blue-stockings harassing Chrysale (that is to say my grandfather).

While I was giving my all for that man whom I had chosen as the one to decide my life, and who had obeyed my choice, I could make out, through the window, two silhouettes in the hotel opposite – a hotel specializing in rooms by the day. It was a couple. They could not hear me, but could see me gesticulating. They could not see Dullin. They kept pointing at me. They kept whispering to each other, they kept laughing. I must be barmy. I spouted my speeches in front of a pantomime, window to window, across the width of the rue d'Orsel.

And it was my whole life that was at stake – and was being enacted. Later on, when I did Kafka's *The Trial*, Joseph K. perceived the same neighbours facing him and commenting with gestures on the moment of his arrest.

When I had done, Dullin said in a whisper :

'Do you really want to go on the stage?'

'Yes, sir.'

'This is serious ! Are you ready to starve?'

'Yes, sir.'

'Have you anything to live on?'

'No, sir.'

'What I mean is, the school charges fees !'

'Ah !'

'Listen. But don't tell a soul. . . .'

And then for the first time I heard him wheeze in the way that was so much his own :

'Not a soul ! Otherwise . . . Well, I'll take you on for nothing. But mind you don't say a word. No one would be willing to pay, any more.'

'Merci, monsieur.'

I followed courses for several months. Chaptal turned me out. My grand-father honoured me this time with a formal curse: *'La malédiction paternelle'*, picture by Greuze, a painter born at Tournus, a reproduction of which used to hang on one of the walls at Beauregard. And on 8 September 1931, my twenty-first birthday, I made my début at the Atelier as one of Volpone's servants.

I was being born for the second time.

FIRST PAUSE

Our births

'You only die once.' Not true. One dies and is born every day, at each moment. And it is on these continual inner revolutions that the population which animates us feeds, day after day. But there are some moments that are more important than others.

The new-born child *is*. After what I imagine as the horrible pain of the break-ing of the umbilical cord, when the whole system of the bloodstream is starting its turmoil, when lungs are beginning to work, when the mouth starts pump-ing at the void, the Being is in himself the whole World. Outside him there is nothing. He sleeps, eats and drinks clinging to the maternal globe, his brow contracted, fists clenched, stamping his feet like an old man in a fury. He is entire, alone and unique. He is the centre of his own solar system, which is developing and spreading, propagating its circumference.

But after a certain time the eyes open, the ears hear, the limbs find their limits and, one fine day, this unique being makes an astonishing discovery. Amazement! So there were Others! So he was seen, was being watched? He becomes aware of the weight of other people, he realizes that he will now not be able to escape them and that, from now on, he will have to come to terms with them. There takes place then a fresh organic upheaval, as terrifying as the moment of birth. The original Being doubles.

The biologists teach us that the passion of a cell is to become *two* cells, doubtless from the instinct of self-preservation.

Our first act of self-preservation, conditioned by the presence of others, is also to become *two*: 'self' and 'our personage' – the character or part we shall play. To protect the life of the Self, the Personage will be entrusted with rela-tions with the others. Self, or the fundamental Being, will shelter behind the shield of the Personage, a social being which one projects for the others. Against them, or in harmony with them. That moment of life deserves to be called a second birth.

Observe a little child who believes he is alone. His behaviour is simple and spontaneous. But as soon as he notices you, he controls that behaviour. Every individual who is conscious of being seen has recourse to 'play-acting'. Espe-cially little girls, who are more precocious than boys. This double game is enough, by itself, to justify the existence of the theatre. On the stage, all the 'selves', in the auditorium, all the 'others'.

When I made my début on my twenty-first birthday at the Théâtre de l'Atelier, I was officializing my life face to face with the Others. To work in the theatre is to seek self-confirmation through the characters that one plays.

In real life do we truly know who we are? One may go on the stage to lose oneself. But, contrary to what one imagined, one may also be finding oneself. Why should one not, by being the Others, become gradually more aware of one's 'self'?

Besides, what happens in life is not so very different from what happens on a stage. Let us examine the Personage. Though he serves the purpose of protecting us, he may also be a trap. By dint of trying to appear, one may unintentionally cease to be; one may lose one's substance. Sometimes, by rubbing up against the environment, the Personage gradually takes himself seriously and, turning against his 'self', that is to say against the original childhood, devours himself bit by bit. This is the risk that adults run, and what is at stake is youth.

Youth is a fight at the end of which a man may lose his childhood. How many people move up and down the streets, believing that they are alive, when they are no longer anything but their personages, that is to say, an empty suit of armour like those in ancient haunted castles. Or, to take another image, a hollow crayfish advancing in little jerks, on its tail. Where has life gone? It has been eaten. The human beings have nibbled themselves away. Those are now only dead people walking about, the colonel, the professor, the businessman, the militant, Mr Mayor, Mr President, the civil servant, the shopkeeper, the schoolmaster, the trade union official.

By contrast, those who have won the battle of childhood are usually discerned by a certain gleam in the eye. Be their age twenty or ninety, in their gaze there shines the little star.

I distinguish, therefore, four possible stages in life: *childhood*, which is the product of the maternal matrix; *infantilism*, in those who have shirked the fight and come to a standstill on the way; the *adult*, in those who have lost their lives in the fight; and lastly, those who have managed to come through and to attain the world of *eternal childhood* – eternally virgin, curious, surprised, full of wonder. That childhood with which death – which, after all, is not the were-wolf but is, to life, what shadow is to light – will find itself obliged to come to terms.

It comes to this: that people look at you with a 'look-that-is-two-of-them'. There is the body, and there are the eyes. In police photographs, what always strikes me is the fact that you have only to block out the eyes with a dark band to be no longer able to recognize the individual. This is because, beyond the eye-sockets, the original being shelters. We live in a body as in a house. We shut the eyelids as one lowers a Venetian blind. Opening them again, there one is, at the window. Do I close my lips? The door to the yard is shut. My nostrils are two chimneys. In our carcass, of bones and blood, we can stand a siege. And yet a mere fork planted right in the middle of the eyes would be enough to extract from us the inner animal, as you do with a snail. All those people wearing dark glasses do so to hide themselves.

Self and Personage, Personage and Self at grips with the Others and both of them intertwining.

To work in the theatre is to exorcize the demons of our Personage. Let me put it this way: my reason for working in the theatre was to avoid play-acting in life.

Of course there is narcissism and there is exhibitionism. That aspect will be dealt with, but in another pause. Unless I leave that chapter to the specialists.

Let us get going again: I had chosen Dullin, and he received me into his Atelier. But before I come to him I would like to add a few words on the problem of influences.

About influence

What numbers of people close themselves so as not to be influenced! That is real fear – fear, not of others, but of oneself. Fear of losing one's 'me'. In my humble opinion they are wrong.

An influence is a meeting. One cannot be influenced except by what one already possesses in oneself. Better than a meeting, a recognition. It is the accelerated revelation of our own personality, with the help of the experience of someone else.

We could not be influenced by something completely foreign to us. Influences are effects of chance which reveal us to ourselves. We were carrying the thing in us, but at the embryonic stage. Now we meet it fulfilled. What a leap forward! One must be indeed pretentious not to take advantage of it. Our elders certainly did so: Rabelais, La Fontaine, Molière; and yet all three of them were libertarians.

Life? It is thirty thousand days, given plenty of luck. Life is short and knowledge is infinite. There is therefore no time to lose, and if someone helps me to meet what I could vaguely feel coming, I am gaining time for some other thing that I want. Let us not miss the short-cuts.

Influences define our outlines. They are never anything but the result of our choice and of our capacities.

Tell me who influences you, and I will tell you who you are.

The doors of the Atelier were open to me. Dullin was about to transplant me. The season of the *grafts* was beginning: I have received three of these – Dullin and the Cartel,[1] the Surrealists, the Comédie Française.

[1] A loose union of French directors founded in Paris in 1926. Besides Dullin, it included Baty, Jouvet and Pitoëff, all of whom opposed both the academicians of the Comédie Française and the commercialism of the 'non-artistic' theatre.

The Atelier

KIERKEGAARD – in his journal, I think – divides the cycle of human life into four periods. The aesthetic period, the ethical period, the period of the absurd (or humour) and the period of the sacred.

At a rapid glance I would suggest, in my case :

1972   at present, we are in between the absurd and the sacred.

1945   the post-war period will prove to have been the ethical time.

1931   was a kind of aesthetic golden age.

Each of them one venerates and serves like a religion. That golden age had its prophets, its apostles and its high priests.

The prophets: Stanislavsky, Gordon Craig, Jacques Copeau. *My Life in Art* and *The Art of the Theatre* were our Scriptures. The Vieux Colombier was our first church. There were also Max Reinhardt, Appia, Piscator, Taïroff. Above all, there was Meyerhold.

In France, the *apostles* were four :

Louis Jouvet, the 'Engineer' – from Sabattini's machinery to the smallest recesses of Molière, he knew every bolt, ball bearing, sailor's knot and mercury lamp. The mechanics of the stage never caught him out. He belonged to the seventeenth century.

Gaston Baty was the 'Ensemble Man'. The stage of the Théâtre Montparnasse, all clothed in black, resembled the bellows of the plate cameras you see in old prints. Baty used to wear a wide-brimmed hat and a loosely knotted cravat. When he pressed the bulb of the camera, he produced miracles worthy of Méliès or Nadar. His theatre was the only one where scene changes made no noise. He might have lived in Flaubert's time.

Pitoëff took for his own the poetry of the itinerant theatre. Pierrot Lunaire, or Hamlet's John o' Dreams. He seemed to have abolished weight. Through all his travels, he swarmed with children and dreams. Even his accent was winged : Chekhov, Bernard Shaw and Pirandello. In fact, an Elizabethan strolling player. At his start, like all the others, he had been opposed by Antoine, the high priest of the 'slice of life'. One evening Antoine, beside himself with irritation, had asked him : 'Where have you ever seen a room that has no ceiling?' 'But . . . in the theatre, monsieur,' he had replied.

Finally, there was Charles Dullin. I shall call him the 'Gardener'. He was redolent of the dyed-in-the-wool mountebank of every day and age.

That movement in the theatre – the Cartel, the fruit of Jacques Copeau's Vieux Colombier movement – was based on essential poetry. He had restored to the theatre its honourable place in the fellowship of the Arts. He had joined Dream to Reality again. He was at one and the same time avant-garde and traditional, western and universal. In his fight against the 'hands in the pockets'[1] theatre of the Boulevard, he had rediscovered the ramifications that bound it to the great traditions: to the theatre of antiquity, to the *commedia dell'arte*, to the great Spanish and Elizabethan moments, to the Mystery Plays of the Middle Ages and also to the exemplary theatre of the Far East.

Thrown (by my feeling for caricature, which is indeed a noble art) into a different walk of life, Copeau – '*le Patron*' – would have done very well at the Vatican as a Cardinal, with a slight Renaissance period tinge; Jouvet, transferred to NASA, would have made modifications in an Apollo rocket; Baty, with a certain mysterious gentleness, would have been an initiate of some secret society; and Pitoëff would be perfect, swinging in the sky of a picture by Chagall.

As for Charles Dullin, I see him as half-cowboy, half-gangster. The one who, all through the film, seems to be the villain and, at the dénouement, reveals his great heart.

DULLIN, MY MASTER

Dullin came of a Savoyard family. He was born at Yenne, at the foot of the mountain which overhangs the Lac du Bourget and is called 'La Dent de Chat'. His father, some kind of lawyer or notary or justice of the peace, used to identify with the horse which he rode through the villages and valleys. In France, when giving a toast at a country banquet, they shout:

> *To our horses!*
> *To our women!*
> *And to those who ride them!*

Charles Dullin, the last born, never knew for certain whether he was the eighteenth or the twenty-first child of the same mother. Malicious tongues suggested that, in the country round about, he had half-brothers as well. Jacques Dullin, his father, had the knife of justice in its right place.

Dullin's elder brothers were tall and bony, proper mountain stock. And Charles had the morphology of a man of great stature – the legs too long for the body. It was only at the upper vertebrae that the body began to stoop, as though under a weight, the weight of all those children his mother's phenomenal womb had had to endure. And yet his mother, in finishing her task, had put the best into him.

By way of balancing the excesses of his stallion temperament, nature had given Dullin's father a strange brother: Joseph-Elisabeth. In 1840 this person had decided, like one of his elder brothers, to go and seek his fortune in India. But he did not get further than Marseilles: he had found the debauchery there rather repulsive, and had returned to the family home, never to emerge from it again. He shut himself indoors all day and only went out at night. He had a

---

[1] The expression is Paul Mounet's.

nice head-voice, but in the songs he sang he suppressed all the words that had
to do with love.

> *Pleasure . . . hum hum . . . lasts but for a moment,*
> *Sorrow . . . hum hum . . . lasts a life!*

He was in fact hermaphroditic; but he was the one who initiated Dullin into
the world of Poetry – his culture seemed to have no limits. When he was on the
point of death, he asked for a glass of white wine and his pipe. He emptied his
glass, breathed in a good puff of smoke, then gave his last sigh. Like Grandfather Barrault, he *'cassa sa pipe'* like an artist.

There they all lived, at the foot of the mountain, at 'Le Chatelard', an old
house which had some bits of stone dating from the fourteenth century. It was
a peasant citadel, flanked by four towers and adorned with a coat of arms
which, when later the house was sold, Dullin and a friend of his sent rolling
into the ravine, after writing on the wall this graffito : 'Resignation is the virtue
of the cowardly'.

Dullin used to speak of Le Chatelard as of a fairy-tale world full of sorcerers,
strange creatures, tales of devils and magicians. 'My vocation for the stage',
he wrote, 'is made up of all these fantasies which peopled my childhood. Its
construction came from outside me, I owe it to the poets, to my old uncle, to
Philippe, to the itinerant workmen, to the nature of the countryside, to many
many things outside the theatre.'

It is surely strange that I instinctively went and chose as my master a man
who had known another Beauregard.

There was in fact a curious kinship between us. My art (if one is still
allowed in our day to use the word) also is made up of everything that we can
harvest outside the theatre. Art is a way, one way, of seizing hold of life and
garnering it. Like those birds that heap together in their nests all sorts of bits
and pieces from heaven knows where.

Charles Dullin, like his father, belonged to the race of oaks, one of those
oaks that have come up against obstacles in the forest. The obstacles had
distorted his growth. His knotty wood was all the more close-grained and
resistant. From his father he had taken two things in particular : the horse
and his fits of anger. We called these his *'foutros'* (fuck-alls). And like the
bird that gathers its life into its nest, he had made the Atelier a second
Chatelard. For me, it was a second Beauregard. The paternal house of my as yet
undreamed dreams. At the crossroads of Destiny, my life, my subconscious or
whatever it was, had made me choose that place – perhaps it was waiting
for me.

In Jean Vauthier's play *Le Personnage combattant*, there is the line :

> *That is why the storm obeyed me when I summoned it, it has answered*
> *me and I have heard it speak.*

All is sign. From which of us, the Atelier or me, had the summons come?
Clearly I was not wrong in calling this a second birth, and Dullin a second
father.

Antonin Artaud had been for a while one of Dullin's pupils, and had made a short portrait-poem about him. I quote it from memory, perhaps not quite correctly but, I think, not far out:

When the bishop died
a devil appeared,
an elderly devil whose stamping-ground
is seedy brothels where accordions
conjure up provincial towns.[1]

Dullin, having started as a salesman in a hosiery shop in Lyons, had taken to the road as a 'poet'. Engaged by a travelling circus, he would recite verses in the lions' cage. Aged philosophic lions, no doubt. Whether the poems were by Baudelaire or by François Villon, I think he found it simpler to announce that they were his. After all, he was taking the responsibility for them.

Then, with the itinerant companies, he had come 'up' to Paris. He had familiarized himself with melodrama in the fringe theatres. The fringe at that time kept him going on absinthe, a curious medicine. He performed in the parnasse and the Théâtre Montmartre – which he was later to turn into the Atelier. He retained some of the tricks of the 'melo' style of which he was particularly fond. For instance, when he was acting, he would always stamp twice with his heel, when still in the wings, before going on stage. For an actor this is like the starter's pistol shot; for the spectators it announces the 'apparition'.

His life had not always been easy; one of his friends, a chemist, had at one time kept him going on absinthe, a curious medicine. He performed in the Montmartre night clubs, for instance at the Lapin à Gil, reciting Jules Laforgue's *Complainte du pauvre jeune homme*, Villon's *Ballade des pendus*, etc. Involved more or less with the Bonnot gang, he palmed off counterfeit money, and received a stab in the back from a knife at the Rat Mort in the Place Blanche.

He wore this past like a halo; we used to transmit it to each other without asking questions about its factual truth – it fitted him so well.

To move on from legend to history: he had been noticed by Jacques Copeau, and created the part of Smerdiakov in the adaptation of *The Brothers Kara-mazov* in 1911. In this way he had entered the Vieux Colombier and been initiated into 'Art Theatre', in company with his young fellow-actor, Louis Jouvet, with a marvellous woman called Suzanne Bing, with Valentine Tessier, Decroux, Jean Dasté, Copeau's daughter Marie-Hélène, etc.

1917   he broke away.
1923   he created the Atelier.
1924   the break-up of the Vieux Colombier. Copeau decided to start again

[1] Dullin was afraid of Artaud. He did not know how to take him. In one play, *Huon de Bordeaux*, Artaud had the part of Charlemagne. He made his entrance on all fours. Dullin, very gingerly, tried to explain to him the extravagance of his interpretation. 'Ah! if it's realism you're after, well ... !' Artaud replied. He did not stay very long.

from scratch. He took his young pupils, nicknamed '*les copiaux*', off to Burgundy. What came of that was a company that had a great effect on me: the Compagnie des Quinze, with Michel Saint-Denis as its moving spirit, and nourished by a young writer who came close to complete victory, André Obey.

That post-war period was decidedly a return to the fountain-heads. While my mother took refuge at Tournus, and Copeau at Pernand-Vergelesses, Dullin departed to Néronville with his young actors. Shortly afterwards Dullin found his second Chatelard: in Montmartre, in the Place Dancourt.

The first period was heroic, poor, mad and patient. His horse had its stable close by his dressing-room. At that theatre Cocteau gave his *Antigone*, played by a young beauty called Genica Athanasiou, who was Artaud's great love. Achard made his début there with *Voulez-vous jouer avec Moâ*: its authentic poetry was a foretaste of *Jean de la Lune*.

The company made up between two bushels of oats. At their feet, in the capital, there was (so it seemed) a community, its life, and beyond that a country, continents. . . . The world might have crumbled to pieces and none of the company would have noticed. This waking dream lasted for several years. It was also the time of the lean kine. The public was faithful but thin on the ground.

And *Volpone* came. It was the hit of the season in Paris. The consumers of successes made their way – a thing unheard-of – to the Atelier. This good fortune lasted for two seasons. The faithful lost the habit of visiting their own theatre whatever was on, and the Paris consumers waited for the next success.

That is to say, there was a relapse. A few changes in the membership of the company, but the general spirit of it had matured. The Atelier adventure entered a new age: deeper, more expert, perhaps a little less spontaneous.

That is when I joined it. Of what had happened I noticed nothing. For me, in my turn, it was adventure, madness, youth, passion: an elected kingdom whose king was so by divine right: Charles Dullin, my master.

During the first two years I could never meet his gaze without trembling, blushing and a chattering of the teeth. I have always needed – and still need – to admire, to love, to trust.

I made a horrible discovery: stage fright. On stage I was afraid I would faint. The presence of the audience terrified me. In *Volpone*, dressed as a *sbirro*, I could feel my body becoming as thin as my halberd; my wig seemed to be perched on a broomhandle. My saliva dried up, my mouth was like a stone, my heart was beating like a drum and everything began to whirl round. That is forty years ago, and I confess that it is not very different now. I haven't made much progress. I have always made a mess of my previews. I only act decently when I am very tired, when I no longer have the strength to feel stage fright, as though in a dream.

Stage fright is not fear. It is the emotion of the tryst, and the obsession with 'rising to the occasion'. Let us call it a potency complex, which could only disappear with a bit of indifference. Sometimes I have envied those who are indifferent – not for long, of course.

When dominated by stage fright, one no longer knows whether to eat or to fast, to lie down or to walk about, to 'warm up beforehand', or to snatch some sleep. One goes through all the illnesses: cerebral congestion, liver, hunger, feeling sick; one is deprived of air, one shivers, has the vapours. . . . Quite simple: 'It's the last chance!'

Luckily, once on stage, after a moment of just plunging ahead, the intoxication begins. The radars come clear, the reactors are working. One is flying above the clouds, one imagines one is extra-lucid. At least, when all is going well and the audience is with you.

What mattered most was the teaching. Dullin used to make us do improvisations. This was new at that time. He was teaching us authenticity in our sensations: to feel before expressing. The birth of life, discovery of oneself, anger, joy, sadness, and all sorts of animals – their resemblance to human beings and the other way about. I adored these improvisations and sometimes did well at them.

Mme Dullin taught us to love Claudel: an ambassador at distant posts, a poet and a playwright, the author of *L'Annonce faite à Marie*.

We also worked at the classics a little, and sweated at gymnastics.

Sokoloff, a direct disciple of Stanislavsky, gave us courses that were fascinating, at least to me: let us not forget the meaning of influence. He would make us observe some thing, at first objectively, then subjectively. For instance, a box of matches. In the first case, you observe it for two or three moments, then you must describe it from memory. In the second case, you become a match, as though it were a person. It is an excellent method, making you pass from the spirit of analysis to autosuggestion.

Charles Dullin's theories, it must be said, were not exactly hard and fast. He was too much of a poet and artist to be a slave to ideas, and he had nothing of the intellectual about him. In this too the play of influence worked to perfection.

When his purse was full he would extol decors; when it was empty, there was nothing more true than the purity of a bare stage. He practised Stanislavsky and advocated Meyerhold. I would have had a crush on Meyerhold, had I known him. If only because of this phrase of his: 'The domain of the theatre can only be approached through the domain of sport.'

Later on, I was to adhere with my whole being to Artaud's definition of the actor: 'The actor: an athlete of the emotions'. In this case my congenital response to an influence received was as quick as lightning.

Dullin's teaching was not cerebral, and that is why I have called him 'the Gardener'. A gardener of men. As, in fourteenth-century Japan, the great master of Noh, Zeami, must have been. No one was better at bedding out, trimming, cutting back, transplanting to heath-mould, grafting, coaxing into bloom, the 'flower'[1] of a young man or girl, cherishing the fruit, watering,

[1] The name given in Japan to the innate gifts of a young actor.

shaking, causing to expand, protecting and torturing a young human being. All this was done by instinct, by osmosis, empirically, by successions of great pains and small happinesses.

Among other riches, Dullin possessed the rarest of them : a daily virginity. Every morning he seemed to have forgotten everything and be feeling life for the first time. This is the most precious lesson I have retained. The really fascinating moments were the rehearsals. With a ferrety expression and the tone of an old fox, stroking his nose with his long fingers, and standing first on one leg, then on the other, he would say to you :

'You understand . . . your character . . . it's . . . let me see . . . you see . . . especially at that moment . . . he will . . . you understand? Well, yes . . . but FOR ALL YOU'RE WORTH !'

And the miracle was that one had understood. He had not said it to us, he had conveyed it.

DECROUX

In the Atelier company there were actors with extremely different temperaments. All acquired a certain unity because of Dullin, but some of them were nonchalant, others liked playing cards or swapping accounts of adventures on tour, others were attached to their home comforts and others to drink. There was even a trade union activist, a rare thing at that time and in any case unimaginable in that lair of pro-anarchist bohemians. True, he acted the swashbuckler parts.

There was one among them who always stylized his part and as good as danced it. His name was Etienne Decroux. That one had ideas. He was looking for followers. From the first approach he made to me I was his man. In fact, his novice.

Decroux had begun at the Vieux Colombier. Guided by Suzanne Bing, he had become interested in expression through the body. He gave me my first lessons. In no time we were great friends. I was gifted. If a gift is something that 'comes to you heaven-sent', whether you desire it or not, I recognize that once in my life I had a gift – that of expressing myself with my body. This is why Decroux made a dead set at me – for me and later against me. He must have found it impossible to forgive me for having neglected qualities which in his eyes I did not deserve.

Very soon we were like two accomplices who had set out in the search for a new art of mime. Decroux is the seeker *par excellence*. He possesses the genius for selection. He lets nothing slip past. I would improvise before him : he would choose, classify, retain, reject. And we would begin again. In this way the famous *walk without changing place* took us three weeks to work out : losses of balance, counterpoises, breathing, isolation of energy. Thanks to him I was discovering that limitless world, the muscles of the human body. Its fine shades. Its alchemy.

We began to codify a new sol-fa of the art of gesture. We established the difference between wordless pantomime and silent mime. It was an inspired, mad period. We had become nudists and vegetarians. Nudists by a religious respect for muscles. Vegetarians, I have to say, rather by necessity. There are as many calories in a packet of raisins or dried figs as in a beefsteak. Kippers cost only 95 centimes. We used to calculate the price of our meals meticulously, reserving 40 centimes for coffee : 4.40 in all. We drugged ourselves chiefly with our own bodies : searching for ways of keeping balance, of slow motion, contraction-decontraction-relaxation, push-pull : the whole gamut. We would have liked to invent the impersonal masque, the music without expression. We did not succeed in that. We had made mini jockstraps, just enough to cover the private parts without hiding the abdominal muscles as far as the edge of the pubic hair. Objective mime, subjective mime – the walls of the Atelier were shaken by our leaps. From time to time some of our irritated fellow-actors would burst in : we were disturbing their card-play. 'If we wanted to become dancers, we could just go and display ourselves somewhere else,' etc. In the name of the God of the theatre, we received these insults with the patient fervour of early Christians. Other pharisees made fun of us, with a condescension tinged with contempt. Dullin encouraged us while joining in the concert of the sceptics. There you have the man. He wanted no bickering in his team. He had plenty of other worries. At the end of two years we acted a fight for him. This time he was converted : in his eyes, two Frenchmen were attaining the technical perfection of Japanese actors.

Decroux's genius lies in his strictness. But his strictness became in the end oppressive. Sometimes it was also comic. I remember a show we did, one evening, in Paris. At one place, right in the middle of our act, Decroux lost his balance. He stopped, apologized and began again from the beginning. People started to laugh. He stopped again, advanced to the proscenium and scolded them, reproaching them for being so stupid that they had no idea of what an artist's sufferings were like, etc. In the end he became unwilling to perform before more than two or three persons : if there are more, he used to say, people are no longer judging freely. It was natural that he should evolve in the direction of a kind of mime which he called 'statuary mime'.

My disposition was a lighter one – 'tarty', he called it, reproachfully. My aspiration was simply to act before the largest possible audience, and, far from showing my faults, I tried to conceal them. Later on, he was to pronounce his anathema against me, what I was doing 'no longer felt like work'. That was precisely what he had aimed at : he could not forgive me for it. I am as sorry as he is that our union could not last.

Our paths were to cross again two or three times. Those moments were again magnificent; but his intransigence absolutely refused to compromise. Yet this does not efface the extraordinary memory of those two years spent with him, with his wife and his son Edouard, then a boy, whom he nicknamed Maximilien because of Robespierre – all naked, gambolling in the corridors of the Atelier. Years of perfect joy. Inexhaustible laughter. A dream come true ! I can still see him as he thanked my mother for having brought me into the world. And a few moments later predicted the worst for me.

'I consider you pretty well done for,' he was to write to me in the end. 'It is essential: 1. that you admit you have wasted your time; 2. that you now change from top to bottom the company you keep; 3. that until further orders you give up acting, and also preparing yourself to play the part of a great man,' etc. The letter goes on and on. It was as if, to his mind, I had signed a pact with him and given him my soul. Which of us was wrong? Which was right? A pity!

From that time onwards my body has become a face. I look with the breasts. I breathe at the level of the navel, and my mouth is at my privates. If I had to convey this impression in a painting, I would choose the picture by Magritte which is called, I think, *Le Viol*.

MY WORK AT THE ATELIER

I did hardly any acting with Dullin. But to me everything served as a means of learning something. At the least opportunity I rose from the water like a carp, and snatched a fly or a breadcrumb.

After *Volpone* I did 'the rain' in *Il faut qu'une porte soit ouverte ou fermée*, rubbing a stiff brush over the back of a canvas, or peas over a drum. In Pirandello's *The Pleasure of Honesty* the second act ends with the entry of the notary, followed by his three clerks. I was the third. At that moment the curtain fell. The public could see the first clerk, the legs of the second, never the third. I always arrived on stage when the curtain was down. I took advantage of this to work at the art of make-up.

'Since in any case I shan't be seen, will you let me make up differently every evening?'

Dullin said yes, and every evening I would go in two hours before curtain up and transform myself into an old man, a chubby one or a skeleton, with masses of sticks, nose paste, wet white, etc. Dullin loved that.

Nonetheless I became his Turk's head and, for some time, everything that went wrong was put down to me. It even came to the point when my fellow-actors petitioned in my favour. It was as though he was trying to test the resistance of a boiler. One evening I met him in the street and plucked up courage to speak to him and tell him how unhappy I was.

'You try to do too well, so you do things wrong.'

There again, that indifference which I never managed to acquire.

For a fortnight I was stage manager: a disaster. If the electric bell would not work, I did 'dring' with my mouth, and the audience collapsed with laughter. I brought the curtain up before the interval was over.

Dullin delegated Decroux to instil a little discipline. He was told to 'tighten the screws' on everyone. Result: next morning M. Charles Dullin's name was on the board for having arrived five minutes late for rehearsal.

Decroux was replaced by the trade unionist, who, finding out that I slept in the theatre, tried to stop me. Dullin was furious and told him, in front of everybody, that he deserved to be thrashed. He then resigned. Such was the order that reigned at the Atelier. The dancer Pomiès (who died prematurely) did his exercises in the basement. In one corner Dorcy would be practising the drum 'in depth'. The dogs barked, the horse neighed, the pupils galloped up and down the stairs – it was marvellous !

With every fresh play put on, a crisis period came. The nights were spent doing the lighting. I volunteered to be the one to stand rigid in any desired place on the stage so that Dullin might judge the intensity of each light. That is how I myself learned to do lighting.

Then would come despair. Dullin's 'fuck-all'.

'I'm done for, it's quite simple, we shall have to close the Atelier. I shall go and work with my hands : I shall get a job doing synchro !'

On New Year's Eve we would all see the New Year in together; the scenery would be shoved aside and we would have a banquet on stage. Helped by the wine, we would move on to games, improvisations. Two of us used to imitate Dullin – my fellow-actor Higonenc and myself. Once, in his presence, we did 'Dullin directing Dullin'. Higonenc played Volpone, I played Dullin directing. The cries of 'Ah, but then FOR ALL YOU'RE WORTH !' followed those of 'I'm done for !'

Dullin received this satire with delight. He laughed till he cried. A few days later : a fresh play, fresh despair. This time Dullin knew we would all be watching his 'foutro'.

'I know I am ridiculous,' he began calmly, 'when I am desperate. That doesn't alter the fact . . . that tomorrow . . . is going to be disaster . . . the laughing-stock of all the papers . . . Oh ! this time I shall say nothing . . . BUT I SHALL FUCKING WELL BLOW OUT MY BRAINS !'

A shout of laughter. He went off to get some fresh air in the Place Dancourt, hitting the tree-trunks with his fist and kicking them, and snorting. There was something of the horse in him. He was lashing out.

But I never once caught him out in any real vulgarity. Four-letter words have nothing to do with vulgar natures. Dullin was extremely courteous, especially with women. Never a word that could embarrass.

He would direct the love scenes with exquisite sensibility. One day he said to a young actress who did not seem to be much moved by the love scene she had to play :

'It is odd, he is kissing you, you are in love with him, you are in bed, you respond by drawing him close to you . . . and yet you are still cold . . . ugh . . . ugh !' – and in the most tenderly suggestive voice and with the sexiest look he added : 'Mustn't be cold !'

VOLPONE'S BED

There he was on his bed, his spirit full of projects. (Homer)

As I was making 15 francs a day and we were not paid, I had given up having a place of my own and, with my master's consent, slept at the theatre.

One evening, after the performance of Volpone (the bed used in the fifth act was still on the stage), I thought I would go and sleep on the great man's bed itself.

Everyone had gone off for the night, the director had shut himself in. I had the building to myself. I slipped on to the stage, found a candle stump on the stage manager's desk, lit it, and opened the curtains of the bed, which was small because, with his mania for perspective, Barsacq (then a very young designer) had made it only about four and a half feet long. And I lay down.

There, plunged in silence, was the stage, and the flies with their load of curtains. Pieces of scenery cast shadows of ghosts. I thought I would go and raise the main curtain. I wanted to feel the presence of the auditorium. The auditorium with its population of seats : a whole potential audience.

I raised the curtain as one does some forbidden thing. I took a few paces on the stage where, not long before, I had been so frightened. I stood for a moment motionless at the edge of the stage. The *silence* of the theatre came over me. I was caught in it as though in ice. There was frost all round me and on me. I was soon covered over with a hoarfrost of *silence*.

I went and curled up in Volpone's bed. I began dreaming. . . .

Each of the stalls at that very moment might well have a personality of its own; indeed some were creaking. They were like me, they were dreaming. What a lot of things they had seen, those stalls! Only the other day, when pulling to pieces one of the stage boxes to make a new way by which the actors could enter, they had found between the panel and the wall a love letter dating from 1840.

That old theatre on the fringe, the life of all those strolling players Dullin had known. Now my childhood dream had come true : I was living, was at that very moment marrying, the life of the theatre. I came to realize in the course of that night of initiation that the whole problem of the theatre is to set that *Silence* vibrating. Unfreeze that Silence. Move upstream. When a river flows into the sea, it dies; its estuary is its deathbed. What has to be done is to go upstream, to get to the source, to birth, to essence.

Art : defiance of death.

That Silence filled with creakings, in that magic enclosure where I could now hear only the inner sound of my body – my 'luminous' body, as Pythagoras puts it – would now always be with me; I shall always see myself curled up in Volpone's bed spending my first night of love at the source of my art.

Ever since then I have been constantly in search of that Silence, and I have sometimes found it again, but this time in the middle of a stage ablaze with lights, in some white-hot dramatic situation and in front of, or rather among, a thousand people, a thousand human hearts that are attentive, open, sharing the present moment with me.

I believe the place where I have experienced this marvellous sensation most intensely has been the passage containing Hamlet's great soliloquy, 'To be or not to be'. When a thousand hearts are beating to the same rhythm, and mine is beating to the rhythm of theirs; when the rhythm of my heart fits in with the rhythm of those other hearts; when all of us have become simply one: then, I can honestly say, I experience human love, the love of a whole group of human beings, love between human beings.

And just as sometimes, in love, at certain peaks, we want to retard the instant of the marvellous tearing apart, I too sometimes want to retard that instant. I sit silent; I have stopped breathing; all of us have stopped breathing. We are palpitating in the motionless; we are finding once more that exceptional silence, that *silence-on-the-march* which alone can procure the physical sensation of the *present*.

THE ARMY

That beginning of initiation was – alas! – to be interrupted by my military service. As one of the conscripts of the Mâcon district, I was called up as a *conducteur de deuxième classe* in the '8ᵉ *train hippo*', at Dijon, along with the young winegrowers of the region.

My first mistake: I had taken with me Lautréamont and Rimbaud. It was not the only one. To punish me, my head was shaved. Since that day my hair has been curly, as a protest. It was in fact an ordinary year: to me it was cruel. My voluntary chastity (I was determined to be faithful), excessive consumption of coffee, my somewhat unsuitable reading and overflowing romantic imagination threw me into the worst extravagances. And more than all that: the stupidity and the physical and moral filth made me furious.

'Your school certificate?'

'No, but ...'

'Not all there! You're being asked a question. Know what a question is? Your school certificate?'

'No, but ...'

'Shut up! Put him with the illiterates.'

'But, sir ...'

'Next! This one's bloody hopeless.'

Next day, there I was on a bench along with the 'illiterates'; a lieutenant who noticed my writing gave me permission to go.

Part of my reason for putting on a Jarry show last year was my memory of that:

> *Soldiers!*
> *Don't forget you are in the army*
> *And that army men make the best soldiers....*
> *To advance along the path of honour and of victory*
> *You place the weight of the body on the right leg*
> *And bring the left foot smartly forward.*

In the mess, someone would take the big ladle and fish out of the soup an ancient dish-cloth, soaked with grease from washing up dirty dishes; or else, in the cauliflower someone would chop in two a huge caterpillar, boiled also, from which the whitish liquid would spread about the bowl. One man who had just swallowed ten pernods in a row, out of disgust, was knocked out with blows from a helmet. He had gone mad.

Till you have been a soldier, you are no man.

Ah, so that is what you call men? The stink of the barrack room, smell of feet, bad breath, unwashed arses, stains under the armpits, masturbation competitions (the one who ejaculates farthest wins) – is that the school of life? A humanity of swine, and no mistake !

One or two of the officers tried to tame me :

'Look here, on the stage you're used to living with other people, aren't you?'

'*Mon colonel*, I don't force you to appear in public at the Châtelet !'

When I had a few hours' liberty, I would rush into the countryside and, naked to the waist, hurl myself into the brambles to make myself bleed; I was beside myself. My behaviour became abnormal, and indeed I did nothing to hold it back. I had had a thought. And in the end the doctor ordered me three weeks of convalescence for '*insuffisance mentale*'. That at least was a gain. But I had to go back.

I had kept up a correspondence with Tosi, my colleague at Chaptal, who had became an Italian teacher at Nîmes. I now indulged in an escapade – I went off and joined him for three days. This brief desertion was not too severely punished. I had arranged things well.

We took walks in the *garrigues* (the hills of Languedoc) and among the monuments of antiquity; at Arles we read Theocritus in the midst of the sarcophagi of the Alyscamps. Between Guy Tosi and me there was an extraordinary harmony. If I wanted an image for the two of us at that time, I would draw two parallels. Our sensations were the same at the same moment. We would be walking side by side and would stop simultaneously. We would speak at the same time, surprised by the same things. Our friendship was total, without any ulterior thought. It was an astonishing, exceptional case. During that short period our cellular structures must have been in phase. As if two meteors, each with its distinct orbit, should suddenly, for a few moments, move abreast in their course.

Life since then has separated us : at intervals we have met again; each time there has been the same harmony.

At Nîmes, then, I discovered *the Friend*. I have experienced the same harmony since then : with Labisse from our first meeting; with Robert Desnos, in the streets of the Marais or in the forest of Compiègne; with André Masson, always; with Pierre Delbée and two or three others.

Friendship is a phenomenon comparable to Love. One does not make it, one meets it. But while love drives us towards fusion, friendship has the genius of communication, of correspondence. Such communication can exist with women also, but inevitably a disturbing element is mixed with it; this is very natural. With men the whole thing is extraordinarily limpid : crystalline blue, no complications.

On the day when I was demobilized, the nightmare suddenly vanished. I returned to the Atelier, and it seemed I had left it only yesterday. But I noticed that I had changed. I had 'grown up'. In a night? Like Alice in Wonderland? Everything I had received before, higgledypiggledy, must have been decanted, sorted out, I don't know how, instinctively. I could feel I was better built, denser.

Dullin was putting on *Richard III*. I did three parts, and he asked me to arrange the battles. The Compagnie des Quinze, which I had admired so much in *Le Viol de Lucrèce, Noé* and *La Bataille de la Marne*, had broken up, and the adaptation of Shakespeare's tragedy was done by André Obey. Copeau's daughter, Marie-Hélène Dasté, played Lady Anne and made costumes. That was for me a great meeting. Maïène (short for Marie-Hélène) was beautiful, pure and feminine, all three. A tall and subtle statue, but warm. In my eyes she became the symbolic figure of the Golden Age, both of the Cartel and of the Vieux Colombier. My feelings for her were a mixture of attraction, respect and timidity. 'A sister for whom I rejected incest.' Besides, she had a life of her own and not exactly a calm one. Our Maïène had other fish, not to fry but to look after.

Richard III was a great success, and the takings kept the wolf from the door for a time.

Another of Dullin's peculiarities: before stamping twice with his heel and making his entry, he was in the habit of warming up in the wings. If he had to enter in anger, he would pick a quarrel with someone – stage manager, another actor, me if I was within reach. One evening he could not find a pretext. No doubt he had not seen me. As usual, he was snorting, looking round for prey, for any old thing, and his eye fell on a hole in a curtain. It should be said at once that the curtains had holes everywhere, they were real sieves.

'Who did that?' he half roared. 'Ah! my curtains! I'm ruined! Done for, betrayed, a figure of fun. Well, who is it has torn these curtains?'

His anger was rising, rising, he was snorting more and more, and then came this sublime phrase:

'Wear out a whole life to come to this!'

Two stamps with the heel and he was off into the light on the stage.

On 6 February 1934, revolution came in Paris. The Atelier did not close its doors. In the auditorium there were about ten people. Dullin, as Richard III, stooping more and more, looked out through the slit in the curtain, and we could hear him muttering:

'After all, I'm more used to getting bad houses like that than full houses.'

Then he called us together and advised us to think only of the people who had come, not of the empty seats. He never gave a better performance than that evening.

Day by day I could feel myself becoming a young male: glances that I tried to make profound, hair dishevelled, clothes and accessories artfully negligent, the gait of a wild animal, something between a puma and a wolf. The esotericism of the East, the new American literature and certain Scandinavian writers attracted me. I was enlarging my field of influences.

This is the place for reporting that I had a new love: a Canadian girl from Toronto. She said she was of Indian blood, and in point of fact she had slit eyes, prominent cheekbones and equal toes like those of statuettes. We lived together for a year. For the first time I was sleeping in a woman's arms. I liked the thought of a couple. At the end of the year she was unfaithful.

Let us reproduce the setting of this sentimental drama. Jacques Copeau, after ten years of withdrawal, had put on a production of Shakespeare's *As You Like It.*[1]

I was acting, as usual, several bit parts, including, at the end, that of Hymen.

My sweetheart had had to go to Provence. We wrote to each other daily. She was expected back on a certain day. The day came. Nobody! Next day, no news. I was like someone who is drunk. Third day, nothing. I had hallucinations. On the fifth evening, as the act was about to begin, my companions were whispering all round me. And just as the three knocks went, one of them said to me:

'Have you seen . . . ?'

'. . .'

'She is in the audience, with her husband.'

I must have been a sight, dressed up as Hymen. In spite of the dazzle from the lights, I managed to see her, sitting beside a creature who looked to me like a hideous half-caste. In fact he was English. Never mind: a horror of a half-caste. My first defeat in love.

Later on, she asked me to help her get a divorce. I agreed. That is how I first came to London: to provide evidence of adultery. But I returned alone. I had been taken for a ride.

Copeau was the great boss. Even Dullin trembled on stage, like a dog before his trainer, when Copeau was in the audience. He had a way of grasping you by the neck and shaking you affectionately until your head was leaning against his chest as though to kiss the feet of Christ. That got on my nerves. Nonetheless, we felt veneration for him. He seemed to possess the keys of our mysteries: intelligence, sensibility, vision.

When in due course I gave an imitation of him as the melancholy Jaques ('A hool, a hool, I saw a hool i' the horest', etc.) he took it much less well than Dullin had taken being imitated directing *Volpone*. Copeau took all the

---

[1] It was he who awakened me to the game – the interplay – of proportions. For example, a small, flat stone from his garden at Pernand, with a few blades of grass around it, became, when enlarged, the device enabling him to stage the play, its palace and its forest. I discovered from that what fun it is in the theatre to play with the human scale. In Anouilh's *La Petite Molière* a piece of scenery, which in an outdoor scene represented a double gate, could be turned in order to represent the fireplace of an inn-parlour, etc.

obstacles one comes up against in the theatre as personal insults. That this should be done to *him*!

The actor who was playing Touchstone gave notice that he had to leave. Copeau did not believe him. The days went by. The actor said that he had already given notice some time ago and he must now leave in two days. No replacement had been provided. What was to be done? Timidly I informed the stage management that I had learned the part. Some hours went by. Next day, that is to say the day before the part had to be taken over, I was told:

'*Le patron* wants to speak to you.'

I went into his office. Copeau had on his martyr expression. As usual, he rolled his tongue along his lips as though detaching them from his teeth, then said in a warm and melancholy tone of voice:

'They tell me you know the part?'

'Patron, er ... ! Well, if I go at it all night, I do think I....'

He picked up the text, held it out to me as if he were parting from an old friend, and said:

'There's nothing for it!'

I spent the whole night with Tania Balachova while she listened to my lines, and next evening I played Touchstone. My chief partner was Raymone, Cendrars' wife.

Copeau did not come to the performance. Was this in order not to intimidate me? Or was it from contempt? I was hurt. And yet he was fond of me and I certainly returned the affection. Copeau was in our eyes the Father of the whole modern theatre. The conclusion I draw, sometimes, is that everything in life is enriching, even the psychological mistakes of our 'masters'.

Though I said the virtues of a master are chiefly in his disciple, I have to recognize nonetheless that the masters sometimes do not make things easy. The insolence of pupils is sometimes a result of the teacher's haughty contempt.

To quote my friend Jarry again, 'there are two kinds of ignorant people, the ignorant people and the specialized ignorant people; the second kind are called pundits.'

In between the pupil's ignorance and the master's, there is a little specialization. In other words, they differ only by a few years. There is no good reason for either of them to despise the other. And neither of them has anything to boast of. If people were taught human respect first, the conflicts between generations would be more than smoothed out. On this subject, here is an anecdote.

We were at the Conservatoire, in a class given by Louis Jouvet, that real master. A young pupil called François Périer (now one of our best French actors) was doing a scene from *Scapin*. As soon as it was over, Jouvet, preparing his effect with a doctoral silence, said to him in his inimitable tone:

'Young man, if Molière heard you, he must have turned in his grave.'

Périer, nettled, replied:

'Well, he must now be back in place, for he heard you yesterday in *L'Ecole des femmes.*'

There is the problem in a nutshell. Contempt engenders insolence. Why not all work together – ignorant people, whether specialized or not? And try to make some attempt at 'understanding'? At 'learning, learning in order to act and understand'?

I mentioned Tania Balachova. It was she who lent me the novel by an American writer not at all well known at that time, William Faulkner's *As I Lay Dying*, translated by Maurice Coindreau. I was hooked on American literature, Walt Whitman, Thoreau (*Walden, or Life in the Woods*), Emerson (that Descartes of the New World), Poe of course, Melville too (I still have a long-standing desire to adapt *Pierre, or the Ambiguities*), Hemingway and – later – Caldwell, Steinbeck and Dos Passos.

Faulkner's *As I Lay Dying* was a revelation: a tearing of the veil, a kind of vision, a window opening in the mountain mists to reveal the whole horizon.[1] It seemed to me that, with the help of that subject, I might be able to pull together all my accumulated ideas and sensations concerning the theatre.

To make my first object! For the next six months, I worked at nothing else.

'AS I LAY DYING' OR 'TOTAL THEATRE'

What, on the theatrical plane, tempted me in that novel? The *silent* behaviour of those primitive creatures. They spoke only to themselves. I saw in this a wonderful opportunity to satisfy longings of mine, which I refused to consider as theories.

In the draft of an old letter dated May 1935, I find this:

> This kind of mime, I believe, has nothing to do with pantomime, education or aesthetics (or that disagreeable thing the *tableau vivant*); it is an attempt to be purely animal. For example, the face becomes a natural mask, the concentration being respiratory.
>
> I don't want to expound theories in detail, practical realization alone counts. I have worked as I breathed.

And, further on:

> As a text this play does not exist. It exists if, and only if, a group of actors and a director work on a stage. It is theatre trying to purify itself.

In a note presenting the show I declared: 'My only theory is to create a work which, as a member of the audience, I would have liked to see.' I now realize that this is what I have been doing all my life.

The subject is well known:

[1] I shall return more than once to this image. It matters to me, and is one of my leitmotivs.

It is the story of a mother who, having fallen ill, wants her coffin to be made in her presence by one of her children, and her remains to be taken on the family cart, attended by all her family, to the town – Jefferson – where her parents lie buried.

To this central subject the father and the five children react in accordance with their own individual natures and passions. The action takes place in our own time, among the peasants of the Mississippi. Season of hot weather and rains. Life is hard, they are poor. In the family there is a 'living lie': Jewel, the natural son of the mother and the village priest. Remorse.

This dramatic action took two hours to play, with about thirty minutes of text. It was a case, therefore, of starting from *Silence* and living in the *Present*. The characters are *there*, they are living at this moment. They don't speak to each other. They act. But they are not dumb. Silence is not deafness. Every sound takes on an importance of its own. No one has separated sound from image. It is 'speaking' theatre in which the people say nothing. If their breathing makes a sound, if their footsteps beat time, this is splendid. The actors assume at one and the same time the characters and their environment: the river, the fire, the rasping of the saw breaking down wood. The actor: a total instrument. The characters have a social behaviour and a fundamental behaviour. They are living on two planes, the man and his double. Each has a passion . . . attached to his belt (the significant object).[1] Nakedness is maximum: the only thing hidden is what might become distracting.

The mother is nearing death. Her eldest son is making the coffin. The wheezings from her chest fit in with the raspings of the saw. All the rest of the family, like an enormous jellyfish, contracts and relaxes in union with the mother and the carpenter. The whole theatre is in death throes – a pump rhythm, an octopus rhythm – and all of a sudden, at the climax of a breath: total stoppage. The mother's hand, which had been raised as when someone wants to look out into the distance, falls slowly in the silence, like a water level going down. Life is emptying out. The movement is prolonged throughout the body until the rigidity of a corpse is reached. She is dead.

Then, quite naturally, without any stylization, she gets up and begins to speak. She can, for she is now alone. She has 'passed' to the other side of life. Real life is Silence. Speech appears only beyond reality.

The bastard son's passion is the horse. It is on his horse that he does the whole journey, beside the cart which bears the coffin. To be at one and the same time man and horse tempted me. Here again I wanted the actor to be a complete instrument, capable of suggesting both the animal and the rider as well, and the two together crossing a ford or pursued by buzzards. To interpret at the same time Being and Space.

I had had a vision of that magic space of the stage as a world of poetry made flesh. It would now never leave me (I shall return to the subject).

[1] See pp. 169 and 190.

And so I worked at the horse. In the morning, on the forestage in front of the lowered curtain, I was able to practise, for the auditorium was lit while the cleaners did their work. They and I were living our own lives, like the characters in the novel. I paid no attention to them. But after several days one of them stopped with her hands folded on top of her broom, and stared at me:

'Hey, young man!'

I stood still.

'I'd like to know what you're up to, like that, every morning, on that horse!' The finest encouragement I have ever received.

I had drawn a dozen fellow actors into my net. When one of them withdrew in alarm, I persuaded another to join. This happened often. In spite of these desertions, I moved on like a sleepwalker.

The publishers had refused to let me use the title of the novel. So I called this 'dramatic action': *Autour d'une mère*.

For some time now I had been visiting Saint-Germain-des-Prés. Outside the Atelier, I had acted with Marcel Herrand and Jean Marchat (whose company was called Le Rideau de Paris). Justice will never be done to the wit, taste and courage that animated Marchat and Herrand. They were extremely important during that period between the two wars, and made a great contribution to the exceptional vitality of the Paris of that time. Under their direction I had created the part of the Soldier in Ramuz's *Histoire du soldat*, with Stravinsky's music conducted by Desormières. Then Gide's *L'Enfant prodigue*, then Vitrac's *Le Coup de Trafalgar*.

I had made friends with Robert Desnos. At the Deux Magots or Chez Lipp I rubbed shoulders with Léon-Paul Fargue, André Breton, Georges Bataille and René Daumal. There was André Malraux, then a reader at the NRF, also Labisse and Balthus. André Derain had painted my portrait; he called me his 'little Florentine sculptor'. And there was Antonin Artaud, whom I observed from a distance – he intimidated me. I would spend my nights dancing at the Cabane cubaine (Eliseo Grenet, Tata Nacho, Alejo Carpentier . . .) or else at the Bal Nègre in the rue Blomet. I have always loved dancing, I like playing the fool. After dancing beguines, rumbas or congas till I could hardly stand, I would take some girl home at dawn, 'in a friendly way'. Unquestionably I was breaking free.

When my friends started to whisper the news that I was preparing a show of my own making, which would be called *Autour d'une mère*, the rumour quickly spread that it would be *'autour d'une merde'*. I was making the acquaintance of Paris.

From Les Halles I had learned *overwork*, from the Atelier I learned *gymnastics*. Those Parisian nightbirds knew neither the one nor the other. I continued on my way, driven by my passion. Blind and deaf, possessed, authentically naïve.

I often went with Maïène, after the evening performance, to eat pickled cucumber with her in some little Russian bistro, and there I would lay out before her my ideas, my convictions, my conceptions, my worries, my dreams.

She was a very kind listener. With her as model, I imagined my ideal audience. 'I know I please those whom I ought to please,' says Antigone.

The rehearsals were now going forward. Those of my fellow-actors who had resisted seemed all in favour. Some of them even agreed to act under their own names, Jean Dasté leading. The others, more circumspect, took pseudonyms. Labisse helped me with the setting and the scanty costumes. Tata Nacho, a Mexican composer, composed the songs (in five parts). No instruments. Simply a tom-tom. André Frank looked after the administrative side, with my brother Max. More a raft than a boat.

The Atelier's season was over. I had hired the theatre from Dullin. As his finances were tight, his business manager did not exactly make me a present of it. So the enterprise was pretty foolhardy.

And now we were rehearsing on stage. The date of the first night was drawing close. From time to time we could hear a curious creaking from the old woodwork of the flies: it was Dullin, who had slipped in, intrigued, and was watching us from up above among the ropes. A theatre is like a ship. The knots are sailors' knots. The curtains float like sails, many sailors do become stagehands. Every evening you 'get under sail'.

Two days before opening, tragedy came: panic among the actors; mutiny on board. The actress who was playing 'the mother' had fallen ill. In point of fact she had fled. I never saw her again.

'We'll open all the same!'

'But how? You're mad! It's the leading part.'

Nerves were cracking. The ridicule that lies in wait in Paris was rotting the morale of the company. Better give it up. Not even put it off, give it up.

'All right, I'll act it by myself!'

'Act it by yourself – that's a bit thick. We trusted you, we were wrong. Besides, this passage ... that bit. ... We don't want to make fools of ourselves. And anyhow it's not possible to be ready in two days. The chief character is missing!'

'I've had an idea. I shall play the mother.'

'And Jewel as well?'

I was already playing the bastard, on my horse all the time.

'I shall play both!'

'Mad! Certifiable! There are times when you're on stage together!'

'Give me twenty-four hours, please. I've ideas coming. This time tomorrow I'll act the new scenes for you, and then you do as you decide.'

'Right, let's give him twenty-four hours.'

My idea, inspired by necessity, was to transfigure the mother so as to give her the dimensions of a totem. I had a mask made out of cheese-cloth, with steel buttons for the eyes. It was the nearest thing to an impersonal mask. The mother had an enormous black wig coming down to her thighs. The skirt was made of broad ribbons in two colours. To finish off the effect, I stripped to the waist. By altering three scenes I could play the two parts.

Next day, 4 June, I faced my fellow-actors and passed a real examination.

They were convinced; I had succeeded – at least with them. We rehearsed up to the last moment.

The curtain rose at nine. Before we started I told them : 'If there is too much row, watch me. I'll tell you what to do.'

I was six feet off the ground.

When I was left alone on the stage, a figure made its appearance. It was Dullin.

'I shall not be at your performance this evening. It's completely mad. Everything that I detest. Compared with this, Artaud is boulevard ! It's like monkeys in a zoo. And that father is just gaga.'

'Of course, he's fifty !'

Insolence, conflict between generations. . . . He went to his dressing-room, trailing his arms behind his back. As for me, I had reached the stage of insensibility. I really believe, if I'd been run through with a sword, I wouldn't have bled.

The time of the performance came. On the other side of the curtain all Paris had come up to Montmartre for the kill. 'Baba's stuff – that's something we must not miss !' (Baba was the nickname they had given me.) The surge of great disasters is what 'all Paris' loves.

Curtain up. It revealed us all stripped, our private parts only just concealed. (We have gone further since then – Living Theatre, *Oh! Calcutta!* – all over the place the nude is routine. Let us remember that this was thirty-seven years earlier.)

A storm of laughter and animal cries. Never mind, we began to act. My comrades watched me out of the corners of their eyes. We went on. The audience calmed down, seemed to become resigned. The house was like stagnant water. Sometimes more than twenty minutes of silence. No other sound than that of the bare feet on the floor and the forge of our breathing. The firemen in their corner could not believe their eyes.

The scene where Jewel breaks in the horse arrived. They're warming up ! They're warming up ! The scene lasts for about ten minutes. I had that cleaning woman in my muscles. We had won ! They were with us, and all the more with us because they had come to scoff and remained to pray.

And then came the mother's death throes, the crossing of the river, the counterpointing of the fire. Dewey Dell's sex scene. Young Vardaman's madness. The end. Whistles. Triumph. After all, something had happened.

The good old English saying : *Put that in your pipe and smoke it.*

The audience dispersed. The other actors went off with their friends. There was a man waiting for me, it was Antonin Artaud. The two of us went down the Boulevard Rochechouart, and together we started off on two imaginary horses, galloping as far as the Place Blanche. There he suddenly left me. He was drunk with enthusiasm. Later on he was to write an article which appeared in *Le Théâtre et son Double* : my best certificate of craftsmanship.

I had been living, since my return from the army, in a studio at the Bateau-Lavoir, of illustrious memory – Max Jacob, Picasso, the whole of that now historic band. Labisse, who had the studio next door, had also gone off with friends. I climbed to my lair, alone, worn out and lost, happy and sad at the same time. Religiously I washed that young horse's body, reached my attic and flung myself on my bed. I had scarcely slid into sleep when I heard knocks on the door. My door was never locked.

'Come in!'

Who was it? A young girl, as beautiful as day. She had been at the performance. She had been happy. She had come to tell me so and . . . to offer herself, if I would like that.

This personal manifesto (for such it was) was given four public performances, before a somewhat small audience. And yet I am astonished at meeting, nowadays, so many people who saw As I Lay Dying; it is like those small Burgundy vineyards – one is always surprised to see how many bottles of good wine have been extracted from them.

Its virtues must have been magical; but it was far from pleasing everyone. One evening a member of the audience leaned over to his wife and said to her:

'If I'd known it was so stupid, I'd have brought the children.'

By contrast, the Paris artistic and intellectual circles found it a revelation. Jouvet and the members of his company sent word, asking me to do a matinée for them. A supplementary matinée was decided on for the various friends in the profession: Michel Simon (whose son Michel François was acting in the play) was one of them; about fifty actors, writers and artists. Jouvet in person arrived at the Atelier. Dullin, astonished, thought he had come to see *him*.

'No, it's not you I've come to see, it seems you have a young lad who's done something that's not bad. We've asked him to act for us.'

After the performance Jouvet said to me:

'I can see the distance that separates two generations. Everything we were formulating in our heads at the time of the Vieux Colombier, you now have in your blood. Digestion is proceeding.'

With As I Lay Dying I made my entry into the theatrical life of Paris. I grew closer to Roger Blin, Jacques Prévert and the Groupe d'Octobre. The surrealists took me up. In the following month Marc Allégret, Gide's nephew, gave me my first film to do, *Les Beaux Jours*, which enabled me to pay my debts. The long exchange between theatre and cinema was beginning.

In the summer, at Beauregard, I received the following letter from Dullin:

26 July (1935)

My dear Barrault,

You must give me an answer by letter to these two questions:

When will you be back in Paris?

Do you intend firmly to return to the Atelier next season?

I will then answer immediately and tell you my plans. In haste and very cordially yours,

Charles Dullin

A deeply human letter, which put me on the spot. I took a leap and left the Atelier. By an act of will: against my inclination.

Often, in order to fight my timid nature, I put myself – simply and solely by the will of my double – in the situation in which I am really compelled to find my own feet. I took four months to recover. Dullin, three years to forgive me.

In a private note I wrote at that moment:

> Four months since I left the Atelier. For some time my mind was torn in two by it; it was 'my animal' that drove me to it. I left the Atelier and at the same time, as I realize now that I think about it, for I did it without thinking at all, I left everything that had caused the Atelier – preceding generation, theories, etc., a time of peace.
>
> What, then, did 'my animal' want? It is only after four months that I think I understand. I understand it because in these four months I have come to see that the movement of real life, at the present day, has no relation with the movement in which I was living. Does this movement really exist? Is it merely in me? I don't know. I don't want to know. What I do know is that this movement is what 'my animal' was after and so is now living more happily. I refuse to judge myself, I recognize that it is all settled, but precisely, it is at that moment that life is beginning. Must I, because it is all settled, live like an image, by heart? To be young is to begin to live, well, I have a physical conviction that I am beginning life. For three years I was carried in the womb of the Atelier, in the month of June I delivered myself; the labour I produced last June has cut the umbilical cord. I have been born. And I have cried out. And I have cried out. And life has risen before me. Its movement is revealed to me. I understand absolutely nothing about it. I accept it.

And so I descended the hill of Montmartre, sad at heart, my soul bewildered, in obedience to that inner command, to 'my animal', and I went into Paris to settle in Saint-Germain-des-Prés: at the Grenier des Grands-Augustins. Leaving the ivory tower of an aesthetic Golden Age, I charged head down into the society of human beings.

SECOND PAUSE

My impression is that, when I chose the theatre, I decided to attend the School of Life. First I had become conscious of the Individual, the 'Self'. Then I had discovered the 'Others', both as nourishment and as obstacle. Then I found the place where everyone meets to raise a quantity of questions: a theatre.

At nightfall, when the sun has set and darkness makes it possible to feel things more clearly – the small frictions of the Present, the below-the-surface rustle of Silence – men assemble in a closed space. On the stage there is a selection of the prototypes of individual human beings, the company. In the auditorium, sitting close together, a collectivity gathered like the spirals of a magnetic coil represents Humanity: the Audience. The game of 'Self and the Others'. The one and the infinite face to face. Paradoxically, the impression of plurality is there on the stage, on account of each individual representing a separate world, while the impression of unity is in the auditorium, because there is a fusion of all the Others into a single body.

The invention of theatrical representation stems from that original situation. It is concerned, unquestionably, with a *game*. Why?

Human life can, in theory, be explained with the help of science, except at five mysterious points through which the religions and philosophies have crept in:

- birth
- death
- the Being's double
- self-awareness
- language

Which of these five mysteries is the first, I cannot tell. Perhaps, after all, the miracle of language, which may have engendered self-awareness, which in turn poses questions (before being born, one was – what? But one must die, to go – where?) and automatically divides our Being into two. It is self-awareness that first perceives death. Life is a kill. From this point onwards one looks for the key to the mysteries, one hazards explanations.

While the progress of science moves forward continuously along the road of knowledge, when we come to the mysteries we have to proceed by leaps.

As long as Claudel is exploring the most secret regions of the human soul, he uncovers for us extraordinary treasures, touches the heart of man and woman: 'One heart only in order to be two.' But when he says: 'The woman is the road that leads to God', he is having recourse to a 'leap'. The personalization of God is the supreme 'leap'. I am not saying that it is bad.

When Teilhard de Chardin describes matter, it is magnificent; when he attributes to it a sort of awareness, he is already bringing in a bit of imagination, but it is still possible. Between the three forces that underlie our life:

- invariance or need for conservation;
- the desire for greater energy – 'to be more';
- and the spirit of selection or freedom of choice;

it must be that the 'to be more' is superior to disorder, to entropy, and that in the last analysis matter is an adventure that can be perfected. Therefore we continue to follow him when he reaches the point *Omega*. But when he announces that this Omega is Christ, he too has to make a 'leap'. I am not saying he is wrong.

Similarly with the man who asserts that after death there is nothing – to know what 'nothing' is he must have recourse to a 'leap'.[1] So the human being

---

[1] To a scientific biologist, death does not exist. Granted, this is true. But it has to be admitted that, to 'ordinary mortals', the 'perpetually living' deoxyribonucleic acid has not the charm of human life. To say this does not make me an anthropocentrist!

is a strange kind of animal that has been granted an awareness which doubles him. He lives and sees himself living. He exists and knows he is dying. He is present at his own life. He is at one and the same time actor and spectator. He has one foot on the stage and one in the audience.

Deep down, he feels he is alone and perishable.

Strange unbalanced puppet on his string, he knows he must move forward and equally well knows that, at the most unexpected moment, the strings will break. And then will come the fall: upwards according to the faithful, down according to the 'unbelievers'. So anguish is born. At first a small, light, tenuous note, which insists on growing stronger with the rhythm of our pulsations, it becomes a cruel booming as time runs out and the tape gets less; and we could easily burst our brain if we did not have recourse to extreme types of action: aggression or flight.

Defiance to death, or pirouette.

Action by grappling direct, or action through the absurd.

Tragedy, or comedy.

> No matter from which side I turn my eyes on me
> Misfortunes that condemn the Gods are all I see . . .
> . . .
> Yes, I do honour thee, Heaven, for thy perseverance . . . (Racine)

Let's attack death, head on ! Or else like Menander: *My joy keeps me from knowing where I am.* Or like Molière: let's laugh at it !

Whether tragedy or comedy, the source is the same: *solitude* and *anguish* bring theatre to birth in us. It is the game ending in the kill.

But why 'play' with what seems so serious? Death is the consequence of the errors committed by the living cells. The fewer errors there are, the longer death will be put off. So everything must be *utilitarian*. To eat, sleep, procreate and work, so as to be able to sleep, procreate and eat. And to play? A fresh mystery. Everyone plays. Animals too play. They remember and they make-believe. They discover imagination. Is play, then, utilitarian? What does a dog do with a ball? He has seen it, he circles round it, he crouches and observes it, creeps towards it, then pounces on it. It has become an enemy; he attacks it, wounds it; after wild leaps, he is the victor. Then he abandons himself to a victory dance. When the victory is complete, he goes and buries the ball, until next time.

What was the dog doing? Exactly what soldiers do in peacetime. He has been doing manoeuvres. He has been training to fight. Play is training to live.

This is what the people in a theatre are doing. They recreate death, danger, crimes, sickness, anguish, solitude, horror – but 'whitewashed'. They get themselves inoculated with a vaccine of death. The plague is rigged up on stage, and we lance the tumour with all our dark forces. This purifies us, and we go away clean and fortified.

This is how the individual drama becomes a thing of public utility. By accepting oneself, one accepts the Others. One comes to see, gradually, that

'Self' and the 'Others' were not by any means two separate worlds, everything hangs together. Fresh discovery!

No living being is an isolated existence, as though under a glass bell, but each is an incandescent centre that is one with its environment in both Space and Time.

Such a concentration is not a simple matter: it goes beyond the limits of reason; it must be sensory. The situation is far too complicated for ordinary intelligence. For example: the three terms 'Past – Present – Future' do not form a straight line, with the past behind and the future in front, but a series of circles of which the Present is the centre, as though, in two opposing currents, the circular ripples of the future were converging towards the centre, and the circular ripples of the past were being propagated outwards, creating an infinity of swirls. And since that centre also is moving in time along a rectilinear trajectory,[1] at every instant 'present', the character keeps running into ripples of 'past' that are struck by ripples of 'future'. This is the great *soup of existence*, of which the theatre is the reflection.

When a man, encumbered with his 'id', his 'ego' and his 'superego', moves out on the stage of life, his 'situation' is the same. He is not alone or isolated. He belongs to the great shared body. A man is a magnetic centre moving in space.

And so what I have lived through, up to now, is something I shall meet again on my way. My past is in front of me. With that manifesto, As I Lay Dying, there occurred a rending of the veil, through which I discovered a world of poetry that was to impose itself on me for life. From that time onwards I have belonged to it, I would never be able to leave it, I would be its slave, it would require of me servitude and the total gift of myself.

But at the same time, since I am not an isolated being but am one with the Others, I have to come to terms with life. From that moment I knew the destination of my journey, but my ship was part of the sea. I had glimpsed perfection, I knew very well what had to be done, but in order to do it I must survive and, in order to survive, one must keep afloat, keep watch, trick, take evasive action, betray. Life is that.

> *Handled, tossed, dandled, scrubbed, struck, knocked over – and that sea, how she pounces on us, the pagan creature! Oh! là là, under that maniac wind ... that hard mistral harrowing the broken water. The whole sea raised up upon itself, bumping, stamping, kicking at the sun, decamping in the stormwind.*
>
> (Claudel, *Partage de Midi*)

With As I Lay Dying I had drunk my first big draught of life! That period at the Atelier had enabled me to get to know Man, the individual. A man, that instrument, creating the art of human conduct, or theatre.

[1] Or geodesic – why not?

To the theatre, the Cartel had been what the Fauves had been to painting. I had received from it the aesthetic graft. But society had had no place in our preoccupations. We had been taking no account of the Others. The artist went on with his dreams; he obeyed his inner claims and made his objects, in other words his work, in consequence. Then whoever wanted to come could. The theatre was exclusively a poetic art, 'The Poetry of Space by means of the human Being'.

But there was no question of the Others. Fundamentally, even though I did not realize it, that was why I tore myself away from the Atelier. Dullin was *the Man*. I now needed to mingle with *Men*. I wanted to move from the individual to society.

Thanks to my first manifesto, the Surrealists held out a hand to me. I gave myself up to their movement and was soon to marry their Rebellion.

The Grenier des Grands-Augustins

I HAD FOUND a marvellous place, in the rue des Grands-Augustins, at number 7 or number 11 – anyhow two good numbers. An old building, sixteenth century. In the evenings it became completely empty. You reached it by going up a few steps at the far end of a courtyard humped with old paving-stones. On the raised ground floor the Bailiffs' Union had its offices. Above them there was a weaving-shop with some very fine old looms. I had taken the top floor – three extraordinary rooms with magnificent uncovered beams. The first was forty-six feet by twenty-six feet. I took it as my workroom, and we gave shows there. (It was later to become Picasso's studio.) The second room, fifty feet by thirteen, became a dormitory, a dining-room, lavatories and box-room all together : the common room. I can still see a notice : 'Le lavabo doit rester bo'. The third, twenty-six by thirteen, I reserved for myself. But often, when I came home late at night, I would find people in my bed.

I founded a 'company', called Le Grenier des Augustins. Jean Dasté was with us at the start – he soon resumed his freedom; he was right, for I was a long way from being mature. I still had a lot of living to do.

Saint-Germain-des-Prés was my new village. The surrealist movement, my new faith. To it, as to the Cartel, I was a latecomer. The split had already happened. The surrealist Revolution had divided into three branches, like a living cell no longer able to co-ordinate its three forces. With stubborn strictness André Breton was trying desperately to preserve the purity of the movement. He agreed to ally himself with left-wing politics, while retaining lucidity and freedom of judgment. Aragon and Eluard, wishing to move on to effective action, had chosen to enter an 'Order' and had become converted to Communism, therefore to politics. Those who were now unwilling to follow either Breton or the others had resumed their liberty : Robert Desnos, André Masson, Artaud, Balthus, Jacques Prévert, etc. – the libertarians. Instinctively I joined these.

I was very raw at that time, very primitive, I had not enough specialized knowledge to become an intellectual; many things must have passed over my head. Besides, I was not being asked to understand. I was won over – that was enough. And indeed the whole business was not exactly clear. To the papacy of Breton, Aragon's communist schism and the diaspora of the individualists, a fourth vein might be added, the one that came from the Dada movement: Tristan Tzara, Dr Fraenkel, etc. All these people continued to mix, Breton and Georges Bataille asked me to let them hold their assemblies at the Grenier. So it came about that, on 21 January 1936, there took place a grave ceremony full of black humour in honour of the beheading of Louis XVI. Humour? Rather seriousness clowning so as not to become too serious.

77

So also it came about that we studied the book of Public Prosecutor Brisset who, by simply stripping words down, traced the origin of man to the frog. *'Je m'examine . . . je me sexe à mine . . . je me sexe à la main'*, and so on. The longer it went on, the more unbearable it became – and the more it was what was needed. What these talented bores and mock exams taught was worth learning.

Up to then I had rubbed shoulders with men who, not meeting with sympathy from the society known as that of 'respectable people', had contented themselves with turning their backs on it. Each camp lived in separation. 'There is not one time for form and another for content,' Valéry used to say; yet they confined themselves to playing with forms without giving any real thought to changing the content. That is why I have called that period an aesthetic period. The bad lots of Montmartre were good underneath. They just had no social sense, they were not interested.

Only Gémier, originator of popular theatre in Paris, had been before his time in having an inkling of these things. To the others society was like some sinister but strongly established citadel. To the Surrealists, on the contrary, the citadel had cracks in it: form and content must be blown up simultaneously. Established society was attacked both on the plane of the individual and of the collectivity. Through Freud and through Karl Marx. Freud's share: liberation of the instincts. Marx's share: liberation of Man. Suddenly the aesthetic ideal itself had been called in question. 'We shall not have demolished everything unless we demolish even the ruins,' says Father Ubu.

This revolution struck me as an extraordinary cleaning operation, beginning with the brains. Automatic writing, waking dreams, hallucinations. To blow up the Others, lock, stock and barrel, is not enough. The real courage consists in blowing up one's own lock, stock and barrel.

> *'Before remaking the world, remake yourself.'*
> *'Every human being is a poet without knowing.'*
>   (These slogans were to turn up again in May 1968)

Soon there was added to the influence of Freud and Marx the attraction of the East. This was natural, inevitable, logical: even cartesian. Freud was called the father of the family. Marx was called the collective Father. The philosophers meanwhile were relentlessly bringing down the Super-Father – there was the famous 'God is dead'. But because the slaughter of God the Father did not do away with the metaphysical sense which everyone carries in him, with that longing to penetrate into the mysteries of existence, recourse was had to the wisdom of the East.

> *You who are aware how one turns back in one's thinking and how the mind contrives to escape from itself, you who are interior to yourselves, you whose spirit is no longer on the plane of the flesh . . ., pitch into the water all these Whites who arrive with those small heads of theirs and their minds on their best behaviour . . . Save us from the rot of Reason . . .*

*Europe with its logic is crushing the spirit ... Save us from these insects.
Invent for us fresh homes.*

(Révolution surréaliste, no. 3, 1925)

The Bhagavad-Gita, Tantric Yoga, Hatha Yoga, the Upanishads and Mil-
arepa, but also the 'golden verses' of Pythagoras and Trotsky's *My Life*, became
my preferred reading. I can still see myself going with Robert Desnos to
Trotskyist meetings at the Salle Susset, close to the Métro Jaurès. Desnos used
to improvise poems to my mime turns; I used to improvise mime to his poems.
Desnos had real genius for automatic thinking, and was the most gifted of them
all for waking dreams.

Was I aware of the seriousness of all this? I don't think so. What I remember
from this period, which lasted for two seasons, is the effervescence, freedom
from care and complete liberty of my behaviour. This behaviour was perfectly
deliberate. I meant things to happen as they did. Anarchy is a kind of nobility.
It consists of an entire and absolute responsibility for oneself. Nothing to do
with the 'terrorists'.

At the Grenier the door was never closed. Anyone who wished came to live
there. I left it to my comrades to run the place. We had fixed up beds in every
corner. An ideal republic. Once a week we organized a picnic. Everyone brought
what he wished. The girls in our group would cook a dish. I see now an
enormous basin filled with calamaris. The imagination of the guests was not
always wide awake, and sometimes forty camemberts would descend on us – we
had our work cut out to finish them off during the rest of the week.

Since there would be fifty to sixty of us on those evenings, we would improvise a show. I liked improvising mime to a record of Varèse's *Ionisation*.
Gilles Margaritis practised for his Chesterfolies turns. His partner Caccia's harmonium was mine. I adored the mind of Gilles Margaritis – his clown's soul
with its subtle melancholy.

Sylvain Itkine was working at the Grenier for his company, Le Diable
écarlate. It was there that he prepared Montherlant's *Pasiphaé* and Jarry's *Ubu
enchaîné*.

I had asked Prévert to adapt Cervantes' *The Wonder Show*.[1] In it two
mountebanks are presenting a show that can only be seen by 'decent people'.
In fact nothing at all is shown, but everyone, in order to be taken as decent,
'sees' something. The subject was a piece of cake for the author of the '*Dîner de
têtes*'.[2]

Another who used to come was Tchimoukov, who was responsible for the
Groupe d'Octobre. This group had just won the Moscow Olympiad prize. It was
the perfect example of the kind of young revolutionary company Jacques
Prévert was so fond of.

Sylvain Itkine was to die under torture in Lyons during the war. He was a

---

[1] *El retablo de las maravillas* (1615).
[2] Title of a poem by Prévert.

perfect human being. Passionate, strong-willed, mordant, with a child's smile and gaze.

We had also several comrades who belonged to the I A F (International Anarchist Federation). Princes, knights. During the war in Spain they were massacred, especially by the Communists.

The gypsy composer Joseph Kosma wrote for us marvellous songs to poems by Prévert. We needed a child: Itkine found me one who was at a loose end in one of the working-class quarters of Paris. He must have been about eight, and was afraid of only two kinds of animals: cops and dogs. His name was Mouloudji. A bed was found for him at the Grenier. The first evening he was there he went off to bed, but we could hear him moving about.

'Aren't you asleep?'

'No, I'm rocking myself to sleep.'

And in fact he was swaying from side to side. Then he curled up and was asleep.

'I've always rocked myself to sleep. . . .'

He had an enchanting voice, and when he sang, with that smile of his, 'Ah! comme elle est triste notre enfance', by Jacques Prévert and Kosma, each of us had a lump in his throat.

And then there was Baquet: prize cellist, acrobatic clown, actor and ski instructor. If someone had taken us in hand, we might have made an excellent commedia dell'arte company. But that was just it: we did not want to be taken in hand.

Prévert used to write his poems on scraps of paper – it would never have occurred to him for a moment to put them together and make a book of them. Anarchist generosity was the rule, an unwritten rule, simply self-evident. Respect for the joy of living came first.

Such liberty was bound to deteriorate sometimes. For example the picnics. At the start we were just ourselves. Then we invited friends. The friends brought others. The first ones got tired of it and stopped coming. In the end there was nobody I recognized. I understood the situation when one day, in the rue de Rennes, a man came up to me and shook hands, saying:

'You don't remember me? We spent the evening together the day before yesterday, at Barrault's.'

I have always wondered who he thought Barrault was.

ARTAUD

We saw each other almost every day. Sometimes we would exchange a rose. He asked me to imitate him. I did so. At first he smiled, followed closely every detail, approved – then grew exasperated, then in excitement started shouting:

'I've been r-r-r-robbed of my p-p-p-personality . . . I've been r-r-r-robbed of my p-p-p-personality !'

And he ran out of the room. Had I hurt him? No. For I could hear him on the stairs, laughing uproariously. Neither of us was taken in by the other. My relation with Artaud was always human, not literary.

Every person gifted with a fertile imagination 'goes through to the other side'. He *moves out of his own circle*, but he is aware of it. And this enables him to come back, to re-enter himself. Artaud never stopped leaving himself. As long as he kept his lucidity, he was fantastic. Royal. Prodigious in his visions. Funny in his repartees. He was completely lubricated with humour. But when, under the effect of drugs or of illness, his escapades submerged him, the machine began to creak and it was painful, wretched. One suffered for him. His body had stiffened, twisted backwards like a person deformed under torture. His teeth seemed to wear themselves out biting his lips. His skull developed monstrously as if from the pressure of the brain. His eye-sockets seemed all the more huge because his glance carried a long way – like a laser beam. He had been particularly handsome, but his inner fire was calcining him. The frequency of the vibrations of his diaphragm made his voice strike against the outer frontal regions of his resonators. His voice was at the same time hoarse and shrill. A child who has set himself on fire. For we had child-like pleasures.

Once, the mother of a young and beautiful actress whom we knew invited us to dinner at Passy. She was a well-to-do middle-class lady who, I think, was eager for her daughter's sake to display an enlightened attitude towards our theatrical community. Artaud took her good intentions literally, as no one else could have done. In the middle of the meal he stripped to the waist, invited me to follow his example and gave a demonstration of Yoga exercises, after which he remained half-naked in front of his elegant hostess, who could think of no better homage to this 'delicious performance' than to wonder, out loud, how it was that the Comédie Française had not yet discovered him. Thereupon Artaud banged the lady's head several times lightly with his dessert spoon and shouted in her ear, in his strange metallic voice: 'Madame, you get on my nerves!'

Sometimes he failed to notice the intensity of his voice. On another evening, Jean-Marie Conty, who was a fan of Artaud's, in order to help him to put on his *Conquête du Mexique*, had organized a dinner with possible backers. All these fine people had accepted the kind invitation, chiefly to see Artaud close to. In the drawing-room our poet was at the top of his bent. Imagining that he was speaking under his breath, he shouted in my ear all that he thought of that honourable society. The least one can say is that his remarks were not polite. Finally he demanded silence and exploded:

'My only reason for letting the lot of you make me feel sick is to give you the chance of returning to the theatre and to human beings a little of the money you extort from the poor,' etc.

Or anyhow something in that vein.

The evening came to grief, and *La Conquête du Mexique* was never put on. It was Artaud who went to Mexico, to recover his health with the help of the magic ceremonies of the Peyotl Indians. He had said to me, after the sublime failure of his *Cenci* :

'Tragedy on the stage is not enough for me, I'm going to bring it into my life.'

He was to keep his word. He made himself into a theatre – a theatre that did not cheat.

It was as we walked down from Passy all the way to Saint-Germain-des-Prés that he made me swear never to take drugs. Between drugs and Artaud there was a corpse : himself. He said a thing I still find overwhelming :

> To *cure me of the judgment of the Others, I have this: the whole distance that separates me from myself.*

His extralucidity. Unquestionably he knew he was ill. Certainly, from early youth, his bodily sufferings were cruel. To mitigate them, he took drugs. But he was aware that under the influence of drugs he lost his vitality. He would beg to be detoxified. His letters are evidence of this. After a few days the torture was such that he would again implore a little of some drug. No matter which, according to how much money he had, or to the generosity of his real friends. Opium, cocaine, hashish, heroin, valerian, laudanum, anything : a little of that 'filth'.

Like De Quincey, he took drugs because he was ill, did not become ill because he took drugs. Anyone who in these days goes on drugs in order to have Artaud's genius has misunderstood. It is the same with alcohol. Poets who drink – and I know some – do so from despair; because the fear of living is strangling them, because they want to suppress themselves : an extreme unction. They know very well that at those times they are no longer anything. This is precisely what they want. They do not do it to realize their dreams and write better. But the misunderstanding goes on.

And so he left for Mexico to be *cured* once more. When I saw him again, he was no longer able to come back into his circle. He left again, this time for Ireland. He came home with Saint Patrick's stick. He gave it to me, as he did Lao-tzu's stick. He was taking on his shoulders his own tragedy.

My last memory of him : at the little restaurant called *Chez Jean*, in the Place Dauphine. He read me the manuscript of his *Taharumaras*. Then the *Correspondance de Rodez*.[1] After that the distance between us grew. In him : the destiny of a crucified man. In me, I suppose, the desire to live, to fulfil my own destiny, and, above all, disgust at seeing him used by certain intellectuals for ends that seemed to me sordid. There was, in particular, a certain perform-ance at the Vieux Colombier, which I refused to attend. It was dreadful, point-less, shameful. The outlandish animal was being displayed, not for his sake but to make use of him. Misery and disgust.

And yet in June 1946, at the Théâtre Sarah-Bernhardt, there was – so it seems – a performance for his benefit. My name is on the programme. An act of solidarity, therefore. I must have had no objection to it, and yet I remember

[1] Put together by André Frank and published by Gallimard.

nothing. Probably I was absent from Paris. I don't now know. The abysses of the human heart. . . .

What did he reveal to me? Through him the metaphysics of the theatre had got right inside me.

Up to then, thanks to the teachings of the Atelier, to the night on Volpone's bed and to those two years spent with Dullin, I had become acquainted with the physique of the human body. It was clear to me that the art of the theatre consisted in recreating life – observed from the angle of Silence and of the Present – by means of the human Being. A man, that instrument. But one's conceptions concerning that instrument were all scientific.

The approaches to oriental wisdom which I had tried to make through my reading, on Artaud's advice, had given me a first glimpse of horizons other than the extremely clear ones of the flesh as matter. The irradiation of our fleshly being carries far further than the contours of our skin. The infinite resources of muscular contraction and of breathing make a man into a battery, producing magnetism. Besides, it would be a false simplification to separate the influence of Dullin and Decroux from that of Artaud: there was not a succession of influences, they were working in me simultaneously. At the Grenier I instinctively drew closer to Artaud, that is all.

Although he found some difficulty in making his ideas concrete because of his frail health, the help he brought me was much greater in the technical field than in the intellectual. And one reason why we came so close together during that short period was that he, in his turn, had discovered in me a quantity of sensations which he already shared. Possibly I reassured him by my spontaneous reactions. In our joint soul, fire and laughter shook down well together.[1] Passion and humour: this alloy has always been the foundation of my nature. It still is. Æschylus and Feydeau. And among the many mottoes I have adopted in the course of my life, there is one which sits firm:

Feel passion for it all and cling to nothing.

This passion, then, was for the human mechanism, the pulse of life and the virtues of their magic.

When Artaud taught me the ternary of the cabbala, I was intrigued, magnetized. I could have made use of it next day, to 'astonish the groundlings'. I can say in my favour: I was free from that snobbery. The word 'cabbala' remained foreign – 'too strong for me'. On the contrary, the phenomenon of the ternary hit me point blank – I recognized myself in it. Artaud was giving me a key. It was for me to find the lock.

Whether it came from Dullin, or Decroux, or Artaud, or above all from my personal experiences and my imagination, I would like now, in a few pages, to take you on a tour of this world in which I then began to live, and which is still mine.

1 'Alfred Jarry's drama gives up any attempt to enumerate all the fragmentary influences it may have undergone: the Elizabethan theatre, Chekhov, Strindberg, Feydeau . . .' (Artaud).

ALCHEMY OF THE HUMAN BODY[1]

> *Ah! my father and my mother, how I have it in for you.*
> (M. Jourdain, *Le Bourgeois Gentilhomme*)

Imagine an alchemist's laboratory.

My instruments: the elements of the human body. My field: life in the Present. The base: Silence. Let us begin!

Life on the move: all the presents succeeding one another like so many successive deaths down to the final mutation. Becoming:

> *A man never bathes in the same water twice.* (Heraclitus)

That has been known since time immemorial: Space is *movement*. In the course of this slow and irresistible march, the molecules meet, rub up against each other, collide or associate: all the dusts of life, in their interplay, ceaselessly establish *exchanges*. And all this happens in accordance with a certain *rhythm*: the 'tempo' of universal gravitation.

To transform into a concrete and palpable object all these elusive vibrations which alone constitute the Present, I need an instrument that can reproduce, in their natural state,

movement
exchange
rhythm.

Now follow me and touch the object. Observe this *spinal column*, as supple as a whip; is it not *movement* itself? The flexibility of a snake. Note these blacksmith's bellows, the *respiratory apparatus*, ceaselessly establishing and keeping up a double circulation between the being and the universe, between the exterior and self. Is not this the seat of *exchanges*? And listen to the tom-tom of that witch-doctor, the *heart*, as it beats a short beat, then a long one. The iambic, as you remark. Does it not fit in with the universal *rhythm*? In life we beat iambics.

Let us observe more closely respiration: the chest dilates, it *receives* air. It contracts: it sends the air out again, it *gives*. It can also clench: it *holds the breath*, it suspends the circulation of exchanges. Let us call this *retention*. There you have the primitive ternary of life: Receiving, Giving, Retaining. The ternary of breathing is: Inspiration, Expiration, Retention. For the moment we are not thinking; indeed we shall not ever 'think'.

But the sensuality of life makes it easy for us to understand that:

Receiving is the feminine time
Giving is the masculine time
Retaining is the neuter time.
There you have the cabbalistic ternary.

---

[1] The reader can very well skip this exposition, if he finds it too austere, and come back to our life at the Grenier on page 88.

Of course it is not a matter of women or of men : whichever our sex, we are all made up of the ternary of life. The ratio varies according to the sexes, and in the artist the whole thing is confused.

Every ternary has six components :

Neuter – masculine – feminine
Neuter – feminine – masculine
Masculine – feminine – neuter
Masculine – neuter – feminine
Feminine – neuter – masculine
Feminine – masculine – neuter.

You ask me what I am leading up to? Let us apply this reasoning to painting. The ternary is :

yellow *neuter*, blue *masculine*, red *feminine*

the three basic colours.

Bringing into play all the components, you add :

yellow and blue =*green*
blue and red   =*purple*
red and yellow =*orange*

the complementary colours.

By play of these six colours you can obtain an infinity of broken tones.

In the same way, by the play of the respiration ternary, you can obtain an infinity of respiratory states.

What is the interest of that? Just as a Being is double, so there are two kinds of breathing : unconscious breathing, which keeps up biological life, the 'self'; and conscious breathing, that of the Personage, who establishes contact with the Others. The nature of a conscious breathing may change the nature of an unconscious breathing. We will call this : being in a certain state. In life this happens quite naturally. But if we can acquire a respiratory alchemy, we can manage to put ourselves into determined states. This artificial recreation of what happens naturally in life is *the art of breathing*. You realize that we are now approaching the science of human behaviour, that is, of theatre.

Before going any further, let us take note of a fresh observation which, once again, painting can make plain. To the six colours (three fundamental, three complementary) must be added two influences : white and black. Light and its shadow. In the same way we add to the respiratory combinations two influences, two currents, two influxes according to which, in action, the individual weighs on the Exterior (active influxes) or the Exterior weighs on the individual (passive influxes). It is precisely these two influxes that make possible the *infinity* of broken tones or of states. I know it is difficult to get inside these perceptions by reading alone, but theatre is, above all, 'the lab of living'.

To take an example : in spite of me, against my will, the exterior forces me to breathe in. This inspiration is therefore 'passive'. I am forced to absorb air which does not suit me. It could just as well be an idea, or the reading of this tiresome text. When I can stand it no longer, I assemble my will and, with all my energy, expel, by 'active' expiration, what someone or something tried to impose on me. Then I shut down. But soon, on pain of asphyxiation, air comes in again against my will, and so on. If I give myself up to that sort of respiratory rhythm for two or three moments, I shall experience *really*, even in my unconscious breathing, *the state of anger*.

If, on the contrary, I breathe out passively, I precipitate myself – in order to survive – into an inspiration for which I have assembled all my strength; at the height of my 'active' inspiration, I want to keep this precious nourishment and I shut down. But soon, not having enough strength to keep this bit of life, I have to obey the fresh expiration, and so on. If I give myself up for two or three months to this respiratory rhythm, I shall experience *really*, even in my unconscious breathing, *the state of weakness, of sickness, then of death*.

Let us now leave that sample of *respiratory alchemy* and move on to gesture. The spinal column, with the aid of the bust, the neck, the head and the limbs, commands and designs our gestures. Same ternary:

Pull	push	retention
receive	give	retain
feminine	*masculine*	*neuter*

(Cabbala).

Same combinations. Same influxes: active and passive. Same infinity of broken tones. In other words, same richly resourceful language.

> *Whatever is not prose is verse, whatever is not verse is prose.*

(The Philosophy Master in *Le Bourgeois Gentilhomme*.)

Thus – having taken care not as yet to bring in ideas – we know that the human body possesses, physically, a language of breathing and a language of gesture. The language of gesture also has its rudimentary grammar: subject, verb, object. In terms of mime these are called: attitude, movement, indication. As for speech, it is the result of combining a muscular contraction and a breath. More or less rapid frequency of the contractions of my diaphragm sends air into the more or less closely moulded cavity of my mouth: so the vowels take form. As this air passes, I *carve* the consonants by the muscular contractions of my lips or tongue. So the syllable is created and the word appears. The word is like a little bag into which I put an image or an idea. We send it off into the air like a shell; it bursts, and the idea or the image is parachuted like radio-active fallout on to people's shoulders. Speech is originally a pantomime of the mouth. There is therefore no break of continuity between a gesture and a word; both of them, physically, are a part of the same creation, the result of a muscular contraction and a respiration. Magic of life; religion, that is, extreme physical sensation.

When, two years later, Claudel gave me the definition 'word: an intelligible mouthful', you will understand with what eagerness I drew closer to him.

Our body contains, roughly, four centres of energy: head, belly, sex and nerves.[1] Most often, one of these centres dominates the other three and takes control of our behaviour. It acts especially on the frequency of the vibrations of the diaphragm. Then the breath comes and strikes upon different points of that complex cavity – mouth, nose and frontal resonators. So the sound of the vowel gets its particular quality. The visceral centre sends the sound against the lower lip; the sexual centre into the throat; the cervical or intellectual centre strikes the palate; and the nervous centre reaches the resonators of the nose and brow. Thus the voice is not a simple musical instrument but an orchestra. The belly uses the trombones; the sex the violins; the head the woodwind and horns; and the nerves the shrill trumpets, piccolos – or musical saws.

It is rare for anyone to say 'I love you' in an adjutant's tone of voice. It is rare for an adjutant to give the command ' 'Shun !' in a throat voice as if saying 'I love you'. And if the girl sitting next to you at table whispers 'Would you give me some wine?' in an ovarian tone, you may safely venture your knee – she is sensitive to your presence. The gap between what one is officially saying and the voice that comes to us for transmitting it gives an extra dimension to our behaviour.

In *Phèdre*, Hippolyte speaks to Aricie of 'reasons of State' in a throat voice, because he is in love with Aricie and her presence disturbs him deeply. His voice 'fails him'. Diction in the theatre is the art of shifting one's voice. Artaud's voice used to lay bare his nerves.

Objectivity – Subjectivity

We look with our eyes. We see with the chest. This is the difference between analysis and synthesis. Subjective concentration is respiratory. If I am listening to what you are saying, but my true being is attracted by the girl next to me, my head will be turned towards you but my chest towards her. The axis of the body is a coil.

Another key: *the understanding of cruelty*, according to Artaud. At least so far as I have understood it. Cruelty is life. It is not an inclination, it is an admission. Where there is most life, there is most cruelty. From this to seeking cruelty is only a step. But it has nothing to do with either sadism or masochism – these are 'failures' of life. As in the case of drugs, one must beware of misunderstanding. 'Kindly do not seek gratuitous cruelty in the name of Antonin Artaud.'

The primordial law of nature is the law of aggression: it is a creative law. To attack in order to get further. But men sin out of misunderstanding: they have invented destructive aggression. This is no longer a liberation of the instincts, it is a sickness: man has lost the sense of his own survival. Freud's notion of a 'deathwish' seems to me now outdated, thanks to the progress of biology.

In a lecture he gave in Mexico, Artaud spoke of my work. I quote a few lines of it to show how far we were in agreement:

[1] This is still Plato's ternary, plus the top of the tetrahedron (volume composed of four triangles).

This theatre in space is more than a social revolt which does not accept the law of Destiny, it is a theatre filled with cries, which are not cries of fear but of rage, and even more than of rage, of the feeling of the value of life.

It is a theatre that can weep, yet has an enormous alertness to laughter, and knows that there is in laughter an idea which is pure, a beneficent and pure idea of the eternal forces of life.

Artaud, before I knew him, had created at the Théâtre de Grenelle the 'Alfred Jarry Theatre'.

Jarry : the clown streaming with tears.

Artaud : the grimace of laughter on the face of a crucified man.

Artaud : the Van Gogh of the modern theatre.

Now back to our life at the Grenier. Decroux had been right up to a point : I was dispersing my energies. Instead of persevering in the underground galleries of theatrical seeking, I was responding to all the appeals of life. My astral conjunction is, apparently, Mercury/Venus. It has nothing Saturnine about it. I cannot help it. A libertarian, sowing my wild oats, I was living like a sprinkler-rose. For one thing, the Spanish Revolution, which had just broken out, was heating people's brains. For another, the film world was making offers to me. I have always – contrary to what people have thought – liked taking part in films. In the film world I have met only charming people; I have made some real friends there. The life one lives there is full of fantasy : outside office hours, like in Les Halles. And lastly, I had understood that, by marrying cinema and theatre, I would be able to run my life successfully. Marc Allégret engaged me again, this time for a part in *Sous les yeux d'Occident* (*Under Western Eyes*), the part of a terrorist.

As regards theatre, I entertained the secret desire to form a company, though I still did not clearly see how. I *intended* to be, some day, responsible for a group of human beings. This was my will, my aim, my voyage, my passage : the destiny I had marked out for myself. But I was alone and had been thrown into society. When one is on the high seas, what else can one do but 'negotiate' the waves? I admire the people who go straight ahead; they doubtless have the means of commanding the elements. Spending a third of my time in the studios, another third living without thinking, I devoted the remaining third to *my* theatre.

I have already said that I am timid – let us call it fear-ridden. I can feel that, as the present introspection goes on, I shall come to recognize this fear more and more clearly. I wonder, in fact, whether fear is not at the source of life, even before the law of aggression. When a cell wants to become two cells, is it not because it is afraid of no longer being a cell at all? When nature discovered aggression, was it not from fear of ceasing to be? Is a man without fear really alive?

Later on, as I now remember, Dr Schweitzer, who honoured me with a touching friendship, was to reveal to me that fear *rules* over life. To be afraid, come to think of it . . . there is plenty of food for thought there, one must admit!

For fear that my fine ideas on the theatre might have only a very relative truth, I was looking for confirmations of them. In ancient Greek drama? Tempting, but difficult. In the French classics? Dangerous. I did want to test my ideas, but on condition that I would find good reasons for going on believing in them. Some of the Surrealists, Georges Bataille for instance, loved Corneille. I was more attracted by Racine. Claudel? Almost unknown to me. Artaud had indeed already put on one act of *Partage de Midi*, of which the script was being passed round surreptitiously. Had he not declared: 'The act you have just heard is by Paul Claudel, poet, ambassador and *traitor*'? And to the question: 'Who is, in your opinion, the best living French poet?' had not Desnos replied: 'Claudel, God help us!' In my circle everyone was anticlerical. I did not care one way or the other.

André Masson (who, at the approach of the Civil War, had brought back from Spain his wife and his two babies, Diego and Luis) said to me: 'Since you love Cervantes, you should reread *Numance*.' I caught fire at once. Masson had been right. I had found what I was looking for, a classic off the beaten track. On the social plane I would be bringing my contribution to the Spanish Republicans; in that play the individual was respected, liberty glorified. On the plane of the metaphysics of the theatre I would be going right into the world of the fantastic, death, blood, famine, fury, frenzy. There would be song, mime, dance, reality, the surreal. *The river, fire, magic, my total theatre.* I threw myself into it without reserve. *Numance* (*La Numancia*): the confirmation that might very well enable me to go further.

André Masson gave me willing support; he promised me his collaboration over the costumes and sets. As for the music, we would see. I was caught, as they say a bitch is caught. With a bitch gestation lasts sixty-five days, with a mare eleven months. With an artist, his spiral ternary spinning like a top – feminine, neuter, masculine – who can say?

At this point another business was grafted on. *Sous les yeux d'Occident* was being shown everywhere. Jean-Benoît Lévy, well known because of his film *La Maternelle*, noticed me. He adored Madeleine Renaud and was preparing a new film for her: *Hélène*. The two of them were looking for a juvenile lead. Madeleine Renaud wanted Claude Dauphin. And quite right too. He had everything: subtlety, talent, intelligence, wit and physical attraction.

'All the same, I have discovered a young man whom I would like to introduce to you. He's not handsome, but he can look and he can smile.'

'Nothing wrong with that. When can I meet him?'

'I'll send him to you. But I warn you, he's wild and he's dirty. Badly shaved, no tie. . . .'

'Tell him to shave and wash, and above all not to bite me.'

Jean-Benoît Lévy was looking for me everywhere. I was at L'Alpe d'Huez with my revolutionary buddies. The Trotskyists were already hooked on holidays in the snow. We were in the avant-garde in everything and everywhere. Even skiing. It was the heyday of the Popular Front. We used to go and recite poems in the factories. The Renault works and the salesgirls in the big stores were discovering Jacques Prévert, Paul Eluard and Louis Aragon. The first holiday camps were making their appearance, and the tandem was being brought into fashion. The branches of the *Printemps* were marketing, in advance of their time, the first little ready-made printed dresses. The girls looked enchanting. The people were shaking free. With prophetic insight, Léon Blum, whom I admired almost as much as Trotsky, was just inventing a Ministry of Leisure. Human beings began to have glimpses of the right to live. An extraordinary period, which the 'respectable' were not to forgive. The right to life? Enjoying liberty and human respect? Anything but that! Rather war! They took three years to react. Three years of respite.

But let us come back to our business.

MADELEINE

It is my duty to say that Madeleine disapproves of this story of my life, which is largely the story of our life. It embarrasses her. I can understand her the more easily because it embarrasses me, too. And yet, when we see ourselves on the screen, we are no longer seeing ourselves. If I go to see a film in which I have taken part, I never think 'I', I think 'he'.

Anyhow, I am less embarrassed than she is, 1. because, being the writer, I am in action; 2. because I am writing the story of 'another' – my double is doubtless helping me. And besides, these are facts. Why not consent to report them?

I was enchanted by Jean-Benoît Lévy's proposal. The part was an important one, and I had an unreserved admiration for Madeleine Renaud. I had seen her in *La Maternelle*. She had just won the Grand Prix du Cinéma for her acting in *Maria Chapdelaine*. She was unquestionably a star and, in addition, one of the queens of the Comédie Française. Luckily my poet and anarchist comrades had the same admiration for her. In my group she commanded unanimity. To us, because completely human, she was the example of the true artist.

And so I went to see her. She lived in Passy in a superb house, decorated with pink cushions and modern glass trinkets. I had shaved, that was all. But do not believe malicious gossip: I was not as dirty as all that. And, though nervous, I was determined not to give up my 'puma' style.

The conversation was delightful. She asked me what I thought of the decoration of her drawing-room. I replied, frankly, that I detested it. I dragged in some literary quotations, and it was her turn for a little gentle mockery. She was charm itself, with her Angel of Reims smile and her large heavily lidded nut-brown eyes. I was above all attracted by her forearms, which seemed to me as appetizing as two warm brioches.

As she was showing me out, she said:

'Jean-Benoît Lévy would like me to make my hair a bit darker. What do you think?'

'As your future lover, I like your hair just as it is.'

We were talking of the part, of course, but I like to slip in the odd piece of foolery. Perhaps I was also making an attempt to charm. Women like a touch of insolence in men. There are two ways of doing them honour, treating them with respect and treating them with disrespect.

We started work on the film at Joinville. I had bought my first car, an old Citroën. Madeleine arrived like a meteor, driving her touring Talbot. It was July, the weather was lovely. She introduced me to her first husband, Charles Granval, whom I already admired, and to whom I took enormously. Like me, he belonged to the race of 'inoffensive anarchists'. When the day came for shooting the big love scene, our meal was served to the two of us in a small private room, with a bottle of champagne to put us in good form. Between shots I told her that I only cared for life as a couple, that I wanted to have a company of my own, to direct plays, to take on a human responsibility, etc. And while I expounded my ideas, which she found too intellectual, I kept on looking fixedly at those two small forearms of hers.

She must have found me funny. She was quite a flirt and was aware of the power of her voluptuous eyes: the look that goes a little further than it should and suddenly makes the lips open.

In short, nothing extraordinary happened. It was the life of the film world – its poetry. It is normal for one to pay court to one's partner when the characters are supposed to be in love, and it is good that the partner should let herself be courted. In the film I was in love with her to the point of suicide.

After three weeks in the studio, the team and the actors went off 'on location'. We stayed in Grenoble, at the Hôtel Lesdiguières. Madeleine took the opportunity to have a short joy-ride in the Midi. To the star, nothing could be refused. I took the opportunity to visit Tournus. I still have a photograph taken during that visit, at the moment when I said to my mother (I remember that moment clearly, the subconscious engraved it in me with exquisite prescience):

'Next time I shall bring Madeleine to see you.'

Was it a presentiment? Love, coming from immemorial ages and spreading secretly into the deepest corners of one's being? Bravado? A kind of wager? How did I know? In any case, a keen desire. My 'animal' wanted it. If Madeleine had known, she would have had a good laugh. As indeed my mother did.

When one is boiling water, the kettle begins to sing, then the water swirls for quite a while and suddenly, with big bubbles, is metamorphosed into steam. Up to then, in the studio, we had been singing – slightly swirling, let us admit. In the Dauphiné mountains, it was the metamorphosis.

During the scenes of kissing among the flowers in the fields, we would go on, forgetful of everyone, long after the camera had stopped. The technicians would come and gently tap us on the shoulder to bring us back to them. And we remained convinced that no one noticed anything. We had become irresponsible. But one day I was extra-lucid.

While the team was making ready for the next shot, I made my declaration, in the state of insensibility that comes at the great moments of life : a formal proposal. We were in the middle of a meadow.

'There is in you the deep down Being which is the one that corresponds to mine. I will take you for life and carry you in my pocket. Your present life is splendid but artificial. At heart you are not happy. Your soul is grey. My life too is not properly adjusted. You are the only one who can make me be what I could be. We shall make the two of us flower, and our souls will be luminous !'

Here again it was the rift in the mountain mist, which they call the 'window', and through which you discover the horizons you were hoping for : it is no longer a view, but vision. I was as sincere as a man can be, as convinced as possible that my Being was speaking to her Being, through me, through the two of us.

Mesa, I am Ysé. It is I.

It was not just mutual attraction, not just a matter of going to bed together, marvellous as that might be. No ! no ! it was far more than that ! It was something that came from much further, something that was bound to go further still. There is no future and no past, there is the eternal Present. Two halves of Being have to be made one. The couple.

'I have met you, now I admit you.'

'Hey ! are you coming ? It's your turn. We're going to shoot.'

Then we got on our tandem – that fashionable vehicle of the Popular Front which the production had allotted to us. I was carrying Madeleine off physically. We were starting out, unknowingly, on a ride which is still going on : thirty-five years of turning, climbing, braking, across winds, rivers, seas, stormy skies, lands, and 'right round the world'.

We returned through Tournus. My 'animal' had been right. Then Madeleine went back to her family; she had a young son by Charles Granval, Jean-Pierre. Indeed, her private life was somewhat complicated. A few weeks later, among my friends, I celebrated my twenty-sixth birthday.

THREE YEARS OF LIGHT

In most people's eyes, Madeleine and I came from two antipodes. I was a young anarchist, no doubt a 'Communist', an untidy, dishevelled good-for-nothing, with no 'morality'. I belonged to the lower middle-class – common, pseudo-peasant. I had learned my art from the Fauves. For example, at that time, never would an actor from the Comédie Française have thought of going to see the shows at Dullin's theatre. We on our side would never have thought of going in for the Conservatoire competition. (Indeed, I would certainly have been ploughed, as was Jouvet.)

Madeleine's life, on the contrary, had been clear and straightforward. At Royan, as a girl, she had recited a fable at a charity fête: by chance Féraudy had been there, and he had advised 'Maman' to have her trained for the stage. 'Maman' had agreed on condition that she should go through the Conservatoire and enter the Comédie Française. Above all, not the Odéon, because she would have to cross the Seine! (Later, because of me, Madeleine disobeyed her mother. I know how much it cost her!) And so the girl passed first into the Conservatoire, left it after taking the first prize, and entered the Comédie Française. One side of Madeleine is that of an eternal laureate. A Being who gets off to a flying start. This innocent, this leading actress, passed through life with an invincible grace: a bulldozer of naïve freshness. So much for the outside.

And yet, without changing the facts, the truth has a different ring. Born into the upper middle-class and firmly anchored in Passy, she is of pure Ile-de-France blood. Her father, an engineer from the Ecole Centrale, had a brilliant mind and was associated with Georges Claude in the discovery of liquid air; he died when she was two. So she, like me, was deprived of a father figure. Her mother, still young, became the elder sister of her two daughters, just as my mother had been to Max and me. And her grandmother was the real ruler, as in my case my grandfather was. Her mother, like mine, thought only of love – she had indeed an extraordinary charm: a sensual smile, eyelashes that curled almost too much, brilliant teeth. A most seductive person.

Madeleine had one idea: to be free. As a small girl she made hats, to earn her independence. Had I not been like that?

As a conspicuous pupil at the Conservatoire she was already, 'in advance', acting at the Comédie Française. De Max nicknamed her 'belle en cuisses'. And when she did reach that highly official 'Maison', on whom did she set her heart? On the one and only avant-garde anarchist there: Charles Granval, who was much older than her. He too had no morality: 'result of enquiries unsatisfactory'!

In spite of everything, at eighteen, our gentle innocent runs off and marries, without her mother's consent, that 'dangerous' individual. Friends lent her a pair of sheets.

As a small child, when required to obey an order, she would say: 'I would like to, but my soul is against it!' Madeleine too has her 'animal'.

She was full of laughter, always putting her foot in it, scatterbrained, flirtatious, but with a will of iron. A real little soldier. Like me, and I was like her: she wanted the lot and clung to nothing.

She wanted to earn her living. She chose her father figure, just as I had chosen Dullin. She chose him at the antipodes, and made him her husband.

I believe that in every deep love there is something of incest. Father or mother, brother or sister, daughter or son. Many country women call their husband 'mon fils'. 'Mon fi-fi, Figaro', says Suzanne in Beaumarchais. And there is nothing abnormal about that. No one has an Œdipus complex because of that. Once again, may Freud forgive me. We are members one of another.

She would have been anyhow a good actress, without Granval. Under his influence she became an artist. She revealed the bohemian in her. At the same time, she knew what it costs to win one's liberty in the midst of other people, without a father. She loved fantasy, but did not want to lose her foundations. She is a tree, roots as well as flowers.

And so, contrary to appearances, it was possible that the two of us, meeting, would at a given moment end by admitting, recognizing, one another. If I had been a woman, I would have liked to be Madeleine. And . . . well, I must say I find life strange! Look at that *sociétaire* of the Comédie Française, living in her own house in Passy: she meets a sort of shaggy young man who goes about with the young people of Saint-Germain-des-Prés. The two of them learned their professions from the very opposite directions: tradition, and Fauvism. In between those two 'enemy' camps, what was called the 'Boulevard theatre' was still prospering in Paris. At its head: Edouard Bourdet. Two months after our adventure, Jean Zay, one of the finest ministers the cultural life of France has had the luck to encounter, brings Bourdet and the Fauves – Jouvet, Dullin and Baty[1] – into the Comédie Française. Madeleine's professional life takes a fresh turn. As if I were bringing to Madeleine, as a kind of dowry, my masters from the Cartel. She, in exchange, introduced me to the only Fauve inside the tradition, a free and rebellious man: Granval. Exchanges and grateful recognition. And I am sure that, at the time, her creation of the part of Jacqueline in the *Chandelier*, directed by Baty, which was the beginning of the great change at the Comédie Française, was more important in her eyes than our idyll.

The next three years were years of light, for the two of us and all over Paris. Three expansive, effervescent years. The rebirth of the Comédie Française. The acceptance of the Cartel. The major works of Giraudoux, Jules Romains, Salacrou and Cocteau. Christian Bérard's designs. The *soirées d'intelligence* – decisive contributions by François Mauriac, Professor Mondor and others, whom, sadly, I have forgotten. The films of Prévert and Carné, of Jean Renoir, of Grémillon. Painting at its summit. The harvest of the Surrealists. The appearance of Sartre on the scene. Social emancipation. Paris, spiritual capital of the world. The most disparate people were willing to associate together. Hardly anyone then was withdrawn into himself. When a barge is moving forwards, the water, before being divided, rises like an erection: one has the impression that, at the approach of the War and its ordeals, life also was growing big.

For Madeleine's sake I had left the Grenier. Picasso took it over. It is there that he painted *Guernica*. I had taken a studio in the Place Dauphine, at number 11 (always a lucky number). We were not living together. She was mistrustful. I had now only one idea: to prove to her my value. Of course I was

---

[1] And three years later Jacques Copeau himself.

acting: in Salacrou's *Un homme comme les autres*; in *Le Misanthrope*, with Alice Cocéa. I was becoming a film star: *Le Puritain, Drôle de drame*. But my value, to my mind, depended on the success of *Numance*. As a poem by Desnos puts it:

Pour le plus grand amour pour elle.

I plunged head-down into this new challenge. All the money from my films went into that. Instinctively I chose a theatre larger than the Atelier. The size that suits me is one that seats about a thousand. I don't know why, that's how it is.

I made a contract with M. Paston, manager of the Théâtre Antoine, to have the use of it for a fortnight, in between two runs of an operetta by Allibert about Marseilles. This time my friends trusted me and there was no defection. Roger Blin was with us. The Cuban writer and musicologist Alejo Carpentier helped me to choose and arrange the music. A great musicologist, Wolff, who had an extraordinary record library, made available some extremely rare recordings. Later on, he was murdered by the Nazis: he was a Jew. André Masson kept his word. And Mme Karinska, the leading costume artist in Paris, had agreed to make the costumes. The fever of the rehearsals was now rising. Madeleine was somewhat surprised – at one and the same time disappointed and touched – to find herself living a love affair with such a maniac, one who would come and collapse exhausted at her side on the bed in the little studio. As my brother elect, Desnos attended the rehearsals. The day for the delivery of the costumes arrived. Mme Karinska insisted that I should pay the money down. I had no money left. She would take her costumes away unless I paid immediately. I was at my wits' end. Desnos was there. He said:

'I have to go out for something. Madame, be an angel and at least wait till I come back.'

Two hours went by. He came back, took me on one side and held out to me the money she was asking for. He had gone to the place where he worked and had asked for two months' salary in advance.

Gide's definition of a friend: 'The person with whom you would put yourself beyond the pale.' To me, after Desnos's gesture, a friend is someone who is willing to put himself out for you. It is a very rare thing.

Mme Karinska was paid. *Numance* opened punctually. It was an event. Paris rushed to see it. At the last performance the box office counter (what we called 'the salt cellar') was swept on to the pavement outside, in spite of the police reinforcements. I had brought off my present for Madeleine. I knew that in her circle, with its population of 'eminent gentlemen', Madeleine was being criticized, politely, by many of them for her inclination towards this 'young rebel'. In reply I was giving them *Numance* in their teeth.

I left the Place Dauphine and went to live near her, at Auteuil, in the hamlet of Boulainvilliers; Granval came to live with me for a while. Our lives were becoming more and more inextricably mixed. I encountered another bohemian life, a gilded one. What did I care if I spent all I had, provided that I was fulfilling a dream? Another film and the crisis was settled.

Picasso has said, more or less: 'I like living poor – with a lot of money.' It did not reach that point, but still we lived recklessly. If Madeleine had three days free from acting, we would spend the three days on the road, stopping at inns.

At Saint Tropez I pitched my tent under the pines and did the springs of the Talbot a bit of no good along the rocky paths. At Pampelonne, at that time, you could wander stark naked along the four kilometres of beach without meeting a soul.

We explored the Ile du Levant, with its nudists and vegetarians. The whole island was ours; one could live. When desire gripped us, we had only to move six feet aside, to 'be together' in the woods. There were perhaps a hundred nudists to fourteen kilometres. We ate nuts like the squirrels, we shared the honey with the bees [1], we washed in springs among the brushwood. We were savouring our youth.

I was dreaming of further shows. With Madeleine I was discovering Kafka. With Granval we deepened our love for Jules Laforgue; with Desnos, for the American novelists. Another real friend, Darius Milhaud, had revealed Knut Hamsun to me. But in connection with *Numance* he had set in train what was to prove a major event: he had brought me into contact with Claudel. He had already tried to introduce me to him after *As I Lay Dying*. At that moment Claudel was still stationed in Brussels. Monsieur l'Ambassadeur was to give a lecture in Paris. The thing had been arranged:

'Meet me there, I'll try and introduce you.'

What a prospect! What a door was being opened to my ambitious imagination! I went. He was there all right, at the other end of the hall, on a platform, a completely round man with that solid bone structure of his. His regular and decisive delivery hammered at my chest, and I could feel rising in me a kind of blush, an irresistible flood of timidity. The hall was full. I seemed to see a terrible lot of ladies; they irritated me. What had Claudel to do with ladies? Would we ever be able, afterwards, to get past that wall of hats? The meeting came to an end – long applause – and the 'elect' rushed forward to congratulate him. I manoeuvred myself into Milhaud's wake. Now I could see, in the midst of the compact group, Claudel advancing at a diplomatic pace, not too quick to be still polite, not too slow to make the thing end soon: the well-judged gait of a professional. In this way he advanced towards us; the group pressed tighter and tighter, everyone was jostling with a noise like an aviary. Claudel's replies reached me vaguely like a bassoon punctuating – and he had gone by. For a second my eyes must have thrown at him a few appealing flashes, a juvenile S O S which he did not see. He vanished – it was over. Darius had not managed to introduce me. In any case, would that rolling mass have noticed me? 'Sledgehammer for women in hats!'

[1] Once, when one of these was circling near my face, I waved my arm. Madeleine said to me: 'Don't move like that, it thinks you want to play.'

I was annoyed that I had let myself be dragged into trying to be introduced to that official block in whom, as it seemed to me, there was no tremor of humanity.

Two years later, Claudel retired. He returned to Paris. Darius Milhaud saw *Numance* and took two seats for the Master. It did something to Claudel. He came again, several times, then invited me to go and see him at the rue Jean-Goujon, alone. Not at all the same thing.

Here, again, a visit which my subconscious engraved, to be there for the rest of my life. For me a memorable interview, in the course of which, to borrow his language, we achieved *co-naissance*, or rather *re-connaissance*: yes, *nous nous re-connûmes*.[1]

In talking about *Numance*, we found ourselves at one on the value of gesture, on the resources of the body, on the plasticity of speech, on the importance of consonants, on the need to be wary of the vowels (which people always draw out too much), on the prosody of spoken language, on longs and shorts, iambics and anapaests, on the art of breathing. He talked to me about the Japanese theatre, and encouraged me, going so far as to say: 'What a pity we did not meet forty years earlier !'

When I left him, I was walking on air. He had just given me the most won-derful leg-up imaginable. Through my timidity – which quickly disappeared – I had seen a simple man, one who could talk like a real worker in the theatre, an artist just as unsatisfied as oneself: a comrade of my own age, hooked like me on those absorbing problems. And he was lavishing on me all his inspira-tions, his observations, his ideas. In short, an authentic passionate man. He must have been sixty-nine, I was twenty-seven. That immediate communion between the two of us filled me with wonder and made me want to say thank you to everything: to God, to life, to the first person I met in the street.

Dullin also had seen and liked *Numance*. He had then forgiven me. I started again seeing him regularly. Madeleine remained protected by the bastion of her house-of-her-own. At night I used to walk figures of eight in the street while waiting for her signal, a light in her bedroom window. Then I would go in. At the slightest unusual detail I would nearly faint with jealousy. Madeleine was delighted. She quivered like a fish in water.

One fine day she telephoned me:

'Can you come now?'

'At once?'

'Yes.'

I arrived. There were some men with her. She was leaving her house. She had sold her furniture. Pink cushions and glass trinkets. We were to leave together. She was changing her way of life. She would be in my pocket. 'My

---

[1] The intimate connection revealed by the likeness of the words *naissance* (birth) and *connaissance* (knowledge) is a theme that runs through the work of Claudel. '*Naître, pour tout, c'est co-naître. Toute naissance est une connaissance.*' So *connaissance* is *co-nais-sance* (knowledge is shared birth). And if two people are fully alive, acquaintance is recognition: to meet is to admit. (*Translator's note.*)

child from immemorial ages' had taken nearly two years to respond to my appeal from that meadow in the Dauphiné. And she was responding totally : by giving her whole self.

That evening we went to stay at the Hôtel Trianon, at Versailles. It was there that I began adapting Knut Hamsun's *La Faim*. Our setting has nothing to do with the inner world that inhabits us.

Some time before, I had bought a superb little Danish caravan, which I towed behind a Ford roadster, designed to go everywhere. It looked like a small mahogany railway carriage. The surprise of the staff at the Hôtel Trianon – pages, waiters, porters, receptionists – was worth seeing, as they watched me arrive with my caravan in front of the main entrance and carry off my *'sociétaire'*, like a gipsy eloping !

We went to Normandy, between Honfleur and Villerville, where Madeleine had installed her brood – husband, child, staff and various other more or less distant 'relatives'. I parked my caravan in a nearby meadow, twenty yards from the sea.

And I went on working on *La Faim*. One evening I read the first act to Charles, Madeleine and young Jean-Pierre. It was nothing but rhythm and counterpointing. Jean-Pierre christened that kind of theatre *'théâtre ta-ga-dag'* (ding-dong theatre) – a phrase I have adopted.

Our life was taking giant strides forward. In September 1938 we took a modern house, with a garden and a small lodge, at Boulogne. I was to live in the lodge; Madeleine and Jean-Pierre in the main house, surrounded by flowers and pine trees.

The series of my films continued : I became a regular matinée idol after having set the fashion for untidy hair. My grandfather (even he had forgiven me) said :

'In those films of yours they don't only need urchins like you, they sometimes have to have old men. I could act in a film like anyone else. Why don't you find me a little film work?'

He was, as he liked to tell people, in his eighty-third year. His income was not increasing, his son was losing money, I paid them small allowances. I was happy.

Dullin proposed to me that I should share the Atelier. He felt that he himself had done all he could with it. He wanted to work in bigger theatres. He was thinking of the Théâtre de Paris – Réjane's theatre. Or the Théâtre Sarah-Bernhardt. I would be his dauphin. We reached complete agreement. I was to return to the Atelier to put on Salacrou's *La Terre est ronde* for the first time, in the autumn of '38. I was to take charge of the second half of the season – March '39. I would put on the *Hamlet* of Jules Laforgue, directed by Charles Granval, and *La Faim*, adapted from Knut Hamsun. And, beginning in the autumn of '39, I would take over the Atelier, while Dullin would instal himself in Réjane's theatre.

Me at the head of the Atelier ! I was Dullin's chosen successor, but he was in a bad way :

'In what spirit are you going to take it over?'

'In the spirit it had before *Volpone*.'

It was as if I had given him a knife blow in the heart. He looked at me with his incisive gaze, withdrew into silence, and then I heard his piping voice say to me:

'I think . . . I think basically you are right . . . I ought to have left the Atelier at that moment.'

Youth is generous but cruel.

La Terre est ronde was a great success.

The character of Hamlet haunted me, but I was afraid to undertake it. Laforgue's Hamlet was a good approach. It is a *Hamlet* written not by Shakespeare, but by another Hamlet. Granval had made an excellent adaptation of it. Stage music by Darius Milhaud.

> *Ophélie, pauvre Lee, Lee*
> *C'était ma p'tite amie d'enfance*
> *Je l'aimais, c'est évident*
> *Ça tombait sous les sens.*[1]

And this couplet:

> My rare faculty of assimilation
> Will contradict the course of my vocation. . . .

Charles was to give me several keys to the actor's technique, which I have never forgotten. He was the man with the best knowledge of the springs of the human body.

La Faim, with costumes and props by André Masson and music by Marcel Delannoy, was another victory. In it I was experimenting with many new resources: the play between actor and lighting (going up a staircase), simultaneous scenes, nonsense scenes – words that have no sense but whose sound plastically reproduces conversation and situation. Spoken text answered by a tune hummed with the mouth closed. Heartbeats, buzzings in the ears, 'physiological' (if I may use the term) musical effects and, above all, a man and his double. Roger Blin was the double. I played the man, Tangen. It was really a duet between us.

While *As I Lay Dying* had had only four performances and *Numance* only fifteen (though that was my fault – I had been asked to keep it on and had refused: I was 'not a business man'), *Hamlet* and *La Faim* exceeded seventy.

May 1939 had come with all its buds. Since *Hélène* and our meeting, Madeleine and I had spent, I repeat, three years of light, all made of youth, passionate love, professional success, emancipation, liberty, imagination and freedom from care. It was much the same everywhere in France and in Paris, in spite of Munich. With Desnos and his wife Youki, the two of us took crazy joy-rides in the forest of Compiègne. With Labisse we strayed through Paris night life. Was it presentiment? We were eating our 'corn in the blade'. Our intoxication was twice broken: by my mother's death, and by mobilization.

[1] The girl Laforgue was in love with, if I remember rightly, was called Miss Lee.

DEATH OF MY MOTHER

In January 1939 (had I strained myself acting Alceste, or shifting my caravan, or practising mime too strenuously?) I was operated on for a first hernia. I took advantage of the enforced rest to reread the whole of Montaigne. Professor Mondor had taken charge of the operation. This outstandingly learned man, specialist in Mallarmé, with his subtle and original mind, visited me often, far more to talk about literature than to check my stitches. Surgery of that kind was of little interest to him: his genius was for diagnosis.

One day my mother had come to the clinic, to spend a short while at my bedside. For some time she had been having abdominal pains. Mondor looked in on me and I introduced them to each other. Such moments are brief, since surgeons economize the time taken by consultations. Suddenly, as he was leaving, he turned back at the threshold, like a dog pulling up short.

'Since I am here, if your mother would like me to examine her, I will do so gladly.'

We had not asked him for anything; it was the last thing we would have done. Already, in my case, his services were an act of friendship.

'As the Professor has suggested it, Maman, accept.'

A few hours later he telephoned Madeleine: he had discovered a hardening in the liver – my mother had an advanced cancer and would be dead within six months. In Professor Mondor the sixth sense had functioned. Like a sorcerer he had seen 'through'.

Of course everything was done to make a miracle happen. Unfortunately my mother, through what she had picked up working in the chemist's shop, had understood perfectly. At her deathbed I was with her for three days on end. It was in June. My eyes never left her, and from time to time I would take a cherry from a jar and eat it. I wanted to rob death of every moment of life that remained to her. My grandfather was brought, after being told what was happening. Perhaps expecting to set eyes on her for the last time, he had dressed in black, ready for the funeral. He looked like a poor old lost animal. When she recognized him she quickly raised her arm across her face, as though in self-protection. A moist cry of 'Baby darling' came from between the moustache and small beard, now thin with age, and he went away: the leave-taking between daughter and father was confined to that. A strange settling of accounts. And now my mother, transformed, gathered us together and gave us our orders, second by second.

'Open that cupboard, behind that pile of linen there is a bottle: it's holy water. Next to it: a sprig of box that I brought from Tournus.' (She was living in a small studio at Montmartre.) 'Put them down here. Now go and fetch a priest.'

'But Maman, it's ridiculous.'

'Children, it's already difficult enough to die, you're not going to make things worse for me. I want a priest. Where is Martin?' (She meant Louis Martin, her second husband.)

'He's lying down upstairs. He's asleep.'

'Let him be. Well, the priest?'

'He's coming. You'll have nothing to tell him.'

'Not much. ... Yes ... was rather unkind to your father. But he's already forgiven me.'

(Once more we saw her roguish smile.)

The pain, at intervals, was cruel. There were moments when we would have liked to knock her out with a hammer or give her an injection, to stop her sufferings once for all.

The priest arrived. They were left alone. She confessed and received the last rites. What? Was my delicious cat of a mother, my little sister, my child, so pious? Would she soon be saying to God:

'Mesa, I am Ysé, it is I'?

The priest left, we returned, we found her at peace. Her gaze was calm.

'Was the priest nice?'

'A young idiot! But that has no importance. *My children, if you only knew how good one feels! It's wonderful.*'

Those were her last words. She had no more suffering at all. Her small respiratory forge had taken on a regular rhythm, like the engines of a ship that has started on a long journey. This went on for another day and two nights. I was no longer doing anything. I was attached to my mother's breath, as I once had been to her breasts full of milk. From time to time she would open her eyes, which shone like two blueberries, would smile, then go off again on her journey. At dawn on the second day she gave her last sigh. A sigh of relief. It was 14 June 1939. She was buried at Père Lachaise, in the family vault. The Mass held in Paris was cold and disappointing.

That summer Madeleine and I made a pilgrimage to the gorges of Chouvigny (Auvergne or Bourbonnais?), cradle of my mother's side of the family. There the old parish priest gave me a photograph of my mother at the age of fifteen. I asked for a genuine Mass to efface the one in Paris. With the help of his server, he took us into the real regions of the sacred, of prayer: a rite as strong and primitive as if we had been in the middle of a tropical forest among witch doctors. Rhythm is the only thing that can take us out of ourselves – I am thinking of trances of the soul:

... *corps de Jésus*

... *corps de Jésus*

... *corps de Jésus*

This time, my mother had been received.

Next we were to pay our first visit to Paul Claudel, in his château at Brangues (Isère). We came a sightly roundabout way by the Col de la Madeleine – the least we could do.

Claudel, Mme Claudel, their children and their grandchildren, welcomed us in the burly château with its hundred-year-old lime trees. It was not I who was visiting Claudel, it was he who wanted to see Madeleine. There was a question of the Comédie Française putting on *L'Annonce faite à Marie*, and they were thinking of Madeleine for the part of Violaine. I seized the occasion to ask him point blank for *Tête d'Or*, *Partage de Midi* and *Le Soulier de Satin*.

'Why this choice?' he asked me.

'Because *Tête d'Or* is your sap, *Partage* is your ordeal and the *Soulier* your epitome.'

He said no, but I had shaken him.

Without knowing, still without knowing, I was sowing at that moment a seed that was to burgeon four years later, just as, in good plays, the author plants before the end of an act the suspense which will serve to arouse interest in the next.

We went back to Normandy. I returned to my caravan and began to attack Kafka's *The Trial*. With a view to a fresh piece of *théâtre ta-ga-dag*. After Faulkner, Cervantes and Knut Hamsun I had chosen Kafka. My path was firmly marked.

It was with André Masson that I had had my last conversation about Kafka. Ever since Munich everyone had been afraid of war, and the two of us were in full agreement that, if it came, everything would be bound to change, and that in any case, whatever the camps might be, we would be recognized by none of them. Neither by the right nor by the left: on all sides we would be considered as felons and outlaws. It was with that future in view that I penetrated into the world of Kafka.

However, we were still on holiday. One August afternoon I went out fishing on the banks of the Saint Georges river. The sun was going down. A chill was beginning to fall. I walked back gaily along the road. As I passed in front of the small *mairie* at Pennedepie (five kilometres from Honfleur), I noticed a few people watching a bill-poster:

MOBILISATION GÉNÉRALE

Those whose card bore the number 6 were to rejoin the colours on 31 August. That was my number – the number for 'specialized workers'. Specialized in what, I wonder?

In my stomach, in my heart, in my head, in my soul, in my double, I felt something coming loose. A stone falling, then two, then three, a collapse. My life was breaking. My love. My work. My hopes. My joys. MADELEINE, MY LIFE. Suddenly, I was no longer in a hurry: I finished the walk with small slow steps dwindling towards zero.

After agonizing goodbyes, with our eyes weeping into one another, Madeleine took me to the station at Trouville. Then she returned to the holiday house, to hear her eighty-six-year-old grandmother mumble into her false teeth:

'What a pity you fell in love with that boy. But for him we wouldn't have a soldier in the family, we'd be nice and quiet.'

She was of the same generation as my grandfather, who was moping in Paris, wearing out the housekeeper who had taken the place of my grandmother, deceased five years earlier.

ENFORCED PAUSE

Phoney war

Geological cross sections often reveal veins which, as they circulate between two strata, are suddenly interrupted by some seismic catastrophe, but then, reappearing further on, continue on their way.

In 1939, on the strength of my training (individual at the Atelier, social with the Surrealist movement), on the strength of my first attempts – *As I Lay Dying, Numance* and *La Faim* – which had won me a place in the front squad of the avant-garde, on the strength of a certain reputation which the cinema was bringing me, on the strength of that tremendous thrust of *reality* which had given me Madeleine, on the strength of Artaud, Claudel, Gide, Desnos, Prévert, André Masson, Labisse, the anarchists, the Trotskyists and all sorts of surrealist artists and poets, and, above all, on the strength of my love of Life, I was all set to take up my modest part in the human revolution of the morrow.

Our energy came from three axes:

> Freud, or the liberation of the instincts,
> Marx, or the liberation of Man, and
> The East, or the recasting of the Western spirit;

these all now seemed like so many veins brutally broken by the world catastrophe of the War.

It is not until twenty years later that we see them reappearing, making their way between the two strata, capitalism and socialism, principally in the beatnik and hippie movements, then in the May '68 risings, in people who, indeed, even today claim kinship with that period on which Surrealism set its mark. What happened, therefore, was not really a swerve in history, but a stoppage deliberately caused by the 'powers that were', in order to confine and destroy a worldwide revolution which was beginning. This *calculated* aspect of that jamming on of brakes was what gave to the 'phoney war' its *false*, ridiculous look: a real mess. 'La Fête (the holiday, the celebration) was suddenly forbidden by the international lords and masters.

Who manufactured Hitler? Who sent, just a year earlier, Pétain to Spain as ambassador? Who fished out of political imprisonment the courier to whom were entrusted the secret papers of the Fifth Army, before it went to join General Duseigneur's squadron? Who had just printed in *Fortune* that the U S A would not intervene in the war until the armaments supplied by them should have been economically absorbed? Who ordered French aircraft to crash-land on strategic points, so that these points might be bombarded a quarter of an hour later? The pilot emerged unhurt from his cabin and arrogantly asked to be immediately repatriated. The whole business was fishy. This was no war, it was a machination. And so, at nightfall, after the soup, when the bistro radio began retransmitting Daladier's speeches with his Vaucluse accent:

Marings della meer
Avyateures dell'l'aair
Paysaings den'no cammpagn' !

the speech of the Président du Conseil would be received with a collective and
resounding '*Merde!*' Our 'brave' soldiers, 'the best equipped in the world',
would switch off the radio and return to their depression. Make war with that?
What next? And whose fault that the country was in danger? Why should
these men, as though by enchantment, have been less courageous than the men
of '14–'18? Because they were being led up the garden path. Humbug! Bun-
kum! Corruption!

I can still see that requisitioned horse committing suicide by a desperate
gallop, which ended with it smashing its head against a wall. I can still see,
most clearly of all, that peasant leading his horse to give it to the military –
a sinister dialogue! All the way, walking at its side, he spoke to it – in its eye.
Then he stopped and, standing in front of it, with his forehead against its
long nose, he spoke to it face to face and wept, wept huge tears.

I was back at Dijon.

'You've got the letter G.'

'Ah? So what?'

'This isn't the place!'

They didn't know what to do with us. Apparently the barracks had not
been informed. They took three days to regroup us. Automatically I kept
going to the station, like a dog who has lost his master, in the hope – not
belief – that Madeleine would step down from a carriage full of travellers. As
for us, we already belonged to the goods trains.

A column of lorries was formed, we were piled into them and went off eastwards, destination unknown. We were flanked by police. Ironically, the last
vehicle was a requisitioned van with, painted on the back of it, this: 'Where
are they off to? To the Great Butchery.'

When we were halted, out in the country, I would go and pick a few flowers
and then call out to the officers:

'*Mon lieutenant*, I've got a flower, but I haven't been given a rifle.'

'Bugger off!'

I had some nerve!

When we got near to Strasbourg, we met the first evacuees with their carts:
bits of furniture, mattresses, kitchen utensils, children, bicycles and a few
useful animals. We began to find the first stray dogs, abandoned by their
masters. Also the first corpses of hanged dogs! Dingheim, a little to the north,
looked out over the Rhine. Next to us, on one side, a battalion of Chasseurs
Alpins. On the opposite bank, the Germans, thinking they were addressing the
children of the region, had spread out a streamer: 'Alsatians, don't fire at
your brothers.' The Chasseurs had replied with another streamer: '*On s'en
fout, on est du Midi*' (Wrong address, we're from the south). There were also
some terrified Senegalese who had been shoved into the front line after being
knocked about by regular officers who had it in for them.

To make good use of my 'specialities', I was put to clean the officers' quarters. They too were 'regulars', that is to say, this life was their trade.

While I was sweeping the floor :

'Ha, the artiste ! A change from the cinema !'

'I prefer cleaning floors to cleaning trenches.'

'*Qu'est-ce que tu dis?*'

'*Tu as très bien entendu.* You heard me. I must ask you, *mon lieutenant*, to abide by the regulations and not address the men as *tu*.'

My days in the officers' quarters were few. The more so because my name had a cross against it, as anti-militarist. I was next given a forage waggon and three horses. This time I had to plead not for my own sake but for the animals.

'*Mon adjudant,* these animals will die, I don't know head from tail.'

The Adjutant was moved with pity for the equine race. I became a grave-digger. Since I could not look after the live animals, I could deal with them once they were dead. I can still hear the drumming sound as the clods of earth fell on the swollen bellies. Dogs, cats, horses, cattle, all sorts went in.

Being in Burgundy, I was in a company of peasants. These mutinied. They went on hunger strike to get the horses given sufficient rations. The rations of oats had to be increased to make the men eat. Splendid people, they reconciled me for a moment to existence.

I met some marvellous Alsatians. Hospitable, serious, resigned. I remember one mid-day meal when I was so moved that I could not swallow any food. Though I clenched my teeth, I could not stop the tears flowing. Luckily I had my back to the window and they could only see me against the light. They found speaking French difficult but spoke it very correctly. Out of affection I gave them Gérard de Nerval's *Sylvie*, 'a pure French style'. I loved them.

Everything that was human was overwhelming. Everything that was military was revolting : (to be polite) nonsense.

On 3 September war was declared officially. End of hope. My life sank, like sand to the bottom of water. I turned into mud. In eight days I was reduced to zero. In my body the blood made its little noise of silence, it came tapping right to the tips of my fingers, my temples went in and out like gills. In a fit of black depression, there is a humming in one's chest, in one's head – there seems to be a humming everywhere.

To humiliate me, they again put me in another company. The further down I went, the more nice chaps I met. We were now at Reipertswiller, near Bitche, in the hills of Alsace. A deeply undulating region, magnificent. In the fields the autumn crocuses were out : like three years earlier, in the Dauphiné, when Madeleine and I were making love, out in the country. On 8 September I was twenty-nine.

I hit on a trick. I volunteered as a washer-up. Usually men feel humiliated when made to peel spuds and scour greasy dixies; but the lower I was on the ladder, the more I found myself in harmony with the situation and with myself. At morning parade :

'Private Barrault?'

'In the kitchen.'

'Ah yes. The chap who washes up.'

A little titter would run through the ranks.

Another trick: I volunteered to go and milk the cows that had been abandoned. A cow that is not milked gets fever. Her milk curdles. She dies of it.
There were a lot of them abandoned. So three of us would go out into the fields.
One of us would hold the head, another hang on to the beast's tail, and the
third would knead the teats. Curdled milk is almost as firm as butter. The poor
animal would bleed. She would puff and kick. At last, after a lot of patience,
the fresh milk would begin to flow. We had just rediscovered Friendship. This
was the only moment when life again made sense. The tenderness that my
mother had handed on to me. . . .

On 19 August Madeleine had given me, to celebrate our three years' love,
a fountain pen, and I had decided to write the diary of our life. Out of my
notebook I can now copy this:

> *Half past nine.* I am on the hill: on watch. My duty is to watch any
> aircraft that may pass and 'if they throw anything out' (projectiles, tracts
> or balloons), I am to whistle. Then the sentry down below is supposed to
> hear me. The sentry is supposed to inform the head of section – he is sup-
> posed to inform the bugler. The bugler must then run to the house where
> the lieutenant is billeted, at the other end of the small village, and tell
> him: 'That an aircraft has thrown something out (projectile, tract or
> balloon), that I have whistled, that the sentry has heard, that he has
> informed the head of section and has sent him here and here he is.' Then
> and only then the lieutenant, after mature reflection, and after having no
> doubt said, like Field Marshal Foch: 'What is up?', decides whether it is
> a case for sounding the alert.
>
> As by that time the aircraft must be a hundred kilometres away, every-
> thing would probably settle down again.

And now we are in another village: Soucht, still in that deeply undulating
part of Alsace, not far from Bitche. I sink into sottishness. I catch myself
spending a whole morning watching the tragedy of a young boy, detailed as a
butcher, slaughtering a pig. An extraordinary spectacle: talk about theatre
of cruelty! The pig tied up. The child trying to smash its skull with a club.
The pig squealing like a human being: 'Oh! oh! what have I ever done to
you?' And the blood spurting, the apprentice spattering it everywhere. What
a lot of *boudin* wasted! A mess, I assure you.

How lucky that the radio was appealing for 'footballs for our soldiers'. The
army was sinking into inaction and boredom. Another of my notes:

> *Half past nine.* We are doing nothing, nothing, nothing. A September
> day, fog which the sun is taking a long time to pierce. The boredom is
> pouring softly, like a spring with a regular flow. The boredom has set out
> on a long spell. It surely knows it will last for a long while. It keeps turn-
> ing with its small, regular, terrible rhythm.

There were indeed some 'impregnable' fortresses, but they were turned in the wrong direction. They had been built by the Germans after 1870, at the time when Alsace had ceased to be in France. Derision!

October 16 – anniversary of my father's death (twenty-one years earlier). On that day, still making use of my 'specialities', I had been detailed to distribute tobacco in the living-room of a small farm. The daughter of the house said to me:

'There is someone asking for you.'

Back to my notebook:

> I answer: 'Right', and move off slowly, limply, "bluesishly", as usual now, to see this someone who is asking for me....
>
> !!!!????!!!!!... it was Madeleine, my little card of a Madeleine. My Being. My love, my sweetheart soul. Madeleine in a little blue coat, a little blue hat with a little challenging feather, who stood blushing and smiling at me, like a little girl who has just 'pulled something off'. Explosion in my head. It isn't true. I'm going mad. It can't be her. But let's join in the game: 'What on earth are you doing here? No!!! but what on earth are you doing here?'
>
> My arm touches her on the shoulder, to *see*: it resists, my hand does not go through. She is not transparent. It is her. She has come all the way here. She is here. My legs are trembling. I break out in sweat. I am suffocating. My voice goes down into my depths. That's done it, I can't speak now. I turn about. Take a step or two, like someone who is afraid of falling.

I had fixed up for myself, in a kind of loft, a sort of room with a high bed, on top of which was an enormous eiderdown shedding its feathers. Access was by a ladder.

> She recognizes everything I have described to her in my letters. We climb the ladder. Enter the 'room'. We are in each other's arms. We are alone. We kiss. Both of us are crying. The beloved mouth once more. The infinity of words. We are weeping gently with joy and emotion.

With the connivance of everyone – comrades, farmers and even the lieutenant – we remained for two days under the feathers of the eiderdown. Apparently by chance, the sounds of a genuine war became audible. A German offensive, according to the announcement. 'A message from Generals Gamelin and George has recalled Joffre's message at the time of the Marne.' Those were doubtless merely the salvo of 121 cannon shots which Madeleine's arrival deserved. I was worried about her, all the same. She would have to return those six hundred kilometres in the rain and the mud, among the convoys.

> And this morning she left at 8 a.m., with a new route I had worked out for her. She has gone. A flood of tears, nerves all to pieces, grief crying out its distress. I clenched my teeth. She has gone, my sweet, my courageous ... adored, admired, revered, my fascinating love, the life of my

choice. I have watched her disappear into the mist, slowly, in no hurry, prudent because I had told her to be very careful. Oh, the cruelty of separating people who are in love, the injustice of it! The horror. Now I give way to tears. Up to now I have resisted. I cannot any longer, my heart is breaking. They stream down my face. And yet, immediately after her departure, I have rushed to be with my comrades. I couldn't say a word but I was counting on pride to prevent me from weeping. Now comes collapse.

Madeleine, without knowing it, had just repeated what my mother had lived through, twenty-five years earlier, in 1915, when she went to join my father at Saint-Mihiel.

These confidences are leading me astray. I am not keeping my word. I did promise to select from my memories only those things that had shaped me, or those that other people could adapt to themselves, or, finally, those that seemed likely to be useful to me for the future. I am stumbling into 'private matters'. The whole of that war period is waste of time, for you, for me, for life. Impotence!

I would now like to fly over the next few months and merely recall the events that have marked me.

There came a chance to find friendship again: I learned that Desnos, with his regiment, was thirty kilometres away. I borrowed a bike and was off. As I went past the lorries stuck in the mud and the half denuded woods acquiring their boars' bristles in readiness for winter, I kept shouting: 'I am flying towards the Friend.'

We met again. Two huge fields transformed into swamps by the rain. A road across, and, halfway, a group of poplars sheltering a small bridge. We talked for hours. Deeply and simply. Desnos was a *man*, a complete human being. I was becoming aware, perhaps for the first time, of what a support he was for me. He had the gift of taking the responsibility for others and for himself. He was really double – the master and the friend of his 'double'. Of peasant and lower middle class origin, a balanced rebel: exactly what I wanted to be and remain.

We had to separate. We did so with an exchange of smiles. What an exchange at that moment! What true human communication! We had no illusions about what was in store for us – I mean for all of us. All the rest was so idiotic, so false: like loaded dice.

At Christmas I had a few days' leave. I took advantage of this to do a broadcast of the first act of *Tête d'Or*, with music written by Honegger. A seed, sown then, which was to burgeon twenty years later.

Back to the stagnation of a nation's youth in uniform, foundering, abandoned. Two months went by.

A gleam of light: Jean-Pierre, Madeleine's little son, wrote to me:

Mon Jean-Louis,

I am writing simply to tell you that Mama adores you. I am very happy about this because I love you like a second papa. Yesterday evening I said to Mama: 'Why haven't you married Jean-Louis?' She told me she dared not suggest it to you and told me you were afraid I might be too young and might not understand you. Jean-Louis, I shall be crazy with joy at seeing you two united and at seeing Mama protected by a man everyone loves. Take care of yourself and come back to us soon. *Je t'embrasse tendrement.*

Overcoming my emotion, I answered my Jean-Pierre, and I wrote Charles a letter, in slang (from masculine modesty), in which I asked him for the hand of his first *'daronne'*.[1] A few days later I received his answer, also in slang. O.K. for the *'maridage'*, but he would advise me to take his second, since the first was not Madeleine . . .

Suddenly I was transferred to the Third Engineers at Suippes, in the barren part of Champagne. Nothing made any sense. After experiencing all sorts of sidings, in which we were parked like cattle, with nasal loud-speakers intoning 'Transport officers, chain up!', I reached Suippes. My surprise was boundless at finding Labisse there, at finding the painters Brianchon, Legueult and Launoy, and various sculptors, Damboise, Colamarini, engravers such as Lemagny, the designer Pierre Delbée who was to become one of my dearest friends, and musicians who had won the Prix de Rome: a regular Surrealist academy issued from a college of pataphysics. I had become part of a camouflage company, Company F1 (christened very rightly: 'the phantom company'). I was moving from annihilation to the absurd. It was Robert Rey, my teacher at the Ecole du Louvre, who had brought this off. He had remembered *La Faim* and made use of the 'regulations'. So I became once more a 'painter'. The absurd, I tell you!

France went on mouldering behind the Maginot Line. We, meanwhile, were living as though in a dream worthy of Alphonse Allais and of Jarry. It was crazy. I painted 'from nature' the mill at Valmy. Derision deepened. I used to do guard duty by the latrines while rereading *Romeo and Juliet*. The one thing about which I was firm was my refusal to put on shows. Settle down in all that imposture? No! The bad farce needed no addition.

There were also quite a few architects. We were made to 'put on our thinking caps' about the problems of camouflage. I remember a project for protecting Paris by altering the course of the Seine, using municipal sprinklers to scatter soap bubbles: at night, enemy aircraft would be mislead by the reflections! I am not inventing.

In the spring of '40 we were sent to 'camouflage' ourselves in the woods of Villers-Cotterêts, and then instructed to protect the château of Ermenonville.

---

[1] *'Daronne'*, in thieves' slang, is 'mother'. And *'maridage'* is from *'marida'*, thieves' slang for married woman. (*Translator's note.*)

It was nearer to Paris. When the great May offensive was let loose, we began to blush with shame. A fine figure we were cutting: strolling about among the swans of those lakes, close by the tomb of Jean-Jacques Rousseau. I was rereading the *Rêveries d'un promeneur solitaire*, I had learned to look for morels, I took walks deep into the forest. I can still see the body of a stag that had been brought down by a polecat: the whole of its inside had been emptied, nice and clean – all that remained was the bones, the teeth and the skin. The polecat had made it his house. The whole animal was emptied of its substance. Why was it at that moment that I was seized by a physical, vegetable, animal love for my Country? '*Amour-passion, non amour-bonbon*', says a note in my notebooks. Thirty years of wrong civic education were effaced by that sight. Not that it reconciled me to the army.

The Fifth Column was in full swing. On guard in front of the wrought iron gates of Ermenonville, it was my lot to show some false generals the way (foretaste of Baptiste in *Les Enfants du paradis*). There was a rain of parachutists. Fires were started in the forest. We rushed to put them out with spades. And when we met the suspicious-looking cyclists armed with sten-guns, we would let them pass and pretend not to notice; for, in the whole of our section, the sergeant-major was the only one with a revolver. But it was not loaded, there was no ammunition. Thank God for that: we would have been massacred, the lot of us.

The exodus arrived.

Our company was so 'phantom' that the General Staff forgot it. Already we could hear the enemy tanks.

Sign of life

It was 11 June. I heard that an air force company was leaving for Chartres and would pass through Paris. Come what might, I would go. I wanted to see Madeleine again and warn her to leave. It was no longer a case of desertion: my company also would be taking to its heels, next day, southwards, mingling with the long files of civilians making their way like frightened cattle along the roads. I slipped into a lorry and hid under a groundsheet. Notice of our marriage, after Jean-Pierre's consent, had been put up at the Billancourt *mairie*: the date given was 14 June. This would be the anniversary of Mama's death. I had not chosen the date, but it was good. She would have consented so completely. She adored Madeleine. She had handed on to her her engagement ring.

The Germans were flooding towards Paris. Rout everywhere.

Over the road huge clouds of black smoke formed a thick, disconcerting fog. At seven in the morning the lorry entered Paris. At half-past seven it dropped me in Boulogne: it would come back and collect me as soon as possible, then make for Chartres. But would it be able to come back? There was talk of declaring Paris an open city. This meant no soldiers there.

I reached our home. Madeleine had left the house barely an hour before, taking with her Blanche and Ya-Ya, our two helps, and the cat. In their haste they had left a window open. They had gone by order of the Comédie Française, which had given, yesterday, a last performance of Musset's *On ne saurait penser à tout*. Decidedly topical!

So there I was, alone, at a loss, a deserter. Where had Madeleine gone? In the direction of the Creuse, where her mother and grandmother had withdrawn? Or in the direction of Brittany, where Granval and Jean-Pierre had taken refuge? I wandered about our disordered house: our books, our pictures, our happiness. What should I take away? Our life was broken, perhaps for twenty-five years. I wrote some notes in my book. The only souvenir worth taking was a flower from the garden: I picked it and put it between two pages. Grief makes one sentimental. In two days it would be the first anniversary of my mother's death: where on earth could her husband, Louis Martin, be? She was now at rest in her tomb at the other end of Paris, to the north-east, in the Père-Lachaise cemetery. No one would be able to go there. And here I was, detained, waiting for the lorry to come back. At least she had been spared this horror.

The hours ticked away. Should I get back into mufti? No! Here came the lorry. 'Quick, slip under the groundsheet. I nearly couldn't get through. We must reach Chartres as soon as possible.' We were ready, as it were, on our way there, at the right exit from Paris, the south-west one, only a short distance from the Porte de Saint-Cloud. But, buried under my groundsheet, I could still feel the jolts from Paris streets. Twenty minutes went by. The lorry stopped. Where on earth could we be? I ventured to peer out. We were in front of Père-Lachaise. Exactly in front of the small door through which you go to our tomb.

'Hey! Just a second, please.'

I jumped out. In my notebook I had a flower. My mother would get a flower in spite of everything. Are the dead really as 'active' as this? (The driver had come all this way round to deliver a letter to a friend's wife.)

We started off again, this time towards the south-west, across Paris again. The streets were blocked, we were diverted, and now here we were on the way to Fontainebleau, to Montargis: the south-east. Who was it had just passed us? It was my captain in his car. He saw me. He braked. I told the lorry driver to stop. Oh well, I was caught.

'What are you doing there?'

'I . . . got lost.'

'All right, get in!'

There I was in the car, on the back seat, with the captain in front. I felt crestfallen, 'like a child being brought back to the fold'. Hoping to mollify the captain a little, I ventured to say so. He answered:

'You couldn't put it better!'

We arrived at Châtillon-Coligny, not far from the Loire. And what did I see? Madeleine, in the midst of my company. The company's column had been diverted, Madeleine had been diverted, my lorry had been diverted, and here we were all together again!

As Madeleine and I were due to be married next day, 14 June, the captain had the right to take the mayor's place. We made a jeweller open his shop. All he had was a pair of wedding rings left over from a marriage that had not taken place. They happened to fit us and, exactly one year after the death of my mother (who had received her one little flower), Madeleine and I exchanged two rings which bore the date May 1937. God is no stranger to humour and the absurd.

Madeleine wanted to go to Creuse, to see her mother; then to Brittany to rejoin her son. She had my car, a Citroën with front-wheel drive (more practical), no map, just the tip of her nose to follow the sun. We parted, and remained without news of each other until the end of July. A harsh ordeal. But life had made us a sign.

The journey, begun in Alsace, ended in a small village of Southern France, Miramont-de-Quercy. I had been right across France in a month – one of the sunniest Junes I have ever known. June : the month of the year's fullness.

Those hills and valleys of France, lovelier than all else.

I thought I was being born yet again, but this time in misery. Up to then I had felt I belonged to the soil of Beauregard; after what I had been through, I felt I was made of the soil of France. As an apple feels its apple-tree.

'A bit late in the day !' some will say.

'You're getting soft !' others will say.

'Your Mother Country? Œdipus complex !' the psychoanalyst might say.

'Purest Jocasta !' mutters Jarry.

The armistice was signed. Pétain took responsibility, with honour and dignity. De Gaulle launched his appeal. The demarcation line passed through Tournus. France was cut in two, in every sense of the word.

I felt that Madeleine was at the other end of the world. I could now think only of the moment when I would be demobilized. I had to moulder for another month. I was torn between despair and the desire to be reborn. To serve, not with all this stuff and nonsense, but with the Faith by which I was animated.

The Quercy region is splendid and has a character of its own. One day, with the painter André Marchand, we were walking in a valley and approached a ruined house. It was very beautiful indeed, an old manor house falling to pieces. In it nature had resumed her rights. The walls were pierced by trees. The leaves were bursting out through the roofs. Round it, springs were flowing, making a low fresh sound. Inside, there were the remains of fine panelling and the worm-eaten floors were 'rich'. Moved by the sight of nature invading, biting, torturing those rags of humanity, we remained silent and held our breath, in respect and a slight dread.

Suddenly, from the floor above, we heard footsteps. *Someone* was descending the staircase. The atmosphere was such that the apparition of a ghost would not have surprised us at all. My heart was throbbing. The 'presence' must be old, for it was descending slowly, limping from step to step. The summer heat quivered beyond the confusion of leaves and stones, the water from the springs was singing like a soul. The 'owner' was drawing near. He came in sight at the turn of the stairs. It was a magnificent barbary duck, with sparkling hues.

What was this living thing doing in this lost place? He stared at us intensely, with a somewhat reproving eye. He wagged his head a little, as a sign of rejection. Having got the message, we slowly backed away, 'Sorry to have troubled. . . .' It was the soul of France in ruins.

No sooner demobilized, I fetched up at Toulouse. I did not know where to go. In a street I met an actor whom I knew vaguely. He at once took me in hand, as things happen in adventure stories; I followed him as one obeys a new destiny. He took me to a house. The door opened. A lady welcomed me. Introductions:

'Madame Martin. I was expecting you. I am giving you my son's room.'

There are moments when really you no longer know where you are.

As at Dijon nearly a year before, I began going every day to the station, watching for, not believing in, the arrival of Madeleine. At last I had news of her. She was in Brittany. I waited, going almost mad. Then, with a desire to be reborn to my country as though to an ancestral womb, I went to the municipal library and plunged into the history of France. My head, my heart and my belly had chosen Villon, the *Chanson de Roland* and *Saint Louis*.

I felt I was convalescent, emerging from some terrible illness. Those eleven months of nightmare had in truth changed me, and at the same time my Double was busy effacing them. It seemed only yesterday that, on my way back from trout-fishing in Normandy, I had seen that notice. Since that yesterday, what layers on layers of events! Now I wanted to be active. But to act one must understand, and to understand one must learn. I wanted to start again from scratch. To go back to school.

On the one hand, there was *my* country and its ruin. On the other, the swarming confusion of Frenchmen accusing one another. De Gaulle was condemned to death by Pétain, the 'traitor', who was giving us to understand that it was all our fault. Sartre, by way of reacting against this false accusation, wrote *Les Mouches*. One newspaper actually printed this:

> There has been the 6 February 1934, then an attempt which failed in '37 (suppression of the Popular Front) and at last this war has just lanced the abscess there had been in France. . . .

The conspiracy was no longer being concealed! To my mind, it was the Spirit, above all, that had to be saved. A note in my book says:

> Return to individual intuition. Reform of the West. To find once more, through a neo-Christianity helped by the East, the universal laws and, this time, to take them on ourselves.

Over and above the general bankruptcy, there was the German occupation – dictatorial, anti-Semitic – the first concentration camps. The spirit, along with the armed guerilla, must be organized clandestinely. Therefore, no question now of working openly at things like *Numance*, at the head of the Atelier.

I thought of settling at Aix-en-Provence, if I could manage to persuade Madeleine. I kept sane by filling my little notebooks:

> The day before yesterday we had gone, at nightfall, into a small church, marvellous in its simplicity, gaiety and love, to play the harmonium. The priest, a splendid old man – quite capable of lighting his pipe at the flame of the Reserved Sacrament, he lived with God on such familiar terms – received us with open arms. When we asked him to switch off the electric lights so that we might feel the atmosphere of the place more clearly, he hesitated for a moment, went and lit a candle, switched off the lights, then went off to pray, like us. An intense moment. At the harmonium, Marcel Landowsky.

I felt torn between Madeleine, whom I could no longer live without, a desperate need to act in accordance with my thinking, and a completely unknown future.

Destiny was waiting for me in a corridor of the municipal library. In between two readings of the life of Saint Louis, whom should I meet but the treasurer of the Théâtre Français:

'So you are in Toulouse?'

'Well, yes, this is where I fetched up.'

'Jacques Copeau is looking for you everywhere.'

Jacques Copeau had also come forward, and had agreed to take charge of the Comédie Française. He was less docile than Pétain, so did not last long.

> People tend to forget the state of mind of the French in June 1940. The speed of what had happened and the strange nature of the conflict had plunged the country into a kind of total misery. People did not understand. At first Pétain's gesture was taken at its face value. No point in speaking of General de Gaulle's long-term 'vision'. We had felt ourselves betrayed on all sides. England, at Dunkirk, had acted on legitimate but cruel instincts of self-preservation. America no doubt had not yet made its deliveries of arms pay off. Italy had been ignoble. Russia had joined with Germany in devouring Poland. The world was secretly rejoicing at the fall of the French Empire. When two wolves fight, the one who is hurt lies down and presents his jugular vein. This is not cowardice but tactics. The gesture produces an inhibitory reflex in the victor, who stops the carnage and moves off, after having lifted his leg against a tree to mark his superiority. The armistice was the offer of the jugular vein: but men are much crueller than wolves. The Germans, alas, would not go home. Without dreaming of disparaging the courage of those who made their way to America or London, it has to be admitted that the French people had to survive, as nobly as possible, and that was all. Not all succeeded, but many were real heroes. *Invictis victi victuri*.[1]

---

[1] The conquered to their conquerors: 'We shall conquer.'

Let us return to Toulouse.

'Jacques Copeau is asking for me?'

'Yes. He sent me a telegram about you. He wants to take you on at the Français.'

The treasurer got me my *Ausweis*. I crossed the demarkation line at Vierzon. I was seeing my first Germans in their green uniforms, wearing boots and helmets.

On 16 August 1940, I signed on for a year. Copeau had said to me:

'I want you to bring in new blood.'

I was returning to school. What was more, to the school of Jacques Copeau, the creator of the Vieux Colombier, the instigator of the whole modern theatre movement. I was going to live with Madeleine. Everything to which, in the midst of the misery, my Being at present aspired.

The Comédie Française

PARIS 1940. Two ways of life. On one side : cars, uniforms and 'privileged people'. On the other : métro, bike, work.

We had sold our cars, the caravan had long been a thing of the past. Curfew was at 10 p.m. or 10.30, I am not sure which. The situation was soon extremely clear. Desnos and Jeanson gave it a fair test by publishing in *Aujourd'hui* an article which they called 'The Revenge of the Mediocrities'. It was their last article. So it was proved : there was no question now of going on working at Kafka's *The Trial*.

When a tree is cut back, it puts more strength into roots. After the Fauvism of the Atelier, after the emancipation brought by Surrealism, I was ready to receive the classical graft, that of the Français.

In the eyes of many of my comrades, I was ratting. Some thought I was really terrified of the liberty I proclaimed in other circumstances. A form of cowardice, a failure of character.

In the first place, they were forgetting Madeleine. Love is love. Above art, there is the religiosity of life without which art would not exist. After a year of separation, which I had found intolerable, we were going to be able to live together, be *one*. I have said enough about my conception of the couple, of two people as one Being. We were going to act together, share the same worries, the same ordeals, the same hopes, the same Destiny.

We were two people and had but one heart.

Besides, just as at the time of *Numance*, I was looking for 'confirmations'.

My timid nature – an orphan's, perhaps – has often given me an inferiority complex. Are the beasts of the forest cowardly when they are timid? Is the wolf who pricks up his ears and puts his tail between his legs, is the puma who hides in a piece of brushwood, showing a lack of character?

Although my poetic vision of my art had deepened during those eleven months of enforced reflection, I was aware of what I still lacked. It was true, I wanted to begin all over again, start again from scratch. After Dullin, Decroux and Artaud, what finer school could there be than that 'Maison de théâtre' whose birth dated back to 1680? Even older than our vines at Beauregard. I loved life, and it was from life that I wanted to draw the substance of this art.

I have no love either for ideas that cancel each other out, or for the game of politics that serves only some people. My heart is on the left, that is all. And life, I repeat, is a trinity – call it a Christian Trinity or the ternary of the cabbala, or, if you are a biologist : invariance, teleonomy and selection. To my mind, life is the balance resulting from the interaction of three forces : need, desire and liberty. Three permanent injunctions working away in our Being. When they get out of balance, need becomes egoism, desire becomes agitation, liberty becomes licence. In other words : excess to the right, excess to the left and desertion. None of this is *life*.

After the uprooting caused by the world catastrophe, I felt the need to replant myself. Betray? Betray whom or what? Ideas? Politics? Leave them to their own betrayals. Let us work at supplying life. This is also a highly valid way of attaining the objectives determined by those ideas and by politics. How often, since then, I have been able to confirm the efficacy of this way! Especially when, first and foremost, it leads to the *human being*.

Desire? It had sharpened. I was more and more eager to see clearly in the matter of my art, to attain self-evidence. The sixth sense again. The Zen philosophy has a small book from which I am never parted : *Zen in the Art of Archery*. A good archer can only hit the target if, instead of aiming 'cerebrally', he becomes the bow, identifies himself with it; if his whole body is torn and his breathing becomes an arrow. Then, even in the dark, he will hit the target. There lies the whole difference between the speculative or profit-making spirit and the vocation of a craft. The one leads us towards the society of consumers, the other towards a civilized world. Give all so as to receive all. You will not be 'paid' unless, in your spirit, you were ready to work for nothing. In fact, paid in return. Before *profiting* from the return, one must *offer* to go. The law of exchange needs to be earned by an act of offering.

In my case the art of the theatre had confirmed itself as being 'the poetry of space by means of the human being'. Before I could go any further, I wanted to look for some confirmations in the classics. Already Proust, when describing the actress who worked with La Berma (Sarah Bernhardt), had written :

> The gesture of these artists said to their arms, to their peplum: Be majestic. But between shoulder and elbow those undisciplined limbs permitted the strutting of a biceps that knew nothing about the role.

This was another small key which I picked up on my way, and which suited me marvellously.

Besides, I was completely out of training. Like someone who has been hurt in an accident, I had to go through a period of re-education – this was where *need* came in. And finally, my genetic nature was playing its part : my peasant fibre has given me a taste for being a 'pro'.

Also it does, after all, happen in the adventure stories that the men who roam far and wide take refuge in convents, especially in the ones where there is a 'Sister Madeleine' living.

And *liberty*? We shall often recur to that. As I grow older, it haunts me more and more. Not all the philosophies and psychoanalyses have removed my taste for it. For the moment let us say that to me liberty is the faculty of being constantly in tune with oneself. It is also the faculty of choosing the constraints one will accept. In consenting to put myself in question all over again, this time on the stage of the Français, I was profoundly in tune with myself and was choosing my constraints. Also, this did not, for that matter, prevent me from living the life of Paris and the ordeals of the Occupation. On the plane of friendship, I dedicate this period to Robert Desnos: we drew closer and closer.

I think I may already have said that I love the ceremony of the table. To me a meal is a kind of rite that has something sacred in it: another inheritance from my ancestors. I love customs, and one comes across plenty of these in the daily life of the theatre. Those of the Français delighted me from the first. When I walked up the staircase leading to the level of the stage, I never failed to stop for a moment in front of the bust of Molière, to touch him with my fingertips or lay before him a small bunch of violets.

In accordance with etiquette, I presented myself to the senior actor. I did not realize that one had also to present oneself to the senior actress (apart from the courtesy due in general to the female sex). She made me aware of it.

The etiquette of the place went, indeed, rather further. The *pensionnaires* were only there by the year. The *sociétaires* for life. *Sociétaires* had the right to use the lift, the others not. But indeed this did not last for long.

The place was famous for its intrigues. It was often said that the *Société des Comédiens français* was 'one big happy family – like the Atreidai'! And yet I experienced there some great acts of friendship. True, some colleagues would not address a word to me. But, once on stage, everyone was reconciled. I call this the 'law of the circus': brotherhood in battle. If one is to understand the divergencies from which the actors of the Comédie Française suffer regularly, one must bear in mind their origin: they are the fruit of the fusion between Molière's company [1] and that of the Hôtel de Bourgogne, and this has given them a bifilar 'genetic code'. Sometimes the 'young company from the country' style is in the ascendant, at others there is a fit of nobility, of solemnity. Rare are the moments when the level is high enough to bring everyone into agreement.

Up to 1914 gold was worth its weight, there was no cinema, no radio, no television, and the dramatic art had no other branches than that of the theatre: the Society of Comédie Française Actors at that time balanced its budget. After the First World War, the State had to refloat it every year. So it came under tutelage. The more the Comédie Française needed the State, the more political intrigues infiltrated and deteriorated the system. This is the tragedy of 'La Maison'.

Later on, when I was a *sociétaire*, I was to put forward a report in which I made this point: the Society of Comédie Française Actors would not recover its balance except by gathering together, into a single activity, all the branches of the dramatic art: theatre, cinema, radio, television. I still believe this. Especially with the development of cassettes and the prospect of recording on

---

[1] Molière, who died in 1673, never belonged to the 'Français', which was created in 1680, but it is to Molière that we owe this theatrical community. Which makes him rightly 'Le Patron'.

videograms. Indeed I think the Comédie Française at present is preparing for this.

LE CID AND HAMLET

I made my début in *Le Cid*. It was a disaster. I was much too 'light' (in category, that is, as with a boxer). In Corneille's play the Cid is not Guilhem de Castro's Spanish bullfighter, protected by the supernatural. He is a Norman ox. In between Marie Bell, that magnificent Chimène, and Jean Hervé as the old Don Diègue, as strong as a Turk, I looked like a grasshopper. Jean Hervé, who was furious at no longer being given the part of Rodrigue, shook me like a plum-tree. Certainly he had no need of his son in order to get rid of the Count.[1] 'This trial stroke is not a master stroke', wrote my old friend André Frank, who had fought on my side over *As I Lay Dying*.

Copeau decided to have the first night of *Le Cid* on 11 November, the anniversary of the 1918 Armistice. For the Germans it was not the best possible date. With the connivance of the students, the thing turned into a real patriotic demonstration. Copeau was sent home. His courage was an object lesson.

My second début, in *Hamlet*, was more fortunate. This time, it was Shakespeare's Hamlet. Granval had consented to direct me and put me through my work. The part was 'my weight'. Hamlet's anguish, his frenzy, his double nature, his black humour, his libertarian spirit – all these things enabled me to feel close to the part. All the same, I did dance it rather too much. I have always liked 'dancing' my roles. This is 'my worst self-indulgence', as Delacroix puts it. But it does give me so much pleasure at the time. Johann Sebastian Bach said:

> *I get so much joy directly from my work, that I cannot take offence if people don't like what I do.*

The quotation is a dangerous one – it has often served me as an excuse for the faults I commit voluptuously.

I was thirty. I have now played Hamlet for more than twenty-five years. He is my friend, my brother. I have tried to climb that peak by all its faces, but it is inaccessible. I see him as the superior crystallization of my nature: as a hero of the higher hesitation. But he slips through my fingers:

> Like a camel, like a weasel, like a whale!

To play Rosencrantz and Guildenstern I had sought out two young people of the Conservatoire, whom the magic wand of the theatre had singled out both for their physique and for their talent: Jean Desailly and Jacques

[1] We had to wait ten years to see Gérard Philipe triumph over this difficulty.

Dacqmine. They were to become two of the pillars of our own Company. *Hamlet* earned me my admission into the 'profession'.

It was Marie Bell who procured for me the finest opportunity of receiving the graft of classic art. She had long wanted to play *Phèdre*; and already, in Edouard Bourdet's time, Jean Hugo had drawn his design for the setting. She asked Jean-Louis Vaudoyer, the new Administrateur-Général, to entrust me with the direction. That so important a production should be entrusted to a young *pensionnaire* was a novelty, but Vaudoyer, that courteous and culti- vated man, did not funk it. The result, for me, was a major enrichment. It gave me the chance to put my convictions to the proof: they emerged reinforced.

PHÈDRE

In *Mon coeur mis à nu* Baudelaire says:

> *What has always seemed to me the most beautiful thing in the theatre, when I was a child, and now still, is the chandelier, a lovely object, luminous, crystalline, complicated, circular and symmetrical. . . .*

In the temple of the classical theatre, *Phèdre* is the chandelier.

Mahelot, who designed it in Racine's time, says: 'The scene is a vaulted palace, one chair at the beginning.' I applied this direction exactly. After Phèdre's first confession, the *confidante* removed the chair. The tragedy was played standing. The men were barefoot, the costumes Cretan in style. The sun followed its trajectory from dawn to night. I have written a whole book about *Phèdre*.

Whether I look at it from the point of view of Racine's poetic adventure, which is comparable to Rimbaud's *Saison en Enfer*,

or from the point of view of the recitative, which is a lyrical enlargement of the soul, a dreamlike extra-lucidity,

or from that of the extremely rich rhythmical combinations of the Alexan- drines; of the metrical craft of spoken French; of the scales of breathing,

or from that of crystallization of gestures in close relation with the crystal- lization of the verbal prosody,

or from that of displacements of the voice,

or from that of the tragic action, which comes into view at the moment when the instinct of self-preservation is left behind,

or from the point of view of that challenge to death, which demands a super- vitality,

or, finally, from that of recourse to rhythm in order to enhance the atmo- sphere of the drama, I kept finding in *Phèdre* striking proofs of the relevance of everything I had thought, up to then, about dramatic art: use of breathing, waking dream, the plastic art of the mouth, art of gesture, rhythm, etc.

The study of *Phèdre* was to mark me for ever: here is the alchemical elixir of the secrets of our art. Quintessence of stage poetry: love, hate, aggression, theatre of cruelty. Racine seemed to me the most musical of the French poets.

I made a study of the symphonic movements in *Phèdre*. I took its metrical craft to pieces, as one might with a Greek tragedy. I studied it so closely that one day, in a Dominican monastery, I was able to give a reading of it without recourse to the text: the 1654 lines issued from my skin.

I returned from that plunge more convinced than ever.

JEAN-PAUL SARTRE

With the success in *Hamlet* and the enlightening experience of *Phèdre*, I had recovered my strength and, with it, my demons. Anguish reappeared. Perplexities gnawed at me again. 'My animal' was hearing the call of the forest. Madeleine, who during the whole of our life together has been understanding itself, allowed my suffering to take its course, as all kinds of torments assailed me.

I had made the acquaintance of Jean-Paul Sartre. I was enthusiastic about *La Nausée* and *Le Mur*, as soon as they came out. We saw each other very often. He had a great influence on me, from which I retain these four points chiefly:

1. The emotions are actions.
2. The theatre is the art of justice.
3. The relations between 'Self' and 'the Others' make up the essential drama of existence.
4. A man, at a given moment, whatever his life may be, is *free*.

I found, confirmed in his existentialist philosophy, the third element in the ternary of life: freedom of choice – that element which Jacques Monod, in his book *Chance and Necessity*, confirms on the biological plane, and which had already struck me in the ternary of Destiny according to Æschylus.

Æschylus, Sartre, Jacques Monod: some references! And what a confirmation of the inklings I had had as a young man! For the benefit of any who still dispute the right to liberty, let us hazard this: is not liberty (when memory has been taken into account) the sister of imagination? The faculty of juggling *in one's own way* with past perceptions, with a view to future encounters?

About liberty

I am sorry that Sartre never treated the subject which he had worked out and called *Le Pari* (The Bet). A couple, two 'displaced' persons, are mouldering in a railway station waiting-room. The woman is pregnant. The man wants her to have an abortion. She is resisting.

He: If the child is going to have the kind of life we have, it's best to have done with it at once!

She: I bet it will cope.

They argue. A clap of thunder. A supernatural being appears, at the same time as a set honeycombed with cells that rather suggest the 'mansions' in medieval pictures. The child's destiny is prepared. His life is there in front of us, complete with the people he will encounter. He alone is not there. The life in store for him will be cruel. He will end up being shot. Blackout. And the supernatural being vanishes.

The parents, left alone, now know the fate of their child. The wretched life in store for him strengthens the father's argument : 'What good is it, his living through that ?' But the young mother is stubborn : 'I bet he'll cope with it.' 'But since nothing can be changed . . . !' 'He'll cope, I tell you.' 'All right, have this kid of yours !'

Part Two: The 'mansions' are again lit. The same life and the same characters are there. This time, *he* too is there. He does not in any way change the *facts* of his life, but by his behaviour he transforms, transfigures them. He will end as was predicted : shot. But he has rendered that life magnificent, instead of sordid. Thanks to the sense of liberty.

About the emotions

I recommend Sartre's remarkable study on the phenomenology of the emotions. Briefly : the emotions are not states that come and add themselves at random to our behaviour, the emotions are *actions*.

I had already come to think that everything serves a purpose, including play. Sartre brought a confirmation extending even to the emotions. Emotion is an extreme, a last resort, a limiting case of behaviour. If someone shows hostility to me, I puff out my chest, speak louder, put myself *into a temper*. I actually make myself stronger than I am. I am having recourse to a 'magic' action. Or if someone is dangerous, I faint : I make myself disappear *out of fear* – either that, or I start whistling and artificially transform the danger into joking. Or again, if I am depressed, I turn my head to the grey surface of a wall : I forget, I suppress the situation, *out of sadness*; etc.

When Théramène tells of the death of Hippolyte, he spins out his narration because, as long as he is speaking of him, Hippolyte still lives. Théramène's narration delays the death of Hippolyte. The invention of the great speeches in tragedy is the result of an emotional action, an extreme action in the course of which one is put magically in communication with the subject.

The invention of dramatic representation – in other words the art of the theatre – is due to a collective emotional conduct, which consists in gathering together in one place in order to fight the feelings of solitude and anguish and to 'represent' – that is to say, to revive in a way that is bearable – the great problems of life, especially the constant relations we have, as individuals, with the 'others'.

Theatre: art of 'self' and 'the others'. Art of justice

Sartre brought me also his insights on this third point. His analyses were brilliantly intelligent. They defined and reinforced my convictions (already expounded), and this applies also to the idea of theatre as the art of justice. I soon saw that this went beyond the justice of Ideas, or that of the various political camps, and extended to the 'biological justice' of life – in other words, *'justesse'* (measure, rightness).

Excesses, passions and questions of right defended egotistically unbalance life in its normal movement. Men who have sacrificed a large part of their instincts for the sake of a questionable kind of intelligence are constantly falsifying, throwing out of gear the mechanism of life. Too often they confuse function, value judgment and knowledge.

It is by facing all these excesses, passions and pretensions to right in a selected place (the stage) that men 'settle their accounts'. The result, when the game is played honestly, is a collective cleansing, a smoothing out of all the wrong creases, a *readjustment* of balance : an act of Justice. Here we have the social utility of the theatre. The theatre becomes an art that is of public value.

One day a member of the audience wrote to Dullin : 'A good play is a play that is going somewhere.' That 'somewhere' is, it seems to me, the ground on which men settle their accounts and *life renders justice*, or, once again, re-establishes the correct running – *la justesse* – of the mechanism.

In our precarious condition as living beings, some more strange than others but all condemned to destruction, what is *just* is what sustains life, and what is *unjust* is what deteriorates it. The theatre is the form of play – that is to say, the physical training – best fitted for showing what is just and what is unjust, what sustains and what deteriorates. When it does that, it can be considered the true science of human behaviour.

TO BECOME A SOCIÉTAIRE?

That professional life at the Comédie Française, my reasonably satisfactory début thanks to Shakespeare and the confirmation of all my convictions thanks to Racine and Sartre, had restored me to health. My faith was no longer vague, it was now concrete. The very heterogeneous ramifications of my education converged on to a single road, broad and clear and firm : complete theatre, total theatre, the theatre as the art of *Man*. My motto became : 'About man, by man, for man'. And at the same moment my demons woke up again : to have a theatre, to be responsible for a company !

As I said, I was not unhappy at the Français : I love craftsmanship. But I was unsatisfied. I was not working enough.

Sartre had written *Les Mouches*. He suggested to me that I should direct it. I had my head full of *Le Soulier de Satin*, and Sartre greatly admired it. He used to recite me verses from it, particularly this one :

What, will he never know this flavour which I have?

Jouvet had left for South America. Pierre Renoir had charge of the Athénée and did not know what to do with it. I asked Renoir to take us in at the Athénée. Sartre had found a backer whose name was Nero. So we were all agreed to use the Athénée for *Le Soulier de Satin* and for *Les Mouches*. At the same time the Comédie Française was offering me the chance to become a *sociétaire*. Let us not forget the Occupation, which was infernally present, conditioning us in spite of our passionate egoism (artists have the irresponsibility of possessed people). Once again I was torn in two. By turns whole-hearted and timid, rebellious and hesitant. Besides, my choice was not concerned only with the really important things. At the Français I was as sheltered as possible from the foreign occupiers and from their French political opposite numbers (these were the more dangerous). Outside the Français I might very well be unable to carry our 'action' through. Yet there was Sartre, Les Mouches, the Soulier – everything that attracted me.

At this point the chronological order becomes confused in my mind. I had a difference of opinion with Sartre about the casting of Les Mouches and about our methods of work. He was courteous but made no concession. Nero's backing vanished. The Athénée project fell to pieces. This was a blow. And yet, I seem to remember, I continued to reject the chance to become a sociétaire. It meant, therefore, leaving in spite of everything. Wilfully moving away from Madeleine, when life had miraculously reunited us – this decision of mine had about it something 'attentatoire' (a word which André Gide was fond of declaiming, to the accompaniment of that diabolical look of his), it was 'tempting Providence'. At the same time my demons were at me and gave me no rest. Along with Jean-Marie Conty, Roger Blin and a few other friends (Rouleau, Bertheau, Jean Servais – my memory is now indistinct), we had created the E P J D (Education par le jeu dramatique). Its object was to get into the schools, enter into contact with the pupils, and make them do carefully controlled improvisations through which, on occasion, we might have an antigovernmental effect. To create a sort of resistance spirit among the young. In a very modest way, of course, but one which might lead somewhere.

To stay at the Français was to confine myself in an aesthetic citadel. To leave the Français meant entering the social mêlée, the battle of ideas and politics. Desnos, who knew me well, advised me against the mêlée:

1. I knew nothing about it (this was true).

2. Deep down in me, I did not like it (also true, but were there perhaps other ways?).

3. As I was doing more and more films, what I looked like was too well known: I could become dangerous for the others.

I was tempted all the same. Divided between so many things of such vital importance, I was extremely unhappy. The end-of-year committees had come round. I had to decide.

'Are you accepting the sociétariat?' André Brunot, our senior actor, asked me one day; 'we've got to examine your case this afternoon.'

'No,' I answered, with tears in my eyes.

That was that. I would leave the Comédie Française. It would be harder for me to live in close union with Madeleine. I would be going once more into an unknown world – or one with which, in the fields familiar to me, I was not always in tune. What was driving me to act in this way? Was it the opinion of my friends? Nonconformist convention? Any real desire to do so? Fear of binding myself for ever? (For it must also be borne in mind that to become a *sociétaire* was, in a way, very like 'taking vows': it meant engaging myself for life, I would never have the right to leave. The committee could simply retire me after twenty years.)

While my case was being debated in the committee (of which Madeleine [1] was a member, having become the senior actress), I had joined a friend of mine at the Brasserie de l'Univers. We discussed the future. Suddenly, in a flash, it seemed to me so amateurish, so unprofessional, so artificial, intellectual and naïvely pretentious (as the 'amateur' spirit always is), that I was seized with panic. Making the first excuse that came to mind, I left my friend, crossed the square at a run, approached the attendants and had a note taken in to the Administrator, saying that I accepted membership of the *sociétariat*. Perhaps it was already too late?

Five minutes went by. The door opened. The members of the committee, in defiance of custom, wanted to receive their new associate. I went in. Great was my emotion. My comrades also had tears in their eyes. In any other managing committee such effusions might have seemed out of place, but in a society of actors they were quite natural because for us living under stress is normal. Abruptly I drew away from them, with my back against the wall, and, shaking my fist at them, cried:

'Mind you, beginning today, I'm going to make you foam at the mouth!'

Shouts of delight, affectionate laughter. I went out, and things returned to normal. Date? Let us say: end of '42.

I, who had dreamed of having a theatre and a company, had just opted for the Comédie Française. Does that mean that I wanted to make it *my* theatre, and the illustrious company *my* troupe? I genuinely do not think so. On reflection it seems to me that there is in me a mixture of craftsman, anarchist and Dominican. Because of my peasant origin, I like to know 'where I am treading'; I am drawn towards 'the craft', towards technique. By my own moral choice, I like to safeguard my liberty to the point of appearing a libertarian. From fear of death, I have a morbid hunger for knowledge and for 'being more', a feeling that one must give oneself: 'Give all and receive all' (Jean Vauthier's *Le Personnage combattant*) – 'To know all so as to be all known' (Paul Claudel, *Partage de Midi*).

Here again the ternary: need, liberty, desire.

The Dominican had just gained the upper hand. The Dominican and also the craftsman.

This time, my 'treason', so my friends thought, was final. Sartre, whom I had asked for last minute advice (we had remained good friends), had replied:

> I think a man like you, who has at least one new idea per day, who is made for trying out new things in all directions, ought to be his own master and every time to commit only himself. I am venturing to make

---

[1] The *doyens* (senior actors and actresses) are the *sociétaires* of longest standing, not the oldest.

these criticisms to you frankly, because you have been kind enough to ask me my advice. You also mention struggle and fighting, but I see in a work of art not so much a fight as an achievement. My fear is that you will have to fight a great deal and achieve little.

As for Dullin, he wrote to me:

Reread La Fontaine's adorable fable *Le Loup and le Chien* and, knowing me as you do, you will understand all that I think. The form of theatre I have always defended is perhaps the one nearest to all those which 'the Français' ought to be defending, and yet the furthest away because of the constraints imposed by false traditions and a State conformism. It is very good that at your age, in the fullness of your strength, you should carry the struggle into the citadel itself. But every concession you will be obliged to make will turn against you even more harshly than in your own theatre, unless your ambition turns merely towards your skill as an actor, which, obviously, you can exercise with a maximum of security. Good work and good luck, my dear Barrault.

Dullin had understood perfectly: I wanted to carry the struggle 'into the citadel itself'. I still had to prove it.

There remained to me Claudel, the man who, in his time, had also 'betrayed the penniless poets', because he wanted to cry out, like Tête d'Or:

Do, do, do. Who will give me the strength to do?

I wonder nowadays whether the Claudel I was already carrying in me had not secretly influenced me – obviously without meaning to, for he was living in the unoccupied zone and we had scarcely any direct contacts. But was there not in him too something of the craftsman, something of the anarchist and something of the Dominican?

I wonder also whether, at that moment, I was not congenitally searching through his work for *another father*.

In any case my honour was at stake. It would be defended by *Le Soulier de Satin*. On this point I received unreserved encouragement from Desnos, my Boileau, my Pylades, my friend, my brother, my defender.

LE SOULIER DE SATIN

The story of how *Le Soulier de Satin* (*The Satin Slipper*) came to be staged is pretty well known. In reality, like the charioteer driving several horses at once, we were in simultaneous action. As early as 1941 I had badgered Claudel again. He had answered: 'What good fortune and how happy I would be to work with you!' But *Tête d'Or* gave him 'gooseflesh'. *Le Soulier de Satin*? What a labour! Couldn't we start with *Christophe Colomb*?

But I wanted *the lot* at one go, and I dug in my heels about *Le Soulier de*

Satin. From the wings Desnos encouraged me. For one thing, Sartre had been in favour at the time of the Athénée project: for another, J.–L. Vaudoyer was anxious to apply some heat to the Comédie Française actors. The camp of the 'moderns' was enthusiastic. The other camp, more reserved.

While I was pursuing my efforts to get the *Soulier* accepted, I was going through all the agonies of doubt I have just described. A journey to Brangues, requiring an *Ausweis* for crossing the demarkation line (oh, irony, the place was Tournus!), and five days spent working with the Master on taking the play to pieces, like two children, had proved sufficient: I left on the return journey with a letter of consent, in which the poet authorized us to present *Le Soulier de Satin* in two evenings of three hours each.

Not long before that, at Marseilles, I had tried the play out on the radio: four broadcasts of an hour and a half each for each 'day'[1]. It was there that Madeleine and I had met Gide, who was on the point of taking refuge in Tunisia, and that was when I persuaded him to finish his translation of *Hamlet*, which he had begun twenty years earlier. Here is the note in Gide's *Journal* about this meeting:

5 May 1942

> I saw the two of them again, on the eve of my departure; at lunch the three of us, invited by them to a very good restaurant in the square from which the broad Avenue du Prado starts. Barrault urges me to finish my translation of Hamlet for him; and I have such great confidence in him that I would like to get to work at once. I learn with lively pleasure that he is a close friend of Sartre.

And so I was bringing back, victoriously, Claudel's letter of consent. I went through Tournus again. The Germans searched us. One of them found my letter. He tore it up into small pieces and threw them into the corridor. The train moved off again. Grumbling, with the unusual calm you may sometimes find in a madman, I picked up the bits of paper. Not one was missing. It is now a relic.

It remained for me to persuade the reading committee. Two sessions were allowed for it. As I wanted not only to read the play but to act it in order to explain how it would be staged, I had asked for a special session, to take place not in the committee room, around the traditional green tablecloth, but in the

---

[1] In its original form *Le Soulier de Satin* is a tetralogy. Claudel called each of its four parts a 'day', being inspired by his memories of the Chinese theatre, with its performances that go on for several days. The first three 'days' of *Le Soulier de Satin* treat their theme tragically, though with a Shakespearian variety of mood. The fourth 'day' takes it up afresh and treats it from the angle of the absurd, as in Athens in the fifth century B C a tetralogy ended with a satyr play. It was from the first three 'days' that Jean-Louis Barrault and Claudel carved a single play for the Comédie Française in 1942/3. In 1972 Jean-Louis Barrault presented – in a big-top at Brangues, and then at the Gare d'Orsay, Paris – a version of the fourth 'day' (*Sous le vent des Iles Baléares*), a bit shortened to make room for a prelude resuming the first three. (*Translator's note.*)

foyer des artistes. The *sociétaires* had permitted this extravagance. What is more, to do the reading, I took off my jacket. Never had the walls of the learned house looked upon such an audacity! A three-hour reading was needed for the first of the two evenings: this part of the play was accepted unanimously, but for one vote (that of a sublime actor who was wonderful in the *Soulier* but confessed that he did not understand it all).

So half my *Soulier* was admitted. A few days later, the other half was rejected. I had to begin all over again. Before returning to Brangues, I persuaded the committee to accept in exchange, and in advance, a reduction of the whole to a single performance lasting five hours. Five hours! Unprecedented! And in the midst of the German Occupation, with curfew at 10.30. Crazy! We would start at 5.00.

In spite of which, the committee agreed to the project. I left again for Brangues. Stopped at Lyons. Then, at dawn, the local train to Morestel. Then a walk of several kilometres, full of hope and apprehension. With my usual rucksack on my back, I went with ringing steps along that smiling road, which wound between alternate rows of poplars, fields of young oats and meadowland. My spirit grew drunk with the rhythm of my steps, I talked out loud, I laughed, and tears came into my eyes at feeling so strongly, in my veins and round about me, Life. I have a melting nature: that is how it is. A *Soulier de Satin* that was still unreal was flying about me like a seagull escorting a ship, a drunken boat, and *'je devins un opéra fabuleux'*.[1]

At the end of a short dirt road, the wrought-iron gate. Behind that, framed by a nave of plane trees, the burly château and, lurking within, the Master. He let himself be persuaded. All that remained was to go into action. That was not easy. Only one point was already clear: unreserved acceptance of Honegger for the music. (A lovely man. This was the beginning of a long, brotherly collaboration.) For the sets and costumes, Claudel wanted José-Maria Sert. I did not: too decorative, too immediately baroque. It seemed to me that Rouault's *impasto* corresponded to that 'intelligible mouthful', the word as used by Claudel. I suggested him. This time the reaction was startling:

'I don't want at any price anything to do with that dauber, whom I abominate!'

I had another idea in reserve; but Les Halles had taught me that the customer has to be softened up before you put the merchandise before him. We went over the list of painters. Claudel, whose Turelure[2] side sometimes made one think of Le Père Ubu, said:

'What a pity the painters have so little imagination! Look at Cèzanne! He never painted anything but apples!'

---

[1] Rimbaud, *Le Bateau ivre.*
[2] Turelure is a character in Claudel's *L'Otage* and *Le Pain dur.* Most people would regard him as, on the whole, the villain; Claudel was always delighted when anyone said that he resembled Turelure. (*Translator's note.*)

2–4 'Beauregard', the family house at Tournus in Burgundy

Jean-Louis (below), aged about two and seven

5   Jean-Louis Barrault, at 26, with his mother   6   His father in uniform, World War I

7   Jean-Louis Barrault and a group of soldiers in World War II

8 Charles Dullin, founder and
director of L'Atelier, in
Volpone

9 Louis Jouvet

10 Paul Claudel

11 André Gide, a painting by
Paul-Albert Laurens, 1924

12 Training in mime

13 In the film *The Puritan*, 1937

14 *Hélène*, a film based on a
story by Vicki Baum;
Madeleine Renaud and
Jean-Louis Barrault, 1936

15 With Madeleine Renaud in
Normandy, 1939

17 *Les Enfants du Paradis*, with Étienne Decroux

18, 19 As Baptiste in *Les Enfants du Paradis*

20 *La Fontaine de Jouvence*, 1947

21 *La Fontaine de Jouvence*, a pantomime with libretto by Boris Kochno. Madeleine Renaud and Jean-Louis Barrault

Plays with Madeleine Renaud

22 *The Trial*, adapted by André Gide and Jean-Louis Barrault from the novel by Franz Kafka, 1947. Marigny

23 *Amphitryon* by Molière, 1947

24 *The Cherry Orchard* by Chekhov, 1954

25 *Les Nuits de la Colère* (The Nights of Wrath) by Armand Salacrou. Marigny, 1946

26 *Occupe-toi d'Amélie* by Georges Feydeau. Marigny, 1948

27 *L'État de Siège* (The State of Siege) by Albert Camus. Marigny, 1948 ▶

28 Jean-Louis Barrault

Humour was something Claudel had in profusion.[1]

When he was 'done to a turn', like a bull that has received his dose of ban-derillos, I moved in with the estocade and got him to accept my friend Lucien Coutaud.

To bring off such an adventure, I needed not only talents but also friends.

After the committee's enthusiastic agreement, each *sociétaire* had resumed his normal cruising speed. Three times the first rehearsal was announced, three times nobody came. I was like Charlie Chaplin in *City Lights*, making the bread-rolls dance as he waits in vain. Desnos, with his knowledge of human nature, had told me:

'Commit them to things that cost money.'

With the connivance of Vaudoyer, whose tenacity about this 'revolutionary' enterprise was admirable, I had immediately ordered some of the sets to be built. After the third attempt at holding a rehearsal had failed, I demanded not only that the managing committee should meet, but that the principal mem-bers of the cast should be present. A stormy session, in which each of them defended his own taste in the name of the interests of the House.

'Why not put on De Létraz's *Bichon*, instead of this farrago which won't draw even a cat?'

'If you give up the *Soulier*, I shall clear out, and I warn you I shall tell every-body you are all on your last legs.'

'But after all, some of the sets are already built.' (Thank you, Desnos, you were so right.)

Luckily the majority had more nobility in them. And it was decided to go ahead seriously, and as quickly as possible, with that enormous affair of thirty-three scenes.

During this time, Claudel kept writing to me on *cartes interzones*: 'I would like to have some news from you. Am I being once more steered towards a postponement?' He had experienced, not long before, the same troubles with *L'Annonce faite à Marie*.

From that day genuine rehearsals started. Usually when one is rehearsing, the technical staff take refuge in their lair and the actors who are not for the moment involved gather in theirs to gossip. If, gradually, you see stagehands, electricians or actors slipping into the auditorium, out of interest or curiosity, to watch the rehearsal, you have the right to be hopeful. This is what hap-pened with the *Soulier*. The general atmosphere betrayed the fact that some-thing was happening. The work became fascinating. The problems inside the house seemed to have been settled. But there were many others: lack of wood, lack of canvas, lack of materials for costumes. . . . The newspapers, influenced

[1] The flat below Honegger's studio was used by a doctor, specialist for venereal diseases. One day, as the two of us arrived on that floor, Claudel pointed to the plate on the doctor's door and quoted Phèdre's line: 'C'est Vénus tout entière à sa proie attachée'. One year, for one of the exams at the Ecole de Beaux-Arts, the director had asked Claudel to supply the essay subject for those who were taking painting. What he sent in was: 'Illustrate Racine's famous line: "Hippolyte étendu sans forme et sans couleur." ' Decidedly he was fond of *Phèdre* . . . and a hoax.

by the German Occupation, were watching us with hatred. Because of these difficulties, the rehearsals were sometimes interrupted. The paper *Je suis partout*, of sinister memory, with its sinister Alain Laubreaux (who has the death of Desnos on his conscience), printed this:

They are waiting for the arrival of Eisenhower to present their Soulier.
Others were already insinuating: 'Lucky there's only one [slipper]!' My own stubbornness was that of a man obsessed.

One day I received an odd visit. There was a German officer asking to see me: a 'courteous and cultivated man'.

'The Kommandantur has chosen you to direct Werner Eck's piece at the Opéra' (I have forgotten the name of the piece).

'Very sorry, but I'm putting on *Le Soulier de Satin*.'

'If we were to postpone the *Soulier*?'

'My inspiration would be postponed by that amount.'

'But we don't like Claudel.'

'We like him. You can't take that away from us.'

'We can ban the *Soulier*.'

'You can, but it will be such a blow to me that I shan't be capable of doing anything else.'

'You would be capable of going to work in Germany.'

'Yes, that also you can do.'

'But I have come here simply to discuss things on the cultural plane.'

'Thank you for that.'

Next day Honegger came to see me:

'You ought to send a nice letter to that gentleman, he has defended you. Thanks to him, you will not be deported.'

I did send a polite letter to the officer, and we went on with the rehearsals of 'my' *Soulier*.

The work was progressing. Ten days before the opening, Claudel made the journey to Paris. The first part lasted two hours and a half. We did a run through for him. He watched his work blissfully and, with the smile of a big baby, exclaimed:

'It's quite simple, it's genius.'

When the interval came, he added:

'Well, they will be getting their money's worth!'

He was enchanted.

The second part, lasting two hours, contained passages that were less successful. Especially the great '*Château-Arrière*' scene (on the poop), in which Rodrigue and Prouhèze have at last met again and unite themselves for eternity by a sacramental 'no', in place of the 'yes' of marriage which would only have united them on the temporal plane. For us this scene was what we call, in our theatre jargon, '*un os*' (a bone). I was not managing to 'place' the scene properly, to get it going; Marie Bell and I could not even get the text by heart.

In rehearsal there always arrives a moment when the play is born and comes alive. From that moment it imposes its will upon the author, the director, the

actors. If they do not listen to it, it resists. At the point I have mentioned
Le Soulier de Satin was resisting. I warned Claudel of this.

'Go ahead, we'll see.'

The second part began. It went well, but once we reached that scene we fal-
tered. We stopped.

'You're right,' said Claudel, 'I'm completely lost, it's gibberish.'

'Don't you think, Master, a small cut. . . .'

'We'll see in a moment or two. Before pulling the teeth out, we should try
curing it. Go on.'

We went at the recalcitrant scene, and the rehearsal ended on the irresistible
emotion of the final words: '*Délivrance aux âmes captives*'. When I think of
France at that moment – what a line !

We went into a huddle and rapidly reviewed the course of the action:

'That Jesuit father in the prologue, who gives a fresh impetus to the
dramatic interest in the middle of the performance, when the ship hits the
piece of wreckage, why shouldn't he intervene a third time?'

No more was needed. Claudel hurried away.

At eight next morning the telephone rang:

'The Master has been working all night. He wants to see you urgently.'

The appointment was made for nine o'clock at the Français. He was a bit late.
He had lost his copy in the métro, had gone back home, picked up his rough
draft and brought it. I saw in front of me that old man of sixty-six – his
thinned white hair, his blue eyes full of tears. His teeth were not lodged
firmly, and when he spoke his emotion made them click. I had in front of me
a twenty-year-old lover !

'God breathed on me last night, I wrote under His dictation. Here, I give
it to you, it doesn't belong to me.'

And in fact the rough draft contains practically no erasures. One can see
that he wrote at the speed of speech, for the words are indicated only by their
first letters. I had in front of me a case of pure inspiration. The really divine
moment, when the artist is present at his own injunction and, because of his
total attention, has now only to *obey* – I will go so far as to say, to *copy*. The
day before, at that rehearsal, Claudel had understood his work: he had just,
twenty years after writing it, rounded it off.

Sixty-six years old ! What power he had ! A real horse ! Marie Bell and I
achieved unison in record time: we felt ourselves being literally breathed
upwards.

The final three days were a continual fever: arrival of the sets, costume
adjustments, the lighting going wrong, not enough room for the orchestra. . . .
Everyone was criticizing the play, pulling it to pieces. 'Too long ! Wants cutting ! Unintelligible ! We're in for a disaster !' The newspapers, in their hostility to this insurrection of the French soul, were waiting to tear us to pieces.
The thing was taking on the quality of a spiritual battle, a national rising.
Everyone was aware of Claudel's Gaullist views. I confined myself to defending 'my thing'.

'Leave the poor beast alone ! *Merde, merde* and *merde,* fuck off !'

In the auditorium J.-L. Vaudoyer, buried deep in his seat, remained imperturbable, under the rug he never parted with. Madeleine, embarrassed by my rudeness, said to him :

'You must excuse him, he no longer knows what he's doing.'

'Oh, as long as he doesn't beat me !'

The dear man ! I wonder if, without him, the *Soulier* could ever have been put on.

> *Order is the pleasure of reason, but disorder is the delight of imagination,*

we are told in the introduction to the *Soulier.* By way of musical overture, I had 'contrived' with Honegger's help a cunning disorder. Putting to use the security regulations imposed at that time by the Occupation and the air raids, I had decided to 'break' the music with an announcement on a wailing loudspeaker : 'In case of an air raid warning, etc.'

It was the day of the opening. The performance took place in the afternoon. The whole, whole, whole of Paris was there. Except for the gold, the velvet, the statues and the solemnity, the thing reminded me of *As I Lay Dying.* They had come to be in at the kill. I had put the whole works into it : mime (the waves), nudity (the negress), madness. Order/disorder, alternating, to the advantage not of reason but of imagination.

Claudel was in the second row. Just behind him, there was Valéry. Conductor, André Jolivet.

The orchestra began tuning up. *Exactly* at the very second when the loudspeaker was supposed to say : 'In case of an air raid warning . . .' the sirens all over Paris began wailing. It was a genuine air raid warning. A jolly beginning ! The audience rose to go to the shelters. But Claudel, already a bit hard of hearing, had not heard the sirens. He stood up, turned round, waved his arms and shouted :

'No, no, stay where you are ! Don't be alarmed, it's part of the show !'

Valéry finally managed to convince him of the reality. A few moments later, the show was able to start again, and it was a triumph. Proof? The only one I will cite here is that given by a certain eminent person, with a considerable following at that time, who exclaimed, in the auditorium :

'*La vache! Il a gagné!*' [1]

On that day the poet Paul Claudel became a popular author. It seemed as if the vital strength of the French was arising again, on their national stage, under the noses of the Germans. All the actors of the Français were galvanized – led on by Marie Bell with her surpassing sensuousness and spirituality. It happened on 23 November 1943. That winter there was no heating : we acted in the cold, sometimes two degrees below freezing point. Sometimes I had to pinch Marie Bell, who was on the point of fainting in her low dress. The

---

[1] 'The bastard ! He's won !'

audience brought rugs with them and, to keep their hands covered, applauded with their feet.

I have heard that in Cologne, after the city had been completely destroyed by that terrible war, the German audience also – some years later, when peace was restored – listened in wretchedness and cold to this same play, *Le Soulier de Satin*, in its German translation, and felt rising in them the same vital forces that had given us life. Who claims that the true theatre cannot serve to bring human beings nearer to one another? Is there not something moving and striking about such parallel reactions in two people who had been led to disorder by the machinations of politics and money when the whole of their Being was capable of throbbing with the same rhythm?

On 11 December 1943 Dullin wrote to me:

> *Cher vieux, cher ami,*
> I am not sure I can call you that any longer! You are too emancipated for me to address you as I used to. I would like to see you and talk to you about *Le Soulier de Satin*. I am completely tied for the moment to a daily job that is pretty depressing. Anyhow, when I have told you that I was very touched by the performance . . . I have told you the essential, for knowing the work, loving it as I do, a kind of song produces in one's mind an idea of how it could be transposed to the stage, and that means that everything you have done corresponds well with that idea, with those rather confused images which aroused my imagination. So I received like a blow in the stomach your whole contribution, that block, like a family achievement; if I may say so, and without being sentimental, I have been deeply moved. I have recognized also that you were right in seeking to create your work in that house. I had disapproved of you when you tied yourself by becoming a *sociétaire*, fearing that you would be lost for the theatre that seeks, or that seeks itself, and you have just proved me wrong. It is certain that nowhere else could one bring together such a cast, and make available to a difficult work those financial resources requisite for a commercial success. You have won all along the line. Only remember that in the theatre one has never won and that at the moment when one has most friends one has most enemies. . . .

Had I been the hound? Had I been the wolf? Let us say: the wolf in the sheepfold. As for what he said about friends and enemies, unfortunately Dullin was too experienced not to be right.

François Mauriac entrusted me with the direction of *Les Mal-Aimés*. It was another success. At my suggestion Shakespeare's *Antony and Cleopatra* was put on in André Gide's translation with Marie Bell and Clariond in the two name parts; as with *Phèdre*, Jean Hugo did the sets and costumes; Jacques Ibert composed the music. I brought Decroux back to the stage – he agreed to join me in arranging the fights.

I also asked for the creation – in a small theatre, such as, for instance, the neighbouring Palais-Royal – of a young Comédie Française, which would have become our experimental theatre. It seemed to me that in this way one could better serve the poetic world which had laid its hand on me some years earlier : total theatre and poetry in Space.

Could I really hope to win acceptance, in this high place of the profession, of my vision, now disciplined by my recent approaches to the classics? To marry the *avant-garde* to traditional customs – was not this to go back through time and rediscover the great universal traditions of the Greeks and of the Far East?

I admired the technical team at the Français. I worked in perfect brotherhood with René Mathis, the stage director, an exceptional man. I liked the craftsmen more and more. Some of them were sublime. Here are two anecdotes :

The first time the set for *Les Mal-Aimés* was set up on the stage, I found that it was deflecting Mauriac's play rather too much towards nineteenth-century psychological drama : it was depriving it of its tragic overtones. At some other time the thing would have had to be thought out afresh and done again. Unfortunately at that time there was no chance of that. No wood, no canvas, all sorts of restrictions. I told the head carpenter :

'All right, we'll set it sideways. That will bring a touch of the unexpected.'

'But, sir, with the rake of the stage, the set will be cock-eyed. The verticals will be leaning. It's impossible.'

'If you slewed it round only a little, the audience wouldn't notice.'

Then he looked hard at me and said :

'But I shall see it, sir !'

It was not the set I was breaking, it was his faith, his reason for living.

I then got the whole team together, to explain the situation and make it clear that I respected their leader's professional honour. Nonetheless, for some time afterwards he remained decidedly tepid. A good lesson !

Another lesson : I had been charged with organizing a poetry matinée in honour of Jean-Jacques Rousseau. A bunch of flowers was required. Preferably wild flowers. I ordered them from the props master. Days went by. Realizing that times were difficult, I said nothing. Still no flowers. Such periods can make the most devoted people lose all professional conscience; still, I was surprised. And still no bunch of flowers. In the end I rushed to the workshop :

'Well, Grumbert, that bunch of flowers? It's too much !'

'Sir, have a look ! I'm just finishing it. But I've had the devil of a job finding the flowers M. Rousseau liked !'

Such was the Maison de Molière, to which I had taken vows. I was not sorry I had. Well anyhow, not too sorry. For I was greedy to have everything. Gallimard had secretly sent me Camus' *Caligula*. How happy I would have been to put that play on for the first time, had the Comédie Française had its experimental theatre !

We went on making films. Madeleine was working with Grémillon. Christian-Jaque engaged me for a film on the life of Berlioz, *La Symphonie Fantastique*.

It was summer '42. Madeleine was filming *Lumière d'été* in the Midi. She, Jean-Pierre and I had managed to go down there together, with our bikes, as far as Saint Tropez. We were again at Pampelonne – among the vineyards – camping in a small hut. On holiday, I am the one who makes the *petit déjeuner*. Madeleine was summoned to Nice, to the Victorine studios, where all the French film world had taken refuge. She went off by train. There I was, alone at Saint Tropez: Jean-Pierre, looked after by friends, was probably in good hands. At ten o'clock at night I thought of the next morning, of Madeleine without her *petit déjeuner*. I loaded it on my bike and rode through the night. A hundred and twenty kilometres. Before dawn I went and lay down on the deck of a boat in the harbour of Cannes. When I reached the Négresco I was looking as scruffy as at the time of *Hélène*. I was shown the service entrance.

'Never mind. When Madeleine Renaud wakes up, take her this *petit déjeuner* and these flowers. Tell her someone is waiting for her downstairs.'

I omit the rest: our 'Woman's Own', romantic side, what-have-you!

I stayed two or three days at Nice. I ran into Prévert and Carné. They were furious. A producer had just rejected a script of theirs. We had a glass together on the terrace of a café on the Promenade des Anglais (where my grandfather had liked to go in his time). Prévert said to me:

'You haven't by any chance an idea for a subject?'

'Yes. You should put the story of a mime into a talking film; in contrast with a speaking actor. For example: Deburau and Frédérick Lemaître.'

Deburau, in the effort to defend his wife, had accidentally killed the attacker with a blow from a stick (he was a single-stick champion). The whole *Boulevard du crime* had rushed to the trial, not to see him acquitted, but to hear the sound of his voice.

A mime in a talkie? The *Boulevard du crime*? Prévert was delighted.

'Write me four or five pages about it, I will do the scenario and will try to make the film.'

'If it excites you, I will lend you all the books I've got.'

Prévert, like the real poet he was, absorbed it all and imagined *Les Enfants du Paradis*. He added the anarchist Lacenaire, the part played by Marcel Herrand. Brasseur played Frédérick Lemaître. Arletty and Casarès the two heroines. Pierre Renoir did 'Chant d'habits'. Decroux, Margaritis, Joseph Kosma, Trauner, all those friends from the Groupe d'Octobre were involved: all our youth. To my joy, mime, theatre and cinema were brought together. This happened in the same year as *Le Soulier de Satin*: 1943. *Annus mirabilis*: a real synthesis of one's life. And all this under the German Occupation!

In so far as one's astral complexion harmonizes more or less completely with certain characters that one interprets, I think the closest to me was Baptiste.

But while *Le Soulier de Satin* and *Les Enfants du Paradis* were the culminating points of this extraordinary period, the time of ordeals was approaching.

DEATH OF DESNOS

Desnos was arrested by the Germans and taken to Compiègne. He might have got off, but for the hatred borne him by certain Frenchmen who *must* share with the Nazis the responsibility for his death. There was no more news of him.

> *Rue Saint-Martin how I once loved it:*
> *Not now that André Platard has left it . . .*
> *My friend, my buddy, André Platard,*
> *One morning he disappeared,*
> *They took him, since then not a word . . .*
> *Rue Saint-Martin – André Platard*
> *Has left it.*[1]

Someone told us that he had sustained the morale of the others during his harsh captivity. That man who, like me, hardly dared cross a street for fear of being run over! Really one knows nothing about the depths of the human heart. He had, apparently, a star on his forehead as a result of the blows he had received. In August 1945, I could bear it no longer. I tried to go off in search of him, but just then, we learned that he was dead. This was discovered in a strange way.

His column, at the end of one of those extermination marches, had fetched up somewhere or other in Austria or Czechoslovakia. On the way he had seen one of his comrades killed because he was too ill to keep up. This comrade had entrusted him with his box, which he promised to take to his wife. To Desnos friendship was something holy. When they were liberated by the Russians one of the soldiers stole the box. At this, Desnos's will went from him. He had caught typhus. He was on his deathbed. There were two Czechoslovak students looking after these dying men. They were crazy about Surrealism and had read Breton's *Nadja*. In that book there is a page of photographs in which the Surrealists had had themselves taken as their imagined death-masks. One of these masks is that of Desnos. When the students saw Desnos on his deathbed they remembered the photograph and looked it up in *Nadja*. 'It's him all right!' They returned to his bedside, bent over him and said his name. Desnos came to and murmured: 'Mon matin le plus matinal' (My freshest early morning). They did all they could to save him: it was no good.

A few months later the two students told me the whole story and, as I remained silent, they added, in the way one speaks of a dead person to console one who was close to him: 'He seemed to be smiling, he looked as if he was

[1] Desnos, *Poèmes de Résistance*, 1942.

resting, he was very handsome.' And then: 'He had the most beautiful bone structure.'

The cruelty of our time. It was under that sign that a whole generation was moulded. Desnos was forty-five.

Within the same few days, my grandfather Valette died of old age.

But the Normandy landings had taken place, and the Allied armies were advancing. We lived through the week of the liberation of Paris: the bells of all the churches pealing – General Leclerc's tanks – the girls riding on the gun-mounts – De Gaulle's walk from the Etoile down to the Concorde – the Republic was returning to us with a sub-prefecture simplicity that we found overwhelming.

But with the Liberation came the settlings of accounts. It was a sordid moment. Jealousy, informing, ambitious intrigue: it was dreadful and discouraging. In adversity people group together, love each other, understand each other, help each other, nourish themselves and each other with things that go deep. As soon as the danger has vanished they become assertive, harsh, pitiless, selfish. Not to mention the absurdity of the last-minute heroes. Let us leave that. France was liberated, at last.

Liberated and injured. She needed to nurse herself, think things over, profit as best she could from the cruel ordeal and get going again soundly. As De Gaulle observed: there is France and there are the French. The best intentioned had each 'a certain idea' of France: the least one can say is that it was not always the same idea. When a pack of hunters and hounds are ravaging the forest, the animals go to ground. When, after the massacre, the pack moves away over the horizon, ears stick up, muzzles venture out, the animal takes three little steps, gives a snort, then they all run and strut in the clearing.

The Comédie Française has always reflected the France of the moment. At that moment each of its members had 'a certain idea' of 'la Maison'. Not the same one. While France was searching for her new way and the French on all sides were ringing the alarm bell, the Comédie Française began looking for its own new way, and there too the alarm was given. This was to end in a grave crisis.

CRISIS AT THE FRANÇAIS. OUR DEPARTURE

Molière, in the seventeenth century, had created a human community, a real republic of actors. Each had his share of responsibility and of giving himself. After Molière's death this private society of actors was attached to the 'traditional' company of the Hôtel de Bourgogne; in spite of the static strength of the latter, Molière's conception prevailed – the Société des Comédiens remained a private society. Because, as history took its course, every government, whether royal, imperial or republican, officially required the Société to maintain the national repertoire and to serve the French language, it was only right for it to enjoy something in return. It therefore received a place of work and a subsidy. Up to the First World War (forgive me for repeating myself) the private society balanced its budget: the subsidy served only to help it to bear the supplementary burdens – in other words, its national mission.

From 1914, its budget went into deficit. From that time on, the State refloated the Société every year. In a civilization based on the power of money, independence of spirit depends upon economic independence. As the State continued to save it from bankruptcy, the Société parted with its independence to a tutelary Minister, whose representative was the Administrateur chosen and appointed by him. Gradually the points of view diverged. In the mind of the government the Comédie Française was simply a State theatre. In the mind of some of the *sociétaires* it remained a private company. What Mounet-Sully said to the Administrateur Claretie is a good illustration of this state of mind. At the entrance to the theatre, Claretie and the great *sociétaire* met, and the two of them competed in politeness:

'After you, my dear *Sociétaire*.'

'After you, my dear *Administrateur*.'

'Go ahead. I refuse to.'

Mounet-Sully had the last word:

'You go ahead, my dear sir. *Vous êtes ici chez moi*.'

He could not have put it better, and his attitude was understandable.

To accept membership of the Société is to engage oneself for life, as in a monastery. This monastery must therefore serve a faith, must have some unity of spirit.

At the time when I took that engagement, the spirit of the Comédie Française had become confused. We were still governed by the so-called Moscow Statutes. They had been drawn up and signed by Napoleon during his ill-fated Russian campaign. Among the *sociétaires* – let us call them the monks – there were some who were determined to keep their independent spirit: these were the militant monks.

In September 1945 the government decided to recast the Napoleonic statutes. And indeed there was an urgent need to think out the Comédie Française afresh and to adapt it to the demands of new times. The Minister responsible for this business forgot just one thing: the private Société of the members of the Français. After Vaudoyer there had been three administrators in rapid succession. Now the fourth was appointed: André Obey. He was a good choice: a great writer, in the direct line of Copeau and the Cartel, with a good Resistance record and integrity of mind. A commission was formed. It included eminent personalities from the worlds of the arts, letters and business, and some senior officials. But representatives of the Société – there were really none. The Minister himself appointed two 'right thinking' *sociétaires*, who showed themselves willing to walk on during the sessions of the commission. A certain number of us protested against this contemptuous way of proceeding.

After all the vicissitudes of the War and the continual slide towards the 'State theatre' style, the Français had become a monastery without God. That people should want to give it a new vocation was perfect! For all that, the future 'monks' needed to be given the chance of taking vows afresh. It would have been so easy to ask the *Société des Comédiens Français* to elect its representatives in complete independence: these would have been extremely useful in the commission! That is what we asked for. That is what we were refused, and in an unacceptable manner: contempt, a smile, irritation. The Minister scolded us and sent us back to 'our cells'. Birth of the dissident monk. We had engaged ourselves for life, we were being asked to renew our vows, we were insisting on at least the possibility of choosing our religion.

The government then took a decision: when the commission had finished its work, the new statutes would be presented to us and the doors would remain open for fifteen days: those who were not content had simply to leave.

The 'eminent' personalities did their work conscientiously. Then they went home again to their nice little private lives. The new statutes were proclaimed. And, to all appearances, everything settled down. The Minister could cheerfully return to his electoral preoccupations. Nine of us took advantage of the open door.

No hard feelings:
– the commission thought it was doing the right thing
– those who stayed thought they were doing the right thing
– we thought we were doing the right thing in withdrawing.

Once again my Destiny according to Æschylus proved the stronger. Once again I 'obeyed' that Destiny. I had just lived six years at the Comédie Française, I had received its craft with faith and passion: a beneficent craft. I had loved from the bottom of my heart that *idea* which I had formed of a society of actors. It was clear to me that it would leave a mark on me for life, like those sabre-cuts that make men's faces more virile. Destiny, my double and myself had now chosen the *life* which till then had been *given*. I was taking to the road again; but this time I had in me a new strength: I was carrying off, on the crupper of my horse, Madeleine.

TWO

The peculiar charm of the theatre is
to live with the rogues because one is in love
   with Justice,
to sink with the rogues so as to preserve Health,
to tremble with those in dread in order to find
   a little Happiness,
to be always braving death because one loves
   only Life,
to move off without rest, suitcase in hand,
   rucksack on back,
in order to try to understand
and from fear of, one day, arriving.

Creation of our Company

FOR THE SECOND TIME Madeleine was offering me her life. It was not now, as in 1937, a matter of selling up her private house, of leaving Passy in order to live an adventure which, after all, was not shaking the foundations of a very solidly established existence. It was now a matter of breaking with a whole past. Up to this point her life had moved straight ahead. From the fable re-cited by the little girl on holiday at Royan, passing smoothly through the Conservatoire like an innocent with a charmed life, to the *sociétaire* who had reached the top of the hierarchy, Madeleine had only needed to respond to existence by embellishing it with her human warmth, her talent and her imagination.

And now she was breaking up everything, to move off once more into the unknown. Twenty years of the Comédie Française; the security of being there 'for life'. Twenty years of success, of comfort and of all sorts of perquisites produce habits, create an attachment, arouse a real tenderness towards the setting which hems you in but protects you. More than a setting, a mould which has fashioned you. Those walls of the Français were hers, her dressing-room was hers, her fellow actors were her family, that special public was her own. And yet she was breaking it all up. Why? Beyond all sentiment, I think the two of us were fundamentally in tune, and it seems to me that we had become totally united.

I can still see that Sunday, 9 June 1946. At the matinée I had played the part of Moron, in Molière's *La Princesse d'Elide*. I was setting foot on the boards of the Français for the last time. I was miserable. Then we went out between the two rows of statues, which stared at us with their white eyes. Molière was watching us go.

We had an appointment at the Théâtre Marigny, to visit the stage in between the matinée and the evening performance; they were doing *Arsenic and Old Lace*. You go in by a side door, descend to the level of the cellar—narrow, dirty corridors. You go upstairs again to the stage. It all seemed to us grey, bare, dusty, uninhabited. We were silent. Madeleine began weeping on my shoulder. I was determined, certainly, but I was unhappy. I was becoming aware of my responsibility. The doors of the Français, which had been open during fifteen days, had now shut. I must say, André Obey had facilitated my decision. He had definitely advised me to go. Did he do so for my good? Since I had heard that many of the actors did not want the Français to become 'Barrault's theatre', I imagined at the time he had given me that advice in order to have a little peace. In fact, I was courteously shown the door. I had been given to understand . . . Again that half-obedience and half-liberty in accordance with Æschylean Destiny.

On the other hand it was the general opinion that Madeleine was wrong to follow me. So the real courage was hers.

Simone Volterra, to whom her ex-husband Léon Volterra wished to give the Marigny, had got in touch with us. After two or three interviews we had reached an agreement in principle. In such cases I like to rush things. At the time of *Le Soulier de Satin*, Claudel and I had chosen as our motto: '*Mal mais vite*' (badly but quickly). It is an excellent motto for a man who wants to live without wasting his time, for one who is aware of our ephemeral condition and in whom modesty is deep-seated.

All the same, the Marigny raised problems. The final agreement depended on Volterra himself, and I had never met him. I liked the theatre. In the first place, it seemed to me viable. We had no money, and it was necessary not only to avoid getting into debt, but to be able to go on. It seated twelve hundred. Not too many overheads. My grandfather's blood was rising in me – the population that inhabits me includes a small shopkeeper. He has his work cut out, dealing with other people, mad ones, who also inhabit me; but among these madmen there was one, the individualist, who likewise loved the Marigny: the building was isolated, had no others touching it. Another too – the peasant – approved of the choice: the theatre stood among trees, in the midst of 'nature'. Lastly, the *bourgeois* in me was not exactly displeased with the idea of being in the Champs Elysées. Unfortunately at that time, on the strictly professional plane, all these excellent reasons ran up against the reputation of that theatre, which had never managed to find the style that was right for it. Formerly it had been a 'Panorama' – the Panorama Poilpot.[1] For a while Offenbach had used it for his comic operas, but since then the operettas produced there had had no staying power. It was rarely used for straight theatre. In short, many people considered it a bad theatre, with no atmosphere.

Raimu, in his southern accent, used to say he would never go and 'act in the forest'. Maurice Chevalier avoided it, and he knew what he was doing. When the decision was already taken, I had an edifying conversation with Jouvet:

'I'm alarmed for your sake, *mon p'tit vieux*. You'll come a cropper in that damned house. First of all, what are you opening with?'

'*Hamlet.*'

'Ho ho ho! *Hamlet* has never made a franc. Shakespeare and the French, you know! And besides, there's a ghost. The Parisians don't like ghosts. And it's interminable!'

He frowned, concentrated on his thoughts like a man aiming a rifle, and concluded:

'A bloody bore! What translation?'

'Gide.'

---

[1] A panorama was a painting that went all the way around a circular wall and was viewed by spectators from a vantage-point in the centre of the cylindrical space. Special lighting, and real objects placed to blend in with the picture, heightened its effect. Panoramas – often of dramatic historical events – drew a large public during most of the 19th century. (*Translator's note.*)

'Good writer, not a man of the theatre. Don't spend money on it, it will run a fortnight. Next?'

'Les Fausses Confidences.'

'Marivaux! Lace. I know Madeleine's good at it. But it's a posy. Try and find an old set. And it doesn't make a whole evening.'

'I'm filling out with a mime piece.'

'I know, your hobby-horse. Perhaps, because of Les Enfants du Paradis . . . But be careful, the French and mime – it's all right for the Italians. With a bit of luck, that sees you through a month. Next?'

'Les Nuits de la Colère, by Salacrou.'

'Don't know it. What's it about?'

'The period of the Occupation. The Resistance . . . the collaborators . . .'

'Too late or too early. I'm warning you. People have only one thought, to forget the nightmare they've been through. Noble enterprise, but can't last. Next?'

'Next? Le Procès, by Kafka.'

'What on earth is that?'

I tried to explain. His face darkened, for he was fond of me and absolutely honest. Finally he laid his hand on my arm.

'Mon p'tit vieux – I don't want to discourage you – but you seem to me to be on the wrong tack. If one day you need help, you've always got your old brother. One last bit of advice: don't make long-term commitments. Beware of disaster.'

The commitment I had made was dragging. Simone Volterra had not yet full powers. Volterra was at his country place in the Midi, at Juan-les-Pins. He too did not like ghosts. There was some question of their putting on an operetta meanwhile – Plume au Vent, if I remember rightly. During this time, 'badly but quickly', I composed my company.

Madeleine and I had gone on a tour in Switzerland with Roger Blin, playing Crommelynck's Cocu magnifique. In Geneva I had met a man in his prime: Léonard Cullotti. A complete man of the theatre, both on the technical plane and on the administrative. He had spent seventeen years with Pitoëff, and had chosen to retire after Pitoëff's death in September 1939. A pure, intransigent character. I managed to win him over: the theatre was his only love, and he was to prove it. We reached agreement: he was to be our administrator. He too, in order to take part in our adventure, was once more breaking up his life. He was returning to his old love, but he brought with him 'the shadow of Pitoëff'. Yet another responsibility, a considerable one! I had also recruited most of the actors: a real repertory company, for we intended, as at the Français, to play in repertory. That was, at the time, unheard of in private theatre.

Great and established actors like André Brunot, Pierre Renoir, Georges Le Roy, Pierre Bertin, Marthe Régnier. Colleagues in full possession of their craft like Régis Outin, Beauchamp, Marie-Hélène Dasté (our Maïène – she too was joining). Young hopes of the profession like Jean Desailly, Gabriel Cattand, Jean-Pierre Granval, Simone Valère. In short, I had put the cart before the horse. To meet these very heavy commitments, I had gone to Brussels to make the film of *Le Cocu magnifique*, which had luckily come my way : once again I was happy that the money earned by film work would enable us to get started.

It was summer again. From Normandy, Madeleine telephoned me the news. One day hope would surge up again, another day all was in the melting-pot. Instead of bringing my money back from Belgium I had ordered 'at a favourable price' (my grandfather again) two thousand yards of natural velvet for the *Hamlet* decor and some rolls of calico for the backcloth of *Les Fausses Confidences* and the Italian-style setting of *Baptiste*.

André Masson – in at the start again, as with *Numance* – was busy on the designs for the Shakespeare play, Brianchon on those for the Marivaux, Mayo on those for the mime. Honegger was writing a score for the Prince of Denmark, Kosma for *Baptiste*, to the Jacques Prévert libretto. All friends. And still no news !

There were Madeleine and I with all those commitments on our shoulders and, practically speaking, no theatre. At the same time the Comédie Française announced that it would now have two large theatres – the Richelieu and the Odéon : in one of them there would be the classics, in the other the moderns, new plays, experiments. It had the strength, the resources, the essence of power. Madeleine kept her Reims angel smile, but one morning she spoke openly to me of her anxiety and uttered this terrible, disturbing sentence :

'Do you understand? Up to now I've never failed in what I've undertaken.'

We were lying side by side, and the window was open on the countryside. Exactly in the centre of our view a superb pear-tree was gleaming in the sunshine.

A silence . . .

'Well, I'm not going to stay here, staring at that pear-tree ! I'm going to see Volterra.'

'Where?'

'At Juan-les-Pins.'

'When?'

'Today.'

She agreed. I made the journey. Volterra was all kindness and straightforwardness. The final agreement was drawn up. We would sign when he came back from his holiday. I returned.

'It's done.'

'You've signed?'

'I have his promise.'

'. . . ? . . .'

Fortunately Volterra was a man of his word. The date of the opening was fixed : 17 October. We started rehearsals at the end of August, at first in our flat. We did not sign with Volterra till 10 October. Seven days later the company came into being, publicly, with *Hamlet*. To play the *ondes Martenot*,[1]

[1] An electronic instrument with a wide range of effects and dynamics, much used by Messiaen, Jolivet and others. (*Translator's note*.)

Honegger had introduced to me a young musician, twenty years old: Pierre Boulez. He in turn had introduced one of his young colleagues, Maurice Jarre, to play the percussion.

In the following week, on 24 October, we presented *Les Fausses Confidences* and *Baptiste* (the complete mime play belonging to *Les Enfants du Paradis*). At the *ondes Martenot*, again, Boulez.

At the beginning of December came the first performances of Salacrou's *Les Nuits de la Colère*: the designer was Félix Labisse, who had been my companion-at-arms at the very start.

These three shows were given in repertory until April 1947. Then we went off on a short tour to Belgium, Holland and Switzerland, with the Marivaux and the mime play. Of this tour, over roads still wrecked by the War, two memories.

In The Hague, on 5 May, in the great Hall of the Knights, in front of the Queen of Holland, we took part in the ceremony commemorating the Liberation, by reciting Resistance poems by our friends: Robert Desnos, Louis Aragon, Paul Eluard and Jacques Prévert.

At Lausanne we held a moving celebration of the hundredth performance of *Les Fausses Confidences*. On the evening before, I had taken the chair at the enthroning of those newly promoted to be 'Bellettriens' at the University: I was returning late at night, slightly unsteady because of the quantity of white wine I had absorbed, when someone came up to me and said:

'Ramuz died this evening.'

Ramuz was someone I really loved. I had come to know him well in 1937, when I was making a film based on one of his novels, *Farinet ou l'Or dans la Montagne*. We had made it near Sion, and it was from there that I had brought home the leather bag from which I have never been parted since. We had become close friends, also, through *L'Histoire du Soldat*, which I had acted with Marcel Herrand in 1932. 'Ramuz is dead!'

The next day at Pully, on the lake shore, we had invited our colleagues to eat fillets of perch and drink *fendant*, the excellent local white wine, under the trellis of an open air restaurant. Up above us Ramuz lay at rest in a small village on the hill. At the end of the meal I asked the proprietor if I might pick a few roses from his trellis. Without anyone seeing me go, I left the general gaiety, climbed up through the fields with their rows of vines, 'my' vines – for vines anywhere in the world will always be 'my' vines – presented myself at the door of Ramuz's house and offered him the bunch of flowers. He lay there sleeping in the shelter of his stiff grey hair. As I went down again towards joy, I could feel myself making contact with that singular mixture of joy and sorrow, of lightness and depth, of folly and wisdom, of dread and intoxication, of death and life, which is the stuff of the life of the stage.

What I had said to Madeleine in the Joinville studios, when we were making *Hélène* – about my longing for the couple, for a human community, for being responsible for a theatre – was coming true. We had made our choice, we had succeeded somehow in 'weighing anchor', and our ship was seaworthy.

ON ENTHUSIASM

Claudel wrote a text for us. Here is an extract from it:

> The human soul is a thing capable of catching fire, is indeed made for
> that only, and when the thing happens and 'the spirit descends on it',
> as they say, it feels such joy, such a cry is wrung from it . . . in truth
> the word enthusiasm and no other is the right one! But material fire de-
> stroys what feeds it, while this sacred fire of which I am speaking, and
> which I would prefer to call a volitional and violent light, far from de-
> stroying, draws things upon us from all sides, and here comes the un-
> known, here come fresh forces arising and running up to us and opening
> out and working together tumultuously! Lucid, agile, the spirit is as
> though cleansed and feels all sorts of wonderful resources coming to the
> help of the idea that is accorded to it! This is not the past, progressing
> prudently . . . nor the present . . . (who could say what the present is, or
> pin down that elusive thing?) . . . It is the future, breathing events to-
> wards it . . .

> Is not our 'job' discovery? Discovery even more than invention? And
> rather than inventing, remembering? . . . Just as, when a person returns
> to a town where he once lived, but has now rather lost his bearings, the
> foot, then, is a better guide than the eyes . . .

Claudel knew what the sixth sense meant. We were on the same wavelength.

SHORT PAUSE: TWENTY-FIVE YEARS LATER

> There must be Ups and Downs in Life; and Difficul-
> ties mixt with our Affairs awake our Ardours, and
> augment our Pleasures (Scapin) [1]

If Antonin Artaud had decided to transport the theatre into his life, a theatre
that did not cheat, it seems to me today that what we wanted was to transport
our life into the theatre, a life that also would not cheat. How not cheat?
Was it possible to live without making concessions, just by one's craft? Was
it possible to owe nothing to anybody? Was it possible to know the world
simply and solely through one's work?

I think the twenty-five years of our Company answer these three questions.
That quarter of a century of labours and trials is simply the story of one
million old francs. Thinking of this subject, we think very often of our young
successors: they have every reason for hoping – yes, even today, in spite of
the increasing hardness of the times. There is always a fissure through which
one can pass and arrive at earning one's living by some work that is happy.

[1] As translated in the bilingual edition of The Works of Molière, London, 1739.

From Brussels, thanks to *Le Cocu magnifique*, I brought back a million's worth. We had scraped the bottom of every drawer we had : the total, in ready money, was fifteen hundred thousand francs. *Hamlet* cost twelve hundred thousand francs; *Les Fausses Confidences* and *Baptiste*, eight hundred thousand. Outlay : two millions. So we were five hundred thousand francs short. We found no one willing to lend us that sum free of interest. No question of ever finding a Maecenas. And we knew 'all Paris'. We had to borrow the sum at a ransom rate. Thanks to success, it was repaid one month later. Our luck was that, in two seasons, we scored six successes running : *Hamlet*, Marivaux and *Baptiste*, *Les Nuits de la Colère*, Kafka's *Le Procès* (*The Trial*), *Amphitryon* and a new mime play (*La Fontaine de Jouvance*), and finally Feydeau's *Occupe-toi d'Amélie*. Feydeau was not, at that time, a concession to the public, anything but ! It seemed possible that, coming after *Le Procès*, the play might cause an uproar. I remember the reserves expressed by our elders : luckily I had an ardent supporter in Gilles Margaritis.

Our first statement was a clear one. Our company? *An international theatre, French language section.* Our aim? By playing in repertory, to build up a repertoire.

On playing in repertory
Playing in repertory is not only a source of artistic wealth, but a means of economic defence. To have at one's disposal a company capable of playing a whole repertoire, one must engage actors whose talents are diverse. These, by rubbing up against different styles day by day, add suppleness to their qualities and make progress. The quality of the company constantly improves. An actor playing a big part on one evening will be willing to play a small one next day. When he is playing one of the big ones, he is happy to have at his side a talented actor supporting him in a small part. The result, inside the group, is emulation, solidarity and homogeneity. So the artistic standard of the company rises continually.

Economically, there is no chance of making a fortune, because the breaking even and the profits of earlier productions are constantly invested in new ones. There is less risk of bankruptcy. Not all the eggs are being put in one basket. If a new play is a failure (these things happen !), it is immediately given a hand by the earlier successes – they are brought in to balance the takings. There are in fact such things as Saint Bernard plays – *Volpone* for Dullin, *Knock* for Jouvet – and we had several of these. The unsuccessful play can remain on the posters for some time : performances of it are gradually spaced out, and when it is withdrawn from the posters everyone has forgotten the deplorable effect.

The social life of the theatre is as capricious as the seasons. On this subject Jouvet, in the interview I have mentioned, had said many wise things to me, and I have often had the chance of confirming them :

'You will have successes with plays you love. That will fill you with joy. You will have failures with plays you were not sure of, but which tempted you. That will be hard, but your convictions will not be shattered. You will also have resounding flops with plays you cherished, and surprise successes that, deep down, left you indifferent. In these cases you will be thrown off balance. Finally, and this is the worst, there will be periods when, no matter how you slave away, you will get nothing at all: emptiness. Nil. General indifference. That is anguish.'

'What they call in mathematics *le phénomène de battement* (the pendulum effect)?'

'Yes! The moment when the pendulum stops moving.'

It is indeed the most terrible thing of all.

The law of the circus

This is my name for what one owes to one's craft. I have, before now, acted with an abscess in the throat, such a temperature that, unable to hear at all, I followed what the other actors were saying by lip-reading. I have seen Madeleine, who was doubled up by pain from a liver attack, go on stage in *Les Fausses Confidences* with all her subtlety and graciousness. She has even acted with a bone in her foot broken. I have seen one of our actors who had torn ligaments in his knee: his colleagues carried him into the wings, he stood up and walked on stage, then collapsed as soon as he was back in the wings.

This superhuman exercise of willpower may seem excessive for something that, after all, 'is only play'. Some young people nowadays find it idiotic, and will sin in the opposite direction: they only consent to act when it amuses them. They have a complete contempt for the public. They even exploit this contempt in order to get themselves talked about. But to us 'the law of the circus' remains a sacrosanct law.

I have said already that there is no exchange without a previous act of offering. In an actor respect for the public is a matter of individual morality. It is the symbol – the behaviour that is the outward sign – of that respect for humanity which ought to be the first among the universal laws.

Jouvet, at the period when he was at the Comédie des Champs Elysées, experienced for a time that static condition, the '*phénomène de battement*'. Everything he attempted merely ended up in emptiness. He was deeply disturbed. One evening the stage manager came to see him about starting the performance and found him not even in costume and make-up.

'How many are there in front?'

'Seven, *patron*! I have counted.'

'I'll go before the curtain!'

He did so, explained his discouragement and asked permission to give them their money back and cancel the performance.

'No, no, monsieur!' said a lady in the front row. 'I've paid for my seat, I don't want my money back, please do the play.' And she brandished her watch. 'I would have you know we're late.'

The whole cast jumped to it. Jouvet remembered that lady with deep gratitude.

Balance sheet
In twenty-five years our Company has presented a hundred plays. A hundred
works of all sizes, some very long, very weighty, others shorter or lighter.

Of these hundred pieces, sixty were 'creations' – were being shown for the
first time. Of the other forty, twenty-two were classics (Molière, Shakespeare,
Marivaux, Beaumarchais, Æschylus, Lope de Vega, Seneca, etc.) and eighteen
were modern masterpieces: *Intermezzo*, *Amélie*, *La Cerisaie*, *Le Bossu*, *La Vie
Parisienne*, etc., which might be considered as, in a way, creations.

The optimum balance for a modern repertory theatre seems to me to be the
following:
 – 50 per cent new creations;
 – 25 per cent 'major modern revivals' or re-creations;
 – 25 per cent classics.
The vitality of a theatre can be judged from its choice of creations; its personality from its choice of revivals; its fundamental quality from the way
in which it is able to respond to the permanent demands of the classics. Here
again the biological ternary: Energy/Liberty/Invariance.

We made another declaration: this *international theatre, French language
section*, would be run as a farm is run – preferably a model farm. Here again
my ancestral inheritance was at work.

Just as such a farm includes nurseries, reserves of quality, which supply
the grafts, as well as fields put to maximum use and maintaining the economic
life of the whole enterprise, so we would have a number of young members
who could rub up against 'old hands' of quality, with a view to replacing
them gradually, though in the meantime these, being in full possession of
their art, would carry the burden of the work. A society is not really alive
except when it is made up of three generations confronting each other freely.
From sap to selection. The ternary again. Practice proved our theory right.
Before having ideas and a political strategy let us be alive. And indeed *life*
and nothing else was our 'idea' and our 'strategy'. Which is why, in the eyes
of some intellectuals, our 'line' was not clearly apparent.

We wanted to build up a living theatre, a theatre that would breathe, would
palpitate, would have volume – the opposite of those restaurants that have
only one speciality. We wanted a theatre as varied, as complex as life. Here
again what inspired us was the model of the living cell, though we did not
realize it. We wanted to rub up against some of the classics and at the same
time to clean them. My impulse to seek confirmation (*Numance*, *Phèdre*)
would find plenty of exercise. We wanted, with the greatest possible breadth
of mind, to serve the modern authors: the law of exchange. But we wanted
also to pursue our investigations, to organize expeditions into unknown regions, to continue along the vein of *As I Lay Dying* and *La Faim*. That is why
I was thinking of *Le Procès*. These were the aims we set before us.

Lastly, I was not willing to give up my experiments with mime.

And so our 'line' was a plait. A plait of five or six threads, for I must add that of exercises in different styles. These always attracted us: vaudeville, with *Amélie* [1]; melodrama, with *Le Bossu*; operetta, with *La Vie Parisienne*; Greek tragedy, with the *Oresteia*; etc. And all these *genres* with the same actors, to help in constantly improving their suppleness [2].

There were therefore bound to be a certain number of misunderstandings: for example, although I got on extremely well with Bertolt Brecht, whom I saw two or three times at the Marigny or in his barn in East Berlin, I was destined to have a good deal of trouble in getting on with the Brechtians – they have a 'line'!

There are, besides, two kinds of artists: warm-blooded artists, cold-blooded artists. The one kind are not better than the other. It all depends on taste and on instinctive choices.

At first we made an agreement with Simone Volterra for a six months' season. Then for two more seasons. Then again for three seasons, and so on during ten years. Our contract provided for sharing: she supplied what is called the 'theatre in working order' – building, technical and administrative staff; we supplied the rest: artists, immediate technicians, company administration, sets, costumes, music, props, etc. In addition to Léonard, who supervised everything, we had a young secretary – Marthe, whom we loved like a daughter and who, after twenty years of sharing our life, died of a cruel illness at the age of thirty-eight. She was beautiful, she was straightforward, she was competent. For the sake of the company she would have gone to any lengths. So would Léonard, for that matter.

There was Pierre Boulez, who also shared our life for twenty years. We shall have more to say of him, especially at the moment when the Domaine Musical was created.

Our social centre was our flat. It still is. I never had a licence as a manager. The corporation only allowed me a licence as *tourneur* – that is to say, a strolling player's licence. If there were now a general gathering of the French show business, we would figure there along with the circus people, the 'travellers'. This, genuinely, delights us: a proof that our first declaration did correspond to the truth.

> French to the marrow of my bones, I have always felt I was a citizen of the world. 'To be French just as one is universal,' said Eluard, and added: 'To belong to one's own time as one belongs to a period.' [3]
> I have made these two points of view entirely mine.

At the end of our first year we received a moral reward that might easily have flattered our vanity: I was invited to return to the Français – as *Administrateur*! It would not have been a good solution. And besides, it was too

[1] Stanislavsky's regret was that he had never dared to tackle vaudeville.
[2] It does one good to watch Jean Desailly in a singing part in *La Vie Parisienne* and, next day, as Pyrrhus in *Andromaque*.
[3] Opening page of *L'Eternelle Revue*, No. 1.

late. Our couple had become 'theatre'. From that moment it was better to make our work a complement to the task which the Français was accomplishing.

The pike law

In (I think it is) *Si Le Grain Ne Meurt*, André Gide cites a law of nature which has made a great impression on me. When the denizens of a pond consist of only non-predatory fishes, these gradually grow sickly and die for lack of aggression. Introduce a pike to 'activate their circulation', and the whole lot (except a few victims!) will become flourishing once more.

Let us help one another by serving each other, in turn, as the pike. The 'predator', as Jacques Monod puts it.

Emulation, or *the pike law*[1].

---

[1] Antoine, who was a true *animateur* and a great one, said a splendid thing when the young Jacques Copeau was starting the Vieux Colombier: 'Ride us down!' He knew that in Art, as in life, everything has always to be begun afresh.

The Marigny period

OCTOBER 1946. France, Europe, the whole world was partially and painfully emerging from the terrible crisis that had come upon the human race. What bloodshed! What destruction! What torments for men's consciences! The extermination of the Jews, the scandal of the yellow stars, shame from which no human being's honour would now go free. The camps, the gas chambers, the tortures, Hiroshima, 'Coventrization'. The bombing raids supplanting the plough. All these horrors recoiling upon post-war life. Add to them the privations, the great fear haunting everyone, an insidiously hunted life and, for the future, only the prospect of a slow and uncertain recovery. It all awakened a strange appetite, not the one that is a sign of health in bloom, but a sort of sickly craving, that of someone desperately trying to recover some strength.

As I was writing the last chapter, about the situation of the Comédie Française, relatively isolated and safeguarded by its centuries-old tradition in the midst of an occupied country, I kept saying to myself: 'With distance we are bound to look like monsters, preoccupied only by our craft and apparently indifferent to what was going on around us.' I think the truth is different. Unless one was an active member of the Resistance, a hero of the Maquis, or had gone to London or the United States (whence indeed some people sent advice that was harder to carry out than to give), what was the right conduct, for the majority of this nation caught in the trap? Was not the most correct behaviour precisely to live an *upright* life within one's own task?

I am not looking for an excuse (in spite of my usual guilt complex), I am thinking, here, of everyone. Was there not, in those circumstances, a clear case of 'emotional conduct' in continuing to act 'as though nothing had happened'? Sartre was fond of recounting the following newspaper story:

One evening, coming in from the fields, a farmer finds his manager hanged in the barn. Suicide. He acts. Takes down the body. Tries to bring it back to life. No good. Calls the neighbours. Fresh attempts, fruitless. They inform the police. The medical expert makes his report. The day of the funeral is settled. The priest gets into his surplice. The cemetery is opened. The ceremony – the whole village joins the procession, then everyone goes home. Apparently the page is turned. The farmer resumes his habits, finishes his meal. In between two sips of coffee he opens the paper and reads: 'The other day, coming in from the fields, Farmer So-and-So found in his barn the body of his manager, who had just hanged himself.' At that point the farmer faints.

During the Occupation there was only one recourse: *to be active*. To be active as honestly as possible, simply that. When the War was over, would one faint?

From 1939 to 1946 there had not been any spring.

The creation of our Company answered to a general need to be reborn. I can see this now: our desire as individuals fitted in, unconsciously, with that vast collective desire.

HAMLET

What can I say about this, that might be useful to us?

The *object* around which the tragedy is organized: *a throne* – Power – and Hamlet sitting on the ground beside it. The Prince himself assumes the role of fool. In discussing my productions we shall keep coming across what I call a *catalyst object*, the significant, generating object, the object that strikes the seminal spark of the play.

Music. Mixture of live instruments and recorded instruments. Live like the actors in the play: the Martenot and the percussion. Boulez and Jarre, with their playing, followed our acting. In this case the instrument attains its maximum human quality. The trumpets and other brass had been recorded by the best solo players available: a quality of interpretation not obtainable in an ordinary performance; no eminent solo player could agree to be immobilized for four solid hours to play for fifteen minutes, over a period of years. With the live instruments I was able to pursue my researches into organic sonorities: buzzings in the ear, heartbeats, etc.

The fantastic. Since in the theatre the launching pad is Silence and Death, dead and living are active on the same plane. A 'ghost' is simply an 'unexpected living being'; a living being is only a dead one who has not yet reached the moment of his mutation. The two are living on the same level. No cavernous 'operatic' voice, but a true Presence, whose gentle voice enters the ear with more intensity. No artificial slowing down, but a pure onwards movement in time with the muscular synchronism.

Ambiguity. I have already spoken of this. 'The twilight hour', the atmosphere of estuaries . . . idea of Death. I had brought back from the islands of Denmark this memory: 'dead leaf floating on the waters'. The deep and milky blue of the Baltic, the verdigris of those roofs, the sand of the sea shores.

The symphonic movements, which had already struck me in Racine. Often the dramatic action of a play is brought out more by the rhythm of its orchestration than by psychological points, for we must address ourselves to the chests of the audience rather than to their heads. The breathing receives *all*, the head perceives only fifteen per cent (that was the percentage Giraudoux estimated).

Hamlet's psychological condition. He receives two blows, like two shock treatments:

1. The vision of his father, which we witness.

2. The adventure at sea between Denmark and England, and the sending of Rosencrantz and Guildenstern to their deaths, which we do not witness.

Before the first blow we have in front of us a prince who is normal, though given to melancholy, and whose tears have been dried up by the extremity of his sorrow. After the second blow we see a man with his psyche cleansed, in the ambiguous time leading from life to death. The 'twilight' of the graveyard, with its significant object – Yorick's skull.

In between those two times Hamlet is double: he is *another*. He is never as lucid as when he is counterfeiting madness. He is never as threatened with 'not being able to get back into his circle' as when he is with himself.

The chastity that is not impotence but sublimated sensuality. It is this that enables him to have for Horatio the feeling of absolute friendship, and to revolt against his mother's sexuality. Hamlet's Oedipus complex? Let us leave that to the psychoanalysts, or to the intellectual speculation of the audience: it is of no use to the person who has to try – I say *try* – to assume the character of Hamlet. To him, the notion of chastity is much more useful.

Lastly, one should not forget the Hamlet of Belleforest, whom Shakespeare certainly knew and who also inspired Jules Laforgue. Hamlet has *political* sense.

The Renaissance spirit. One human cycle is ending, another is on the point of being born. The night is no longer night, and it is not yet day. As in *our time*, as in that of Æschylus when he wrote the *Oresteia*. A real stroke of genius: the moment when Fortinbras' trumpets blare. Here again we are up against the musical composition of the play. At the darkest moment in the tragedy the heralding theme comes in from the plain of Denmark. Fortinbras' cape, white and a tender green, like the apparition of the Angel of the Last Judgment. Announcement of the moment when life will be redeemed. No further mention of it. The theme has been stated in the midst of the tragedy. It prepares for the finale's sentence: return to creative life.

> *I do prophesy the election lights*
> *On Fortinbras*

Every year, towards the end of January, bang in the middle of winter, a false springtime bursts out for a day or two. The air becomes pale green, the sun is all white, like a mirage of the first leaf. When this brief outburst is ringing in the air and in nature, I say, nowadays: 'Here are the trumpets of Fortinbras'.

The higher hesitation. That painful and pure vibration of the soul with which Shakespeare goes beyond the universal:

> *But howsoe'er thou pursu'st this act*
> *Taint not thy mind ...*

Without having at my disposal all the elements of the case, I shall need at least five acts to accomplish nothing !

LES FAUSSES CONFIDENCES

The history of France is passing through an autumn. The aristocracy is declining, like the Sun King. Brianchon chose his palette well: faded yellows and dead leaves. The *bourgeoisie* is like a manure through which the spring will be born again.

Meanwhile the capering goes on, in Italian style. First Zany: Dubois. Second Zany: Arlequin. Araminte has premonitions. Dorante will become a Jacobin – for the moment he is only a steward.

> – A *steward's lot! What a fine thing!*
> – *Why should he not have a lot?*

A pleasanter way of announcing the French Revolution could not be devised.

The objects. Screens, behind which society hides and eavesdrops. A piece of furniture: the desk, an object symbolizing *money*. And the whole thing fizzes like champagne. Italians who have drunk wine from the hill slopes of Suresnes. A Parisian art.

A game of collective acting. Les Fausses Confidences must be played like a set at shuttlecock. Even when it was not our turn to be acting on stage, we always remained in the wings, ready to dart out and take the ball as it flew. As Feydeau said:
> I was limbering up, waiting for my turn.

BAPTISTE

One small anecdote: I had called auditions for the part of Arlequin. Result, two young men on my short list: Maurice Béjart and Marcel Marceau. I engaged Marceau – slimmer, more flexible. If the part of *Hellequin* had been in question, I would have chosen Maurice Béjart, with that irresistible, authentic Devil's look he has. Later on, Béjart told me that this choice of mine had decided his career. What luck for him and for all of us !

LES NUITS DE LA COLÈRE

The object. Not easy to hit on. The action is in two places – the inside of a house and a railway track – and includes both the time of the living and the dialogue of the dead: a mixture of everyday life and the abstract. We did hit on the object: a footbridge across the tracks and their ballast, then becoming the gallery of the living-room and indicating the first floor.

I had been struck by one of Jouvet's experiments in Cocteau's *Machine Infernale*, for which Christian Bérard was designer. At the moment when Jocaste and Oedipe learn the dreadful truth, the set exploded into the flies, in complete harmony with the explosion of their lives. What was seen fitted what was lived. Remembering that lesson, I arranged that, at the moment when the living are killed and stand up again dead, the set did disintegrate, bit by bit, like the parts of their bodies.

The exceptional quality of the play. Salacrou's intellectual and moral honesty. Theatre: art of justice. As I write this, a film is being shown in Paris, called *Le Chagrin et la Pitié*. It retraces that period with the same care. Salacrou had had the courage to 'commit himself' in this direction just as people's minds were still heated by the fever of the Liberation. Since then, twenty-five years have passed.

I can still see, abandoned on the bare stage, that metallic footbridge from which the 'terrorists' were reliving 'in advance' their past and remembering their future.

From Salacrou's footbridge let us now survey that highly fruitful 'Marigny' period and glean from it what may nourish us now and tomorrow.

ANDRE GIDE AND LE PROCÈS

Le Procès belongs to the line of 'the aims we set before us': it followed up my adaptation of Faulkner and Knut Hamsun's *La Faim*. The desire to do it dated back to 1939. I had mentioned it to Gide in 1942, during our meeting in Marseilles. When he heard I was friends with Sartre, he advised me to join with him in order to carry out the project. By 1946, unfortunately, this was no longer possible.

In the preparation of *Hamlet*, Gide and I had worked closely together, looking at the English text again word by word. We had got on extremely well. Gide had the straightforward simplicity that true professionals have.

At the time when he was flirting with the Popular Front, he had written a social play called *L'Intérêt Général*, which he had showed to me. (It was just after *Numance*.) It had seemed to me pretty weak, not worthy of him, and I had told him my opinion with the brutality of my youth. His answer was a phrase which has been a lesson to me: 'You may be right: *I have spread my net too low.*' So many people, in a desire to sacrifice to popular theatre, feel obliged to 'spread their net too low', when in fact, to reach the heart of the people, one can never spread one's net high enough. Just look at *Le Cid*. What we call 'the people' has the purity and intransigence of childhood, of the true childhood, the second one, the one we must attain at the end of life. The Childhood of God it may be called, by those whose thought loves taking leaps, like Teilhard de Chardin and so many others, myself among them.

Because of this, I felt myself on a footing of complete confidence with Gide, and was glad to express myself without beating about the bush, to lay myself open to observation by his microscope of an eye. For Gide had the art of examining you like a scientist, with the same friendly curiosity that a biologist must have towards his monkeys or his mice.

Besides, after my experience with *Phèdre* and *Le Soulier de Satin*, I had acquired a taste for using, for my 'avant-garde' explorations, scripts by real writers.

And so I asked him if he would be willing to collaborate with me. I would do the scenario (I had a lot of ideas about this, as Claudel might have put it), and he would write the dialogue. He took fright, as any scrupulous person would; he said to me that the subject would be better suited to the cinema.

'It's just because cinematographic acting seems easy that one must avoid it at all costs if one wants to treat the subject afresh and in depth.'

He liked what was difficult; he was tempted, but still hesitant.

'Let's do this. I write *my play*, and read it to you and you will decide.'

He agreed to this.

One day I went to his place and found him in bed. It was a small room. The only heating was from a gas stove. The restrictions had not yet ended. From the ceiling there hung a small chandelier. By its light I read him my own personal version of the play. I can still see him as he listened to me, with his cotton cap on his head, and a cigarette between his fingers. At the precise moment when Joseph K. dies, butchered by the warders and muttering: 'Like a dog', the chandelier came loose and remained suspended above my head by the electric wire only! Gide leaped up, in great excitement:

'It's a sign, it's favourable, I'm with you. You can count on me.'

And so there we were, in association, to do this 'dirty deed'. Our friends were hardly encouraging. Madeleine was decidedly not warm. It seemed to her a crashing bore. Roger Martin du Gard, who was Gide's literary 'confessor', kept ministering friendly discouragement. In spite of it all, Gide came regularly, rang our doorbell and read me fresh pages. We were two young people out of the *Faux Monnayeurs*.

It goes without saying that, after that memorable first reading, we remade the play together, dovetailing our respective contributions closely. My defect is always to pack too much in. His was an extreme strictness, dryness even. We reached agreement halfway. I pass over the details, the enthusiasms and the moments of despair. Labisse, who always came to the rescue of each of my personal ventures, was busy painting design after design. Boulez and Kosma (yes, that's the way we worked!) gave me their kind help.

The *générale* (public preview) came – it was the opening of our second season, and it winded them. I had two unexpected and convinced supporters: Henry Bernstein and Paul Claudel. Claudel indeed wrote such an article about it in *Le Figaro* that even Gide was touched.

Gide and Claudel had for a long time been brothers and enemies. Claudel was rather jealous, never mentioned Gide to me. Gide, on the contrary, was always asking me for news of Claudel.

'Would you like to meet him one day?' I said to him.

'Oh, no ! If he saw me he'd make the sign of the Cross !'

Claudel never missed a matinée of *Le Procès*. After that fine article, Gide confronted him at the end of the performance and, taking his hand, said to him point blank :

'Thank you, Claudel, for what you wrote about *Le Procès*.'

Next day I went to see Claudel – between the two Masters I was playing more or less the part of Scapin – and he, having still hardly recovered from that sudden apparition, said to me :

'I suddenly saw that wrinkled face like an old woman's coming towards me. I was so bewildered that I *let him take my hand*.'

A few months later, when we were celebrating the hundredth performance of *Partage de Midi* by a party on stage, I had managed to get Gide and Claudel to come, among the other guests. I was absolutely determined to reconcile them. I had *manigancé* (a favourite word of Gide's) this meeting with Mme Claudel. I was standing at Gide's side, near the buffet. Claudel was not far off, sitting on a bench. Mme Claudel came over to us :

'Bonjour, Gide. Why don't you go and see Paul ?'

To my great stupefaction I saw Gide close up, bow slightly and, saying 'Madame !', move away.

I can therefore bear witness that, in this quarrel, Gide, 'the indulgent', was the one of the two who was unwilling to renew an old friendship [1]. I was deeply disappointed.

With *Le Procès* I was confirming my old idea of having simultaneous scenes. Dovetail several places, representing in them several different situations, and make these live simultaneously. They do not exactly answer each other, but correspondences do result that create a new situation : the real one. Just as Dali had invented the soft watch, in *Le Procès* the ground was sometimes soft, especially the steps. By means of mime, of course.

My guilt feelings were having a field day. We had also the chance of transposing on to the stage the notion of claustrophobia. The result was evidently positive, for it prompted in one member of the audience this observation, which sums up the event rather well : as he emerged from the Marigny, he stopped on the steps and, looking up at the sky, muttered :

'And into the bargain it's raining !'

The technicians had not been exactly delighted by the rehearsals. That kind of anguish seemed to them a bit exaggerated. Nonetheless, some time afterwards one of them said to me :

'Ah, monsieur, today I understand your *Procès* : I've spent four hours kicking my heels at the Social Security Office !'

From then onwards, every time he ran into any difficulty, he would exclaim :

---

[1] Friendship? Let us not forget that in 1905 Claudel, who was then consul in China, had entrusted Gide with correcting the proofs of *Partage de Midi*.

'It's quite simple, *c'est du Kafka!*' [1]

The phrase, since then, has become general.

Our success built and built, and from the start we had little to hope for from the 'snobs'. I must, however, say that I am sincerely grateful to the people whom it is customary to call 'the snobs'. In my experience they are extremely valuable to artists who are seekers. The snobs are those who help us, support us and encourage us while waiting for the others to have understood.

So Kafka entered my close family by the side of Baptiste and Hamlet. I love his startling realism. My imagination is in tune with it. When Joseph K. has Léni on his knees and is caressing her, his hands run over her normal body and suddenly come up against the little membranes she has between her fingers:

'Oh, a slight physical defect!'

The startling point about the *real* Léni: she is web-fingered. So realism becomes dreamlike. It does not take much for the dream to become nightmare: but everything must remain within the limits of humour and anguish, without spilling over into any romantic or fantastic deformation of the Doctor Caligari kind. If one manages to keep within the true, the real, the valid, then the slightest shock of surprise becomes terrifying.

Kafka does not allow himself to make a 'leap'. He offers no answer to the questions he raises. The only answer one can suggest in his place is, precisely, the sense of liberty as understood by Æschylus, Sartre or Monod. He felt he was shut in, yet there was a door he could go through; he was unwilling to use it. His doodle shows this clearly – the barriers are not joined together:

One more reason, not only for admiring him, but for loving him: he lives in ambiguity.

As long as a man has not proved his innocence, he is considered guilty. Is this law imposed on him? Or does he not reflect it upon himself through a personal propensity?

I knew that, in putting *Le Procès* on the stage, I would be attracting the thunderbolts of the 'high priests' of Kafka, not to mention the 'parish priests'. Max Brod had given his blessing. And I myself was convinced that I was serving Kafka's memory by what I did. I wrote an article on this subject, called '*Cas de conscience devant Kafka*'. After having followed up *Le Procès* with an adaptation of *The Castle* and another of *America*, my conscience is still at rest. That is how it is.

[1] 'Straight out of Kafka!'

Kafka brings us a truthful vision of our period and, at the same time, connects us with Biblical times. He builds a bridge. Claudel, who was not very indulgent towards other writers (and their names might be Corneille or Victor Hugo), said to me one day:

'There's one of them to whom I do take off my hat, it's Kafka.'

My own feeling tends to be that I am one with him, and, when I need help in continuing to endure life, I like to repeat to myself this phrase of Joseph K.'s:

Don't take things too seriously!

Which brings us, quite naturally, to ...

FEYDEAU

Courteline said: 'To be taken for a cretin by an imbecile is an exquisite pleasure worthy of a good Frenchman.'

We might add: 'No pleasure is more exquisite than that of seeming a madman in the eyes of those who believe they are normal.'

I love everything that has in it a spice of folly. I love those Beings who possess a Fool. It is one more reason for believing that human nature is comparable to a kingdom. At the King's side, among his people, there must also be a Fool.

Claudel has his Fool. Kafka has his Fool. Feydeau *is* the Fool. The King's Fool. In this case the King is the Parisian *petit-bourgeois* who spends his night at Maxim's. The man of means, 1900 style.

Recently, trying to prove once and for all the insanity of the *boulevard* theatre, an intellectual who had been asked to speak observed:

'In the boulevard plays the people have no profession!'

In Feydeau's plays too, apart from '*cocottes*', '*commissaires de police*' and the '*petites bonnes*', I see very few people with jobs. The only professions that exist among his characters are the ones that re-establish *order*. Glandular order, domestic order, public order.

The whole of his poetic art consists in a 'breaking out of the circle', as the mad or the fools do, but through the doorway of the absurd.

Amélie's father is a retired policeman who has concentrated, all his life, on controlling the traffic. Amélie receives a basket of flowers. Amélie's 'close friends' are wondering who has sent it. A few moments later the doorbell rings. Who is it? The Prince of Palestrie! Immediately, in her father, conditioned reflexes are triggered off. It is for him to control the traffic. He pushes everybody behind the basket, crying out as he does so: 'Behind the trees! Behind the trees!' At once the street is there, the procession, the official welcome. It is a case of pure poetic transposition. The Fool's imagination has worked.

The absurd reigns!

All Feydeau's work is embellished by such metamorphoses. With him, logic itself breaks out of the circle. And it breaks out with such precision, such mastery, such perfection of clockwork and science, that there is nothing left to do but to go along with it : with the logic of burlesque frenzy.

Feydeau's genius had received a first recognition in Vaudoyer's time : the Comédie Française had included in its repertory a small masterpiece in one act : *Feu la Mère de Madame*. That was an initial tribute; but no one yet had had the courage to venture on one of his full-scale vaudevilles. Now the Renaud-Barrault Company brought *Occupe-toi d'Amélie* into its repertory, along with Shakespeare, Marivaux, Molière and Kafka. It was dangerous. The effrontery succeeded and we are proud to have helped Feydeau to enter the society of the classics. For a classic he is : the writing is extremely taut, his stage directions are very strict – sometimes even musically notated. Acting Feydeau is as exhausting as acting tragedy. In his case too one can only get away with it by the help of rhythm. At the slightest failure on the part of one of us, the whole building crumbled. What afternoons did we not spend making 'adjustments' !

To perform Feydeau well, there is nothing like being able to use the talent of actors broken in by a classical training. It must be said that Madeleine was made for Feydeau. On stage she has absolutely no shame. To her everything is natural, it all flows as from a spring.

May I be allowed to add that, in daily life, she is the same? A case in point : one evening, at the end of a performance, she had gone back to her dressing-room and was changing. She was naked. An admirer comes in, sees her, apologizes and makes to withdraw : 'It doesn't matter,' she says, 'don't go . . . I'm not looking at you !' The remark 'breaks out of the circle' with the most perfect logic. You only, in fact, become conscious that you are naked if you look at the person who sees you.

Amélie travelled all over the world, from Buenos Aires, Rio and New York to London, where she had the honour of acting before Queen Elizabeth. Her Majesty had chosen 'the play which had made her grandfather laugh so much'.

Thanks be given to the art of comedy. It distributes to human beings nuggets of happiness. But what a cruel art it is to serve ! I can still see us in the second act, during the so-called 'blanket scene', crouching behind the sets, sweating, anxious, tense, on the watch for the slightest hitch, while out there in the dark of the house there were gales of laughter. At the end of the scene the full blaze of lights returned. Amélie, quite out of breath, would cry out : 'Ah ! we had some good laughs this evening !' The technicians were wiping their foreheads !

> *Let us laugh, because that is good,* says Claudel, and adds : *Farce is the extreme form of lyricism and the heroic expression of the joy of living.*

FIRST ORDEAL

L'Etat de Siège was our first failure. To me a bitter disappointment.

A man of the theatre only acquires his real face if he has the good fortune to unite with an author. Jouvet had had Giraudoux. Pitoëff had joined with

Pirandello, Dullin with Jules Romains and Salacrou. The Compagnie des Quinze had André Obey. In spite of *Le Soulier de Satin* I was not yet tied up with Claudel. To be sure, I wanted to be; but, at least looked at from the outside, we were not of the same generation. We would not be able to explore the unknown together.

I had missed Jean-Paul Sartre. I shall indeed continue all my life to regret not having managed really to work with him. We *ought* to have got on together. Is it perhaps my fault? Sincerely, I do not think so.

I had just met Camus, and our enthusiasm was, I believe, mutual. I have already mentioned his *Caligula* when dealing with the Occupation period. In the Artaud time a project had been born : to give concreteness to the meaning of the phrase 'Theatre and the Plague'. Artaud and I decided to put on a show inspired by Daniel Defoe's *Journal of the Plague Year*. The years of horror intervened. And now, in order to pursue the way I have taken ever since *As I Lay Dying*, a way which passed through *Numance*, *La Faim*, *Le Soulier de Satin* and *Le Procès*, I had just taken up again – alone, unfortunately ! – this project, *The Plague*. The heart of the project was the purification of a Being by the mad inroad of the dark forces in us. A kind of passage through Hell : divine tragedy.

I had a longing for Artaud's lyricism and, at the same time, a realistic appreciation of the limits as a writer. Then there appeared the novel by Albert Camus : *La Peste*. From that moment the project could come to life again. Camus had no lack of realism. He was intelligence itself. He had written for the theatre. The optics of a novel are not the same as those of a play. I asked Camus if I could see him. I was hoping to renew with him the happy experience I had had with Gide over *Le Procès*. After all, the distance between Gide and Kafka was quite as great as that between Camus and Artaud. Besides, if he consented, the project would become a new one. Since our original project, war had swept over the world. Humanity had lived *its* plague.

Camus agreed enthusiastically. I was overjoyed and already saw myself associated with Camus for a considerable part of my life. Camus was my 'chance'. We understood each other perfectly. He was still, at that period, involved in the life of the newspaper *Combat*, that hope of the post-war years.

We worked in a mood of euphoria. I might even call it innocence. We felt we were 'in the ascendant'. We had only to slap death in the face for it to recoil. During the whole period of composition, and then during rehearsals, we tasted a kind of happiness. The right word would be joy. The joy of creating, of modelling a special object [1].

As regards the form of the play, I had won Camus over to the idea of certain investigations designed to carry further the experiments he had made earlier on.

---

[1] We played about like children. To settle the title, we had invented a game. With the audience in mind, we imagined that the title must answer the following question : 'Get dressed, darling, we're going to see . . .' *La Peste?* No ! *Le Bubon?* No ! In the end our choice fell on *L'Etat de Siège*.

The company was at its best. Pierre Brasseur and Maria Casarès were about to enrich it still further with their talents. Once again Honegger was with us. Balthus designed a marvellous setting, an extraordinary stage place – one that was perhaps too perfect, an object that even today might be complete in itself. That was the first snare. There was another which we did not notice: insensibly, the subject slipped from the metaphysical plane (Daniel Defoe, Artaud) to the political (Camus, Hitler, Nazism); and the fallacy became apparent, unfortunately, too late.

The horror of the Nazi concentration camps had no longer anything to do with the saving epidemic, the power of a plague to bring good through the forces of evil. This, it now seems to me, was the deep-seated origin of our misfortunes – in any case the noblest one. L'Etat de Siège was a failure.

It is nonetheless a fact that 'le Tout-Paris' rubbed its hands with malicious joy. What? have the Renaud-Barrault people, after two years of success, just discovered 'their author'? They've gone too far. Put someone on a pedestal – well and good, on condition that one may have the satisfaction of pulling him down at the first opportunity.

What made me very unhappy was that this should have occurred to us precisely over our union with Camus. Camus himself was deeply disappointed, even wounded. We remained good friends, but we never again found an opportunity of working together.

L'Etat de Siège was not our only failure. There were a few others in those twenty years. They were all cruel. Dare I say 'resounding'?

It was no part of our destiny to live in a lukewarm element. The post-war period was bringing a new climate. The aesthetic stage of before 1939 was succeeded by the ethical stage (as Kierkegaard had predicted). The individualist and poetic theatre of the Cartel was giving place to social theatre. The year 1950 marks the advent of that great and true poet Bertolt Brecht, but also the apparition of the Brechtians. The 'artistic' approach was now 'contested' by the intellectuals, who made themselves apostles of distancing and of all sorts of theories which Brecht himself was not applying – not, at least, to the Berliner Ensemble.

The objective of these 'brains' was a highly valid one. Up to then, apart from the enterprise of Firmin Gémier, the creator of the Théâtre National Populaire, theatre managers had not concerned themselves with the audience 'politically'. The artist was once more obeying the commands of his dreams, of his poetic world: he gave birth to his work, then people came if they wanted. The more aficionados there were, the better; but good plays were more often performed before empty seats than to full houses.

From 1950 onwards, the audience has been bound more closely to the stage. Administrative strategy was developed. Groups were organized. There were buses laid on, sometimes even regular round-ups of people. The spirit of propaganda spread. Militant politics infiltrated the theatre. Individuals directed opinion by their writings, and by certain kinds of intimidating conduct. They have what I call the Cid complex: in other words, when they have made somebody their target, they believe they are obliged to murder the whole family. As for me, having begun 'before the War', I was not 'their thing'. I had existed before them, therefore I must no longer exist.

When people are not sure of themselves, they have recourse to the scorched earth policy. It is simpler, more practical, less embarrassing. But indeed how could they have been sure of themselves, since they mingled with the world of the theatre by means of the head and not, as one should, of the senses? In this way, gradually, the theatre became politicized, and electoral activities spread within it. Men spent their time in unsolicited attempts to teach other men how to live.

We had several times to bear the brunt of attacks. People came more than once to give our tree a shake, to see if it still held. Some newspapers even honoured us with banner headlines, such as the following: 'New play at the Marigny – Barrault worse than ever'.

I had invited Jean Vilar – who was not yet head of the TNP – to direct Gide's *Oedipe*. This gave them an opportunity to jeer at us for putting on Maurice Clavel's play, *Maguelonne*, which formed the first part of the programme. Yet where, in that business, lay the courage and the risk?

Again, when we gave a fraternal welcome to André Reybaz and his young company in Ghelderode's *Faste d'Enfer*, we were treated as 'bourgeois' for having done Kafka's *Le Procès*. All this, certainly, was not serious, but at the time it did us real damage. And indeed, over the last twenty-five years, every time I have tried (and I have, again and again, always with conviction) to help some other director to express himself, the mongrels have always turned on me. It is sad, but a fact. Let us call it the 'bullfight' side of public activities.

One day Cocteau's friends were advising him to put on a show of his paintings and drawings in Paris; his reply was: 'A Paris on n'expose pas, on s'expose!' (In Paris you don't exhibit, you expose – yourself.)

In our profession we experience a strange kind of suffering that is hardly to be met with elsewhere. Every evening everything has to be begun afresh. If the play is given rough treatment, hissed and barracked, if you yourself are not popular, you have to prepare yourself every evening for 'punishment'. Then why not resign yourself and stop the whole thing? Because sometimes, by dint of insistence, one manages to win opinion round. So you tell yourself, each time, that you will succeed in that exploit: you persist and you continue to suffer.

The theatre is the finest school of humility, the finest school of willpower also. On the other hand there is no joy in the world greater than the joy produced by a well-oiled success. If the theatre's business is to bring life itself to the moment of truth, each theatrical performance also is a moment of truth from which one must emerge as victor, brandishing the two ears – the bullfighter's. The theatre is the most living, therefore the finest of professions; it can at the same time be the most absurd – like life itself when it is disenchanted.

The experience of *L'Etat de Siège* was to deprive our company of the collaboration of Camus. That was the heart of the ordeal. The rest, really, does not matter.

Failure strengthens the strong, said Saint-Exupéry.

At the same time, immediately after *Le Procès*, I had set to work again on Claudel. The gestation of *Partage de Midi* was going forward. I was, so to speak, 'nearing my time'. He must now be 'forced' – or at least begged, in fact convinced. An arduous task. I wrote to him, he gave me an appointment; I went.

PARTAGE DE MIDI

It was a decisive meeting. Our almost physical knowledge of one another, which had been accumulating day by day for nearly ten years, made it possible at last for us to put our cards on the table.

He: You know I have never been willing to listen to any talk of putting *Partage de Midi* on the stage, and long ago withdrew from circulation all copies of the first edition. The play is about an ordeal from which I suffered so intensely in my youth that its effects have been with me all my life. Even today, the wound still hurts. It isn't only that I am trying to spare anyone living – time, alas, blunts all things – there are certain inner sensations that torment me without ceasing. What still holds me back is more a kind of shame: there are cries that a man has no right to utter. *Partage de Midi* is that cry. I would be as embarrassed as if I were stark naked.

I: Your fresh grief does not matter. *Partage de Midi* is at the heart of your message. It is the key to the whole of your work. Interesting though it will always be to read, it will only ever strike people with its full Life when it is performed. For the sake of all those who love you and follow you, you owe it to yourself, even if to you it is a sacrifice, to let us have your *Partage* for our nourishment. And this nourishment will not be total except on stage. That struggle of the flesh against the spirit will only come across physically if human beings bring to it their voices, their breath, their heart, their gestures.

That authentic and raw drama which you have continued to live for nearly fifty years is something we can only get clear if we in turn live through its ordeal of Sin. I became you as Rodrigue, I want to live you again as Mesa. I want to tread again the path which led you to the Ordeal by Fire, like a piece of pottery placed in the kiln. *Partage* is the kiln in which you and your work were fired and took your true colour. It is the play of your metamorphosis. Everything in your work that dates from before that ordeal converges towards *Partage de Midi*. Everything that comes after it springs from it. It completes the ring of your poetic adventure.

On the plane of moral influence, what are you afraid of, since in that struggle between flesh and spirit it is the spirit that triumphs in 'the transfiguration of Noon'?

He: In any case I would not now consent to that erotic fantasy in the second act – it makes me shudder.

I: That erotic fantasy no longer belongs to you; you have uttered that cry, it lives on without you, you will never now manage to stifle it.

He: Ah! You believe all that no longer belongs to me and that I don't still feel its torture, in spite of my age?

I: One day you will give in, and then it will not be to me that you will give – I won't say that joy – the word joy, in this case, is too weak – but what would be a kind of real life. You owe that to your generation.

He: You are shaking me. Come back and see me in three days' time.

Such, if I remember rightly, was the substance of our interview. Three days later I went back.

'There you are, tempter. You have won: I give you *Partage de Midi*.'

I was speechless, dazed. He added:

'I must confess to you that you owe that to a Dominican monk to whom I am very attached, who guides me and to whom I went with my problem. He advised me strongly to let you put the play on. Apparently it is the one of my plays that has caused the most conversions.'

I asked for the Dominican father's telephone number and at once rang him up to thank him for having pleaded so well for *Partage* and for me.

And in fact, a few months later, when we were performing *Partage*, Claudel forwarded to me a letter, with these words written in his own hand:

> My dear Barrault,
>   Read the attached letter. I think it will give you as much pleasure as it does to me. *De tout cœur et à bientôt.*

It was a conversion letter, from a young man who had returned to God after having seen the play at the Marigny.

The fewer characters a play has, the harder it is to cast. When well cast, it is halfway directed. We had luck with *Partage de Midi*. Leaving aside the part of Mesa, which I took for myself without beating about the bush, without discussion and without bothering about the fact that it perhaps required ideally someone more stocky, more obviously carnal, Pierre Brasseur delighted us by accepting the part of Amalric, for which he seemed to be made; but everything depended on Ysé, the visual centre of the drama and the mysterious instrument of God.

Partage de Midi has in reality not four characters but five. To that splendid but unsatisfied and transplanted female, to that complacent husband, to that adventurer doing his stuff and to that rejected 'little priest' all dried up in his avarice and spiritual self-centredness, there must be added God. It is the con-

stant presence of God which turns that ordinary subject – bordering on the
commonplace like *Bajazet* – into one of the most important subjects in the
theatre of any period. Like a sword being unsheathed, God draws it out of the
temporal world to brandish it in the sky.

As regards Ysé, in our view Edwige Feuillère was the obvious choice. Luckily
she accepted. The day came when I took her to introduce her to Claudel. He
saw her. He considered her – examined her as a trainer examines a thorough-
bred – was non-committal, almost rude. Afterwards he rang me up and apologized: 'I could not speak. She's *her* !'

De Ciz, the least important of the four characters, was allotted to Dacqmine,
whom I admired for having, in spite of his youth, the authority required for a
big leading part. Claudel found him too handsome: 'De Ciz,' he wrote to me,
'is the male insect, apparently puny, but gifted with the sexual prowess for
coping with the splendid female. There is no need for a very good actor. Physical appearance accounts for almost everything.' All Dacqmine had to do was
to adjust to the part, and he did it perfectly.

Labisse, my friend from the very beginning, would do the sets. Christian
Bérard, as everyone knows, the costumes. It now only remained to set to
work.

I had awakened in Claudel the major drama of his whole life: 'It involves
my whole life, whose meaning I have been led to try to understand. It involves
much more than literature. If I manage to convey into your heart and Feuillère's what I feel, the whole audience will be in tears . . .' 'If you cannot come,
could you at least send me Feuillère? I need so much to convey my soul into
hers ! This is not a play like any other . . . I wrote it with my blood . . .'

Harsh Night, Rimbaud said, *the dried blood is steaming on my face.*

Caught up in his passion for that play, which brought the past to life again,
Claudel wanted to rewrite *Partage*.

His creative machinery was starting up again. Claudel liked tinkering with
his plays; having at first, like a true poet, obeyed only *desire*, he was now
trying to understand.

I had been nourished, like all my generation, on the first version, that of
1905 [1]. His retouches terrified me. Was I going to be able to safeguard this
play, which had been the enthusiasm of my youth? But, looking from another
angle, had I the right – or, simply, was I right – not to go along with Claudel
in his present direction?

Besides, Claudel was not only rethinking the content of his play. As a true
man of the theatre who had acquired an admirable skill, he saw at once, with
a still fresh, still virgin eye, the play's technical imperfections, and immediately, with the mastery I have always admired, he set to work correcting them.
I had no trouble in accepting those corrections – on the contrary, my agreement
was total.

And so, during this preparatory period, we were working on two planes:

[1] It had just been republished by the *Mercure de France*.

the technical plane and the spiritual. Just as the play itself is astride what Claudel called 'the two sides of a book' – the visible and the invisible, the real and the surreal, the physical and the metaphysical, the flesh and the spirit – so our activity also bore on two points: the clockwork of the piece, and its profound conclusion. Claudel rightly considered the ending too literary, too aesthetic, too hollow in its lyricism. 'Five words,' he wrote to me, 'should characterize this dénouement: logic, simplicity, *suavity*, intensity, mystery.' While in 1900 Wagner and Dostoievsky had been his inspiration for a time, the distance between them and him had widened long ago. 'You know, on the other hand, that I did study Beethoven, and he taught me a great deal from the point of view of composition.'

I was torn in two: I still loved, as much as ever, the *Partage* he wrote in his thirties, but I could not help being attracted by each of his new proposals. In the end the version we acted was, to some extent in spite of him, very close to the original version, barring the technical modifications.[1] As a result, the rewritten version which was published six months after our opening is very different from the one we usually act.

Like a speleologist, he was exploring the labyrinthine galleries of the flesh and the Spirit, and he discovered a new key:

> The Spirit . . . yes . . . but self-centredness, avarice, harshness, dryness, pride, what the good God hates most in the world.
>
> The Flesh? That's true, the need for the other person, slavery to the other, and the awareness of a bar to attaining it, something not so very unlike Hell.
>
> But above the Flesh, there is the overflesh – there is the *heart* which is also part of the flesh, this heart which has made us and which is wiser than we are. God put it into our breast simply for it to find its echo in the breast of another person . . .

Here, once again, I was in deep agreement with him: I too feel, above the Spirit, the divine Presence by a *carnal* perception. The sensation of the divine, before belonging to the soul, belongs to the sense of Touch. To me, Touch is the sense which attains mystery. We touch with our eyes, with our ears, with our whole Being, which is, before anything else, a magnetic centre.

When you are sufficiently attentive in the presence of a great starry sky, you notice something: it is *that the stars make a noise.*

Claudel too was vibrant. He followed the rehearsals almost every day. He would grimace with shame at the 'erotic' scenes (but I held firm: we had made a bargain and I had said to him: 'I give you the finale of Act Three but you leave me Act Two'). He was in an ecstasy of happiness when God managed to find His way in. Excellent ideas kept sparking from him.

As for me, outside the rehearsals, I soaked myself totally in Claudel. I went to the ceremony of Tenebrae on Good Friday at Notre Dame, and stood near

---

[1] 'Our' version is to be found in the *Oeuvres Complètes*, edited by Robert Mallet and published by Gallimard.

the pillar where, in 1886, the young pagan Claudel had received his conversion. Claudel was now sitting in one of the choir-stalls, among the canons.
I was stifled by my emotion at that ceremony, which twenty centuries of
practice had perfected : that extraordinary business of the candles being put
out, one after the other, and the last of them being taken and hidden behind
the altar as if to safeguard the last flame – the soul of the world burning low
– during the time when Christ is dead. At the end of the ceremony I saw
Claudel walking by. I stood where I was, embarrassed by my emotion; he
noticed me, close to 'his' pillar. We simply shook hands.

Our weeks of work were intoxicating. Nonetheless, at the last rehearsals,
nervous tension made itself felt. There comes a moment when the actors' work
reaches its ceiling. It is time, then, to consolidate, otherwise the work that
has been done comes apart, everything is rubbed away, grows sterile; there
is a general falling off. But it was clear that the poet, oblivious of the first
night, had become permanently plunged in his History. I had to leave the
camp of the author and cross over into that of the actors. This upset me, exasperated me. Claudel imperturbably went on working on us. At the end of my
tether, I said to him :

'I can't go on under these conditions, I shall stop the rehearsal.'

There followed a long and dramatic silence. I heard a sad voice, that of a
punished child :

'You're turning me out ...'

'Er ... No, Master ! Not quite that.'

'Anyhow, you want me to go away?'

'Well, yes, I would prefer it.'

A fresh pause. Claudel :

'Is it far to Saint Philippe-du-Roule?'

'No, I'll show you, it's a few steps.'

'I will go there. Please ask Reine' (that is, Mme Claudel) 'to come and fetch
me there.'

Crestfallen and reluctant, he went off. I was miserable.

Next day, at lunch time, I telephoned :

'Is the Master angry with me over yesterday?'

Mme Claudel answered :

'No, not at all, but he would like to know if he can come in now.'

'Of course !'

'Good, he was afraid you were still keeping him away.'

The sets arrived at last : they were quickly got under control. The tryings-
on of the costumes, at Piguet's, were delightful scenes, thanks to Bérard.
Christian Bérard wanted Feuillère to wear a sari. Someone objected :

'The sari is worn in India, not in China.'

'Ysé bought it there,' said Bérard.

'But the audience doesn't know that.'

Then Bérard, as he always did when he wanted something badly and was
determined to get his way, began humming like a small boy at play : 'She'll

wear it all the same! She'll wear it all the s-a-a-me!', while with his magi-cian's fingers he draped the sari over Edwige, to splendid effect.

The first night came. It was another battle. It was a victory. Claudel was in the audience, as always. To fight against his deafness, he had acquired a splen-did apparatus, which he used with brutal impatience. The poor machine lasted only a few days: it did not take Claudel long to break it completely – he needed tougher toys. But the apparatus caused us, that evening, during the first act, an extremely disagreeable shock. While Edwige and I were whispering the great love scene in the first act – 'Say that you will not love me . . .' 'I shall not love you, Ysé . . .', etc. – suddenly a strident whistle was heard in the auditorium. It was Claudel torturing his 'damned inefficient machine'. He was never seen with it again.

Claudel often came back to listen to his play. Every time he came back stage to see me, he seemed overcome – it never wore off. His eyes were always red. *Partage* to him was like a mirror. He saw in it his life all over again. He would talk to me of Amalric in the present tense: of how the man made him drink vermouth after vermouth, told him bawdy stories and vaunted Ysé's charms to him, the poor little priest.

One day I said to him: 'Won't you go and see Ysé?'

He frowned and said gruffly:

'I've nothing to say to that woman!'

'But Feuillère?'

Then, as though suddenly waking up:

'Ah! yes, Feuillère, of course, she's marvellous!'

Edwige Feuillère was an unforgettable Ysé. The parts we were playing bound me to her with a tenderness that can never die. There are roles that unite people for ever. It was the same with Prouhèze and Rodrigue.

L'ECHANGE, OR THE SPIRIT OF ESCAPE

Like a trout swimming upstream, I wanted to live Claudel's poetic adventure by moving back up his life. My objective, for I am obstinate, was still *Tête d'Or*: to start him from cover at the moment when, as a young man, he was floundering in between Æschylus, Nietzsche, paganism and conversion, as though caught in an eel-trap. Claudel's refusal, as regards *Tête d'Or*, was categorical. I then changed direction and persuaded him into the thickets of the still young America: sometimes under the skin of that young savage Louis Laine, fugitive as water, sometimes under the skin of the future captain of industry Turelure who, in *L'Echange*, is Sir Thomas Pollock Nageoire, with his 'Blessed be the Lord Who has given the dollar to man'; sometimes under the skin of the irresistible and 'crazy' Léchy Elbernon, that youthful but pro-phetic prefiguration of Ysè (whom Claudel had not yet met)[1], or again under the skin of that daughter of the Church, the woman who leads to God, Marthe.

[1] An instance of how, from birth, a poet carries his whole Destiny in him – all that remains for him is to live it.

This time I hoped he would leave the play untouched. After all, he had told me, in his reply to my request: '*L'Echange*? There's nothing in it I want to touch up. It's perfect!' Sez you! As soon as he had put his nose into it, there he was, wanting to rewrite it entirely. The work became really diabolical: he was smashing the whole thing, to remake it all.

Page by page he sent me a second version. I replied with a third, derived from the first two, and so it went on. He would concede me one passage to be able to bargain with me about another.

I kept defending, as best I could, the young attaché of 1891 against the decorated patriarch. Some scenes were mutilated for ever; others, on the contrary, were heightened in a masterly way. The idea of the swing, a stroke of genius, emerged in the course of this work, as the seminal spark of the play.

Marthe's monologue which opens the third act gives some idea of what that struggle was like: sacrilegious and harassing. Instead of the Marthe whose suffering in the first version makes her cry out 'Justice' on the sea shore, we have the new Marthe of the second version sending her parish priest a letter in which she asks *forgiveness*. Disaster! Saint-Sulpice! Unacceptable! I persisted. He negotiated – wrote a new letter. What does it say?

> You remember that book, long ago? That person in despair walking on the ocean shore and crying out 'Justice! Justice! Justice!' She would have done better to cry 'Forgiveness! Forgiveness! Forgiveness!' and to wring her hands as well!

The poet's whole life shows there, in a flash. The whole of his poetic adventure becomes intelligible in that change of words. The phrase contains the whole trajectory of Claudel's life. At the age of twenty-three he was crying out 'Justice!' At eighty-three: 'Forgiveness!'

Now we were rehearsing. The swing was a great help. Claudel followed the work with lively attention. These were hours passed in a state of joy. When he could get his teeth into something he was in his element. When he was demonstrating to Jean Servais [1] the trembling knees of an old man overcome with sexual longing, his eyes were screwed up maliciously, his mouth watered and laughter shook his frame in time with the clicking of his teeth.

He stood in the midst of us like a pole, and we revolved about him like horses on a tether.

Nonetheless the first night was approaching. And on the day before the preview I had to ask him to leave us to act freely and to go and watch us from the auditorium. This was his disarming reply: 'Oh, let me stay among you once more, today. It's the last time I shall hear it!' His deafness had in fact got worse. And so we installed him at the centre of gravity of the stage and acted, with much emotion, describing elegant figures all round him.

Acting the part of Louis Laine in *L'Echange*, with Madeleine Renaud playing Marthe, was to me – I was going to say: voluptuously unbearable. Living

[1] Jean Servais interpreted the part of Thomas Pollock, Germaine Montero that of Léchy Elbernon.

the treachery, disloyalty, unkindness and rottenness of the young savage opposite the human being I loved most in the world put me into a condition which I have not experienced on any other occasion, either in life or in the theatre. I felt not only naked, but drawn and quartered. It was a waking nightmare. And indeed Madeleine felt the same discomfort, and we still often discuss the suffering, foreign to art, which we then went through.

The success of *L'Echange* was compromised by the half-success of Musset's *On ne badine pas avec l'amour*, which filled out the programme. The two plays did not go well together. I had composed the show badly. I had put too much in.

After *L'Echange*, I returned to the attack over *Tête d'Or*. Claudel remained irreducible. I remember one of his replies, a telegram answering a letter in which I had once again asked him for that 'poetic tidal wave' of his youth. One word only : 'No'. Somewhat short, but clear.

Then I set out to absorb him whole.

CO-NAISSANCE DE CLAUDEL

I had long wanted to experiment with a new form of show, in which one would go in search of a man through the whole of his work. The trajectory of a human being is a drama. I wanted to take this 'primitive' drama and try to reproduce it in Space with the help of that crystallization of life which a body of poetic work is.

For a creator carries two categories of works :
– those that fall from him like fruit,
– those that remain attached to him till death.

L'Annonce faite à Marie, Le Pain Dur, L'Otage and *Le Père Humilié* are independent objects that have liberated themselves. The umbilical cord has been cut. They live their own life. They are the Harvest.

On the other hand, *Tête d'Or, L'Echange, Partage, Le Soulier* and *Christophe Colomb* remained attached to Claudel, and one could feel clearly that in these cases the adventure could never terminate. A long journey that would have no end ...

Madame Bovary is a 'fruit' of Flaubert; *La Tentation de Saint Antoine* is his drama for ever.

Terre des Hommes is a fruit of Saint-Exupéry; *La Citadelle* stays attached to him – it would remain forever unfinished.

And so I started out like a hunter in search of Claudel. I submitted my work to him. He sent the manuscript back with the following note:

> *I love this kind of show. It moves me as a spring does. It is specifically theatre in the state of being born. There is in it a kind of fresh start which could bring us gradually the material for a new style, capable of cleaning up many things.*

I was attempting a kind of show that had no precedent. I did not suspect that I had started along a new road which would later make me familiar with Sartre, Molière, La Fontaine, Saint-Exupéry, Rabelais, Jarry – and it does not seem to me to have come to an end.

Pernickety intellectuals have often reproached me for it. How can I help it? I find it fun. Who could prevent me from having fun?

The thing is becoming for me like one of those 'series' of books publishers go in for. This one might be called *Connaissance des Français* (getting to know the French); and why not extend such studies to Shakespeare, Nietzsche, Zeami, etc., and make a *Connaissance des Hommes*? After all, that is my trade.

There is nothing heretical about transforming a body of work, written on flat sheets of paper, into a three-dimensional show. The two are different things, with different problems.

We have a perfect right to do a portrait of anyone we wish, provided we assume responsibility for it. In the case of these programmes, it is 'my' Claudel, 'my' Rabelais, 'my' Jarry. *They* are not compromised; and their 'parish priests', whether they be academicians or pataphysicians, have no reason to take exception.

Connaissance de Claudel had excellent results. At Port-au-Prince, in Haiti, we were obliged to double our performances. It won its greatest honours in Canada. French-speaking Canada began its emancipation in 1952, but this was not yet known. Indeed such things are never known. Claudel himself had written to me: 'Take care, it is the Tibet of Catholicism.' However, His Eminence Cardinal Léger, Archbishop of Quebec, took (I think) the initiative, for the first time in the history of Canada, of making the clergy join the audience in the theatre – Her Majesty's – on the occasion of this 'Connaissance'. He had received me with great kindness in his residence in Montreal – he sitting on a throne beneath a canopy, I on a chair at the other end of the carpet. And he had announced to me the good news. He came to the performance in full dress, surrounded by his bishops; they filled the stalls. That evening, thanks to Claudel, the clergy was rehabilitating the theatre. We have treasured the film of it.

This 'Connaissance' is easy to transport, since it needs only the presence of human beings to make it exist, and we have acted it all over the place.

But my *Tête d'Or* was still sticking in my throat. For a moment I thought I had convinced Claudel. He plunged into the piece once more and, of course, wanted to rewrite it entirely. He made a loyal attempt. It would be set in a concentration camp – the only place, according to him, that could give him the equivalent of that materialist prison in which, at the age of eighteen, he felt he was shut up by the Molochs of the nineteenth century.

He was inspired by the ideas we shared about the 'theatre in the state of being born'. The prisoners would act *Tête d'Or*, and so on. The attempt failed. He gave it up.

I preferred it that way. There was now too great a distance between the crude and cruel young Claudel at the age of twenty-one and the eighty-five-year-old poet, loaded with a very full life and thinking only of becoming simple and familiar with his God.

He suggested to me a compromise: 'I give you *Tête d'Or*, but I ask you not to put it on until after my death.'

What else could I do but accept?

The theme of departure (that central theme of his poetic inspiration), the mad passion for the imaginary and the theatre in the state of being born made me then lay hold on his *Christophe Colomb*.

CHRISTOPHE COLOMB

There is something of the manifesto in *Christophe Colomb*. It is my 'Numance 53'.

A long while before, in response to a commission from Max Reinhardt, Claudel had written a kind of libretto on which Darius Milhaud composed a major opera. Already in 1942 Claudel had advised me to take up the text again and put it on the straight stage. He saw in this a way of leading up to *Le Soulier de Satin*. This would certainly have been a mistake: the density of the *Soulier* supported and guided me. But now it was up to me to 'carry' *Christophe Colomb*.

Knowing Darius Milhaud's straightforwardness and having had proofs of his friendship on many occasions, I asked him to forget his grand opera and consent to compose a score which would become integral to our stage performance. He agreed to this sacrifice, and it was a success.

To give a body to that series of short scenes – this was the challenge facing us. We must confine ourselves to a cast of economically manageable size: I stopped at a total of thirty-three.

After my puzzle on paper had been taken to pieces and put together again, I started work with Milhaud. I acted the whole play for him bit by bit, square by square, and I would hum to him whatever came into my head at the exact places where I 'heard' music. He would measure this to the second, and we would then discuss the spirit, the human content required of this piece of music. Thanks to Darius Milhaud, the music fitted into the play like one of the characters. In fact, it acted with us.

There were so many changes of place that any set was impossible. I had to hit on a catalyst, a magic object around which the slightest accessory would acquire life. The need for a screen for the cinematographic parts and the constant presence of the sea, the wind and Columbus's caravel determined my choice of this symbol-object: the sail. Like the music, the sail in turn showed itself as human as ourselves. I wanted the whole theatre to be man: objects, notes of music, words, characters.

Men and objects act together: the men act an object and the objects a man. While the humanized object is 'saying its words' in the action, the actor in turn, without being shifted out of character, from time to time becomes an element. For example: the waves of the sea (human beings) hurl on to the beach 'an old sailor, nearly dead'. Christopher Columbus goes into the water to rescue the sailor. The two actors interpreting respectively the sailor and Columbus must express at the same time, and without leaving their character, the element of water and the tossing power of the waves.

So the actor is no longer merely representing the human condition, but also nature, the elements, objects. He is at one and the same time man and environment. He is at the centre of life. He is bathed in it. The actor is interpreting not only human beings but also the whole 'theatre'. He belongs to human beings, but also to all the rest. He is in the middle of it all, he adheres to life in its totality: he is a centre of life.

To the author and to all those who are serving him, *the theatre is man*; and 'as soon as there is, on four raised planks no matter where, a man, and nothing round about him, expressing himself in the whole range of his means of expression, theatre will be there – and, if one likes to call it so, *total theatre*.'

That was the spirit of that 'manifesto'. It had been the spirit not only of *Numance*, but also of *As I Lay Dying*, and it came out of me through the pores of my skin.

As in the case of *Partage* and, to a certain extent, in that of the *Soulier*, I was once again in trouble over the last stretch. Is is because Claudel proposes positive endings that these are difficult to accept? Is it because he invents solutions for the mysteries of life? That is possible: life, death and survival inspire poets with ethereal but imaginary conclusions; as I have already said, they have recourse to a 'leap'. The theatre, that art of Justice, is more implacable. And Kafka was right to confine himself to interrogation.

This time I was the one who wanted to change the ending. I asked Claudel for help. I put his inspiration to the test, hoping to renew the miracle of the *Soulier*. But one day he gave me his answer: 'Too late, Barrault, I'm too old now, my inner flame is, from now on, burning low.'

It was at Bordeaux in May 1953 that *Christophe Colomb* was first performed, at the invitation of that city's young sportsman of a mayor, General Chaban-Delmas. When we left for Bordeaux, we had already done a great deal of work in Paris; but in order to adapt our work to the municipal theatre, that magnificent eighteenth-century building by the architect Louis, we had practically to begin the whole thing again, and this in two days.

Morning, afternoon, evening and night I kept the company hard at it. The final dress rehearsal went on far into the night. It was four in the morning and we had not yet finished. My comrades were at the end of their strength and nerves. That is the moment when the animal lies down, in spite of the whip. I saw some of them sitting, exhausted, on bits of the decor, others standing up and leaning on their props, like sleeping sentries on their rifles. The musicians' heads were nodding over their instruments. Boulez kept letting out echoing shouts of '*Nom de Dieu*'. The eldest had gone to lie down. Make-ups were dirty, eyes had rings round them. It was not the eve of Austerlitz, but of Agincourt.

I stopped the whole thing and we went back to our hotel rooms.

Collapsed on my bed, I could not get to sleep. *'It is impossible you should not find a solution before this evening.'* I relaxed. I tried to forget what was at stake. And once again, for myself alone, I went through the whole show like some beautiful dream. Was I asleep? Was I awake? All I know is that, round about six in the morning, a solution came to me. I sat up like a jack-in-the-box on my bed. *Come on, let's rehearse!* I cried. But the whole hotel was plunged in slumber. All those people were re-po-sing! *What are all those shits doing, sleeping, when in a moment the house will be full!* This absurd exclamation brought me to my senses and put me in a good mood. I got up and put down on paper the new version. We went to work again, and worked all through the day. The performance took place. The company went into action, and Claudel had his triumph.

Once again the saying was proved true: bad dress rehearsal, good first night.

DEATH OF CLAUDEL

Alas, Claudel was growing old: not his head, thank God, but his old campaigner of a heart. He was the one who felt it most. He became gentle, more tender. When one went to see him, he would discreetly prevent one from leaving. (I had lived through the same thing during the last days of Charles Granval, who died in 1942.) They were becoming rare, those moments when he would suddenly escape from you, leave you sitting in your chair, while he went off in pursuit of his formidable imagination. Now he would keep his eyes fixed on you for longer. His joy and his pride had not disappeared, but one could feel that he clung closer to those of whom he was fond.

A friend gave me the news at seven in the morning. I rushed over at once, throwing propriety to the winds, for I was propelled towards him by an impulse of my whole being.

In the drawing-room, which was plunged in darkness, a bed had been prepared, and there lay Claudel, dressed and with his crucifix in his hand. What struck me was the resemblance of his dead face to the bust in which his sister had depicted him at the age of eighteen, as a young Roman emperor.

Astonishing nobility, serenity, beauty . . . I pass over my own sorrow, Claudel is what matters.

I was told that death had come for him while he was reading Professor Mondor's book on Rimbaud: death had waited for the circle to close. *'Let me die quietly, I am not afraid.'* These, they told me, were his last words.

I left almost at once; already Paris was converging on him, and the ceremonial of a national funeral was descending on his family.

> *Already many times we have gone away*
> *But this time is for good . . .* (Claudel, *Ballade*)

Claudel was taken to the crypt of Notre Dame, and his funeral service was to take place in the square in front of the cathedral. Two platforms had been raised. It was bitterly cold. Snow had fallen. There was a cutting wind, and the icy temperature was made still colder by an organization that was too austere. The square was too big, the cold too discouraging, the catafalque looked lost and was too far from the stands. And there were too many barriers, which kept people from approaching.

I would have liked the whole of the youth of Paris to take charge of the farewell to Claudel. I would have wished the people of Paris to be there to jostle around his coffin. I would have wished, for this national homage, a fine disorder: that there should be some feeling of a fair, improvisation, warm blood. It was not the poet that they buried that day, it was the ambassador and academician. After that official and completely frozen ceremony, he was taken back to the crypt of the cathedral where, seventy years earlier, he had received the sunstroke of Grace.

The whole business seemed to me miserable.

Fortunately there was still his work. In opposition to that sinister departure a different Claudel had just been born or, more exactly, revealed. It is easy to understand human beings having invented ghosts. The dead Claudel was giving place to a new Claudel.

It was this Claudel who was at my side in 1959, for *Tête d'Or*.

Claudel remained for six months in the crypt, and it was in August that his real funeral ceremonies took place, at Brangues, near Morestel (Isère). Mme Claudel and her children asked me to pronounce our farewells over his tomb.

Summer had come. The day was magnificent, one of Péguy's '*journées de juin, de juillet et d'août*'. The appointment given to all parts of the world, and to the countryside with its summer visitors, was at his château, quite close to the Rhône. The pure sky, the bright sun and the green fields and trees sang of life. Here was something resembling Claudel!

The château of Brangues came in sight. I recognized the great avenue of plane trees and the two windows of Claudel's study (their shutters now closed), where I had so often gone to find my old master. We went straight to the church. On the road we had passed people gathering from all sorts of places: official guests, fervent admirers of Claudel, curious holidaymakers, journalists, photographers – all sorts.

As soon as I went into the little church I recognized the soul of Claudel. There it was, quiet and good, waiting for the seal to be set on it.

His body, invisible under the flowers, was surrounded by the village firemen in uniform. Above the doorway, close round the harmonium, a whole swarm of village men and women was rehearsing the hymns aloud and independently. Some improvisation at last! The pleasingly authentic red faces of those peasants dressed up as firemen seemed to exhale an atmosphere of both reality and operetta. The disorder of the choir brought a feeling of the 14 July. Small flags mingled with the hangings in the church, and the fire brigade's pennons completed the festive appearance. Only fireworks were missing.

As the church was too small, there was tremendous jostling, and most of the people remained outside under the trees in the square, where a small platform draped in black, complete with a microphone, had been erected.

On one side of the church there was the small chapel of the Virgin, not beautiful but simple in its purity, to which I had often seen Claudel withdraw (he went there every morning). And the whole of that turbulent crowd was sincerely moved.

As soon as the firemen with their naïve zeal came to attention and the first hymn managed by a miracle to get itself organized, I understood that France was arriving. It was, in fact, fully represented: Catholic France with the red-robed Cardinal Gerlier and, like a shadowy replica of him, the Bishop of Belley, followed by their canons and parish priests. And, like a pendant to them, secular France: Edouard Herriot, in academician's robes. Claudel had loved Herriot, and he, in spite of his age, illness and tragic condition, had insisted on coming. He was, to be sure, the second citizen of France, but also – a rare thing in the highly placed – he stood for friendship.

This time, without any doubt, everything was right. The firemen, the choir in their disorder, the Cardinal, the Government, the friends, the curious, the peasants, his wife, his five children, his eighteen or nineteen grandchildren – at last we had Claudel's proper funeral. We were à même, as he liked to say. God was sketching his portrait. Nothing was grudged him: the firemen did their duty; the choir sang more with their hearts than with their voices. It is much finer like that. The choirboys were well behaved and the faithful united in a silence of meditation. The poetry of religion was palpable.

I had the impression that the two prelates differed as to who should say the prayers of intercession. A question of precedence, of course. That too was necessary. Cardinal Gerlier seized a mike which had been placed near the coffin, gave it two or three taps with his fingernail to see, like a true professional, whether it was switched on, and spoke.

At the Académie Française it is traditional that the person who is welcoming a newly elected member should include a witty but penetrating criticism of his faults. He is being accepted, but being put through the mill a little. It is a passing, light tap on the cheek of the happy academician, no doubt to remind him of the day of his confirmation.

Cardinal Gerlier, being a great orator, a man of real wit, a Renaissance prelate, had not forgotten this tradition, and he interlarded his words of praise with a few taut and condescending criticisms, to make it clear to us that Claudel was henceforth a fellow member of the celestial academy.

At the end we walked round him, with the holy water sprinklers, and then regrouped outside in front of the church.

The crowd had grown still greater. Its centre was wearing mourning, but the more the circle widened the more multicoloured the crowd became: little printed dresses, shorts, summer shirts, white, blue, red and brown caps. This medley of colours worked in with the glancing tiles of the roofs, the varied greens of the leaves, and the shades of blue in the sky.

We formed a circle round the black platform and Herriot nerved himself to say farewell to his friend. He was already exhausted and had to stop several times for a violent fit of coughing.

My turn would come when the body was lowered into the grave. With growing terror, I felt the moment approaching.

Then the village firemen took Claudel on their shoulders, and the procession spread out along the white dusty road shimmering with heat.

I took up position slightly to one side of the column so as not to lose sight of Claudel. He passed through the wrought-iron gates. The lodgekeeper's fine black dog watched the great man go by. Now Claudel entered the zone of shadow, under his great umbrella pine trees. He stood out as in an etching against the light green of the château with its carefully closed windows. He took the narrow path leading down to the far end of the grounds, and disappeared. We had to wait for the gravediggers and the kindly firemen to do their work, arranging the wreaths. My heart was throbbing, my head was hot, I had become insensible. I came to only when I found myself facing the same crowd – it seemed as numerous as the leaves – delivering, with a fury that rose up to control my emotion, my last profession of faith to Claudel.

Then everyone dispersed and went off to lunch. Sky, earth and men had responded to Claudel. He had had his real funeral.

Mme Claudel – who was an extraordinary woman, an example of tenacity, dignity and devotion – had herself, in spite of everything, presided over the arrangements for a lunch for forty-five to fifty people.

During those hours spent at Brangues there had not been a single second of stiffness, hypocrisy or formality. The lunch was natural. People talked. Life was continuing. After rising from table the grandchildren began *naturally* to play croquet on the lawn, just as on others days – but on that day, perhaps, so as not to think too much. Others, and I along with them, went down again to the tomb. The gravediggers, with craftsmen's pride, were rolling the slab level above the cavity. The architect who had designed the stone was overseeing the work. They all knew how much Claudel had loved work perfectly done.

The children took a last look down on the bier covered with flowers before the stone hid it for ever, and the smallest of them pointed to an empty place at Claudel's side and said, quietly and naturally : 'Look, that's where they will put Grandma.'

Close by the tomb there was another, smaller stone, of the same kind as the big one, like a chick close by a hen : it was that of one of Claudel's grandchildren, and he had been accustomed to come and tell his beads at its foot.

Soon everything was done. There remained, to remind us of Claudel's presence, only these engraved letters :

Ici
reposent les restes
et la semence
de Paul Claudel.[1]

[1] Here repose the remains and the sowing of Paul Claudel.

And above all – oh, above all – on all sides the fields, the trees, the coming and going of farm labourers at work, those hundred-year-old lime trees, the château full of children and grandchildren, the pale willows on which the aged poet, at the end of his travels about the world, had hung up his harp:

et ce peuplier mince comme un cierge
comme un acte de foi, comme un acte d'amour;
et là-haut dans le ciel, cette étoile resplendissante (n'est-ce pas Marie
dans le ciel?), cette planète victorieuse de la mort,

and that poplar thin as a candle
like an act of faith, like an act of love;
and up there in the sky, that resplendent star (is it not Mary in the sky?), that planet victorious over death,

which we shall not cease to contemplate.

Ever since that day I have known a kind of loneliness which, I fear, will never be effaced.

EXODUS OF A GENERATION

The death of Paul Claudel (February 1955) closed a great exodus which, in three years from 1949 to 1952, had removed, one by one, all those who had more or less made me what I am.

October '49: Jacques Copeau. A stroke had gradually reduced him to a vegetable life. He had withdrawn to his property in Burgundy. To us it was very painful to see that beautiful intelligence suddenly undergo an eclipse, to recover his full light the next moment. He suffered, not a mental enfeeblement, but sudden blackouts. Maiène, his daughter, was acting in *Le Procès* that evening.

December '49: Charles Dullin. 'A long and serious illness' of the pancreas, the reports said: actually, it was not long at all. We had a project at that moment: to add *George Dandin* to our repertory, with Pierre Brasseur in the lead and my Master directing. But he was forced to break off a tour of France in *L'Avare*, and was admitted to the Hôpital Saint-Antoine.

A great deal has been written and said about Dullin's death 'in hospital'. Certainly he was not rich but he had his spiritual children, including Salacrou and ourselves among others, watching over him. Where, in our time, can a person be better looked after than in a hospital, especially when his name is Charles Dullin, and when, from the highest ranking doctors to the humblest nurses, Dullin met with nothing but affection, respect and admiration?

Once, however, when I was visiting him, he had a moment of weakness and told me he would like to be moved to a clinic. Salacrou and I discussed this with, in particular, Professor Mondor, who decided that the quality of the medical care was what mattered most and advised us to keep him where he was. The hospital then set aside for him part of a small lodge. He had 'his clinic' there.

The last time I saw him he murmured, half asleep:

'Were you acting yesterday?'

'Yes.'

'Was the house well filled?'

'Yes.'

'Ah! so much the better! so much the better!'

It is all very well, our being defiant about empty seats, it is nonetheless true that we choose the stage as our life in order to make contact with human beings. What is the nervousness that grips us every evening, if it is not the lump one has in the throat on the way to a lovers' appointment?

The actor is a man in love. The member of an audience sometimes plays the flirt. Dullin, close to death, was living over again the anguish of those missed appointments. The people who now wax pitiful about his fate would have done better to go and see his performances. Posthumous glory is all very well, but response to the person who is 'giving himself' is no bad thing either!

On the Sunday after that visit, I was acting in a matinée of *Hamlet*. Madeleine had gone to visit him. She telephoned me during the interval: 'It's all over.'

The performance began again. I can still see myself between Ophelia's legs, saying: 'And my father died within two hours.' A cruel game, that of life and death!

When Dullin left that hospital, watched from all the windows, at which patients and nurses, male and female, had gathered in one and the same communion, the bier that carried him away carried also my youth.

Then came Jouvet's turn, in the middle of August 1951. I was called back from Saint Moritz, where Madeleine and I had gone to get a little rest. Pierre Renoir and his fellow actors asked me to speak the funeral oration.

At the customs I was let through without trouble. Everyone knew the sad task which awaited me. Jouvet's death had a considerable impact: it was *The Actor* who was disappearing. The Place Saint Sulpice was black with people. From the Left Bank to the cemetery of Montmartre he moved slowly between rows of Parisians who knew 'who was going by' and stayed watching. The people of Paris were saying goodbye to him. He seemed like a Head of State – a Head of State from some other world.

The magic of the theatre! Yes, it is at such moments that one has confirmation of the reality of our vocation, friendship, love and death. This being so, how can it not be given absolute freedom of expression? The petty quarrels about perfectly or imperfectly successful shows fade away, and all that is left is the memory of the man who has given everything and received everything.

Jouvet had collapsed with a heart attack on the stage of the Athénée.

As a line in Vauthier's *Personnage combattant* says:

Men have raised up their works and slid in underneath them to die; to die in triumph or despair, but they had to die, had to give, had to consent . . .

Gaston Baty also was extinguished a few months later, gradually stifled by an angina pectoris.

But the one who had opened the procession, in February 1949, was Christian Bérard. He died at the age of forty-seven, struck down in the central aisle of the Marigny theatre, opposite the fourth row, in front of his setting for the *Fourberies de Scapin*.

Before the War, when I acted *Le Misanthrope*, Jouvet had criticized me severely and told me: 'Alceste is not a part for you, you are Scapin.' And so, ten years later, I asked Jouvet to come to our theatre and direct *Scapin*, so that I might be able to work at the part under his guidance. I love going back to school and putting myself in question all over again. We wash and dress every morning, why should we not rid ourselves of the mannerisms and bad habits we acquire in the course of working? Jouvet, aided by Sauguet for the music and Bérard for the settings and costumes, did an extraordinary job of work. Christian Bérard even more so. It was a great lesson for us.

I have said already that in the theatre one should always put the cart before the horse, otherwise you end by achieving nothing. I had occasion, during this adventure, to realize that in the theatre another proverb also is reversed, and that one should say: 'The habit makes the monk.' That is not surprising after all, since the theatre is the mirror of life.

Jouvet had entrusted Pierre Bertin with the part of Géronte. Jouvet knew the part particularly well from having played it when he was a young man, during the Vieux Colombier time. He passed on to us its traditions: a sunshade, the fat chain attached to the man's purse, the exactly right gait for the old man's body. That is how, in the great family of the theatre, the 'traditions' pass from one generation to another. That is also how 'civilizations' are forged, whatever the practitioners of the scorched earth strategy may say. And so Jouvet was torturing Bertin, who simply could not acquire the greybeard's deep-seated mischievousness. His body resisted.

Bérard meanwhile had said to me: 'Give me a thousand yards of grey stuff and I'll make the costumes on the actors, direct.' He had had enough of theatre that smells of the painter's sketch, of the gouache. A man's sweat has a better smell.

We decided to make a trial. We went to the costume makers. My faithful Karinska once again. Bérard, while he enveloped Bertin in the grey stuff, asked him to act a little of his part. He crushed his shoulders downwards, made his knees give way, gave him pockets that drooped to the ground; Bertin's arms grew longer and longer, a suspicion of a hump formed, and Bertin bent double. We were watching the gradual psychic transformation of Bertin. Caught in that costume, which enclosed him, corsetted him more and more, Bertin was becoming Géronte.

Jouvet had magnificent, inspired ideas. To begin with, he carried farce to the level of high poetry. Scapin, in black and white, inspired by Scaramouche, became the 'prince of valets'. Jouvet's mastery was worthy of Molière's. He no longer bothered with the trifling common tricks which generally worry directors – the logic of entrances and exits, for example. Fully to possess a craft is to become free from it. The whole thing began to flutter at his fancy's sweet will, without for a moment ceasing to be true.

I think, in fact, that in the theatre what matters is not so much to be sincere as to act true. As in music, always as in music. Each play leans on a tonality which is right for it. It may be major or minor, but everything must be made to pass through that imperative.

For me the experience of Scapin with Jouvet and Bérard was a salutary 'confirmation', a great piece of teaching.

Tempo is also extremely important. I got in the habit of going, after the first act, and asking the stage manager for the timing. If we had slowed down by three seconds, I had the word passed to everyone that we must 'pull ourselves together'. I have retained this practice.

Le Personnage combattant, which I am acting at the time of writing, lasts for an hour and fifty-four minutes without a break. Every evening we time it. The time taken varies by about thirty seconds, hardly more. But I amuse myself by guessing whether I have been slower or faster. I am rarely wrong.

'Yes, Monsieur, today you did one hour, fifty-three minutes, thirty-five seconds.'

Or again:

'Today, Monsieur, one hour, fifty-four minutes, four seconds.'

And yet, in detail, the acting changes. One is forced to believe that one's sensations silently obey some secret rhythm which has to do with breathing.

I have never understood this business of the importance of tempo so clearly as in Scapin – which is one of the most exhausting roles in the repertory. One's blood pressure goes up by six or seven points. Molière had only **eighteen months** to live when he created the part, and he knew the actor's craft thoroughly: after the famous sack scene (throughout which Scapin is taunting the old man in the sack), he sees to it that Scapin, for his last big scene, is himself carried by servants.

We had reached the last few rehearsals. We were performing Partage de Midi at the same time, and Jouvet was acting at the Athénée. It was time to do the lighting. We decided to do it during the night. During the performance of Partage Bérard was in my dressing-room, doing the sketches for the luggage. This was to be his last drawing—

Remerciant son hôte et faisant son paquet, says La Fontaine.[1]

And now the public had left the house, and the stage staff were dismantling Partage and putting up the set for Scapin. Bérard came and sat in the stalls. His little Tenerife bitch, Jacinthe, was by his side, as usual attentive to all that was happening, and never leaving her master.

[1] In La Mort et le Mourant:
> Death was quite right: I could wish, at that age,
> A man to leave life as he would a banquet,
> Thanking his host, and doing up his packet.

So there were the three of us looking at the decor and waiting for Jouvet. Bérard's decor was marvellous: grey with a few touches of pink.

Bérard said to me:

'I like the set very much, it's a stage for dogs.'

He had dedicated it to Jacinthe. Then suddenly he stood up, walked a few steps, took fright, came back towards me and asked:

'I've changed colour, haven't I?'

In fact, his face was becoming purple. I had not time to answer before he collapsed in the aisle.

Telephone, doctor, ambulance, police. After a few death-rattles there was silence.

Jouvet arrived, saw, and his eyes stood out from his head. My old friend Doctor Fraenkel (a member of the Dada movement) decided to try the impossible: Bérard was taken to Beaujon, for an attempt to restart his heart. I had wrapped Jacinthe in his raincoat and was holding her in my arms.

It was close on two in the morning. We waited for the result, without much hope. The doctors returned. They had been unable to do anything. There was our 'Bébé' dead in a hospital.

The law forbids taking anyone from there. The policemen, seeing how unhappy we were, agreed to break the law on condition that we took the dead man out on his feet, as when one supports a drunkard.

We took Bérard out of the hospital, holding him under his arms. A police van. We reached his home, in the Rue Casimir-Delavigne. We rang the door-bell, and the sinister cortège reformed. Bérard, upright between two police-men, passed through the doorway. We shouted to the concierge: 'Christian Bérard.' And step by step we took him up the stairs. I still had little Jacinthe in my arms.

By four in the morning we had dressed him. The policemen, who had be-haved with great kindness, had gone. Bérard's friend Kochno was there to watch over him.

We were afraid of the effect on Jacinthe. We decided that I should take her with me. I put on Bérard's raincoat to induce her to follow me passively, and there I was in the light before dawn on my way back from the Carrefour Danton to the Trocadéro, on foot – for really I was in no hurry any more and was not going to wake Madeleine up to give her the news. From her tenderest childhood she had adored her cousin.

Where does one go in such cases, except to real friends? I rang at Pierre Delbée's door. We had formed a small band which the Occupation years had made indissoluble. It still is.

Two days later, on (I think) 17 February, anniversary of Molière's death, Bérard's funeral took place. This time the procession went from Saint Sulpice to Père Lachaise. All Paris was there. All socialite, aesthete, artist Paris, all the 'crazy' ones, all the 'night birds', all the 'snobs', all the 'aristocrats', all the simple people too, the public, the people – all classes of Paris society were suddenly, for a few hours, united in tears.

For Christian Bérard was loved and recognized by *all*, from the Boulevard to the Avant-garde; his genius produced unanimity. On the evening of the same day, that same public met again at the Marigny for the first night of *Scapin*.

The law of the Circus : the show must go on !

Law of the circus and sign of life: at the end of the performance when in accordance with custom I was making the announcement: 'The decor and the costumes are by Christian Bérard', the curtain fell abruptly like a guillotine and would not go up again; the hemp cables had broken.

The theatre too had decided to go into mourning.

CLASSICAL REPERTORY AND MODERN AUTHORS

Nothing is more favourable to the life of a theatre than confronting the classics with the moderns, Racine with Giraudoux, Æschylus with Claudel, Feydeau with Molière.

Of the forty-eight titles that appeared on our posters during this period, a dozen were classics. The remaining thirty-six were given to the moderns; and among these thirty-six there were twenty-four first performances. This diverse fare rubbed shoulders every evening, 'in repertory'. One day a lady came to the box office, listened while she was told what the programme was, and then said: 'Give me the whole assortment.' I like a programme to make people think of a menu.

In spite of the increasing difficulties and the politico-aesthetic discussions of all kinds with which we were showered by certain intellectual papers, not to speak of the stick-in-the-mud and reactionary critics, we managed to do at least two first performances per year: Salacrou – Kafka – Camus – Claudel – Brückner – Jean Anouilh – Montherlant – Gide – Maurice Clavel – André Obey – Cocteau – Giraudoux – Georges Schéhadé – Ugo Betti – Christopher Fry – Georges Neveux – Jules Supervielle – Jean Vauthier.

Such – taking only the first performances – are the names which honoured our posters.

Malatesta

I got on very well with Montherlant. The critics were harsh towards him and towards me. They would not allow that a condottiere could be only five and a half feet tall. To them a condottiere is the Colleone statue.

As an illustration of the mysterious atmosphere that prevails at the moment of a performance :

In *Malatesta* the curtain rose on the empty set.[1] In the wings the hero was fighting with his Master-at-Arms; the two came on stage fighting. On the evening of the *générale*, the curtain rose at the right moment, and I was there with my comrade Beauchamp, the two of us ready to go on stage slashing at

[1] Settings and costumes were by Andrieu.

each other. At that second we received from the house such a feeling of 'ice'
that I cried: 'The bitches! They're against us!' It was true. We had to *row
hard* all evening. What seems to me interesting in this case is that:

1. 'They' were already hostile before the thing began.

2. When we were still not on stage we received that hostility through the
walls, like a blow in the face.

If there are fine moments in the theatre, there are also some abominable
quarters of an hour.

Pour Lucrèce

This was the only one of Jean Giraudoux's plays not 'brought into the world'
by Louis Jouvet. I remain sincerely grateful to J.-P. Giraudoux and his mother
for the confidence they placed in us. It is an admirable play, and it had the
advantage of an unequalled cast, especially the women: Yvonne de Bray,
Edwige Feuillère, Madeleine Renaud, Simone Valère. The men included Servais
and Desailly. Sets by Cassandre in his chiselled language. Dresses by Dior:
perfection.

The creation of *Pour Lucrèce* had as its twin, that year, the creation of
Christophe Colomb. 1953: a good date.[1]

The law of the imponderable

Edwige had two red dresses, Madeleine one white dress. At the first dress
rehearsal, Edwige's two red dresses were 'knockouts'. On the other hand
Madeleine's was a regular *crème* Chantilly. Christian Dior sent for a piece of
natural shantung. Things can only be seen properly on the stage, which
magnifies or destroys anything at its own sweet will. Dior draped Madeleine
in the stuff. It rang true. Then a doubt occurred to me.

'Wouldn't it be a good thing if Edwige tried on her dresses again next to
that stuff?'

'But they're already perfect!'

'Please ... just a precaution.'

The caprice was allowed me. One of the two red dresses was still all right.
The other, also red, not many shades different, suddenly became impossible.
Was this due to very small changes of colour, or to the rivalry of two materials
that did not agree? Feuillère's second dress had to be remade.

I call that *the law of the imponderable*. The thing would have been impossible to discover in a dress shop: *it was the stage that said no.*

At the time when we were putting on Molière's *Amphitryon* with Bérard,
I had had to take a decision on the diameter of the columns of the temples in
relation to their height. I had a dozen cardboard dummies cut out, each
differing by a centimetre.

With 'Bébé' one was always playing; at least, pretending to be.

[1] 1953 marks also the inauguration of the Petit Marigny, the creation of the Domaine
Musical, and the start of the *Cahiers Renaud-Barrault*, published by Julliard, under the
responsibility of André Frank. The *Cahiers* were edited from 1958 onwards by Simone
Ben Mussa and published by our friend Claude Gallimard.

The ten dummies were hung up on stage. We stood at the back of the stalls, facing away from the stage and each with a paper in his hand.

'Now we'll turn round and write down, without consulting each other, the number of our choice.'

It was the same number. Out of ten columns, only one *asked to act*. The others were clods. *Law of the imponderable*.

The sail in *Christophe Colomb*, which had served for the creation of the play in the big theatre at Bordeaux, seemed likely to be too big for the Marigny. It was 10 × 10 yds. I had a new one made, 8½ × 8½ yds. We tried it out: it had no soul.

'Oh, well. Let's try the first one.'

'It's bound to be too big.'

'Let's try, all the same.'

The first one was put up; I don't know how it managed, it made itself small – in short, it did the necessary to be taken on. *It wanted to act*. We shall often meet with this same phenomenon again.

Who would dare to claim that objects do not possess 'humanity'? This is why I have two friends: my old leather bag – it dates from 1937 and is a mass of patches, but I could never bear to abandon it until it abandons me; and an old Indian poncho, dating from 1950, full of holes and with frayed edges – we also cannot separate, and I have even wondered whether it might do as my shroud. I am perfectly sincere: my bag and my poncho are my two travelling companions. Why should we part when it comes to the last journey?

I can understand those men who had themselves buried with their horses. You can look at them in the basements of the Leningrad Museum. And our relations with dogs? That law of the imponderable, so imperious on stage, exists elsewhere in life. It is the bouquet of the sixth sense. I do not think our lords and masters possess it yet. That will come, perhaps.

Alas, the increasing difficulties of life are forcing us nowadays to do without that law sometimes. The spirit of accountancy, standardization, expendability and the gadget are destroying that last nobility, which belongs to the artisan. And yet that 'imponderable' is what makes civilization. A certain way of showing that one is a human being. An exacting courtesy towards one's trade and extending to the mysteries of life.

I shall not review here all the pieces we put on. But here are two more, from before the creation of the Petit Marigny.

Bacchus

A very fine play by Cocteau, one which will remain. When I think of Jean Cocteau, there comes back to me a sentence of Péguy's about the people of Paris: 'It is called trivial because it is quick.' Cocteau went on deepening until his death.

Just one false note in that adventure: the out of place reaction of François Mauriac, caught by a sudden fit of excessive zeal for the Catholic church. Ridiculous, a piece of wrinkled infantilism.

And God knows I admire Mauriac in his writings and his conduct (I had almost said : in his showing off, too). What a pamphleteer of genius ! On that particular evening, I can't think what had bitten him.

La Répétition ou L'Amour Puni

Jean Anouilh and I were friends at school, at Chaptal. He took 'philo', I took 'math élem'. He was always spick and span, I liked being scruffy. When he entrusted our company with *La Répétition*, we were enchanted. He is the most expert playwright of our generation. He knows the theatre to the tip of his nose and of his pen. Working with him is a pleasure : his reactions are always right.

And yet, what a tormented character ! When he suffers, everyone has got to suffer with him. It's horrible. Then, when the storm is over, well, he disappears. But when one meets him again, he is charming, and one's only desire is to go on working with him.

I love Paris but she has been hell to live with : our relations reminded one of those between Célimène and Alceste. We gave the play its first performance in the middle of the 1950 season. Anouilh was the author for whose next play everyone was waiting. And we were in full glory : we were just back from a resounding tour in South America. And yet, on the evening of the first night, the advance bookings were worth no more than a house and a half. Such is Paris, the cruel, the cold, the indifferent. The first night was dreadful. A real catastrophe. I spent all the next day walking about the streets in despair, raging, with my eyes full of tears, discouraged, on the edge of a nervous breakdown. That evening we had to pass the press : the customs ! Our morale was at its lowest. Well, it was a triumph. Two days later, the theatre was turning people away. That too is Paris.

> *What a hard trade ... but what excellent results!* (line from a play by Schéhadé).

No wonder I have gradually learned to adopt as my own motto : 'Feel passion for it all and cling to nothing.'

THE DOMAINE MUSICAL AND THE PETIT MARIGNY

Just as playing in repertory makes a company supple, keeps it progressing and gives it a certain economic solidity, so also the vitality of a theatre should extend to playing *simultaneously* in different places. At the Comédie Française I had already understood the need for adding to the large house a small one, which would have been used more particularly for experiments.

The façade of the Marigny contained room for the installation of a house with two hundred to two hundred and fifty seats. After seven years we managed to persuade Simone Volterra, and in January 1954 we opened 'Le Petit Marigny'. This also made it possible for us to help Pierre Boulez.

We had soon become aware of the exceptional qualities of our young musical director. His powerful aggressiveness was a sign of creative passion. His encyclopaedic knowledge of music, the adaptability of his talent, a particular blend of intransigence and humour, the way his moods of affection and insolence succeeded one another and the sharpness and attractiveness of his temperament – all these had drawn us near to him and had given birth to closer and closer bonds of affection between him and us: a real filial love.

Along with the Petit Marigny the Domaine Musical came into the world. That time, as regards contemporary music, at least in France, was the period of the catacombs: Boulez was determined to save our honour.

The German conductor Scherchen was in charge of the first concerts. We did Stravinsky's *Renard*, with a fresh approach. Thanks to Boulez we gained wider experience of Schoenberg and Webern, and he made us discover Bério, Stockhausen, Nono, etc. Those were particularly memorable evenings, glamorous with hisses and ovations. Nowadays, when I go to a Boulez concert in New York, my heart throbs with a parental pride.

But for the May '68 explosion, we would still be in harness together! 'Feel passion for it all and cling to nothing.' My passion for Boulez's work has not wavered as he continues, independently, his triumphal career.

The Petit Marigny was to welcome new playwrights: Georges Schéhadé and Vauthier in particular.

In fact, I am far less attracted by novelty than I am by quality. Is this a defect? I don't know. *That's how it is.* On the one hand, my training rests on deep foundations of technical knowledge, and on the other hand my professionalism has always urged me into economically difficult enterprises. To me the nursery is not an end, but a reservoir.

Which does not prevent me from being attracted by new qualities. I had been struck by Schéhadé's poetry when I read *Monsieur Boble*. I got in touch with him. We put on *La Soirée des Proverbes*, an admirable play. It was to be followed, in the course of our peregrinations, by his *Histoire de Vasco* (Théâtre Sarah Bernhardt) and *Le Voyage* (at the Théâtre de France). We are constant to those we admire.

After that revelation, *Le Capitaine Bada*, Jean Vauthier sent me his second play, *Le Personnage combattant*. I am still acting it now, fifteen years later. Need I say more?

What with playing in repertory, with using two houses simultaneously, with the marriage between music and the theatre and with our big tours in various parts of the world, we had in nine years carried out our programme: 'An international repertory theatre, French section.' But, as always in our life, Destiny in the Æschylean sense was waiting for us at the corner.

To my mind the double aspect of that 'Marigny period' is reflected in two works: the *Oresteia* of Æschylus, and *The Cherry Orchard*; the strange sonorities of ancient percussion, and the Chekhov play's small band of itinerant musicians (four violins, one flute, one double bass).

THE ORESTEIA

Shakespeare, Claudel, the masque, the mime, total theatre, the cabbalistic ternary, the ups and down of our travels, the presence of Boulez, the different forms of speech from prose to song via *Sprechgesang*, physical trances and the magic of the sense of touch, were bound, one day, to bring me to a halt in front of the *Oresteia* of Æschylus.

Already in 1941, at the Roland-Garros stadium, I had made a first attempt with the *Suppliants*. In spite of valuable aid from Charles Münch and Honegger, I had not succeeded very well. At that time, under the Occupation, it was forbidden to act at night. We were defeated by the June sunshine. The theatre is a moon art.

It is through a small detail that one falls in love. Madeleine's delicate forearms, or the scene of Sept Epées and the butcher's girl in *Le Soulier de Satin*, when they were swimming in 'the pretty sea'. After which, one's whole Being is thrown in.

It was in Brazil that I contracted the need to launch myself into the *Oresteia*. At Rio I had been present at occultist séances. White magic, from which the Devil is excluded, and in which the Indian and African spirits 'possess' the adept. When he is seized by the Spirit, a kind of inner dialogue begins. I noticed that the trances had three waves, and this at once reminded me of the scene where, in the *Agamemnon*, Cassandra is possessed by Apollo. I recognized the three waves. A perfect juxtaposition.

At Bahia I was present at the ceremonies called *candomblê*, which reminded me with the same exactitude of the ceremony of the Choephoroi, when over the tomb of Agamemnon those 'daughters of the saints' are heating Orestes up to the temperature of his crime.

Lastly, in the Brazilian forest I had been present at *macumbas* – a kind of magic ceremony with, this time, the presence of the Devil (Ishu), and whose purpose was originally vengeance. These ceremonies recalled precisely Clytemnestra's black masses in the midst of her Furies.

I was now obsessed by the Æschylus trilogy. During a stop at Dakar, visiting the market in Maiène's company, we had recognized the colours of the costumes – they were all *vegetable*: mineral dyes had not yet become the rule.

For this new 'operation' to have its full meaning, the trilogy had to be played in a single evening. There was in existence a very fine translation by Claudel, in which he had taken over from his 'Master'. That was already something. But while Claudel's language is powerful, it is also copious: his *Oresteia* would have lasted at least seven hours. Besides, his translation of the *Agamemnon* dated from his youth, the time of *Tête d'Or*, while his *Choéphores* and *Euménides* belonged to his maturity, the time of *Le Père Humilié*: placed side by side, their differences of style showed, as though the first play had been written by Bonaparte and the two others by Napoleon.

The duration of the Greek text was much shorter. I invited André Obey to risk the adventure. Obey was open to enthusiasm. He accepted.

Stop-watch in hand, and with the help of several Greek scholars, including a Dominican father, a lecturer at the Sorbonne, and a Greek friend who knew Æschylus by heart, we worked during nearly a year at unpicking every line of the trilogy. We had imposed on ourselves equivalent rhythms. The *Oresteia* was dissected into its various members. We put together a whole marquetry corresponding to the Greek rhythms. For example: for the iambic we chose verses with six feet. For the anapaests: the alexandrine. The trochaics: eight or ten feet. The cretic: six and nine. The diochmiacs: rhythmic prose, etc. And always checking with the stop-watch. The *Oresteia* became actable in three and a half hours. Slightly less than *Le Soulier de Satin* !

As regards the Chorus, I read a great many learned books. I gradually perceived that, in reconstructing the plastics of gesture from the study of vases and statues, our nineteenth-century scholars had been more attentive to plaster casts of the Parthenon sculptures than to the archaic civilization.

For example, one may read in those learned books that the Greeks knew the poses of classical dance, in particular the *quatrième croisée*, except for the use of the points. But I had been able to observe in Brazil that a man who is in a trance turns where he is and, because of this, does the *quatrième croisée*.

Painting and sculpture freeze movement. The attitude in question is in fact not at all hieratic or smooth, as one might believe from the vases or reliefs: a person who is depicted in the *quatrième croisée* is in fact *in trance*, like a whirling dervish.

It became also clear to me that Salamis was an even more important battle than Verdun or Stalingrad: it marked the break between the East and the West. Æschylus had taken part in the battle of Salamis.

His theatre is bound up with archaic Greece – when theatres were of wood. I could imagine that time pretty well by comparing it with what I had also seen in Brazil – a few palaces of marble in the midst of shanty towns such as the *favelas* of Rio.

The gestures in our performance were inspired by African dancers rather than by evolutions in the style of Loïe Fuller. Pierre Boulez, whom I asked to write the music, was in agreement about this. Once again Labisse did the décor, and Maïène the costumes. They had all taken part in our South American tours and had been present at *candomblês* and *macumbas*.

I thought I could see, also, that influences can come from everywhere through Space and Time. The *Oresteia* is one of Æschylus's last works. By then Sophocles had already won the prize several times. Sophocles is said to be the inventor of the psychological treatment of characters. In the *Oresteia* a character such as Clytemnestra has, compared with Æschylus's work in general, a remarkable psychological dimension: does this mean that Æschylus in his old age was letting himself be influenced by the success of the young Sophocles? I like to believe this. Now that the years have gradually deprived me of my elders, who could influence me today if not my juniors? This is something that has happened to me a number of times, and I am the better for it.

In the course of this fascinating work I was able to go deeper into 'the life' of the ternary of creation, that ternary which reproduces the three phases of an act. Neuter. Masculine. Feminine.

Æschylus seems to me the poet most closely in harmony with the reality of life. In each of these three plays there are three phases: the first phase is long, agonizing. It is the time of preparation. It makes one think of the forty-eight hours that precede a storm. The air is heavy, the clouds are piling up, there is a smell of ozone everywhere. Return of Agamemnon and cortège with Cassandra. That is the neutral phase, the mysterious one.

Suddenly the lightning strikes, the thunder roars. This only lasts a few seconds; the bloodstained bodies of the king and the slave are thrown on the stage. The bolt has fallen. Masculine phase. A lightning-brief phase, the spark of fecundation.

Then the gestation begins, just as, after a storm, the rain begins to fall straight, leisurely, penetrating. The act has fertilized History. Now the Fruit has to be brought to maturity: feminine phase; which will be followed by another slow preparation. The mass celebrated by the Choephoroi over the tomb of Agamemnon. Another neutral phase, slow, heavy, agonizing.

Then the lightning assassination of Clytemnestra. History again fertilized by a blinding flash, the spurt of the seed. Second masculine phase.

And then the long pursuit by the Furies: feminine phase of gestation. And so on.

If one does not respect this organic rhythm, if for instance one shortens the 'neutral' and the 'feminine' phases and draws out the 'masculine', one moves from Action to Intrigue. Not at all the same thing. The one is life, the other is agitation. Theatre of intrigue, peripeties, etc.: a modern conception, which has lost its roots.

Later on, studying Jacques Monod's book, *Chance and Necessity*, especially the passage about the 'double helix', I was amused to read that one of the elements in the function of life is called 'the messenger'. 'The messenger has a somewhat short life,' we are told. I cannot help thinking of the messenger in the *Agamemnon*. As in biological life, he brings exactly and only what the life of the tragedy requires. Scientifically, this may seem approximative: I think, all the same, that it is 'a good likeness'.

We acted in masks. It was a wonderful experience. Far from limiting expression, the mask makes us discover new instincts, and serves as a springboard for expression by the whole body. I have dreamed, ever since then, of a modern tragedy, treating a present-day subject and played in masks. It is the only case where total nudity would seem to be acceptable. If you wish to show your genitals, hide your face.

Lastly, like *Hamlet*, the *Oresteia* is situated at the moment of a Renaissance. One human cycle is ending, a new cycle is beginning. The sun has set, the long night of the Furies is finishing, Athena appears at dawn to announce a new day. A 'happy ending' – over which there floats a certain doubt. At least, that is my impression. The Greece of Pericles and the Platonic view of the world do not seem to me to have been a happy invention. But all this passes my understanding and is merely a quite personal impression. Are we not always seeking to reconcile the East and the West?

THE CHERRY ORCHARD

In telling the story of this ten years at the Marigny I have purposely not followed chronological order. In parallel with our life in Paris, our company had also an international life. In April 1956 we again went off on our travels, but this time we were not due to return to our lair in the Champs Elysées.

Because of our work, people had come to believe that the Marigny was our theatre. Simone Volterra, its manager, could no longer stand this. Our contract was not renewed. Were we perhaps not accommodating enough? I have the impression that we would have had to be very accommodating indeed. In short, when we flew off from Orly to Mexico on that spring day in 1956, we had no link with Paris to look forward to. More and more we were becoming strolling players. This was not to our distaste, as yet.

We had just *given* the fullest years of our lives. The prime of life, as they call it. We had succeeded in creating a true theatre. It is perhaps not modest for me to say it, but why should I not? And I had steeled myself to ask the official bodies for help in finding us our means of expression. A certain Minister one day had replied: 'You come into no category that can interest us.' I still had only a gypsy's licence. And so we could only pursue our way and carry our 'living democracy' about the world.

I have already suggested that a memory acquires its full value only when it has a feeling of the 'Present'. If I now sniff the scent which our company had at that moment, I find in it a touch of *The Cherry Orchard*. A family and a house. The house from which one is to be driven. The family in danger of being scattered. A past which must be forgotten. An uncertain future which will have to be lived. Each member of the company fitted exactly with each character in Chekhov's play. We had given our first performance of *The Cherry Orchard* two years earlier. Georges Neveux had made a remarkable French version. The Russian temperament and the French temperament, different though they seem, harmonize with an astonishing subtlety.[1] May I be allowed to say that we have never *acted The Cherry Orchard*, we have always *lived it*?

When we first did it, our company was grown up. But does one ever arrive at being grown up? In any case its body was fully formed. And we were well aware of the fragility of that body, constantly at the mercy of the fluctuations of theatrical life – and of life. Every time we performed that masterpiece of Chekhov's, what happens in Act Four was being enacted no longer just on stage but in the wings.

(On stage)
Madeleine: Anya, put on your coat.

[1] I had occasion to verify this impression when we visited the USSR (Leningrad and Moscow).

Simone: Let's start! let's start!

Pierre Bertin: My friends, at the moment of leaving this house, have I the right to say nothing, can I silence the emotions I feel stirring in my heart...?

Maiène: Please, you mustn't!

Desailly: Epihodov! My coat!

J.-P. Granval: Thirty-six misfortunes, hoo!

Madeleine: Has all the luggage gone?

Dominique Arden: Goodbye, house; goodbye, the old life!

J.-L. Barrault: Welcome the new life!

Madeleine and Pierre Bertin were left alone on stage. They were weeping over their past life.

(From the wings): Ay! O!

Madeleine (in tears): We're coming!

Then André Brunot, the oldest of us, would appear, in the uniform of the old servant Firs:

Life has gone by, it's as though I hadn't lived...

In the wings, we were trying not to cry. It seemed to us, each evening, that our company was going to fall apart.

Yes, the scent that remains to me from that Past-Present is of *The Cherry Orchard*, the 'nursery'. In ten years we had lost all our elders, we had become responsible; were we going to manage to continue? To last? To pursue this wandering life?

The wandering life

'TO TRAVEL ALL OVER THE WORLD, thanks to our work.' Such had been our dream when we created that 'international company, French section'. The attributes of an actor are the suitcase and the scarf. My bag and my poncho.

Why does one go on the stage, if not to meet human beings? To get in contact, to exchange, to share, to get to know one another, in order to try to understand.

In one of his prose poems, Baudelaire says:

> The poet enjoys this incomparable privilege, that he can at will be him-self and someone else. Like those errant souls in search of a body, he enters when he wishes into the Character of each one ... The man who is able to unite with the crowd draws a strange intoxication from this universal union. He adopts as his own all the joys and all the miseries that circumstance presents to him. What men call love is pretty small, pretty narrow and pretty weak, compared to this ineffable orgy, to this sacred prostitution of the soul that gives itself whole, poetry and charity, to the unforeseen as it shows itself, to the unknown as it passes.

That seems to me exactly the actor's essential condition.

We acquired the habit of flying off, every year, in the spring, as the first swallows appeared. But we took with us something other than our wings. In the case of a repertory theatre, a tour resembles both a circus and an army on campaign. Nothing must be forgotten, down to the smallest details, costumes, stockings, shoes, wigs, ribbons, accessories of all sorts – everything that acquires a meaning, a personality on stage. The least little bit of wood, the least bit of chiffon, becomes a precious object.

The customs officers sometimes stood staring, 'comme canes' (like dogs) as Rabelais would say, when faced by a padded skip containing some improbable piece of ancient rotted stuff.

And so we had our inventories – plenty of copies. We used to take with us our lighting switchboard, our lights, our cables, our sound equipment, our 'campaign' office equipment and my portable library.

I was as happy as a child again at the feeling of being half ambassador, half a military commander.

Once, at São Paulo, we were put into a 'deconsecrated' theatre, as bare as an empty barn. Eight hours later, we had a theatre in working order. I love that kind of organization.

LÉONARD

Léonard, at these times, proved himself irreplaceable. I mean what I say: Léonard is *the* example of the man of the theatre, and I mean by that that he is a 'nomad'.

Squarely built, strong and solid, he is equally good at being the most robust of the stage hands and the most precise of administrators. He has the stature of a Roman tribune. An Italian from Fiume, son of a great architect, he had studied chemistry; then, caught by the demon of the stage, he had entered the Pitoëffs' company. As an actor, as stage manager and then as the pillar of the company, he had spent seventeen years with the most poetic of our men of the theatre. I imagine him doing the accounts or repairing the props with, on his knees or on his shoulders or clinging to his jacket, three or four of the children of Georges and Ludmilla.

I like to hope that with us Léonard had found the human warmth which he had shared with that famous couple. I can say now that, along with us, he was the founder of our company. I suspect that, never having been able to rid himself of a certain foreign accent, he always had in some corner of his heart a longing to be an actor: so it happened that when one of our company came timidly to ask him for a rise, Léonard would at once send him packing to his dressing-room, with a shout of: 'You ought to pay for being an actor!' The troupe, nicknamed him '*Léonard de vingt sous*'. That did not prevent him from being kindness itself and a stickler for real justice.

He and I lived for more than twenty years like two accomplices. Léonard is my dearest comrade-in-arms. No one, except of course Madeleine, can imagine the worries, the moments of panic we have shared together. A few years ago he decided to retire, but he is always around and, on the slightest occasion, I appeal to him and we are off again on the road.

That is what I call a man of the theatre! The road, the skips, the suitcase and the poncho, and there we are, off in quest of human beings . . . *Ohé! les Hommes!*

The poet Georges Chennevières, whom I quoted at the beginning about the 1914 War, had written a long poem called *La Légende du Roi d'un Jour*. In our life of travel about the world, there is that 'King-for-a-day' aspect. We have travelled Europe, from Edinburgh to Bucharest, from Warsaw to Naples, the three Americas, Japan, Soviet Russia, the Middle East, North Africa. Several times round the world. That makes an immense album of memories. Let us leaf through it, for fun.

LE FLORIDA

That is the name of the ship that took us to South America for the first time, in 1950. At that moment, although we were well and truly in the ascendant, our purse had run dry. The tour came at the right moment. The Minister Louis Joxe suggested to us this mission. We accepted with enthusiasm.

On curiosity

A company of actors does not deserve the wandering life unless it is made up of people who are curious. To me, curiosity is life. My curiosity shakes down well with my timid temperament. Have you sometimes observed cats venturing on their first steps into a wood? They stretch out their paws as far as possible from their body, try a touch, leap backwards, put back their ears, arch their backs, begin to crawl forwards, put out a paw again and finally, from alarm to alarm, advance. In them curiosity is stronger than fear. They set us an example.

Without curiosity, what would we do with our fear? It is curiosity that saves everything. Madeleine and I have incurable curiosity. This 'noble feeling' was luckily shared by most of our comrades. And if we add to curiosity that faculty of astonishment which every human being ought to maintain and develop so as to remain young in heart, we certainly belong to the category of 'wonderers'. We ought, in the course of our tours, to have founded a Wonderers' Club. The morose people can just stay at home.

The *Florida* was an old boat, doing its last voyage. We took possession of it at Marseilles, for an 'absence' of more than three months. Rio, São Paulo, Montevideo, Buenos Aires.

In our baggage nine shows, the material embodiment of eleven plays. Weight: over twenty-four tons. There were thirty of us, actors and technicians. Labisse and Pierre Boulez were of the party, and so was an old friend, Samy Simon, one of the pioneers of the radio at the time of Robert Desnos: we had agreed to send to France regular 'radio letters' describing our travels. As part of this we recorded the monologue of the Jesuit Father, the prologue of *Le Soulier de Satin*, against the rhythm of the waves as the *Florida*'s prow cut through them. The rhythm of Claudel's verses fitted in marvellously with that of the waves breaking against the ship.

At that time such voyages were real expeditions. The War had separated the peoples. We had been charged with renewing links that dated back a long way. It was a great responsibility. We would be treading again in the tracks of Sarah Bernhardt and Lucien Guitry, and reviving these with a modern spirit, with the first attempts at exporting the *avante-garde*. It was also still the period when actresses brought with them the Paris fashions.

Since then, easier communications have made this needless, and if the actresses now have to wear any clothes at all, it is in order not to appear out of fashion. As for the *avant-garde*, it now comes back to meet us: a plant that has grown and flourished from what we sowed.

The ship had just cast off; it was sliding away from the port of Marseilles. Behind us, above the wake, the iron bridges swung to. France was closing. The adventure was now irrevocable. Length of crossing: fourteen days.

It was my first real voyage by sea; up to then I had travelled only on the ship in *Partage de Midi* taking me to China with Brasseur and Feuillère. I recognized the same atmosphere and began, like them, to pace the deck, as though on 'a board that is breathing'. I can feel even now that dilating of one's whole being, when it is at grips with Life. The air, the sea, the responsibilities, the fusion of a whole group of human beings which is now only a single body. What we are leaving behind, what is in store for us. Every moment of the day the awareness of living a 'memory for tomorrow', unwilling to lose the least bit of what is presenting itself to us, from the green flash at the setting of the sun to the daily decline of the Pole Star and the gradual apparition of the Southern Cross, at which the swaying mast pointed its finger. The moist air of the Doldrums. The nervous tension one feels there – a kind of giddiness that reminds you of mountain sickness.

As head of a company I was in the seventh heaven. I held all those actors in my hand, they could not escape me now. In the dining-room I pinned up a worksheet. I made them rehearse. We went into training: gymnastics and overwork. In the enchantment of adventure they all accepted these things with a good grace.

There came the first squadrons of flying fish. We sighted our first hammer-head shark. We kept the watch, each in turn. Every morning we went down into the galley to devour pizzas cooked by the sailors. We took our baptism at the crossing of the Line.

I had only one painful duty to perform. (The law of the circus.) After being summoned by the radio officer, I had to give Maiène the news that her mother, Mme Jacques Copeau, had just been found dead in her garden. I loved that woman – she had been an admirable human being all her life. . . .

One fine evening, after sailing for some time in sight of land which seemed to me a particularly pure green, we saw emerge the Sugar Loaf and the Bay of Rio, haloed with a sun in glory.

We were home and dry !

The season went like a dream. To describe it is really impossible. Thanks to the *abonnements* (season-ticket system), the public went to nine different shows within a month. Taking into account the parties, everyone knew every-one in a few days. There was soon no anonymity.

We were becoming the 'actors in ordinary' to ten or twelve thousand people. Festivities were organized. We visited universities, schools, hospitals.

The Brazilians, especially the women, had an admirable knowledge of French. At night I went to classes in samba-carioca and learned the dances from Récife and the North. By an amusing bit of luck I brought to Rio the *Frevo* of Pernambuco. And this obtained for me the rare friendship of a famous Brazilian, Assis de Chateaubriant. With guides, we went deep into the forest to witness *macumbas*. On our way back we would stop on the summit of Corcovado, to watch the sun rise over the Bay of Rio. We felt as if nothing could tire us.

I remember one Sunday in particular. We had agreed to give an extra per-formance of *Les Fausses Confidences* and *Baptiste* at 10.30 in the morning. Popular prices – almost token ones. We had got in at 5 a.m. from an excursion in the forest. Our breastbones were still resounding from the tom-toms that had beaten at us all through the night. The square was crowded. We went in through the stage door and said to the doorkeeper: 'At least we shall not be wearing ourselves out for nothing!' 'But, sir, the house is already full; the people left outside are waiting to take the places of the ones who faint.'

At the end they invaded the stage and despoiled us of parts of our clothes. Thanks to their generous, spontaneous temperament, the theatre had been transformed into a Carnival of Humanity.

It was much the same at São Paulo.

I shall never forget an hour spent on deck in the Bay of Santos. The sounds of life. The sea had begun to fray its edges against another sea – that of the banana trees – while a tawny sun was sinking imperceptibly.

> Goodbye, my fine sun, you and I were fond of each other . . . and besides, you are the only one! (Partage de Midi.)

On board ship there are two things I particularly like to watch:

The transition from day to night. I try desperately to follow its absolute continuity, and never manage it. There are moments at which it seems that nothing any longer is moving, developing, changing – a foretaste of Eternity – and then abruptly, as if with a click, one has moved on to something different. The day has gone down a notch. And so, notch after notch, click after click, day ends and night comes. And at the precise moment when the sun's final fingernail disappears behind the horizon, the influx which we were receiving from in front, from the side of the light, is reversed and the influx of the night is enveloping our backs. Night is putting its cloak around us.

The arrival in a port. I am always struck by the slowness with which, very rightly, the boat approaches the quay. This gives me time to observe attentively the moment at which the land's magnetic halo *touches* the magnetic halo of the ship.

From the rail you have before you at first an image, as though on a screen. The quays, the swarms of people, the town becoming distinct behind and then, further away, the land filling the background: a two-dimensional image.

The picture imperceptibly draws nearer. The image grows bigger, but remains still an image; then, suddenly, without one's being able to seize the continuity of the transition, here again as if with a click, *one is inside.* The volumes appear in relief. We have just passed from the abstract to the present, from drawing to flesh, from dream to the vibrancy of the real. Sight and hearing perceived the spectacle, now life is appealing to all our senses. The two magnetic currents have collided and are violently becoming inextricable. And there is still some time to wait before the hawsers bring the vessel trim against the quay. It is at that frontier that theatre makes its appearance.

At Montevideo there is always a nervous depression in the company. Nothing to do with the welcome or with the theatre. While the Brazilians are splendid boon companions with whom to savour the orgy of life, the Uruguayans have the gift of friendship. We are even, in a strange way, related: did not Isidore Ducasse, Count of Lautréamont, and Jules Laforgue and Jules Supervielle come from Montevideo? The Teatro Solis is one of the pleasantest anywhere. Everything is of wood: one might be inside a violin. And yet it seats eighteen hundred. The wind over the rose-pink waters of the Rio de la Plata estuary, the transparency of the light, the fat lands populated with herds of black and white cows like ink spots in a horoscope – all this is beautiful, mysterious and spellbinding.

But in the square the leaves are falling. When we left France we were emerging from winter, leaving the spring rains behind us. A few days later we were tasting the heat of the eternal tropical summer – a summer, in Brazil, that was still continuing, hot and luxuriant. Now it is June – in France the best of months, the richest, densest, the one most in the ascendant; and here, in the square, the leaves are falling. It is the approach of autumn and winter. We are being cheated of our summer.

Then you notice that the sun moves the other way. 'At home', when you look at it, it moves from left to right. Here, from right to left. You walk head downwards.

Add to that the fatigue which is beginning to catch up with us. In Montevideo the company must get its second wind. The actors are depressed, the technicians have had enough. Any failure on the herdsman's part and the herd would start fighting. Three times we have done this journey: on each of the three I have met with the same phenomenon.

How we would have loved to go upstream, deep into the land, as far as the Iguassú Falls and even Paraguay. But we are not grumbling: even when you merely lick the continents, you taste their bouquet.

Buenos Aires is not unlike Paris. The Calle de la Florida reminds one of our rue Saint Honoré. Our theatre was the Odéon.

By now, winter had come. An enchanting young lady gave me, as a souvenir, that poncho, handwoven by the Indians of Mendoza.

At last I got my outing on a small boat through the maze of canals that divide the land. Rotting tree-trunks on the banks. From time to time the blue-green back of a fish. The beauty of the estuary.

It is all flat, almost flush with the water. Small films stuck on a sheet of glass. We are under God's microscope. The ambiguous transition from life to death, from muddy fresh water to the brine of the sea, to the Communion of Saints. A melancholy picture, touched with colour by a horizontal sunset.

And now we are meeting another sea: the immensity of the Pampas. The archipelago of the *estancias*, with their terrace roofs which have cannons on each corner. Along the tracks, skeletons of cattle – horses, oxen, cows, victims of the migrations of the herds – like hulls of boats.

The dances no longer have the sexual exasperation of those in Brazil; here they have the sensual melancholy of the tango or the refinement of handkerchief dances.

The same system of *abonnements* brought us in touch with the same kind of society. Lectures at the Faculty of Law, visits to the young theatrical companies and discussions with them. Here artistic activity is intense. It is true, the Perón government did not facilitate relations. Eva Perón decided not to come. Somebody had slashed whole skips of costumes – I have no idea who. In Paris I had been 'advised' not to present Kafka's *Le Procès*. I was obstinate. It was Kafka who won the palm. At the gala first night a young man came round to congratulate us. He was the Minister for Foreign Affairs.

As for *Occupe-toi d'Amélie*, it was recommended to us that we should cut certain lines. We refused. And when the Prince of Palestrie introduced his 'General' with the line :

> I don't know how he would do in a war,
> but in a procession . . .

the public laughed up its sleeve.

The final evening was sensational. Legend has it that, for Sarah Bernhardt, the public unharnessed the horses and pushed her carriage by hand. We received the same homage. The bus which was taking us to the port at one in the morning was pushed by the young people, and then it drove at a foot pace to the quay, surrounded by members of the audience.

For three months Léonard and I had not had time to look at one another. We were exhausted, emptied out by all that we had given. When we reached the port our eyes met at last, control broke down and we fell into each other's arms, sobbing with happiness.

I took thorough measurements of the *Florida*. I was dreaming of making her into a world theatre. The idea remained with me : later on, with the French line, the project went quite a long way. Even the watertight compartments corresponded to the safety curtain separating stage from house. The great majority of the world's principal cities are ports : New York, Tokyo, Rio, Buenos Aires, San Francisco, London, Hamburg, Marseilles, Beirut, Algiers, Venice, Athens, etc. With a boat of twenty to twenty-two metres beam, you could have an auditorium seating eight hundred to a thousand. Plus projection rooms, exhibition rooms, concert halls, fashion parades. The theatre uses sailors' knots. Why not turn a ship into an itinerant embassy of a country's civilization?

I have kept picturing myself ending my life as a traveller about the world, mooring at the end of Forty-second Street, New York, and flying the French flag.

To serve the cities of the interior, we would carry on the ship a big top and lorries, and from Santos we would go up to São Paulo – we would go to Milan, to Berlin. When we moored at Leningrad, we would be on our way back from Moscow.

All the activities of French science, technology, craftsmanship and intellectual and artistic life would be brought together in a single festival of mind and imagination. It would not cost much more than a national theatre. And the impact it would have! One of those dreams it is sad not to have been able to realize yet.

And why not, at the present day, make of it the real international theatre in all languages?

SOUTH AMERICA

We did three tours in South America.

During the second, in 1954, the Argentine had a smell of civil war. That time we visited Chile. Bolivia and Paraguay are the only Latin American countries we have not visited.

Buenos Aires, 14 July.

Christophe Colomb at the Colón. We were to give two performances, a free matinée in celebration of the taking of the Bastille, chiefly reserved for students, followed by a gala evening performance. The work was hard. I can still hear Boulez yelling in time with the beat: '*Et merde, et merde, et mille fois merde!*'

On the day before, I was summoned by the Mayor:

'It seems that you have invited some Communist students?'

'We have invited all the students.'

'There are Communist students among them. There will be demonstrations. You don't want to be called: Barrault-Communist!'

'As we are doing a play by Paul Claudel, that would seem to me rather out of place. Well, how many of these students are there?'

'We know of a dozen.'

'That seems to me a small number for a régime as strong as yours.'

'We are not ordering you to cancel the performance, but if I were you I should give it up. If there is violence, we can take no responsibility.'

'*Monsieur l'intendant*, knowing what *agents provocateurs* are like, I do in fact think it would be better to give up the matinée.'

A great number of students had come a long way, some even from Cordoba and Tucumán. Disappointed, they were massed round the theatre, and they received, 'surreptitiously', tickets for the evening performance. We distributed these.

That evening, to a packed house, we acted *Christophe Colomb*. There is a line for the Chorus which says:

Il vaut mieux faire un petit effort que de perdre tout! (Better make a little effort than lose everything.)

Dog matters

At that time we had an adorable poodle bitch: Amie. Every time we brought out our suitcases, it was despair: 'the end of everything'. She would lie down under the furniture, would hide in corners. It was painful.

Just before this second visit to South America, the ritual of the suitcases had begun. Amie was in despair, as usual, and as usual we were miserable.

At a certain moment we searched for her, in order to cuddle her, console her and console ourselves. She was not to be found. We gave up and went back to our suitcases. She had slipped into one of them, among our clothes. As flat as a shirt, ears extended, imploring look. Forty-eight hours later she had her papers, her health certificate. The tip of her tail was quivering with joy. On the boat she soon recognized all the hours of the day. At noon, after the passengers had bathed in the swimming-pool, and while they were taking their apéritif, one would hear a splash. It was Amie: she had waited for the last bather to leave in order to take her turn. At tea-time she would be waiting for the tea-rooms to open, just like an English lady.

The Desaillys had their Briard, an enormous dog who knew how to pass unnoticed through the customs or at parties.

We had also a pair of doves for the Claudel play. The female laid an egg high up in the Andes.

Santiago de Chile

A strong, virile people, both peasant and intellectual. With them an instant alliance. I got to know Pablo Neruda better, a man I already admired so much. I came upon the traces of Jouvet and his companions. Jouvet, who had gone into voluntary exile during the War, had been very unhappy. Personal misfortunes: the death of Giraudoux in Paris; and the death of one of his oldest companions, Romain Bouquet, a charming actor, naïf and full of poetry. He was buried at Santiago.

Chile – was it because of the Andes? – felt further from France than the eastern side of the continent.

One day I was in a melancholy mood. Madeleine let me go off alone. I went first to the cemetery, a magnificent garden where the students go with their work. I found R. Bouquet's niche, like a compartment in a beehive. There were flowers. Two Chilean women keep up the memory of 'our comrade'. And then, in those streets of one-storey buildings, I went looking, near the railway station, for a certain restaurant which apparently Jouvet liked. The name of a hotel 'said something to me': I thought it must be there. I knocked. A door was opened, it was a brothel. Two of the girls, half in half out of their chiffon wraps and very sleepy, came forward. It was not there. 'The restaurant is a bit further on.' 'Sorry !' I reached the restaurant.

What I found was a 'French' bistro – that is to say, the walls are covered with French notices, such as one sees in a railway station in France. The proprietor, so as to keep the memory of Jouvet green, had surrounded himself with all our provinces. A photograph of Jouvet was enthroned among these relics.

While I had something to eat, I thought about that great family of actors who travel about the world: we place our feet in the footsteps of our friends, whether they belong to our country or to neighbouring countries. A life that is something like that of pilots and something like the life of explorers – explorers of the human heart.

Our third visit nearly ended tragically: 1961 was a chain of catastrophes. The tour, as usual, had made a fine start in Brazil. This time – if I remember rightly (it is not very important) – we went on straight to Buenos Aires, meaning to visit Montevideo afterwards, and we had been invited to play at the celebrated Teatro Cervantes.

The first performance was sparkling. Next morning I was woken up early. From the telephone a voice said to me:

'The theatre is on fire.'

I hung up. I took it as a bad joke. All the same, as a precaution, I went. To tell the truth, I ran. I arrived just in time to see the roof of the stage collapse. In place of our twelve tons of decor there was now, at the bottom of an immense hollow, merely a huge pile of burnt materials.

Our chief electrician was mourning for his old friend, the lighting switchboard which we had been lugging around for fifteen years, now swimming in water. The most striking thing about a fire is the disharmony between the smell of smoke and that aquatic effect. Moving along the corridors in the dark, your feet splash through a regular stream and you slither on great bowels, as if you were Gulliver struggling in the belly of a Brobdignagian.

This catastrophe took place on a Saturday morning. Thanks to the devotion of Argentinian friends, we were welcomed by our old theatre, the Odéon, and on the Monday evening we managed to resume the series of our performances. Thereupon Madeleine, in a badly lit passage, missed a step and broke a foot. She acted in spite of this, at the cost of incredible pain, still gracious as usual.

Buenos Aires ended beautifully all the same: at the farewell party, which was all the more affectionate because everyone was aware of the efforts we had made, Madeleine had an enchanting thought which delighted everyone there. Speaking of the mutual exaltation, the close communication and the exceptional understanding which had united us with the Argentinians for more than ten years, she said:

'Once again we have succeeded in setting the town on fire!'

The ruins of the Cervantes were still smoking.

I had promised to pay a visit to Tucumán, in memory of the time of Christopher Columbus. We left on board a military DC 3, not heated and not pressurized. I think this time Desailly could have killed me. I can still see his black looks. It was the only time I brought my comrades to the limit of endurance.

Tucumán: smell of sugar cane. As we went north it became hotter and hotter. The welcome we received was wonderful. It was the anniversary of Independence. I went to lay a wreath, surrounded by young girls in white dresses. I noticed a fine table and fine chairs which would do marvellously that evening for our improvised decor. I asked for them.

'It is the table on which the Treaty of Independence was signed!'

'Oh, sorry!'

That evening lasted till five in the morning. Those people were aware of everything.

'Tell us all about the death of Robert Desnos.'

At Tucumán, yes, it was like that. *And it is like that everywhere.*

On our return journey there was the threat of a cyclone. We had to land at Cordoba. We were due to leave the Argentine next day and must not miss the Boeing: Montevideo was waiting for us. By describing an enormous detour, we managed to pass the flank of the cyclone.

Next day, departure. The Boeing, not having enough room to climb above it, was caught in the cyclone. Lightning struck one of the wings and the tail. The hundred and thirty tons did a loop. There we were, bruised, under a pile of cases. In the gale, the pilot made a violent landing: he literally let himself fall so as not to overshoot the runway. The undercarriage stood up to it.

Then we left again for Bahia, one of the most beautiful cities in the world. San Salvador. When we got to the hotel Madeleine discovered that her jewels had been stolen. All the beloved souvenirs of our life together. The emerald I had given her to celebrate Anouilh's *La Répétition.* The sprig of sapphires for *Occupe-toi Amélie,* the aquamarine from our first stay at Rio. . . .

Despair. What with the fire, the cyclone, her broken foot and now being robbed of all these treasures, she was near a nervous breakdown. Anyone would be.

But we had to go and open the theatre in Brasilia: Brazil had decided to honour France by inviting us to give the first performance on the stage of the future capital.

The two-fold impression made by Brasilia was extraordinary. On the one hand a skeleton town, with very wide roadways, several kilometres long, ruling rectangles across fields of untrimmed grass. The avenue meant for embassies was for the time being flanked only by billboards. The French Embassy was a wooden shed. The central square, surrounded by palaces, was complete. The theatre was being finished. While we acted, enormous rats scuttled between our legs. The cathedral, which is splendid, is surmounted by an enormous concrete crown. I asked the architect, Niemeyer:

'Is that the crown of the Virgin?'

'I don't know. I got the idea from a bunch of bananas.'

Never mind. The effect is successful.

On the other hand, by the side of that virtual capital destined for the future, there was a town swarming with people, a kind of giant encampment housing the vast population recruited for the building of the other town. A life of trappers. That is how one imagines America being built.

And we returned via Rio, hopeful that this was the end of our ordeals. . . .

There were still ten thousand kilometres to be covered. It was midnight, and there we were in a heap at the airport in the midst of a stifling crowd. Madeleine, exhausted and still in pain, was at her wits' end to get some rest: she seemed, as they say, at the end of the reel. And so she sat down on a dressing-case. There was a crack. I opened it: she had broken her looking-glass. One evening at the start of the tour we had been thirteen at table. I looked at my watch. It had stopped. Time itself was not working. Nothing was working any more.

We were called to go aboard. There again, as our pilot, was the commander of the Montevideo Boeing.

'I hope this flight will be better than the other day....'

'My dear sir, if it goes any worse, none of us will live to tell the tale.'

Toil and ... trials.[1]

NORTH AMERICA

Our first visit dates from 1952.

Jouvet had preceded us, one or two years before. He had performed *L'Ecole des Femmes* in a small theatre. His success encouraged the French Government.

Our assignment was to attempt a real season. A big theatre: the Ziegfeld. A repertory of six shows. To last six weeks. It was risky. For us a regular gambler's throw. On the programme: Marivaux, Molière, *Hamlet* in French(!), Kafka's *Le Procès*, Feydeau's *Occupe-toi d'Amélie*, Jean Anouilh and the pantomime from *Les Enfants du Paradis*.

We were to go there via Montreal and Quebec. The route we took to Canada seems curious nowadays, but twenty years have passed since then. Paris to Glasgow by train, then an English boat (in the evening they played 'Shake the bag'[2]), and then up the St Lawrence. It was autumn when the maples lavish their gold over the land. The squirrels.

In Canada our objective was attained. I have already reported the entry of the clergy into Her Majesty's Theatre.

We went on to New York by train. Sol Hurok, the celebrated impresario, friend of Chaliapin, welcomed us at Grand Central Station. We got into a yellow taxi, brilliant like a huge beetle, and there we were in Fifth Avenue. What do I see in the windows of the big stores and luxury shops? Models of Baptiste! The reputation of *Les Enfants du Paradis* had prepared the ground, and Sol Hurok had seized the opportunity. So they expected a great deal of us? I should say so! I felt rather sick.

After the first night there was a big party at the Waldorf. Our ambassador and Mme Bonnet were giving us marvellous support. The audience had seemed adorable. And yet Sol Hurok was pale. I really could not understand what was happening. At the end of the supper Hurok went out, paler than ever. And yet the evening seemed to me to have been a success. The reception was charming. A few minutes went by, and Hurok returned – he was pink and bouncing: the notices in the *New York Times* and the *Herald Tribune* were excellent. It was in the bag! In New York a whole season is gambled on the first evening.

We did our fifty days in an increasing euphoria. Hurok had had an enlargement made of an article by Walter Kerr: 'French can do everything!' We had become the 'kings for a day'. I report this because of what followed.

---

[1] *Travaux et ... traverses*: the author's first choice as title for this book. See p. 321 below.
[2] A game of chance.

From the United States we were due to move on, at the beginning of January, to Egypt. Our New York season was ending in festivities and our cabins were reserved on the *Liberté* for New Year's Eve. From Le Havre, where we were to land, we would go to Marseilles, and from Marseilles another ship would take us to Cairo.

Les rois des rois ... d'un jour!

In truth the success had been so great that we were entitled to believe we were safe and sound.

We felt sad as we left New York, that 31 December. Would we have the chance to live such moments again? To that, I would like to answer at once that we have never yet brought back a bad memory from New York, or from the United States. I think I know why : I will say in a moment.

And so, accompanied by our friends, we went to the port, which is right in the city. In New York I love the ships from all over the world, coming and mooring at the ends of the streets. That city 'standing upright', those smoking roadways, that simplicity of life in which all classes of society rub shoulders, those delicatessen shops where you can go in evening dress or black tie to collect in a paper bag the food you will cook for tomorrow's meals in the kitchen which is part of your hotel room.

In the luxury cabin which the *Liberté* had reserved for us, we opened our post. The Egyptian Ambassador to the United States wished us a good journey and a great success. We learned that the season in Egypt was entirely sold out.

Outside it was freezing hard : in fifteen days we would be in the sunshine beside the Pyramids.

With emotion we felt the transatlantic liner begin to move. The lights of the city vanished into the mist. The Statue of Liberty saluted us. The wind was blowing. A storm was coming up. Everyone or almost everyone was sick. At the New Year's Eve dinner I can see Pierre Bertin and myself sitting alone at a long table, in front of a mountain of caviar, while the head waiter sang the praises of the menu in tones worthy of Sacha Guitry.

The storm raged. When that happens, I never stop moving about. I think it is wrong to lie down. I went down below, to the level where the swimming-pool is. The water was oscillating by forty-five degrees. The liner was rolling in sixty-foot troughs. We were forbidden the deck – we would have been blown away.

Thirty-six hours go by in this pleasant broth. The purser has a telegram delivered to me : Egypt is closed to us. There is a revolution. Neguib wishes to 'spare us difficulties'.

So there we are, all of us, unemployed – ridiculous in our luxury. '*Grandeur et misère des baladins.*' [1]

It was *force majeure*, of course. Still, one has to live and I felt responsible

---

[1] Grandeur and misery of mountebanks. Allusion to Balzac's title *Grandeur et misère des courtisanes*. (Translator's note.)

for our community. The next three days were spent over telegrams. We would organize an extempore tour.

The *Liberté* reduced speed. Calm had returned, and we were now in the 'pea-soup' of an icy fog. The foghorns were moaning in the grey unknown. Ghostlike Le Havre was scarcely visible in the dirty-cotton morning. We ourselves were as pale as the twilight. As damp as the air. Up to the eyes in our scarves.

We had managed to make an arrangement with the cinema at Le Havre, and we improvised a decor for a performance of Anouilh's *La Répétition*. Next day there was a bus waiting for us, and we travelled the slippery roads of France to Reims and on to Colmar. In Alsace Madeleine had an abscess in her throat.

Not all our travels were done by bus: there were also trains, hours of waiting at stations, warming ourselves at the cast-iron stoves of the S N C F.

A fine fix they were in, the 'kings for a day'!

But the best part of the story is that, leaving aside the difference in comfort, we met with the same human warmth, the same welcome, the same fervent enthusiasm and the same friendliness as in America.

This experience has made a great impression on me. No matter where in the world, *man* is the same. Everything that comes from his heart, from his head, from his belly, provided it is sincere, finds an echo, a response. Whatever the differences of language, education, social and political training, the theatre passes all barriers and addresses itself to what is fundamental in the human condition.

In New York we had received one of our finest rewards, one of our best encouragements: in the winter frosts of those regions of France, with equal straightforwardness, those encouragements and that fervour were the same.

Through the medium of the theatre, man is completely naked, outside his shell. The reason for this, once again, is the awareness of death. Life is seen as a whole. It is, at one and the same time, full and ephemeral. There is a truth of all interests. Even for those who have no God, life becomes something religious. And this profane religion is that of the theatre.

Our company went back to New York several times. In the heart of Broadway, to the Winter Garden – 'The Pride of Paris'. To the City Center, where, with Offenbach's *La Vie Parisienne*, our takings equalled those of Radio City. And we visited many universities. I will speak of that further on.

Each time, we brought back from our stay in the United States an unforgettable impression. I think it is because we share with the Americans this common sentiment: sincerity. The American public is, right from the start, sincere: it takes you on trust. If you disappoint it, it moves away and strikes you out of its personal geography. If, on the contrary, it meets with the same sincerity and the same trust, and if it receives some real nourishment or simply some propositions that excite its curiosity, then it adopts you and stays loyal to you. What has always attached me to the American public is that it is young in heart. Our last big tour there is quite recent, with *Rabelais*. Let us keep that for the end.

We took off from Orly one morning on board the Air France Super-Constellation called *Le Parisien Spécial*. We were bound for Mexico via New York. Our job was to open a new circuit: Mexico, Peru, Ecuador, Colombia, Venezuela. In the course of the journey I extended the adventure to take in the Caribbean. Return via Puerto Rico, on the good ship *Antilles*. (She would have made an ideal floating embassy. That was exactly the type of ship we would have needed.)

The whole thing went off well, though with its fill of vicissitudes – it was one of our best tours. To begin with, the interest in these human meetings lies in *exchange*: we receive as much as we give. Because I was aware of the exceptional character of this journey I decided that, at the risk of losing a little money, all my comrades should get the best out of it: I had arranged to give them, now and then, thirty-six hours' leave.

So let us set aside the success, the repertory, the lectures, discussions, official receptions, etc. All right, it was a successful tour: let us now concentrate chiefly on the adventure, though returning here and there to theatre matters.

Mexico

There are many points in common between the Mediterranean and the Caribbean basins.

The Mayas make one think of the Greeks, Assyrians and Persians. The Aztecs are their Romans. The Toltecs remind us of the Italian Renaissance. The Olmecs have the slit eyes of the Asiatics.

This impression is formed when one travels through Mexico. In the course of our three weeks in Mexico City at the Teatro Bellas Artes (which is steadily sinking into the lagoon) we were able to pay enchanting visits to the temples in the surrounding country.

For Teotihuacán I had a very special guide – Dolores del Rio. She also showed me round that extraordinary place Guadalupe Hidalgo, with its shrine of Our Lady of Guadalupe.

What I love in Mexico is the fusion that has been realized, so successfully, between Indian and Catholic elements. The result is a particularly vigorous, virile human type.

The architectural beauty of the temples still reflects the atmosphere of the high Indian civilization. The traces of human sacrifices are still there. At the same time, I have never felt the power of the Catholic faith so strongly as at Our Lady of Guadalupe.

Dolores del Rio possesses all that vigour and all that faith. She seemed to me beautiful, both physically and in the fire of her temperament.

Thanks to the protection we received from our ambassador George-Picot (whom we had already come to know in the Argentine), to the influence of our cultural attaché and to the kindness of the Mexican Government, a special aeroplane was lent to us at the end of our season, so that we might visit

Yucatán. At Mérida the sea is hot. We visited Chichén Itzá and Uxmal. There we were at heart of the Mayas. The peasants do not plough: they burn. Travelling over these fields devastated by fire is a striking experience: to us, whose eyes are used to the orderly stripes of the furrows across our lands, the impression made by that atmosphere of chaos and devastation is a strange one. But the ashes serve as manure. The rock is close to the surface, and plough-shares would make no impression. What we see there is not barbarousness, but a different method of agriculture. The Maya civilization was as canny as the Chaldean.

I recommend young married couples to take a honeymoon in Maya country (Chichén Itzá), provided they do not get stung by those small oval spiders, which send you *ad patres* in a few hours. We spent part of the night, in the moonlight, in the stadium of Chichén Itzá, listening to guitarists. It was almost as moving as Delphi.

Everything there is elegant, related to the scale of the human vertebral column. At Uxmal the abstract patterns from the Maya period make a magnificent contrast with the decorative coils of the Toltec serpents. In Yucatán, like an attentive and intimidated small child, I had the feeling of entering into contact with those ancestor-citizens of the world. I would gladly go back there.

During those two days of relaxation and recovery of ourselves, our band had dispersed, some to Acapulco, others to Palenque, and others on other excursions. We regrouped at Mexico City airport, each one bringing his catch. If one accepts that actors are carriers of humanity, they should from time to time be allowed to recharge their hearts and minds.

An orchestra of mariachis played us goodbye in the flowery garden of the airport, and then we took the 'milk plane'. This was the nickname given to the DC 7 which was taking us to Lima, because it stops everywhere: Guatemala, Salvador, Nicaragua, Costa Rica and Panama. You remain an hour at each stopping-place.

We were glued to our port-holes. So many beautiful visions in so short a time! It is hard to keep it all distinct. The Wonderers Club was quivering with excitement. At every stop I would have liked to go out into the country. When the doors of the aircraft opened, we received a blast of heat as though from a stove, and all sorts of strong and attractive scents pricked our noses. Huge green forests, lakes of every conceivable colour, the black smoke of the volcanoes.

It made us happy to set foot, if only for a moment, on the soil of those tiny countries with their – at least there and then – welcoming populations.

At Panama the aeroplane could not move on. Why? Because of the law. There has to be a spare part to match every part that is broken. The aeroplane had this. The broken part was therefore changed. But from that moment there was not a spare part, so the aeroplane could not take off. This meant two days of waiting at Panama.

We were taken by bus into the town, to the Hotel El Panama. If I were a novelist I would go and spend three months at that hotel. It functions for twenty-four hours in the twenty-four, welcoming travellers and doing duty as both gaming rooms and an ordinary hotel. It is the hell of humanity. In among the piles of suitcases and the harassed tourists there circulate women in long dresses and men in dinner jackets; breakfasts alongside whiskies.

One room for the men, one for the girls. The damp heat and the air-conditioning sent us shuttling between showers and rugs. As for sleep – a thing impossible, unthinkable, forgotten. Madeleine and I ended by finding a small room in which to get a little rest. At three in the morning the door opened and a folding bedstead was thrown against us. We drove the chambermaid out and tried to get to sleep again. At five in the morning the door burst open afresh and we jumped up wildly at the noise of an enormous vacuum cleaner. Several times there was an alarm and a rush : everyone bundled into the bus for the aerodrome. We arrived at the aircraft : false alarm – the spare part had not yet arrived. Back by bus to the hotel. Coffee with milk. Close to us, card-players were swigging champagne.

In the town the colour of the trees – flamboyants – was dazzling.

I made my way to the famous Canal. Sturdy Indians with their long black hair crowned with white straw boaters, were carrying their children on their backs. The ships glided by, almost touching the banks to port and starboard.

The consul collected us and improvised a pleasant reception. We would have had time to give a performance at Panama. I am sorry we did not.

Perhaps it was there, also, that I visited a marvellous cemetery? A vast garden in the English style, with flowering bushes. Small stones level with the turf discreetly indicated the graves, and from all sides there flowed, 'noiselessly', like a murmuring of souls, classical music. It was memorable.

At last we took off again. At Lima, where they had gone on ahead, Léonard and his technicians welcomed us.

Peru

When we left France, Peru had not been placed on the programme; apparently there was nothing there to justify the presence of the French theatre. Luckily a new French ambassador had just been appointed, M. Léon Brasseur, a young and dynamic man, a quick worker. He did the rounds of the several French industrialists who had prospective interests in Peru (roads and railways) and collected money, which enabled us to make a detour. He was certainly right : it would have been a glaring diplomatic error, to have us pass through Ecuador and not visit neighbouring Peru.

At first only one or two performances were contemplated. We stayed nine days there, playing in Lima not only at the theatre, a charming one, but also in the gardens of the Embassy. One evening in particular was worthy of the viceroy of Peru. The Embassy gardens contain a magnificent open-air theatre; the yew hedges are cut in such a way that they reproduce the plan of a theatre in the Italian style. We performed Molière's *Amphitryon* there. The trees were so thick that, at a height of seven metres I could stand on the greenery, with Mercury's caduceus in my hand and wings on my feet.

The ambassador had had an enormous dais built. He had invited the gentry of Peru, headed by the clergy. The festivity continued late into the night, with plenty of food and drink. We drank gaily with bishops; it was the great reconciliation of the Church and the Stage.

Peru is a glorious country. The road along the Pacific Ocean passes successively through broad desert regions and narrow luxuriant valleys. In these the verdure is intense and the farms flourishing. That is where the *estancias* are : vast domains in which a patriarchal system rules. At that period Peru seemed to me a bastion of aristocracy of Castille. An *estancia* was not a village but a family. Its master enjoyed absolute power. In his study he kept the military conduct books of all the men. The *estancia* also had its prison. But in the evening masters and servants danced and played the guitar together. That, at least, is what we saw in the course of a party.

Maiène was the most excited of all our 'wonderers'. She gave cries of delight at each rock covered with guano, at each turn of the road, at each garden vista.

'Oh, what's that strange animal?' she cried at one point.

'But, mademoiselle, it's a donkey !'

Wonder too has its mirages !

As in Mexico, I had set aside for the company a holiday, forty-eight hours this time, to let each of them do a little exploring. It was filled by an expedition to Macchu Picchu, via Cuzco. Madeleine, who was not feeling very well and was conserving her energy for the tyrannical role of Célimène, once again sacrificed herself and remained at Lima.

The light aircraft there are equipped with four engines to get across the high mountain ranges. Because of the height (over eight thousand metres) we breathed oxygen through tubes. In spite of my claustrophobia I felt no apprehension : curiosity was stronger.

We landed at Cuzco on an airstrip of red earth, at an altitude of nearly four thousand metres. There we saw our first llamas. The city of Cuzco is splendid : half Inca, half Spanish of the great period. From there a small train winds its way across mountain country, descending slightly. Then a lorry of sorts took us climbing again, to the famous ruins. All along our route I was struck by the work of the Incas : immense terraces on the heights of Macchu Picchu (I kept remembering Pablo Neruda's magnificent poem); an assemblage of enormous cyclopean stones, above lianas and orchids, on the flank of the Andes; unbelievable blocks cut in such a way that they can hold together without any cement and stand up to severe earthquakes. You can feel the presence of giants. As for the forms, Picasso could not have done better.

As we returned down a rocky path, we heard the cheerful singing of Indians. Then we met them; it was a burial. They were carrying the corpse on a stretcher. I can still see the feet of the dead man tossing about in time with the steps of the bearers regulated by the songs. A kind of metaphysical gaiety flowed in the air.

Forced landing at Talara

Once again Léonard and his men had preceded us and left for Quito. As we left Peru we had the great pleasure of learning that Molière, Claudel, Anouilh and Marivaux – and to some extent their interpreters – had served the industrialists who had helped us to go there: the orders for roads and a railway were, it seems, confirmed.

Lima is often covered by a low bank of fog. The aeroplane takes off in pea soup, but five minutes later the sky is pure and the heights of the Andes stand out in strong light, like the white fangs of a dog.

To give us pleasure the pilot of the Panagra DC 7 made it execute a dance between the peaks. The spectacle was overwhelming. In the sky, every shade of blue and green, from sapphire to pale green. Down below, the emerald green of the lakes at the bottom of the ravines contrasted with the crude greens of the forests and the dazzling rainbows of the glaciers. It was so fine that it seemed to me tempting Providence. We must not engage in rivalry with the Gods.

I had just asked the pilot to take us out of this insensate splendour when the aircraft received a powerful shock. One of the engines had just packed up. The aircraft, no longer able to hold its height, began slipping downwards. Insinuating ourselves into the valleys, we managed to emerge from those jaws of rocks and ice, evading the fangs of that enormous beast. The narrow strip of cultivated land came in sight; there in the distance were the fringes of the ocean. Dark streaks, the pipe-lines, guided us to an industrial settlement called Talara. A fairly large airport. The landing went off well.

So there we were, delayed at Talara, on the south shore of the Gulf of Guayaquil. Guayaquil itself was to the north, on the opposite shore. Torrid heat. We were due to open at Quito that very evening, with Le Misanthrope. It looked as if the performance was seriously threatened: catastrophe! We got into touch by radio. Quito replied:

'We are sending you a DC 3.'

During this time the mechanic of our big aircraft was trying to repair it. On the burning sunlit surface of the airport he had taken his engine entirely to pieces and reminded me of Charlie Chaplin performing his autopsy on an alarm clock. We stood round him, idly watching, and from time to time he would say to us in French:

'C'est le vie!'

Honi soit ...

Other members of the company had gone to refresh themselves in the swimming-pool. Suddenly it occurred to us that the doors of a DC 3 are not the same size as those of a DC 7. The greater part of our stuff had been put into the DC 7 and could not be got into the other aircraft. I decided therefore to unpack the cases. And there we were, on the ground, side by side with the mechanic, unpacking. Louis XIV costumes, sticks, wigs, red-heeled shoes, etc. We despatched the empty cases via Panama to Caracas, where we would recover them, and got ready to load the DC 3 like a hay-waggon.

At the beginning of the afternoon it descended towards us, glittering in the sunshine. We shoved everything into it higgledy-piggledy, piled ourselves in as best we could and took off again.

Talara, sea level. Quito, three thousand metres up. We had to cross passes that are four thousand five hundred metres high.

The aircraft roared with painful effort. To right and left the mountains rose. The sky was black with smoke – volcanoes on all sides. The top of the pass was scarcely sixty metres below the cabin. Would the aircraft make it? We practically crawled over the saddle. The aircraft was dragging its mass along like an ox. At last we could make out, on the horizon in front of us, horizontal bands of light – yellow, rose pink, green. It was magnificent. We completely forgot the danger. A fresh mountain range was there in profile, going down gradually towards Quito.

We landed there at 18.00. The performance was at 20.00. We could almost have dressed in the plane and walked down on to the airfield in Louis XIV costume, like extraordinary parrots.

On the dot our 'brigadier' struck the three blows, under the protection of Molière.

To go from sea level to an altitude of three thousand metres is pretty stupefying. I confess I had painful buzzings in my ears as I acted Alceste. Léonard was not at all pleased: the Wonderers' Club had cut things a bit too fine.

Quito

The theatre in Quito, on the big market square, is a ravishing building, the work of a French architect at the beginning of the nineteenth century. (Forgive me if I am wrong.) It was not much used for acting – our first night was the eleventh performance that season. On the other days it was used for stabling cattle. We had had to move the hay to one side before putting up our *Grand Siècle* setting.

I noticed the woman custodian squatting at the entrance to the theatre with her little girl in her lap, as she combed out the child's hair and squashed the lice. It reminded me of my childhood at Tournus when my mother used to do the same for me.

While in one way Quito breathed an atmosphere of the Middle Ages, the *maison de la culture*, by contrast, brought together eight hundred persons who were absolutely up-to-date about everything.

'Why haven't you brought Vauthier's *Le Personnage combattant*?'

The *avant-garde* was what they were keen on, not the classics. A lecture I gave to them the next day was followed by a fascinating discussion. These few hundred people were at the leading edge of modern thinking.

It has to be admitted that we came across nothing to follow that up. When we did a matinée for the schools, all the children were dressed in black and we were greeted with inextinguishable laughter: the Louis XIV marquesses with their *tonnelets* and their curled wigs seemed to them to have come from another planet.

On Friday evenings alcohol was distributed to the Indians, who drank themselves silly on the pavements. Has this sad custom, which seemed designed systematically to destroy a race, disappeared by now? I hope so.

Some of us, during an excursion in the high mountains, became acquainted with the mysterious 'Andes sickness'. It consists in being overcome by irresistible hilarity. A kind of giddiness which can prove fatal.

A bit further north there is a mark at the place through which the Equator passes. Villages with astonishing markets. I felt as if I had reached the far end of the planet – if, that is, a globe can have an end.

Bogotá

Colombia, where we landed a few days later, is much more 'Parisian'.

The valleys near Cali, with their long trails of clouds, are singularly beautiful. Sometimes, when the spine of the aircraft is gliding along the ceiling formed by the clouds, it feels as if one were a fish, swimming just under the surface of the water. Down below, in the half light, the villages, forests, water courses and tracks look like scenes on the bottom of the sea.

At Bogotá our audience was an easy matter. The great majority of the audience spoke French. Colombians seem to me to have a temperament very close to ours. Gay and irreverent, they love the humour that rises from wit. They too know how to be frivolous because they are quick. They seem completely Latin. We were on the same wavelength straight away, and the performances were continued late into the night by delightful parties from which gallantry was not excluded. Our comrades must surely have nostalgic memories of their stay.

Visit to the salt cathedral. You go there in cars. These plunge, one after another, into immense tunnels lit only by the headlights. A long labyrinth. No chance of turning back or reversing. Suppose one of them went wrong? It is oppressive. After driving for a quarter of an hour in that night, you come out into a vast nave: this is the salt cathedral. For all those rocks are simply salt. I brought back a piece. We visited the church in detail, then got back into the cars and, ten minutes later, saw the sky again.

Often in life we experience a double pleasure: that of having seen something exceptional, and that of realizing that the ordeal is over. Double pleasure of landing: having been Icarus and being back on earth. Double joy of an effort accomplished.

It was just outside Bogotá that I observed how perfectly certain modern houses, entirely of glass, fit in with nature. The trees grow in the midst of rooms. You no longer know whether you are sleeping at home or in the woods. It is very attractive, even though I personally feel I could not live there. I am much too fond of stone houses and small windows: they take me back to the 'little huts' of my childhood and to my peasant ancestry. Glass is an isolator. When surrounded by panes of glass, it seems to me I am losing contact with things. The paradox of transparency and enclosure: through glass you see everything, but no longer feel anything. Through stone you see nothing but feel things.

Besides, does not the East teach us that *prana* – that energy which exists in air, and which appropriate systems of breathing enable us to keep, even when we breathe out – passes through stone. It is a force which also goes through the body.

Venezuela

The aircraft taking us from Bogotá to Caracas flew over the Maracaibo oilwells. Those diminutive Eiffel Towers emerging direct from the sea, and each with its plume of dancing flame, were our first acquaintance with Venezuela. This country has in fact a special position: its industrial interest has marked it with the seal of Wall Street. People tend to pass only a few years there, long enough to make their fortune. And yet there are still traces of ancient civilization: I brought back a primitive statuette.

From the airport, which is by the sea, the road climbs a cliff, and passes through a kind of natural gateway. On the plateau the city of Caracas comes in sight; in it the old small houses are being more and more crushed by modern developments.

Whereas in Bogotá human 'exchanges' flowed naturally, here it was necessary to expend seduction in order to win over the business people. Once again the women gave us valuable help.

We made friends at once with a highly cultivated élite who took us to their hearts. I found once more my old Cuban friend Alejo Carpentier, who had helped me over the music for *Numance*. It was years since I had seen him. He was in charge of programmes on the radio service. He later became Fidel Castro's Minister for Cultural Affairs.

We lodged in an awe-inspiring modern hotel which 'sweated' Beethoven, Mozart and Bach from every corner of its buildings – the corridors, the dining-room, the lift, the swimming-pool and even the lavatories. Silence no longer existed, it had been suppressed by modern life.

This was not far from torture.

As regards the theatre, there was a battle to be fought. While in all the other places the performances had been sold out in advance, here on the evening of the first night the takings did not amount to half the house.

The battle was won, but we had had a narrow escape. Tours at such a distance from home are run on a very narrow enonomic margin, and although the French Government did as much as it could to help us we were still financially responsible. In the case of this journey only, we had not been stingy about the expenses and I had taken risks. The cost of air travel at that time was inordinate. We could therefore not afford any setback.

We were regaled with sublime festivities at swimming-pools perched on mountain tops. And the Minister of the Interior made us a fine present: he provided us with a military aircraft for a strange expedition. Once again I had reserved a tourist holiday for my comrades: I set the company free for three days. Some of them left for Trinidad, others explored the neighbouring country. We, with a few fanatics of wonder, chose adventure. The aircraft was a DC 3 : there were two devil-may-care pilots, a sexy air hostess, whisky, guitars and an enormous wreath of gladioli, whose purpose, at first, I could not see.

Objective – Canaïma. An encampment deep in virgin forest, on the banks of the river Caroni, a tributary of the Orinoco, in the south part of Venezuela, near the frontier of British Guiana. The purpose of the journey : to see the Angel Falls. The tallest waterfall in the world : a single jet falling nine hundred metres.

We took off in the morning, and stopped on the way at Ciudad Bolivar, on the banks of the Orinoco. We were received by the notables, and a lunch was put on in the Town Hall. Nearby, there was a small market. The Indians come there and sell nuggets of gold which they have found in the countryside. I bought two or three : genuine crude ingots. After the meal we were shown a small number of those famous fishes, the piranas, which devour an ox in a few minutes. Someone threw a leg of an animal in. A minute later the bone was completely clean. Conclusive experiment.

We took off again, and flew over mountains that were both black and silvery. These are enormous hills containing 95 per cent iron ore. Then the tropical forest thickened. We skimmed above the foliage.

'What would happen if we fell?'

'Half an hour later there'd be nothing left : the debris of the aircraft would have been covered up and we would have been eaten.'

Clouds were building up above us. Among them, gradually, we began to make out cloud masses that looked rather more solid. These were rocks, cliffs. We climbed. The aircraft began dancing. It passed through impressive black, white and pink agglomerations, pierced by sunrays like swords. It was Dantesque. The climb went on, and suddenly, almost above us, we could see a nugget of aluminium, crumpled and glittering in the sunshine. From that small silvery leaf the waterfall seemed to take its source and plunge into the abyss. It fell long and slender, in an airy halo of mist. The angel's leap ! The little metallic mass was in fact the remains of a small aircraft which had crashed there. We in turn plunged down among the clouds and rocks.

For what seemed decidedly too long a time, our aircraft made its way through those masses of water vapour. When one can see nothing, one falls silent. Silence took possession of the interior of the aircraft. A mixture of dread and hope. Then the forest reappeared below us, with lakes and other waterfalls. The water was as dark as Coca-Cola. The aeroplane began circling. It was looking for the landing strip. This was simply a long corridor between the trees, and we landed at last in untrimmed grass.

In spite of everything, the sun was still there. The two men in charge of the camp welcomed us : a Lithuanian and a young German as handsome as Siegfried. Possibly former Nazis, who had been condemned to death and had taken refuge in these primitive recesses? The virgin forest was all around us, with orchids sprouting from tree trunks. I felt as if I had gone back to the time when man did not yet exist.

The wreath of gladioli was carried out of the aeroplane by one of the pilots. Instinctively we followed and arrived at a small hillock of earth with a Catholic cross on top. The gladioli were for the pilot who had been killed on an earlier journey.

Canaïma is simply a hut, with a shed beside it containing camp beds. In the open, not far away, a few hammocks were suspended from the trees. We were allotted our beds: Madeleine and I a hammock each, next to that of the Lithuanian who would keep watch over us. Our other comrades would sleep in the shed. For each person, just a sheet.

There was a kind of pebble terrace. From it, on a gentle slope, the coconut trees went down to the black water of the lake and bathed their feet in it. What was that, flush with the surface of the water? The backs of turtles. Some way off, three waterfalls, spread out over the width of at least a kilometre and at least a hundred metres high.

The air was very damp, and every now and then the pilots had to go and set their engines running.

There were streams everywhere, running beneath virgin forest. We went over in boats to the other side of the lake. Then we plunged into a thicket, almost crawling under the branches. I kept close to my guide. We slid forward between the lianas. He said to me :

'You put your feet where I put mine.'

'Why? Because of snakes?'

'They're not all that fond of the ground . . . more likely hanging in the trees.'

From that time on, I had one eye looking up and the other looking down. We managed to climb to the top of the falls. From there one saw still higher cliffs rising into the sky and, at a distance, the Angel's Leap falling majestically. Its beauty was beyond belief.

That evening was spent drinking, playing the guitar and singing. I think one of the girls of our company was much moved by the blond Siegfried.

During the night the noise of the forest prevented me from sleeping. Courageous, but not foolhardy. Howls of tiger-cats. It was lucky we had no horses or cattle with us – they would have been eaten. Only man frightens those animals. They are not mistaken.

Next morning, after washing at the edge of the lake (I cleaned my teeth by sucking at the water as cows drink), another excursion by air.

Pierre Bertin had had enough and would stay at the camp. The rest of us had become numbed. The aeroplane took off for a flight of twenty minutes through that chaos of rocks, forest, clouds and waterfalls. We came down and landed in the middle of a kind of meadow. The camp is called Cabanaïen. It was set up by Franciscans and Poor Clares. A few of each of these along with a 'colony of Indian brethren'. Warned by radio of our coming, they had prepared a magnificent meal of delicious fruit – and no doubt other things, but all I remember is the taste of the fruit.

They had a jeep, and by using the waterfalls they had managed to be lit by neon lighting.

I asked one of the fathers:

'If the aircraft couldn't leave, would we be able to get back to our camp?'

'With the jeep it would take at least eight days.'

Luckily the return journey went off well. I brought back a small church of terracotta modelled by the Indians. That evening, as we sat by the camp fire enjoying the whisky and the songs accompanied by the guitar, and hearing the distant cries of the tiger-cats, a cacique came to visit us. He refused to guide our boats under the boughs of the trees, because a huge monkey of the orang-utang type was prowling in the neighbourhood with his family. We did not insist.

That night Gabriel Cattand was half emptied by a vampire bat. Luckily vampire bats are clumsy drinkers. Their first bite anaesthetizes part of the leg, but because the blood flows as far as the buttocks, the sleeper is woken by the dampness of his bedding. When he wakes up the vampire bat has disappeared.

Guadeloupe and Martinique

Since administratively these big tours came under Foreign Affairs, the original plan was that we should stop at Guadeloupe and Martinique without giving performances there: these two islands, being French *départments*, are under the Ministry of the Interior(!).

I had ventured to draw attention to the absurdity of this situation, but had run up against administrative routine. I had therefore gone to see President Monnerville, a native of the islands. He had at once telephoned to the appropriate person, and the reply I received was:

'Dans ce cas-là, adressez-vous à l'Odéon.'

'... ? ...'

'Yes, to M. Lodéon, senator of Guadeloupe.' (Or of Martinique, I forget which.)

And so we had managed to organize a visit to Pointe-à-Pitre, Basse-Terre and Fort-de-France.

In addition, as soon as we reached Mexico, I had met the ambassador of Haiti there. A lecture at Port-au-Prince had been fixed. Then at Lima, then at Quito and Caracas, going from one Haitian ambassador to another, we had improvised a regular tour. I confess I was insatiable.

So there we were, leaving for the Caribbean, after recovering those of our comrades who had gone off to dance with the pretty girls of Trinidad.

And now we made acquaintance with the voluptuous charm of those islands. The quick sensuality of the beguines. Those tongue and lip songs. Words from which the 'r's have been removed, no doubt because they scratch one's thoughts.

We lived in bungalows in a sublime place – 'Le Gosier', a kind of hostelry kept by a new friend called Mario.

The two staples of Guadeloupe are sugar cane and bananas. The mongooses have eaten the serpents. The only place where Adam and Eve were in no danger.

At Basse-Terre, where we went to give a performance, I danced in the evening with coloured girls. The notables looked at me askance. I did it on purpose – racism disgusts me.

I made a pilgrimage to the tomb of Christopher Columbus – one of the two, three or four places where his bones are said to be buried.

Those few days of enchantment came to an end, and we loaded our stuff on to a small ship called *L'Ile d'Emeraude*. (The boat and its captain – his pipe rivalling her funnel – came directly out of a Walt Disney cartoon.) An aircraft carried the human material to Fort-de-France. We were to act in the Municipal theatre, which is part of the buildings of the Town Hall: a charming theatre seating seven hundred, entirely of wood, and worthy to be Deburau's theatre.

While waiting for the arrival of the *Ile d'Emeraude*, we explored the region. On the main square there is a statue of Joséphine de Beauharnais. Having sometimes interpreted the character of Bonaparte for Sacha Guitry, I addressed a special thought to her. If one may judge from the sex appeal of the Creole girls, she must have been a very captivating person.

We danced with the black girls to the rhythm of the steel band. Still no sight of the *Ile d'Emeraude*. The day of the first performance arrived. Still nothing on the horizon. I now spent my time on the quays of the small harbour. An old tub was moored there, ready to cast off and leave the berth for our ship when she arrived – but when? The old tub was a circus. There was an elephant tied to the main mast. The elephant's great ears flapped like sails in search of a breeze.

Four o'clock in the afternoon. The performance at nine. The thing was becoming tragic. In the distance, a small black dot, a small cloud of smoke. There could be no doubt, it was Captain Popeye's pipe.

'Come on, elephant, get a move on, leave the berth to us!'

Someone came to tell me that the audience was already queueing in front of the theatre. She made fast and was unloaded. During this, the house had filled. There was only one thing left to be done: bring up the curtain and allow the audience to watch the set being put up – of *Les Fausses Confidences*.

The choice of play was inevitable; here, as in Guadeloupe, we are brought right back into the French eighteenth century. The people talk the language of Marivaux. As in *Les Enfants du Paradis*, clusters of spectators hung from the balconies.

Next day we performed *Le Misanthrope*.

The firemen of Fort-de-France. During the performance the heat was torrid. everyone was wilting. We could feel the sweat flowing like springs under our costumes. The windows backstage gave on the courtyard of the Town Hall. In between two scenes the Marquesses Acaste and Clitandre went there to get some fresh air. The two firemen, two superb blacks, were also there, to enjoy the cool for a bit. One of them pointed to the two Marquesses (J.-P. Granval and G. Cattand) and said to his mate:

'See? Those young men – their costume belongs to the youth of Louis XIV, but their wigs are Louis XIII.'

It was true: they had Louis XIV *tonnelets*, while their wigs, with partings at the side, were Louis XIII. Paris firemen, please take note !

Pierre Macaigne, who was writing a piece on our tour for *Le Figaro*, was on his way back by car from the north of the island. The driver had switched on the radio, which was relaying *Le Misanthrope* live. As he went through the villages he passed their inhabitants out in the street, all gathered round loud-speakers. They were listening to the broadcast of *Le Misanthrope*. The whole island was echoing with the words of Molière. By this means Macaigne knew that he must hurry if he wanted to record the end of the performance.

We were becoming aware of the eternal France. It made us, at one and the same time, proud and ashamed. Proud of our past, ashamed of the little that is done about it nowadays – and yet 'one does what one can'. But seeing the importance which men attach to our civilization all over the world, it is permissible to think that more might be done.

On a path I came across an old woman. She was a poor peasant, perhaps a beggar. Her black face was a network of wrinkles. By her side, some fruit and, in a bit of newspaper, some fish. Flies buzzed around her. She said to me – and this is word for word:

'*Serait-ce un effet de votre bonté de m'offrir une cigarette?*' [1]

I gave her several. She thanked me and addded:

'*Je vois, vous êtes de la métropole, je vous souhaite un prompt retour et de retrouver vos parents en bonne santé. Je vais fumer une cigarette après mon petit repas, et ce soir, quand je serai couchée, je bourrerai les autres dans ma pipe, car, voyez-vous, maintenant je suis vieille, et quand le sommeil a quitté mes yeux, j'aime m'envelopper dans la fumée.*' [2]

To think that such distinction of spirit came down to her from the time of slavery.

Haiti

The government of Haiti had had a DC 3 sent to fetch us, but the director of the airport of Fort-de-France forbade us to take off: the aircraft was too heavily loaded.

'Have you another aircraft?'

'Yes, another DC 3. We can get it ready for you tomorrow morning. At what time?'

[1] 'Would it be an effect of your kindness to offer me a cigarette?'
[2] 'I see you are from the metropolis I wish you a prompt return and to find your relatives in good health. I shall smoke one cigarette after my little meal, and this evening, when I have gone to bed, I shall stuff the others into my pipe, for, you see, now I am old, and when sleep has left my eyes, I like to envelop myself in the smoke.'

'Not too early. I will leave the company behind and we will go on with the technicians. Let us not tire the actors.'

'I advise you, all the same, against leaving too late. Cyclones get up in the afternoon.'

'You decide the time. How much is it?'

'800,000 francs.'

'All right, 800,000 francs.'

A real millionaire's life! No wonder we brought home no profit. But the two feelings uppermost in me then were of a different order : to do good service to my country's spiritual reputation, and to collect 'memories for always'.

And so I left with the baggage and the technical staff, under Léonard's command. Madeleine would leave next day with the company.

In Haiti, which has been liberated from France since 1804, they have remained so French that the Haitians say 'clûbe' instead of 'club'. Our stay there was this journey's apotheosis. As I have already said, we had to repeat the Claudel performance. We were living in a ravishing hotel. As we bathed in the swimming-pool, we could drink water used by Real Hollywood Stars! – at least in imagination. At night we danced the cha-cha-cha – or went to Voodoo séances – or shuddered at the sight of cock-fights.

And yet, at the market, some blacks jostled us, with evident hatred. When we spoke to them in French, they grew gentler but remained mistrustful.

On the day after our last performance, we had taken an aeroplane to Port-Haitien, so as to go from there on horseback to the citadel of King Christophe. This was a happy excursion. The whole company in single file on small mountain horses which needed no attention. Magnificent scenery, huts like the ones in the engravings and high up, among the old cannons and cannon-balls, King Christophe's lair.

On our return, there was our last party. Our host was handsome like an ebony statue: a god. He had the support of a Canadian Cardinal, for the church in America had sent to this island a French-speaking ecclesiastic. In that drawing-room three centuries of French history stood side by side. The Canadian Cardinal spoke like a seventeenth-century nobleman. The Haitian grandee spoke pure eighteenth-century French. As for us, we tried to manage in the best possible modern French. It was a joust of imperfect subjunctives. All the resources of grammar went into it.

In his speech our host thanked us for having paid a visit to 'what *our* great Giraudoux called *la France imaginaire* . . .' I think France ought to offer a double passport to the men of all those so-called foreign countries that have opted for our language, whether it be their national language or the first language of their choice. To think in the same language is surely to share the same sensibility. Is it not to have the same turn of mind? Is it not to communicate with life under the impetus of the same soul? 'The most intimate genius of each people, its deep-seated soul, is above all in its language,' said Michelet. That surely is worth a few customs concessions.

For our return journey to France we were to embark on the *Antilles* at San Juan, Puerto Rico. Madeleine and I tried to blaze a trail there by giving a recital. Not many people came. Excepting a few persons, the bulk of the population seemed to us hardly 'concerned'. I can still see those close-packed groups of rather poor-looking wooden houses, built on piles in the water, their roofs bristling with television aerials. Leaving aside the Puerto Rican flag, we were in a mere United States colony. I have never really understood the 'colonizing' spirit, and this includes 'economic colonization'.

While the boat was taking us back to Marseilles, I was becoming aware that I had never felt so strongly that I am a citizen of the world and, at the same time, French. 'French, as one is universal' – that motto again. These journeys were giving me a new native land – the Earth; and at the same time each country I travelled through sent back to me the image of my country of origin. A magnified image. I realized how much French civilization is an international property of which the French are the managers, and therefore responsible for it. Never have I met with a look of envy in the people we visited – they seemed, on the contrary, glad to find that that 'common wealth' was being reasonably well looked after. (I exclude, of course, certain instances of conduct under the remote control of political slogans.)

I had learned that, in the world, people learn French chiefly to understand Descartes, the Encyclopaedists, and poets and the French Revolution. This last will always remain the symbol of liberty and of the emancipation of human beings. Yes, the world was making me more and more French and a citizen of the planet. It had enlarged my breathing. And so, as we reached Marseilles, my heart was caught in a vice : I was returning to the family, a family that is of my blood, but ... a family all the same.

Having still not found a theatre in Paris, we had to set off again for a year, on the roads, on the seas, in the air, across the world. We visited Europe, we paid our second visit to America. I can still see us in Canada in January 1957 in 40 degrees below zero Centigrade, and at Beirut that July in 60 above.

In New York Mr Dag Hammarskjöld did us a great honour. He had chosen us to bring the theatre into the United Nations. He asked us to act in the great hall of the Assembly. And he chose *Le Misanthrope*. We had placed the bust of Molière on the Speaker's platform. We had set our action among fine Louis XIV tapestries. And we performed around our master as though he himself were speaking. It was a fine sensation to hear Molière advancing this sentiment at the UN :

> *Je ne trouve, partout, que lâche flatterie*
> *Injustice, intérêt, trahison, fourberie,*
> *Je n'y puis plus tenir . . .*[1]

Hammarskjöld was jubilant. He had lent us his office for use as our dressing-rooms.

[1] 'I find nothing anywhere, but base Flattery, but Injustice, Interest, Treachery and Knavery; I can hold no longer . . ." (*The Works of Molière*, London, 1739, vol. iv).

The theatre's role is that of the Fool in relation to his King. By the liberties allowed to the Fool one can tell the strength of the King. If the King is afraid, the Fool is muzzled. In our day and age the king is humanity. Let humanity therefore allow complete freedom of expression to the theatre – it would be a sign that humanity deserves to reign.

We went on working at Georges Schéhadé's *Histoire de Vasco*, which was first performed at Zurich, then at Lyons, and then given at the Baalbek Festival. I was also preparing an adaptation of Kafka's *The Castle*.

As for our tours in Europe, these went on and on, and leaving out the years I can sum them up as follows:

Italy: 14 cities.

Germany: at least a dozen cities, and more than once.

Poland: between Poland and ourselves there are special affinities. Our two countries are not just two peoples, but two nations: because of their uncomfortable geographical situation they have experienced, in the course of their history, some rather burdensome neighbours. Courage, faith, intelligence and the spirit of resistance have forged their character. They recognize each other by this – it creates bonds. Poland was only just emerging from its horrible sufferings, and the time we spent in Warsaw, Poznan, Wroclaw, Katowice, Cracow, was overwhelming. It was in Poland, in 1958, that we heard of General de Gaulle's return to power.

We visited also Rumania, with its Latin quality; Czechoslovakia, with its intellectual vitality; Austria; and of course Holland, Belgium, and Switzerland as if it were France. I am keeping Greece and Yugoslavia for later, as well as England, which we visited six or seven times. It would take too many pages to report the details of each encounter, each exchange. Memories that do not die.

In October 1957 we at last settled again in Paris. This was to be for two seasons – but our tours were not broken off. And indeed, for us, it came to the same thing: the circuit of our tours went through Paris, that was all.

THÉÂTRE SARAH-BERNHARDT

A.-M. Julien welcomed us for a few months to the Théâtre Sarah-Bernhardt. The success which *Histoire de Vasco* had had at Lyons, in Switzerland and in the Lebanon made us decide to open our season with that fine play of Schéhadé's. This provided us with the opportunity, after more than a year's absence, to meet our 'dear' critics once more.

If at present Schéhadé hardly writes any more, if in any case he avoids having his work put on in France, French criticism bears the entire responsibility. I have never understood its severity against that man, who writes French as agreeably as Supervielle. The thing turned into xenophobia – a particularly vicious xenophobia.[1]

For me, as I have said, every man on earth who receives life, observes life, recreates life by thinking in French is of my blood. The colour of his passport

[1] Georges Schéhadé is Lebanese. (*Translator's note.*)

has little importance. Schéhadé is a real poet. There is nothing mawkish about him. He may not roar, but he stings with an insect's virulence. He may remain courteous in his rebellions, they are rebellions nonetheless.

But vulgar minds recognize only roarings and facile crudity. Politics also came in. We had a rough response, the public was influenced. Paris stayed away form Vasco, when other countries had appreciated it so much.

We then created Le Château. The Kafka purists were up in arms. There were more and more purists, including the ones who had discovered Kafka by going to see Le Procès. I think, all the same, that our stage version of Le Château (made in collaboration with Pol Quentin) came closer to Kafka's ambiguous world. It was, nonetheless, only a half-success.

The Sarah-Bernhardt is a heavy theatre, we were losing a great deal of money. Were we going to be able to continue? Our ship was leaking badly.

In such cases, one tries caulking. Our thoughts turned to a masterpiece of popular theatre. We had already put on Le Bossu, and that exercise in style, which had enabled us to work at melodrama, had succeeded well. Victorien Sardou's Madame Sans-Gêne is even more expertly contrived than Le Bossu. To direct it, we thought of Pierre Dux. He consented. The part of Sans-Gêne could be presented in a new light by Madeleine – Amélie, as Napoleon's mistress! It was a triumph.

Once again our ship could sail on a calmer sea. A bad moment was over.

I had the chance, at that time, to make certain observations. Camus had won the Nobel Prize. 'A good choice!' Sartre had said – and the two of them were quarrelling just then. Everyone was delighted at Camus receiving that high reward. There was a gigantic reception at the Swedish Embassy. We were invited. During the evening I amused myself by going around among the intelligentsia of Paris. The fifteen hundred most highly perfected, most refined, most aware persons, those that guide the thought of tomorrow, those that take upon them the progress of mankind.

None of them had been to either Vasco or Le Château. They had all rushed to see Madame Sans-Gêne.

Madeleine, Dux and our comrades had saved the company. A.-M. Julien having projects of his own, we set out again across the world.

ROUND THE WORLD

The French Government had asked us to take a new route. These were its stages: Paris – Hamburg – Anchorage – Tokyo – Osaka – Western Japan (Nagasaki region) – Hong Kong – Saigon – Bangkok – New Delhi – Tel Aviv – Jerusalem – Haifa – Athens – Belgrade – Zagreb – Sarajevo – Ljubljana – Venice – Paris.

Time: about three months. In short, round the world in eighty days.

Anchorage
We left on 16 April 1960. Nothing but fresh countries to be added to our bag. We were to pass from the Zen and Shinto temples to the Synagogue and the

Holy Sepulchre, from Byzantium to the Delphic Apollo, from Apollo to Karl Marx. It was a tour of gods!

Our eyes, gazing at the streets and the shops, would light upon Japanese ideograms, Turkish, Hebrew, Greek and Cyrillic characters, spiced with a number of variants – we would be travelling no longer among writing but among drawing.

As early as February our decors had gone ahead by ship. The two doves taking part in Claudel's *Christophe Colomb* were also sent ahead and were to be kept under observation by a vet for three weeks.

We had two programmes. The second would take us through the Middle East.

The aircraft, a super-liner, was to be our last one with propellers. I still have a certain tenderness towards these 'piston machines', especially the long distance ones. They had the feel of adventure.

It was Good Friday, and we took off for a thirty-six hours' journey. As far as Hamburg, our first stop, one's magnetic waves are still in contact with Paris, with the noises and the voices that we love, our small house and the sad ears of my poodle, whom this time we had had to leave behind: the thread binding us to France stretches but is not broken.

After Hamburg (it was midnight when we left, and this lap would be seventeen hours), the adventure really was beginning. The machine moved slowly towards the Pole. Day, night and the sun would now play hide-and-seek. In the course of this we would lose a day of our lives, jumping straight from Friday to Sunday.

Flying over the ice-cap, I felt a new form of fear. The earth is no more than a skull, an old dirty grey skull. It is the nothing, the perfect image of death. The same depressing grain, the same shade of grey that the old skulls in our cemeteries, with their configurations and networks of narrow crevasses, offer to our eyes. Even more fragile-looking, a surface of plaster tarnished by dust.

> Skull, old skull,
> Their oil's too foul to feed your flame
> Then night all round, then sell you for a song
> Ding dong dell, Ding dong dell
> Then night all round, so what the hell
> Ding dong dell, Ding dong dong   (Laforgue)

Suddenly a sickly dawn-grey cast its pallor over the sleeping faces. Ahead of us a parchment-like sun tried and failed to become wholly visible.

We were served with a *petit déjeuner*. Night returned. Champagne was brought round. Three hours went by, and now we were lit from behind: a new dark yellow sun seemed attached to our aircraft like a copper saucepan to a cat's tail. We were brought a tray of food wrapped in cellophane. Day, a stillborn child, disappeared. Another glass of champagne. Was it Saturday or Sunday?

Disorder had seized hold of time. Ambiguity of life and death.

On our left now, the sun reappeared – a feeble gleam, one could not call it day, filled the aircraft for a while. It earned us another *petit déjeuner*.

What was becoming of that polar ice-cap? Oh ! mountains, high mountains of pink snow. It was Alaska. We had passed to the other side. The sun was still weak, but this time it looked really young. The air was limpid. Rose-pink, blue, pale green. We were passing close by the McKinley massif – six thousand three hundred metres high. And look ! Vegetation. Woods.

We landed at Anchorage on a cold, luminous, sunny morning. An admirable situation, crystalline light, mountain ranges that made you long to go there: you hunt bears and catch enormous fish. The temperature was relatively mild. Anchorage breathed liberty, exploration, adventure. It would have been lovely to stay there for some time, but the stop was over and we took off for Tokyo: this time a thirteen hours' flight.

It was Easter Sunday. Jesus was risen and the Buddha was expecting us. I brought out my surprise and offered the company, the other passengers and the crew chocolate eggs. To our right the Bering Straits, and beyond them the pack ice which the spring was riddling with cracks. Dinner is served.

And now we were above the Pacific. Land – Japan – came in sight. The journey was almost over – a few hours to go. The captain kindly invited me into his cabin.

Japan, whose name had been echoing in me like a dream, was there at last in all its reality, and with it, the whole weight of our tour. We were to give performances in fourteen towns in barely three months. Fourteen times we would have to pull ourselves together, open our eyes, prick up our ears, establish a favourable contact from the first moment of our arrival. Fourteen times we would have to throw off the fatigue with which the preceding town would have burdened us, and to find a virginity, a freshness, an entirely new enthusiasm which we must offer to the new town. Fourteen times our technicians would have to pack and again unpack the fourteen tons of material necessary to us. We were taking everything with us, down to the last little spoon. Nothing must be lost – not a cup, pair of stockings, glove, ring, portrait. The whole of that weight which was in store for us, ahead there, now fell on my neck.

In the cabin, suddenly, the deluge: water from all directions. General laughter from the crew, astonishment on my part.

'It's always like this,' the captain told me. 'The plane is unfreezing. As we descend, the ice melts. See that smoke in the distance? It's Tokyo.'

Junks could be seen. On the surface of the sea the fields of seaweed, with their hatched surfaces, offered to our view the first Japanese prints.

Japan

Ever since the day when I dedicated myself to the stage, I have been attracted by the Japanese school. Those dynasties of actors, their science of the body, their way of using the voice, their feeling for the movement to be found in a certain slowness, the density of their concentration, their art of the masque, the full use they make of the means of expression of the human being – all this was to me an ideal to be attained.

For us, of course, there can be no question of feeling like an Oriental in one's intimate self; but, while remaining loyal to our complexion as Westerners, we can bring ourselves into harmony, at least through the form, with their native complexion.

If we analyse the theatrical style of the Noh, does it not remind us of archaic Greek art? The *shite* is the masked actor. The *waki* is the leader of the chorus. In both genres there are a chorus and musical instruments. The ways in which their scenes succeed one another are related.

At one time the two temperaments were complementary. Relatively modern times are responsible for putting a distance between them. It happened after that diivision of the cell 'Humanity' into two cells, East and West, which must have taken place after Salamis, in Plato's time.

In the Yoga of contemplation, if I understand it rightly, the object is to forget the world in order to find oneself. One says then that all is illusion.

In the Yoga of action, the object seems to be to forget oneself in order to identify oneself with the world. One says then that all is allusion.

There is no antagonism: these are two different energies as are the masculine and the feminine, which are not contrary but necessary to each other. I call 'masculine' what gives and engenders, and 'feminine' what receives and conceives.

As for the neuter, it perceives.

Forgive me for repeating myself once again: every human being contains the three elements of that ternary. And humanity, like a single human being, also comprises these three different temperaments.

History finds highly ingenious ways of setting them against one another as though they were rivals and enemies. But seeing that their functions are not the same, they cannot be enemies. People use them for all purposes, that is all.

In the course of that extremely varied voyage, I kept noticing the two currents.

The Japanese soul appears to me essentially feminine. What I am here venturing to say is far from being pejorative. On the contrary. When the world is sick, it is from woman that all is reborn.

Japan was founded by a woman – the sun goddess Amaterasu. Nara was built by an empress – Gemmyo (eighth century); there are many empresses in Japanese history. One of the strangest, Ko-Ken, was a kind of Japanese Catherine the Great. The greatest Japanese novel, *The Tale of Genji*, was written in the tenth century by a woman, Murasaki Shikibu. Japan is one of the few countries where, in a marriage, the woman can give her name to the couple. In daily life the importance of woman is respected, and this dates from very far back. This is certainly the source of the peculiar spell which Japan casts over us.

Japan, with its deeply feminine sensibility, has the gift of receiving, reproducing, reflecting, conceiving. In the remote period of the nomad hunters (the Jomon), of the settled farmers (Yayoi) and of the great burials (Kofun), from which ravishing funerary statuettes in clay (Haniwas) have come down to us – a period that extends from the second century BC to the sixth century AD – China constantly pressed with all the weight of its influence upon Japan. Japan bent, received, imitated and suddenly, in a defence reaction, closed up.

Just as a woman, in regular periods, pulls herself together, closes her thighs and recovers her own self, so Japan has regularly stiffened herself by means of military governments whose leaders (Shogun) have revirilized the nation. And so the cycle of Japanese culture is a ternary one:

1. Influence from outside, principally China. Japan, through its extraordinary sensibility, transforms what it receives into an original creation.

2. Reflex of closing up, an 'iron curtain' reflex: absolute isolationism, which allows Japanese refinement to make all the grace of its genius blossom, to the point of decadence.

3. Recovery and military stiffening, contempt for death carried to the pitch of cruelty: these restore to Japanese history its heroic character, making it possible for the gates to open again, at the cost of receiving further influences.

At each about-turn the Japanese change capital. Thus Nara was the first capital (seventh and eighth centuries), at a period of Chinese influence (T'ang). Then the capital was moved to Heian (the earlier name of Kyoto) for the next two centuries, a period of isolation. Then, with the rise of the military government came the turn of Kamakura, again for two centuries, on a decision taken by the military leader Yoritomo. Then again Chinese influence. The leaders who followed attempted a synthesis of the two tendencies and returned to Heian, which became Kyoto, and the result – again for two centuries – was one of the greatest periods of Japanese culture, the Muromachi period. Then, during fifty years, refinement led to an enchanting decadence – the Monoyama period. This period led on to three centuries of isolation under military government, and to the setting up of a new capital – Edo (the earlier name of Tokyo). It was not till 1868, at the Meiji restoration, that the gates fully reopened – this time towards the West.

Woman is the being who bears and nourishes. Woman is carnal.

Daily life is physically religious. The religious exchanges are homely.

Among us there is a tendency to keep religion at a distance. In Japan religion is like eating and drinking. There is identification with nature. Soul and body are not separated. Not, as with us, separated during the week: on one hand Sunday for the Mass, on the other the remaining six days during which God is relegated to the sacristy.

At least, that it how it seemed to me: because I like it that way, because I find myself again, because I desire it.

I can see no break of continuity in my being. I have a soul that is moist.

> Que je ne perde pas, mon âme,
> Cette humidité intérieure de moi-même, says Tête d'Or.

(Let me not, my soul, lose
This inner humidity of myself)

We spent only a month in Japan, and we worked excessively. This prevented us from going really deep into things, and yet they acted upon us. I remember a Zen meal in one of the Kyoto temples. The moment of meditation I had at the tomb of the tea master Rikyu. I love the two symbolic elements of the Shinto religion – the sword and the mirror. I would gladly take them as the attributes of the actor: the sword which, from the stage, penetrates the house and is at the same instant its reflection. I love the tea ceremony. I love, above all, the Japanese art of flower arrangement.

The basic type of those bouquets is made up of three branches: the largest rises vertically, directed towards the sky (*shin*); the lowest slopes towards the earth (*gyo*); the one between represents man (*so*), who holds and unites sky and earth. In this way the humblest bouquet of flowers is a reminder that man is the mediator between the spiritual and the earthly.

> *Comme tu tètes, vieillard, la terre*
> *Et le ciel, comme tu y tiens.*
> *Comme tu te bandes tout entier*
> *A son aspiration, forme de Feu* (Tête d'Or, the tree passage)
> (How you do suck the earth, old man,
> And the sky – how you cling to it.
> How you brace your whole self
> To its aspiration, a form of Fire)

These three phases of communication recur in the tessitura of the Japanese actors' voices. They tear from the root of their being guttural, rough, clayey and muddy sounds; the voice climbs, shapes itself, purifies itself and ends as a song in a head voice.

We whose voices have only a few notes like those of a shepherd's pipe are at first rather surprised, and it makes us laugh; but one may ask oneself which of the two gamuts is the more laughable.

And so in Nara, in Tokyo and in Kyoto, in those temples where we spent so much time taking off our shoes, we received the emanations of an ancient and authentic civilization.

At Osaka we acted in a theatre that holds more than four thousand people. We had brought with us *Hamlet*, *Les Fausses Confidences* and *Baptiste*, *Le Misanthrope*, and *Christophe Colomb*.

The train taking us from Tokyo to Osaka stopped at Yokohama. What was my surprise when I saw on the platform my doves, in the arms of a station official! I got down, took the cage from his hands, thanked him and returned to my place in the carriage. He made no resistance.

The Japanese appeared to me – was I perhaps wrong? – to be the Far Eastern equivalent of what the Germans are to Europe. One finds in them the same cyclical rhythm, feminine, poetic, seductive, decadent, military and cruel. One discovers in them the same seriousness, the same conscientiousness, the same inventiveness.

In preparation for our coming, they had placed our repertoire on the year's programme for the schools and universities. Bilingual texts had been published, their television had given extracts from the plays, with full commentaries. No wonder the houses were full. The spectators followed the performance with the text on their knees. Indifference is unknown to them. Their response to the performances was comparable to that given by German audiences.

I have never seen so many technicians on stage. Indeed, I have never seen so many human beings all over the place. When a colony of children in their little black uniforms descends like a flight of starlings on some exhibition, it is really impressive. When trains disgorge their passengers in a station, there can be no question of trying to walk against the stream.

And so the setting up of our plays happened in the midst of a real mob. One day, surprisingly, the head electrician was not there at the switchboard. We were wasting time. I became tense and in the end exploded. Our lighting was only just ready for the evening performance, which went well all the same. Next day I asked to see this electrician so as to make it up with him.

'Oh, monsieur, he won't see you!'

'Why? Is he that angry with me?'

'No, monsieur, but he disgraced himself yesterday so he has shaved his head to punish himself; and he is unwilling to let himself be seen!'

Since then I have sometimes told this story to our French electricians: they have gazed at me, round-eyed.

Osaka is the city of the 'Bunraku'. This is a puppet theatre. More precisely, it is theatre that has puppets. Beginning in ancient times, and inspired by the marionette shows, it found its own style in the sixteenth century.

This is how the acting is done: on one side of the stage the narrator tells the story, while the marionette lives it; this marionette is about one metre tall and is manipulated in full view of the audience by three men. The principal manipulator has his face uncovered; with his left hand he holds the marionette at the height of his chest, and with his right hand he directs the movements of its right arm. His second, clothed and veiled in black, manipulates the left arm. The third assistant, also clothed and veiled in black, takes care of the marionette's dress, and of the attitudes of its body and legs. So three living beings are busy, visibly, about the marionette.

The narrator is a prodigious actor. He does all the voices and, thanks to the extraordinary synchronization of the acting, we are never confused.

The way in which the manipulator holds his marionette – breast to breast, heart to heart – is a wonderful sight. As he watches over it, his face is both indulgent and severe. He watches over it as God watches over us. Delicate, lively and busy, it seems to entrust itself wholly to him. It believes in him, as we in God.

He has put his large, grey-gloved hand into the little creature's sleeve and, with his fingertips at the level of its wrist, guides all the articulations, for all the knuckles of that small white hand are independent.

He is silent, of course, but his whole body dictates his will to that creature, which listens and acts, moved by a destiny which we see becoming concrete before our eyes.

In the most simple way in the world, this is metaphysical theatre. It is poetry rendered palpable by the concrete presence of the natural and super-natural. The marionette is man. The manipulator is God. The assistants are the messengers of Destiny.

With unparalleled grace and poetry the man-puppet is animated by a supernatural trinity. The ternary?

To me the Bunraku is the highest form of theatrical art. From it the Kabuki was born. In the Kabuki the actor has taken the place of the marionette, abolishing manipulations. In this way the gods are relegated and man becomes the centre, determined to assume his destiny. In the process, metaphysics has lost its virtuosity; in spite of the genius of the actors, I thought I perceived in the fundamental principle itself a certain degeneration.

We had the opportunity of seeing the same play performed by the two kinds of theatre. With the puppets the result was more intense, more cruel, more total, more absolute, more credible.

The Noh. The slowness of the acting makes one think of universal gravita-tion. I, who have always been fascinated by the signifying object, was com-pletely held by the fan in the shite's hand.

The fan is like thought. Thought opens slowly, and in small jerks. Then it begins vibrating. It expresses itself in time with the voice. Like the vibrations of the light in the warmth of the sun's rays.

A dry click, and the thought has closed.

The swiftest means of locomotion is walking. There are so many things to be captured all round us that one has the impression that the whole thing is moving too fast. You no longer know which way to look next. You would like to slow down. In the Noh there are so many things to observe that one has absolutely no impression of slowness, only an impression of something too full. While, just now, the shite was directing, at a distance, my concentration upon the vibrations of his fan, as if I had penetrated into his soul, I had not noticed that, imperceptibly, he was turning where he stood. And when the fan closes, leaving me once more 'to the open air', I discover that that astral body of his has made a turn of forty-five degrees.

That is the mystery of the Noh. As Claudel put it: 'With us, in the theatre, there is something that happens; in the Noh, there is someone who happens.'

In the field of exchanges, Claudel's Christophe Colomb brought to the Japanese something special. The style of our company's acting, completely Western though it is, is strongly related to theirs. This comes from the fact that Claudel had been strongly influenced by their traditional theatre, and so were my own dreams which, from the beginning, were drawn towards their poetry of the theatre.

With us this style is modern. It could adapt itself very well to contemporary life; for instance *Le Procès*, *L'Etat de Siège*, *As I Lay Dying*, *La Faim*. With them, on the contrary, there has been a rupture between the traditional theatre and the modern theatre. They are suffering from it. At least in 1960 (the date of our visit), their modern theatre was trying to be in harmony with the Anglo-Saxon theatre. It seemed to them impossible to use the traditional materials of the Noh, the Kabuki and the Bunraku for the treatment of present-day subjects.

Through our *Christophe Colomb* they could, on the other hand, glimpse a possibility of joining up the two periods, which had been separated by a no-man's-land of more than a century. We discussed this question with them. Many of them were longing for their great theatre and were dreaming of connecting up their traditional style with modern preoccupations. According to them, our style of acting gave them encouragement and hope.

From Osaka we went towards Nagasaki, to Fukuoka and Yawata. This meant we could fly over the Inland Sea, one of the most beautiful regions of the world.

Imagine, for instance, emerging from that sea with its infinite shades of blue, a completely green clown's hat on the top of which a small crater has formed a perfectly round, absinthe-coloured lake. That is only one example. There are a good hundred of these islands, all different. They are like a population of extremely gay and individual persons. A nature invented by God for children. Further on, alas, Hiroshima.

Landing at Fukuoka, we found ourselves in the Catholic district of Japan. We saw small churches with their belltowers pointing skywards. I was amazed, and rather reassured: they reminded me of our villages. Plenty of people there understood French. There were old and highly cultivated Japanese who had already admired Madeleine and Pierre Bertin at the time of their débuts at the Comédie Française.

As our performance started at 6.30, we were already wandering through the streets by 9.30. Like good tourists we moved insensibly towards the alleys of the red light quarter. Here the Japanese lantern was clearly in place. It is a charming, attractive quarter. The pimps really protect their girls. At one street corner, two of them came over to speak to me:

'*Les Enfants du Paradis!*'

'Yes.'

'Baptiste!'

'Well, yes!'

They moved off out of sight, and we went on with our visit. Five minutes passed, and there they were, returning, carrying a bouquet of flowers. We ended the evening drinking glasses of saki with them in an inn.

> *On peut dire tout ce qu'on voudra*
> *Moi je trouve charmants*
> *Les souteneurs de Fukuoka!*

M.T. —9*

In Tokyo our happiness was complete. What with the Noh schools, the suppers with the geishas, the parties given by the actors in the city, our competing improvisations, the music and dancers of the Imperial Palace (Gagaku), the fights of the Sumos, our close friendship with the Kabuki actors, and so on, I began to feel I was becoming a Japanese. I must have been one in some other life. I made friends with a *shite* of the dynasty of the Kanze (Isao Kanze). I would gladly have gone through a course at the Noh school.

We ended our season with a performance of *Hamlet*. Actors and technicians, we were all exhausted, emptied of our substance. In hurling a torch from the stage into the wings, I nearly killed Pierre Bertin: the stagehand whose job it usually was to catch the torch had got mixed up in the clutter of our props. I heard a noise like someone breaking an egg and saw Pierre Bertin-Polonius crumple up.

Why at that moment, while my character went on acting, did my 'double' recite an *Ave Maria*?

Luckily, Polonius had finished playing his role (it only remained for me to kill him through the arras), and Bertin was not taking part in the rest of the tour. He returned to Paris by the first Boeing. His head was as black as an aubergine. His only words of reproach to me were:

'When you act Hamlet ... you go crazy.'

On such tours we never had understudies. We cannot afford the expense. The law of the circus becomes tyrannical. Every actor therefore instinctively screws up his willpower to the utmost. But when the last day arrives, there is a succession of small catastrophes: a tonsilitis, a loss of voice, an inflammation of the ear, a slipped disc, an acute sciatica, a monstrous liver attack. Like the aircraft that has flown us over the North Pole, our willpower unfreezes.

We are often questioned about the more or less real double character of an actor. Personally, I remain always conscious that I am in a theatre; but my private reactions are altered by the nature of the character I am trying to embody. For example, if in *Hamlet* one of the lighting effects has gone wrong, I react as the Prince of Denmark, director of the production; I am at the same time conscious – conscious at least of how ridiculous I would be if I believed it 'really happened'; and yet I am no longer altogether myself. In such cases a real use is being made of the Being and of his Double.

Another example: as soon as I have put on my costume, my wedding ring worries me and I have to take it off. But when I undress after the performance is over, the absence of my wedding ring worries me, and I have to put it on again.

Why do I feel the desire to wash all over before acting? I have the impression that I must free myself from all sorts of miasmas.

It was raining when we left Japan: another Japanese print. We were very sad, both they and we, at separating. When one consciously surveys certain exceptional moments in life, there is melancholy in the air. We had just spent an unforgettable month : a whole past that deserved prolonging.

Night in Bangkok

The Bay of Hong Kong merits its reputation. You land on an airstrip that seems reeled out over the water. The Chinese air hostesses, with their skirts split up the side, leave open a view of long legs fit to set young men dreaming. When we took off again, the Air France captain had obtained permission to give us a tour of the Bay. The sampans, the floating streets and houses! I would gladly have idled away several days there.

The stop at Saigon was stifling. Animation, jostling and the atmosphere of a stove. Then came Bangkok. Four members of our company, who were not in the second part of our tour, asked permission to leave us there: very intelligently, they wanted to go and visit Angkor at their own expense. We wished them *bon voyage* and they disappeared into the night.

It must have been very late by local time, for the airport appeared to be asleep. The time seemed long. The air outside was mild, and we made for a terrace on which resigned travellers were dozing in chaises longues and enormous wooden armchairs. Nobody spoke; our exhaustion was making itself felt. The only living things were those huge insects which, with an infernal noise, rolled along the airfield to the foot of the terrace and executed a slow waltz about the small rampant insect directing them with his flag – a midget animal-tamer putting elephants through their paces.

The whistle of the turbines tore our ears, but had no power to awaken the deeply tanned person snoring close by me, his chest bared and his feet in the air – a traveller whose posture was that of a defeated warrior.

At intervals a long-drawn-out roar of thunder shook the atmosphere, and a fiery monster took off for some unknown destination.

When somebody is asleep, everything round him seems dead. The only signs of life remaining are his breathing and, at regular intervals, low belly rumblings. It was like that with the earth all round us. It seemed fast asleep, almost dead. Only, at regular intervals, yet always unexpectedly, the formidable noise of the aircraft tearing themselves away from the ground and the unpleasant whistle of the ones gathering their strength on the tarmac made us feel that all was not dead.

At that moment, as we meekly accepted our destiny, we felt as if we were no longer in any determined place, simply on Earth covered by night. Up above, in the black of the sky, all the torches were alight. It was God's hour. It was the moment when you hear Him breathing.

In seaports the infinite is horizontal: here the 'sea' is directed upwards and stands vertical. The sailor who puts out looks into the distance: here our longing to be gone forced us to look into the air.

Between the kindled constellations and the bit of earth delimited by the dark, the space seemed empty. From time to time, in that nothingness, a small light would show – two spaced-out headlights like eyes with a nose between –

and a metallic monster appeared by spontaneous generation. The flying machines showed us that the rest of the world was still living. Our sleeper went on snoring, regularly, sedately, civilly.

More time passed – we were late. We should have left two hours ago. Some of us moved about a little, the slow march of time was becoming palpable.

Molière, what things you involve us in !

And yet we are deeply happy, at the heart of our adventure. Japan was now far away: all round us, those mysterious countries, India, Thailand, Ceylon, which we would not be able to see. But this stop would leave in me a memory of a very modest, very sincere meditation : my prayer in Bangkok.

A student revolution had closed the doors of Turkey to us. I had therefore decided to go to Tel Aviv direct.

The aircraft took off. All the bodies in the cabin looked disjointed. Legs stuck up in the air, arms trailed on the carpet. Two heads seemed interlocked, like horses embracing.

A sardonic dawn was following behind us, slightly to our right. The chain of the Himalayas at first looked a hostile black, then pink, then white. Below, a huge wet bowel was writhing across greenish-brown lands : the Ganges.

Day came.

New Delhi : the monkeys on the roofs of the hangars. The blue saris of the hostesses who sprayed us with disinfectant.

Noon.

The flight from New Delhi to Teheran is especially splendid. The Indus, the Thar Desert, the salt deserts. The geometrical chessboards that are born in the midst of the desert tracts at the approaches to cultivated regions, and the big towns. The palette is extraordinary : shade upon shade of beige, pale green, absinthe yellow, and layers of mother-of-pearl. In one place, former lakes, dried up and covered with salt, stare at us like eyes. In another, tilled fields with their bistres, chestnut browns, beiges and greens, form abstract pictures which Braque might have signed. In another, the banks of the Indus display sinuosities of many colours. Then come lunar landscapes. Gradually, over the mountains, multitudes of specks of water, like wormholes in sand, reveal the presence of man. It was a fine limpid day. Our noses were pressed to the port-holes, and now we looked to the right, now called the others to admire something to the left.

Israel

After travelling for forty-two hours we at last reached Tel Aviv, in the middle of the night. In such expeditions we have always to adjust ourselves to local time.

Israel would be worth at least a month : we could stay there only two weeks. And so we went at it greedily. In spite of a muddle about quarters for the company, trying to people who were submerged by fatigue, we soon got into the rhythm of the country. At Tel Aviv we performed in the Habimah theatre. In Haifa we camped in a cinema. At Jerusalem again a cinema – this one more comfortable. From that stay I now retain three sources of enrichment:

– the exemplary courage of the Israeli people;

– my encounter with fundamental Christianity;

– the geographical position of the country, where Hope and Tragedy ferment simultaneously, under the sign of the Eternal.

There is a saying, I think, somewhere in the Scriptures: 'This land shall be his who shall restore its greenness.'

That is what the Israeli nation has succeeded in doing. Nothing but orchards everywhere: orange trees, lemon trees, grapefruit trees, vines, cereals; irrigation canals; reafforestation. The Caesarea of antiquity is today reappearing from under the dunes.

> *Je demeurai longtemps errant dans Césarée,*
> *Lieu charmant où mon cœur vous avait adorée* (Bérénice, Racine)
> I remained a long time wandering in Caesarea,
> Place of enchantment where my heart had worshipped you.

Israel is a people in arms, as the French nation was at the time of Valmy. Can one be anything else when one is threatened from all sides? And how not be on edge because of it?

It is also a people with ploughs and trowels. By an irony of fate the winds bring the sands of Egypt and are constantly trying to make this land a desert.

It is a continual struggle against men and against nature. The Israeli people have an acute sense of this. Anyone would, after what they have had to suffer over the centuries and – in the course of that terrible war – from cruel genocide. Their courage exacts admiration and respect. In spite of their ready aggressiveness, one loves them; one takes their side.

Unfortunately, that does not resolve the cruel ordeal of the Palestinian population: this too we share. It is more than a matter of conscience: the problem seems almost insoluble.

I seemed to find there again those two main currents of humanity, the Yoga of action and the Yoga of contemplation – the East and the West. Only there, instead of being complementary as they should be, they announce that they are contraries and are drawn up facing each other.

The Arab civilization, with its great refinement, is the advance post of contemplative humanity: it comes from the East and debouches on Palestine. The civilization of Israel is the advance post of active humanity: it is attached to the West and, in the opposite direction, debouches also on the Sea of Galilee. The two waves have for centuries collided at that point and become transformed into turbulence.

This is why the present conflict is the same as the one described in the Bible. During thousands of years nothing has changed.

The problems produced by the oil industry seem secondary here – the only such case in the world – and yet they too exist.

Is there a solution? On the day when humanity proves capable of trans-figuring those two currents it will have become worthy of what one has a right to expect of it.

Did not Christ try? We can follow His life to the age of nine. We come upon Him again at thirty. From nine to thirty, there are twenty-one years. In the East, that is the time of initiation. May He not have spent it soaking Himself in the whole of humanity in order to try to reconcile it? In my love for Him, I like to imagine this.

One day I asked a monk that question – that 'stupid question':

'What did He do during those twenty-one years?'

'... well, he was a carpenter!'

The mystery is maintained. To my mind, He wanted to make love triumph. At once they killed Him. They would not have reconciliation. Again and again people reject the ones who have come to unite and not to divide.

We went to visit the kibbutz at Eingev, on the east of the Sea of Galilee. In the midst of green things, of fruit, bananas and muddy canals, we made acquaintance with a wonderful community. Genuine communism?

Between the shore of the lake and the cliff which forms the frontier with Jordan – or Syria – there is only a strip, about five kilometres broad. A strip as fertile as an oasis.

On the top of the cliff a desert plateau begins. If you raise your head you can make out, as though on a balcony, Arab sentinels squatting, with a rifle across their knees, waiting for the order to fire.

Down below, in the orchards, the Jews are working. They have shown that they are peasants, craftsmen, creators. They have restored to this land its greenness, they deserve it.

If for centuries money became their speciality, this was because it was the only material that 'those dogs of Christians' and the others allowed them to manipulate. I have acted Shylock, I have felt that rage, and Shakespeare is a just man.

In Jerusalem we were received by Ben Gurion. The man was impressive: a mixture of sage and saint.

From the roof of the Convent of Notre Dame de France, which is on Israeli territory, you have a view of Jordanian Jerusalem. We could not go there. Three years back, when we were in the Lebanon, at Baalbek, members of our company could go there. Politics, politics!

The place is all the more overwhelming because it is very small. Scarcely a ventricle of the world, yet one feels its pulsation there.

On the last Friday, a day of rest, we set off by car. Our guide, Father Roger, was one of the very few Catholic priests authorized to show people round Israel. We retraced chronologically the journey of Jesus from Nazareth to the Mount of the Beatitudes. An unforgettable day. The village of Mary Magda-lene; Capernaum – Jesus is there in the synagogue; the house of Peter's parents; and here, the small hamlet where the widow's son was brought to life again; here, Saul fainted at the witch's predictions; here, Jonathan was killed. The

Jordan, with children bathing in it. The climb up Mount Tabor, where each donkey we meet seems to have, beside it, a mysterious shadow. Reading the Scriptures that refer to the various places we went through put us into a strange state of mind.

The Sea of Galilee is two hundred metres below sea level. Over the lake, on top of a slope, among neat vineyards, is the place known as the Mount of the Beatitudes. The Father read us the Sermon on the Mount (at a hundred and sixty yards below sea level!). The truth coming from the well. We remained silent. A silence loaded with the eternal Present.

At sunset, we passed through Cana. The village seemed untouched, the girls of Cana still carried water on their backs, but the earthenware pitchers are now tin cans.

In the twilight the glowing hills about Nazareth stood out against the sky. The upper part of the town is spoilt by development – those blocks which are the same everywhere and are ruining the whole world: universal planning that suppresses the juice of personality, of the individual – heartbreaking.

Fortunately old Nazareth is intact. We went into the cave of the Annunciation. By now it was night. The Reverend Father had to take some letters to the Little Sisters of Jesus, disciples of Father de Foucauld. Like pilgrims asking for shelter, we knocked at a big wooden door. A young Sister, beautiful and frail-looking, breathing an air of happiness, opened the door. In the courtyard, among the shadows, we could make out the well where Father de Foucauld used to draw water. Not far from there, the lights were on in a small kitchen where three Sisters were singing cheerfully as they made soup, which smelt good. Their radiant poverty filled me with envy. What spiritual wealth enveloped them! What a victory over existence! What a solution they had found! I felt a need to be alone. I left the group and, at the other end of the courtyard, went into a tiny chapel. All I could make out, on its bare walls, was a cross, also bare. Only the light from the candles kept dancing in the gloom. Prayer for the people I love. An inexpressible emotion, which I cannot now bring myself to describe.

In Japan, the Buddha had fascinated us. Here Moses left his mark and we had found Jesus again. Tomorrow the Delphic Apollo would appear to us. Yes, it was a tour of the Gods.

That short stay produced in me a small nudge of conversion. Somewhat the same kind as the conversion to my own country, which I had received during the 1940 exodus. A secret, intimate thing. A kind of illumination. I find it hard now to express myself clearly.

But let me try. Having been of French nationality when I came into the world, in 1940 I became French. Having belonged to the Catholic religion from my baptism, I had now just become a Christian. Result: I draw near to the source and move away from the church; whatever the religion or philosophy or aesthetic may be, I draw near to what wells up. I move away from the practical use which men extract from that welling up, for profit, not for fulfilment.

I couple myself to that Being who brings me, in the slightest signs of life, the desire for absolute love and for self-giving in order to assume the human condition. This at every instant of existence and at the lowliest moments.

The 'great' is for the church. It is heavy, oppressive, stifling. The 'small' is what wells up from us – from Him. Whether He be man or God, matters little. I have not been gifted with radars capable of knowing *physically* what a god is, but in me at every moment, in the best part of me, I feel *the real presence* of that Being – it is *He*.

And from that moment we are free, the two of us together; as in the human couple, there is a fusion of two beings, and one acts freely *à deux*.

I want communion, I want the Mass, but in the Masses in the churches, on Sundays, at weddings or funerals, I end up still hungry. And that is not good when, precisely, it is a meal, 'the meal'.

This applies not only to the Christian sensibility. Human societies have a mania for taking that impulse towards 'being more' which is 'grace', and falsifying it to their advantage – making Churches out of it to satisfy their will to domination.

Would Descartes recognize himself in cartesianism?

Though I love Brecht, I distrust the Brechtians. It is the same with Freud and Marx.

Does the suppression of 'the springtime of Prague' affect the Communist ideology? No! It is a Church business.

Let us distrust the Church spirit. It protects the Pharisees.

I love 'Him'. And I feel I am very unworthy. Not from submissiveness, shame or false humility; but because we never do enough for love, and because He did. Who can say more?

It is the same when I feel myself French, just as a plant feels it is a certain kind of plant and not some other. The reason I am so fond of travelling about the world and entering into communication with all the human beings of the earth is surely that I am trying to understand them, to take their side, to share their miseries and their joys and to fight at their side against anguish and solitude; but it is also that in them I feel the desire that I *should be in their eyes entirely myself*, like a vow they are compelling me to take, like a response I owe them. No frontiers or passport or flag come into this, it is simply a matter of the kind of man who grows in this square of earth comprised between

> *l'Océan et le Rhin*
> *l'Alpe et les Pyrénées.*[1]

The Africans, the Asiatics, the Americans, the Europeans make me 'their countryman', and I owe them an account.

In the same way it is *my* religion. My doubts reappear only when I arrive at Marseilles or Le Havre or Orly. There the place is full of 'Churches'. Religious ones, governmental ones, political ones, intellectual ones. Friends,

[1] François I.

beware! It is full of new catechisms, new curricula that are trying to turn you into conditioned animals. Claim the responsibility for yourselves, distrust Churches, think of the hare and do not become rabbits.

> Et le lièvre tâche d'échapper en bondissant
> à angle droit entre les sillons,

> (A hare tries to escape by leaping at right
> angles across the furrows . . .)

Panurge does the same. Rabelais calls it 'navigation'.

I love Rabelais, I love Villon, La Fontaine, Verlaine. I love Artaud, I love Dullin, I love Jarry.

Claudel had understood perfectly. During nearly twenty years when we worked together, he never questioned me on this subject.

And yet, an important distinction has to be made between a 'Church' and an 'Order'. I have a weakness for monks.

But I am digressing: let us complete our tour. We took our first Caravelle. The gayest of aircraft, the youngest: the young girl of the air.

Athens

Just as the ship in *Partage de Midi* had taught me the feel of the sea and I had recognized that sea when I was on board the *Florida*, so Æschylus and the other Greek tragedians, and Homer, Pythagoras and Heraclitus, had taught me Greece – I had built up in myself so clear an idea of Greece that I recognized it at once.

The defection of Turkey gave us a hole to fill, three days wide. The company was at the end of its strength: we had been made quite ill, in fact, by the changes of climate we had been through, the changes of food, the sleepless nights and the long hours spent getting stiff on board aircraft. Our organisms were out of true.

But as soon as we landed in Athens, we had to face what seemed to us an extremely Western press conference – intelligent, rational, critical and blasé. We patiently did our best to pass this customs examination in 'knowledge and wit': then we said goodbye to all our comrades. 'Have a good rest and enjoy yourselves!' They had well deserved a deep drink of ancient Greece.

So there we were, Madeleine and I, torn between our fatigue and our curiosity. Curiosity won.

First objective: Delphi. At every moment of the drive I vibrated like a drum. All the early seeds my reading had planted in me and my imagination had made grow now suddenly kept exploding into flower at each crossroads, as though brought on by a miraculous spring. I was bursting in all directions. A mythological nature was coming from the pores of my skin. I became tree, bird, animal, sphinx.

We passed through Eleusis, we took the left turn at Thebes, at a place where three roads meet I shouted:

That's where Oedipus killed Laius!

The driver of the car said it was indeed the place.

Delphi welcomed us with its regulation eagles and its appropriate thunder. I went crazy with – not happiness, but communication with things. The theatre, the temples, the dwelling-place of the Pythoness. We were well aware that we were at one of the most radioactive places in the world. The Omphalos, which is kept in the museum, is well sited, like the centre to a circle.

The greatest shock I received was in the stadium. Close to the stone on which the five rings of the Olympiads are engraved, we were united with *silence*. And what a silence ! – charged with life, with time, with past-present. The athletes were there, running naked, like transparent shades. A white eagle was gliding in a circle exactly above us. Behind us the craggy mountains rose sheer. Below and in front of us, after a small oak wood, there sloped right down to the sea a sea of olive trees.[1]

Another day of deep communion. Another nudge of conversion.

I may be quite mad, but it always seems to me that, at a certain altitude of the Spirit, everything becomes alike. There is nothing left but our earth, nature and *man* – as a Whole.

Next day some friends took us to Epidaurus, via the plain of Argos. The man who was driving was a theatrical director – I had found once more an old colleague from the Atelier : the actor and stage designer George Vakalo. We were all taking nineteen to the dozen, and the car was moving through the Peloponnese. A moment came when I asked our driver :

'Hey, aren't you passing by Mycenae?'

'Yes, sorry, I was thinking of other things.'

'Isn't that, up there on the left, the Palace of Agamemnon?'

'Yes, yes. I'll turn round.'

I was at home there.

And we passed through the Lion Gate. Up at the top, the watchman was still waiting for the news from Troy.

The theatre at Delphi is a small experimental theatre. It seats two thousand five hundred. The one at Epidaurus, with its capacity of fourteen thousand, attracts me less. I picked a strange bouquet of flowers there – they still exist and I keep them carefully.

From my walks in Athens, on and around the Acropolis, I chiefly remember the *korai*. From the Museum, the treasures of Mycenae; the gold death masks reminded me of the Mexican ones, fifteen centuries distant in time. Also the *kouroi*, those young men with their archaic forms. And finally, the vases with geometrical decoration.

I spent hours wandering about the ruins of the theatre of Dionysus, that sanctuary of my passion for the theatre. Never have I had such a desire to steal. I would gladly have filled my pockets with stones.

We also took a ride on the sea, in the private yacht belonging to an eminent

[1] The plain of Amphissa, extending to the harbour of Itea.

Athenian surgeon. Still with Vakalo, we visited Aegina, Poros and Hydra. The return journey was full of incident: the leaps of a sword-fish, the fin of a shark, the islets like a seated lion or ship turned to stone; living rocks emerging from the sea; and the talk of the sailor who told us stories of sirens. (For example, when you go aboard in the evening, it is no rare thing for one of them to rise ahead of the boat and to ask if Alexander, the great Alexander, is living still or is dead. You must answer: 'He is still living and reigning.' If you do, your journey passes without a hitch).

I remember, lastly, the storm we ran into at the very moment of the sunset. It made me live all my reading of the *Odyssey* over again. Within a quarter of an hour the horses of the sea had bolted. Neptune was stirring the water. The waves rose, terrifying, above us. The mast kept cracking. The sails kept laying the boat on her side. We were literally riding the billows. Day was darkening rapidly. Doctor Saroglou's pretty blue boat was in travail from bow to stern. I remained standing, barefoot, with my toes clutching the wet planks of the deck. And I adopted the wild movements of the sea. I who am timid, especially on the water – as a child I witnessed several drownings – had lost all consciousness of danger. I was happy, passionate, drunk. The spray whipped our faces and I responded with a shout of defiance.

Neptune had put on for us a little reception of his own.

Now our season of performances began. It was victorious. Expecting a charming, informed but difficult audience, we gave all we had.

At night, in the old Plaka quarter, we imagined we were recovering some of our strength by devouring *brochettes de foie* and swilling the resinated wine I am so fond of.

The accumulated fatigue, our mad excursions, the emotion we felt in that country, the special efforts we had been obliged to produce in order to win that particular battle and the ailments we were now feeling (lumbago, fever, shiverings, general stiffness, limbs almost paralysed) had finished us off.

One last round was in store for us – Yugoslavia – before we would return to Paris via Venice.

One day, at seven in the morning, the company piled into a bus among heaps of suitcases – a troupe of actors, ghosts from the night, odd revellers exhausted by life's orgies. We were mere somnolent paste.

The tour of the gods was continuing. After Buddha, Moses, Jesus, Apollo and all the others, Karl Marx was waiting for us.

The bus started towards the airport. Madeleine, her head nodding with sleepiness, gave a last glance towards the Acropolis and, with one of those gestures that are her secret, one of those gestures she has derived from the whole of the grace of the eighteenth century, she murmured: 'Goodbye, Venice!'

Yugoslavia

After the Japanese gardens, the oases of Israel and the Mediterranean dryness of Greece, it was a delight to land near Belgrade in the middle of freshly cut hay, tall grasses, plump chestnut trees and lime trees in flower. We were in the country again, with the foliage that buds, is born, is green, turns yellow, falls and dies, manuring the soil for other leaves to appear in turn, fragile and tender. The foliage that slakes one's thirst.

The magnetic contact with our own landscapes was being re-established. Nonetheless in Belgrade the continental climate seemed to us oppressive. Politically tense. The Algerian F L N had its headquarters there.

At Sarajevo we moved into a mountain climate: storms and rain. And certain political militants tried to teach us socialism by making us eat with our fingers.

At Zagreb, glorious weather again. An eminent personality of that city, a frank and charming young man, gave us a brotherly reception. It took place in what had been an aristocrat's palace. The rooms, furniture and objects were scrupulously preserved, evidently in their former places. The impression was striking. One dared not talk. One sat on the edge of one's chair. In short, the masters of the house were missing. And yet no one could be nicer than our hosts. The uneasiness of revolutions: may this not be another field where the theatre could help human beings to become reconciled?

And finally, at 'beloved' Ljubljana, we were moved by the charm of the natural setting, which is equal to that of the human beings there.

So, within a single country, we came upon extremely different regions and people. But all these people had the same enthusiasm and kindness. Our stay there proved to be an admirable conclusion to our long voyage. The houses were full, the audiences remarkably knowledgeable and our meetings with fellow actors close and easy. We joyfully gave the remains of our strength. Ljubljana being the last city, the stock of love we had taken with us for the tour was expended there completely.

The final evening arrived – I dared not believe it. In two and a half months we had done a hundred hours of flying, nearly sixty thousand kilometres. Once and a half round the world. We had visited fourteen cities. We had avoided accidents, illnesses, losses of our stock-in-trade – a thousand hitches that can arise and get in the way of performances.

As the last performance approached I kept telling myself that this time something was bound to happen. And as our effort began to demand less and less willpower, my nerves grew more fragile. For this last evening we did *Le Misanthrope*. All through the performance the demon of perversity kept whispering in my ear: 'You won't get through it. Your nerves are going to crack. You will collapse before the end.'

During the interval it was cruel: again and again I asked if it was time to continue. I was on the verge of giddiness. Another hour and I would at last be able to set down the weight I had had to carry without respite ever since we left Orly.

At last Alceste's nine hundred lines had emerged from my mouth, and when the curtain fell I expressed our thanks. I was not very clear about whom I had to thank, but I said thank you all the same.

According to custom, flowers were brought to us on the stage: a bouquet for each of the ladies, then another bouquet for the men – and then a whole table covered with flowers and presents.

And that was not the end: now a gilded laurel wreath with ribbons uniting the colours of France and Yugoslavia. All this happened, curtain after curtain – and still it was not the end. Now from the orchestra pit, in which part of the audience had taken up position on chairs, there came a flower, then another, then ten more, and more from the balcony. The audience gradually stood up to throw flowers, and the stage was strewn with them. In our surprise we appeared awkward and intimidated. The noise of applause came from all over the house, and at the same time, between the pit and the stage, a zone of silence was maintained – the trajectory of the flowers. I was struck by this simultaneous existence of the noise from the audience and the silent murmur of the flowers.

Célimène, who had raised smiles in the Japanese babies, was getting her recompense at Ljubljana.

Still deeply moved by this welcome, we went to bed late. Our mission was accomplished. All we had now to do was to end at Orly – after passing through Venice – this world tour in quest of Man.

Man, whether Japanese, Jewish, Greek or Yugoslavian, we had come on him afresh everywhere, identical with himself: a creature tormented by death, disquieted by his loneliness, who remains throughout his life a child.

PALAIS-ROYAL

For a long time Pierre Bertin had been advising me to put on Offenbach's *La Vie Parisienne*. After all, why not? We had some agreeable voices in the company. The piece had been first performed by actors and not by singers, with the exception of two of the women's roles. I adore Offenbach. Had not my friend Dr Schweitzer told me that, when he used to teach music at Strasbourg, he never failed to make his students work at Offenbach to improve their sense of rhythm?

We had not yet tried our hands at operetta, nor at *opéra-bouffe*. And besides, I was reminded of my grandfather, who used to hum the Offenbach tunes at table.

The first performance of *La Vie Parisienne* had been at the Théâtre du Palais-Royal. It is a delicious theatre. I had even written a letter in 1941 to Quinson, its then director, about hiring the theatre at the time when I wanted to leave the Comédie Française. Since then it belonged to Madame de Létraz. Bold as brass, we made a contract for two years. I was as happy as a king. The theatre is a bit small, but it is a box of chocolates. It is in the historic quarter. It is Paris. It is my city.

Economically, it was a folly. We must play to a hundred per cent capacity or we would be heading for ruin. And the folly did not stop there. I had decided to go on playing in repertory. Since Madeleine and I had left the Français, *Le Soulier de Satin* had gradually been dropped there. I reached an agreement with Mme Claudel and her children that we should put on the *Soulier* at the Palais-Royal. On that tiny stage? How?

And not only the *Soulier*. We would do a new play by a young author: *Le Tir Clara* by Roncoroni.

It was like cramming a regiment into a 1900 cab. It was mad, I agree. Never mind.

All very well, but where could we rehearse? We had nowhere, and the Palais-Royal required modification. At our expense, of course. The stage part of this cost us a packet.

The old Bal Tabarin was closed; we took refuge there. Claudel's Prouhèze and Rodrigue went through their scenes with Gardefeu and Métella on Tabarin's stamping-ground. Claudel, Meilhac and Halévy shook down well together. 'Strolling players', even in Paris.

On *La Vie Parisienne* we put in work as meticulous as we had on the *Oresteia* of Æschylus. Training in singing, training for the cancan. I had engaged Roger Stefani, an extraordinary dancer, unique in his own specialty. He later committed suicide; we have never really found out why.

André Girard was our new conductor. After our enforced departure from the Marigny, Pierre Boulez's Domaine Musical had 'alighted' at the Salle Gaveau. I say 'alighted' because I automatically compare us with birds. In all senses:

> Birds give me the impression of having no heads.
> Birds are killed, are cooked, and you suck their bones.
> Birds are useful. They eat insects.
> Some of them, the carrion ones for instance, even do our scavenging.
> Yes, but birds steal our cherries.
> Birds are hunted. And yet birds sing, and have pretty feathers.
> Birds are cruel.
> Birds bring luck.
> There are night birds that tell our fortunes.
> There is the bird of wisdom. The bird of Spring.
> Lastly, nature without birds would be very sad.
> Like humanity without theatre.

And so, one evening in November 1958, the curtain of the Palais-Royal rose on an aviary of birds, singing for all they were worth Offenbach's operetta. Were they the sparrows of Paris? Jean-Denis Malclès had distributed their plumage. We were more like birds of paradise.

I, in their midst, was living through a terrible moment, like the death of Christian Bérard just before the opening of *Scapin*, I had buried my brother Max that morning.

For some years Max had been suffering from multiple sclerosis. It was a long Calvary. Towards the end he was in a clinic at Bordeaux and asked to see me. We had a heartbreaking conversation, very affectionate and to me unbearable. Was it so to him? I hope not. There is a grace in death. He talked about our mother, and about Bob (my uncle had died a few months earlier). He told me he was 'going to see them again'.

On the morning of the opening of *La Vie Parisienne*, we had gone to Père Lachaise, with (among others) his two children Alain and Marie-Christine, to see him buried close to the remains of our mother. We had always been close friends. Max was *my brother*. On his deathbed he had once more called me '*ma Nénette*'. There would be now no one left to use that nickname.

The law of the circus...

The opening of *La Vie Parisienne* was one of the most sparkling evenings our company ever experienced. A triumph by common consent. The audience, when it left the theatre, sang and danced in the rue Montpensier. In the house the audience were crowded on top of one another, so were the musicians in the pit, and on the stage the actors jostled: the Palais-Royal was bursting with people and with excitement.

The 'folly' had come off.

And the folly continued. Three months later we recreated *Le Soulier de Satin*. Because the stage was so small I had imagined a new production. Catherine Sellers interpreted the part of Prouhèze. Marie Bell, my beloved Marie Bell who had been a divine Prouhèze, never forgave me. I understand what she felt, for I know how that sort of thing hurts.

On the first night, various bits of decor fell on my back, and I exclaimed inside me: 'I'm being punished, I'm being punished.'

Claudel's poetry won. People rushed to see the play.

The folly had still not ended.

We created *Le Tir Clara*. And we played in repertory. The average attendance exceeded a hundred per cent.

Jean Anouilh loves intimate theatre. He approached us. Not long before then, he had written a film script on the life of Molière; the producers had cried off at the last moment. He gave it to me to read, and we decided to stage 'the film'. The experiment excited me. It became *La Petite Molière*. We gave the first performance at the Bordeaux May Festival in 1959.

That was the third time we worked for the Festival in Jacques Chaban-Delmas's theatre: after *Christophe Colomb*, we had created the *Oresteia* there.

We could not rehearse at the Palais-Royal, there was no room: with all the stuff we had there we could hardly move. This time we took refuge on the stage of the Gaieté Lyrique. And the folly continued.

It nearly turned into disaster. I had completely let myself go.

Marionettes and actors were performing together. We had lost count of the number of scenes – it was a succession of 'dissolves'.

We were not even able to finish the production of the play in Paris. I sent everyone away and, at the last moment, we remade the scenario.

In the end, we just scraped through at Bordeaux.

The Paris critics, who had come to the Festival, gave *La Petite Molière* a warm welcome. This was a good omen for its opening in Paris – but wait till you hear what followed !

Since the return of General de Gaulle to power, André Malraux, now a Minister, had been given the job of creating the Ministry of Cultural Affairs.

He was bitterly envied. Malicious tongues said that 'he was already introducing chaos into a ministry which did not exist'. But nothing stopped him; not even himself. He was determined.

One day we had been asked to lunch by a great and longstanding friend of ours, Charles Gombault. André Malraux was among the guests. It was an informal lunch. I think I had not seen Malraux since before the War. In the course of conversation I realized with surprise and deep satisfaction that he had been following closely all our efforts.

Madeleine Renaud and he were sitting side by side. Suddenly he said to her :

'And now, *chère madame*, when are you going to settle at the Odéon?'

'But . . . when you like, *monsieur le Ministre*.'

He had just created the Théâtre de France.

What would have happened if I had not committed all those 'follies?' Would Malraux have asked us to create that modern national theatre if we had been content to trade on the success of *La Vie Parisienne*? Had not those thoughtless audacities contained, on the contrary, some pointer capable of appealing to both de Gaulle and Malraux?

I have always believed in folly. Surely 'to become more', as Teilhard de Chardin put it, is to break out of one's own circle at a given moment.

Enthusiasm – the quality Claudel loved so much – puts us into a kind of condition of weightlessness, the 'folly' of wanting to 'be more'.

Dancing in slow motion on the moon, conquering the Himalayas, taking a tenth of a second from the hundred metres record, managing a new figure on the trapeze, making a bonfire of one's furniture for an idea, setting sail westwards in order to reach the East, ruining oneself to create a new rose, cutting off one's ear to paint a new picture, losing one's sleep to get a poem right, shutting oneself up for life so as to speak with God, getting oneself burnt as a heretic for the honour of humanity, and, finally, slowly killing oneself at 'play-acting' – all this is part of Folly.

To break out of the circle is to bathe life in colours. To normal people life is grey.

Sometimes, it is true, a man can no longer get back into the circle – like Van Gogh, like Artaud. Often a man's reward is merely injustice or ingratitude – like Columbus. There are the ones who collapse exhausted – like Molière, like Jouvet, like Bérard.

Teilhard de Chardin, whom I have just quoted, distinguishes three species of people : The tired ones – The enjoyers – The ardent. Another ternary.

'To the ardent,' he says, 'living is an ascension, a discovery. What seems to them interesting is not just being, but *becoming more*. A being is inexhaustible, like a hearth of heat and light to which it is always possible to get near.' And he adds: 'It is easy to make fun of these men, to treat them as naïve or to find them embarrassing. Meanwhile. it is they who have made us, and they are the ones from whom the Earth of tomorrow is preparing to emerge.'

Wonderers' Club, club of the ardent: club of the crazy. We realize now that my 'follies' had been very small beer. Who cares, provided such folly is destined to become, for me, an ideal, a line of conduct? Anyhow, on that occasion, as sportsmen put it, it 'paid off'.

The period of the Théâtre de France was born.

Théâtre de France or from Tête d'Or to Tête d'Or September '59 - September '68

THE PERIOD OF THE THÉÂTRE DE FRANCE, at least in the memories of the 'Other People', has been darkened by the events of May '68; and indeed, these did put us through severe ordeals – of which I will give a short historical summary further on. But time clarifies things. Let us remain faithful to what we set out to do: of that Past let us retain only what has the vibrancy of the Present. At once joy returns, and I find in it, all over again, the enthusiasm by which I was animated at that moment.

Our company had just lived through thirteen years of full bloom. The Marigny period had brimmed over with vitality. It had enabled us to create a *repertory theatre*. In saying so I am perhaps not being modest, but I am objective: never in the history of the theatre had that phenomenon yet been produced by private means.

In addition, our years of wandering life had given this repertory theatre an *international reputation*. In the eyes of the whole world our company enjoyed the same esteem as did our national theatres, the Comédie Française and the T N P.

Of the fifty or so plays we had put on, a good thirty were still fully active. With *La Vie Parisienne*, the renewed *Soulier de Satin*, and Anouilh's *La Petite Molière* which had just triumphed at the Bordeaux Festival, our last season had been one of the most brilliant. Our value, therefore, was rising.

At the same time the Palais-Royal theatre, whatever its undeniable charm, was too small for our company. Sooner or later we would have had to limit our productivity.

General de Gaulle's government was still fresh. André Malraux, Minister of State in charge of Cultural Affairs, was already planning to clean the luminous stones of Paris. No doubt he considered that the old Odéon also needed to be cleaned from the inside. Since he found, ready to hand, a fully functioning but homeless repertory theatre, why not instal it at the Odéon and baptize it 'Théâtre de France'?

This is in fact what he proposed to us. He was 'nationalizing' our company. Why did we spontaneously accept? I still answer unhesitatingly: for two reasons – because it was Malraux, and because we like to serve.

And yet it was hard to put on one side that 'moral person' called 'Compagnie Renaud-Barrault'. Perhaps we were, after all, unjust and ungrateful. In any case, we put it to sleep and did not dissolve it. The peasant side of me thought: 'You never know'.

To hand ourselves over to 'officialdom' was risky. Would we not be sucked in? By becoming Théâtre de France would we not, in the eyes of many people, be 'academizing' ourselves? Was it not a trap, the prelude to some kind of betrayal? What did my 'double', the libertarian, think of it all?

But there was Malraux and, backing him, de Gaulle. I like men who have dimension.

Life must be grappled with; it is wrong to haggle, it is mean. 'Give oneself so as to receive all.' The Dominican I carry about in me advised me firmly to accept without hesitation.

'Do, do, do. Who will give me the strength to do?' Tête d'Or kept whispering to me.

Faced by this typically Æschylean opportuneness of chance, I decided our Destiny. Once again, Madeleine shared my point of view. All that remained was to cope and, as usual, plunge in 'badly, but quickly'. It was up to us, from then onwards, to avoid the ambushes.

Nonetheless our community was uneasy. Pierre Bertin, for instance, knew the Odéon well, having worked there in his youth. He was well aware of its disadvantages. The younger members of the company were afraid of losing the life of adventure and liberty which had been its charm. Some, still more lucid, foretold fresh economic difficulties.

The risk was in fact considerable. The Odéon is expensive to run; our subsidy, which was settled in a hurry and without any point of comparison, turned out to be insufficient, and according to the licencee's contract which I signed my liability was unlimited. I agreed to this contract nonetheless, for the heavy and dangerous financial responsibility which it involved safeguarded my artistic freedom.

And besides, once again, there was Malraux. During nine years of the Théâtre de France he never tried to subject me to influence or constraint. There were at his side men like Gaétan Picon and his colleagues, including Biasini, with whom we shared the same tastes, the same aspirations.

On the spiritual and artistic plane that 'Théâtre de France' period of our company was pure and joyous, a time of full bloom. If it had not been so, why did men like Ionesco, Roger Blin, Billetdoux, Beckett and Genet, and women like Marguerite Duras and Nathalie Sarraute, come and join us?

On the material plane it was nothing but constant difficulties, and nearly brought us to ruin. Life was much more dangerous than in the time of our 'private enterprise'. The general belief is that, being subsidized, we had a comfortable life. The opposite is true. Whereas at the Marigny we broke even with average attendances of 60 per cent, during nine years at the Théâtre de France our break-even was as high as 72 per cent, and we did not attain it.

The Odéon is like one of those châteaux which in our day the occupant can no longer afford to maintain. And since then that kind of contract has now been abolished. Ours, indeed, was badly drawn up and filled with contradictions between the two Ministers involved – the Finance Minister and that of Cultural Affairs. The articles and conditions were only signed three years later.

I had been put in the position of a lieutenant who receives from his colonel the order to attack. André Malraux's decision had aroused jealousies, 'righteous indignation', in many quarters: for a long time we had to struggle against bitter hostility. Just as we had been an object of charitable compassion when we had no theatre, we were now visited with anger for having received one. That is Paris.

For thirteen years the name 'Odéon' had not been used, since the theatre had become the second house of the Comédie Française. The proposal to call it Théâtre de France aroused a sudden storm of protests. What? our dear Odéon?

To calm this down, I strongly urged Malraux to call it 'Odéon-Théâtre de France'. He agreed reluctantly. He did not like concessions.

I paid a courtesy visit to an eminent official in the Ministry of Finance. This gentleman received me politely, paid me innumerable compliments on the 'cultural' past of our company, and then added:

'To tell you the truth, I don't see the reason for your visit. For me you are only a *project* of Monsieur Malraux's, who is himself only a project of Monsieur de Gaulle.'

The atmosphere, it is obvious, was tense. In the whole of our professional life we had never taken on an adventure like this: it was certainly the one with the greatest risks. What is more, the Odéon's inherited reputation did not help matters.

THE ODÉON

This theatre was built by the architects Peyre and Wailly, round about 1780, for the Comédiens Français. The rue de l'Odéon was then named rue du Théâtre Français. There, in 1784, Beamarchais' *Le Mariage de Figaro* had its first performance. It caused a memorable row. We were to be involved in others.

During the Revolution there was a split among the actors – between the Royalists and the Revolutionaries. These last, led by Talma, moved over to the gardens of the Palais Royal and formed the present Comédie Française. The others had trouble, even went to prison.

The Théâtre Royal, occupied by two large statues of Marat and Jean-Jacques Rousseau, was named Théâtre du Peuple, and then Théâtre Egalité.

In 1795 after many ups and downs the house, now directed by M. Poupart-Dorfeuille, took the name Odéon. What was its vocation? A document of the period says:

> The Odéon is an institute whose object is to train a new generation of dramatic artists, to produce not only interpreters but tragic and comic poets; in short to give new life to all the talents that can embellish the French theatre.

Under Napoleon I the Odéon changed its name to Théâtre Impérial. Under Louis XVIII, again, to Théâtre Royal. Under Napoleon III, to Théâtre de l'Impératrice.

From 1946 to 1959 it had been called the Salle Luxembourg.

Meantime it was constantly lapsing into the Odéon. Now it had to be turned into the Théâtre de France.

So the life of that fine building had been a tormented one. Its object, nonetheless, seemed clearly defined: promotion, creation, youthfulness; a theatre whose plays should be *at the starting-point* of artistic activity. No wonder this object involves it in battles, controversies, shocks. There, right at the Carrefour Danton, it is always the first thing to be touched as soon as there are social troubles. It is covered with scars.

On the plane of economic success, if we except one or two directors who turned it into a neighbourhood theatre, all the others – the ones who, in the course of a century and a half, were determined to remain faithful to its mission of creation and combat – went bankrupt, even the greatest of them, Antoine, Gémier, etc.

The number of cartoons one comes across, on the subject of the Odéon being dark! *'Les rats s'y sont mis, parce qu'on n'y voit pas un chat'*, etc.

When Malraux entrusted me with this 'exploit', the stones were black, the arcades outside were empty, the whole place was dingy. From time to time people would come to the box office and ask for a railway ticket to Sceaux – they were confusing the Odéon with the Gare du Luxembourg.

But inside, the stage was crowded with stage hands. I had to sack a good half of them – a detestable job. But for that, it would have been unworkable. Even the Union recognized this.

I still had no director's licence, but all the worries fell on me.

For the ceremonial opening, André Malraux and I chose *Tête d'Or*.

My *Tête d'Or*, so much longed for, even since 1939. Twenty years of patience and dreams. André Masson, who always turned up at the various fresh starts in my life – *Numance*, 1937 – *Hamlet*, 1946 – agreed to do the sets and costumes for *Tête d'Or*, 1959. Boulez would take Honegger's unfinished score and complete the music. Alain Cuny, Terzieff and Catherine Sellers would be the protagonists.

On 21 October 1959, opening of *Tête d'Or* under the auspices of General de Gaulle, President of the Republic, together with the whole Government.

Paris ground its teeth.

The critics went for us.

The students came.

The clan of 'fans' formed.

There were some fifty performances, and I know young members of the audience who, during that series, saw it as many as thirty-one times. Receipts were not exactly good, but we reached 50 per cent. Morally it was a great success; materially it was a flop.

The company's existing repertory was there to fill out the season – *Les Fausses Confidences*, *Baptiste*, *The Cherry Orchard*, *Christophe Colomb*, *Occupe-toi d'Amélie*: the 'good old St Bernards'. Plus – most important –

Anouilh's *La Petite Molière*, which had already won such a success at Bordeaux in the preceding May. We expected great things of it, very reasonably.

It opened on 11 November 1959 – three weeks after *Tête d'Or*. The same press that had given it a chorus of praise in May now fell upon us. What had become of the time when – in 1946 – Paris applauded each new venture of our company? This time André Malraux's Théâtre de France *must* be brought down in failure.

The battle was now not on the stage, it was in the house: underhand, mischievous, virulent, sordid. It was a psychosis. We carried on.

I announced a third new venture: Ionesco's *Rhinocéros*. Malraux confessed to me his alarm, not on account of the play's quality, but because its *avant-garde* character might result in my going too far for the first year. I took the risk.

> A still present memory. One afternoon, while we were rehearsing, we heard the news of the death of Camus, in a car accident. I can still see Ionesco's face of consternation, even panic. Death, his old enemy, was there in front of him. We stopped the rehearsal, unable to go on working. We were a family of theatre people and had just lost one of our nearest and dearest.

20 January 1960. Opening of *Rhinocéros*. General condemnation. Lips pursed. 'Ionesco is settling down, it smacks of the old Odéon'. Boring and dull. In short, good arguments for destruction. 'Ah! it's no longer the Ionesco of his early days.[1] Here he is now writing propaganda', etc. He was piously attacked for a failure to be *avant-garde*. 'As for Jean-Louis Barrault, he is trying to appear young', etc.

Today some people recognize *Rhinocéros* as one of Ionesco's best plays.

Such were the relations between Paris and the Théâtre de France during the first season. The snarling and rancour were not to disappear decisively until the end of the third year.

Meanwhile, *Julius Caesar*, acted in an extraordinary setting by Balthus, had the same hostile reception. In this particular case, I recognize, I had made serious mistakes. The criticisms were deserved.

On the other hand, Schéhadé's *Le Voyage*, a captivating play which we brought off, was also condemned. We were even discouraged, such bias was shown – I would go further and say, stupid and out-of-place xenophobia.

Guerre et Poésie, a remarkable show which we and Pichette had composed together, with the help of a highly talented young artist of the cinema, Vilardebo, very nearly became a scene of civil war; it was at the time of the Algerian putsch.

---

[1] When his plays used to be given to empty houses. The number of people who were present at the early Ionesco performances to empty houses would be enough, certainly, to fill the Opéra for a whole year.

When Max Ernst consented to do sets for Giraudoux's *Judith,* which is one of his greatest plays, perhaps the strongest of them, the newspapers did not even mention his name.

When André Masson was commissioned to repaint the ceiling of the auditorium, people were taken with a sudden access of affection and admiration for J.-P. Laurens, who had designed the old ceiling.

The first two successes were Brendan Behan's *The Hostage,* directed by Georges Wilson and with our beloved Arletty in it, and the *Merchant of Venice,* directed by Marguerite Jamois, with Sorano. Sorano was to die suddenly in the following year, at the age of forty-one – a real loss to our profession.

At last the storm calmed down with Christopher Fry's *La Nuit a sa Clarté* (*The Dark is Light Enough*) in the French translation by Philippe de Rothschild; *Andromaque* was a victory; and Ionesco's *Le Piéton de l'Air* [1] divided opinion, but favourably on the whole. The cabal against us had grown tired.

Our plane had taken three seasons to get off the ground. Now we gained height. We were flying towards the fine weather.

Jules Supervielle's translation of *As You Like It* did wonders; it was directed by J.-P. Granval. The third production of *Le Soulier de Satin,* with Geneviève Page and Samy Frey as Prouhèze and Rodrigue, was a triumph. And there was the sensational success of Samuel Beckett's *Oh! les Beaux Jours,* in Roger Blin's production.

Then *Le Mariage de Figaro* (sets by Pierre Delbée and costumes by Yves Saint Laurent), Billetdoux's *Il Faut Passer par les Nuages*; and Marguerite Duras' *Des Journées Entières dans les Arbres.*

We had paid our tribute money. Paris recognized it, the battle was won. It had lasted four years.

Now the new productions were as successful as the well-tried favourites which we kept in our repertory – *Amphitryon, The Oresteia, Le Procès, Hamlet, Partage de Midi, Intermezzo* (in the beautiful settings by our true friend Brianchon), *Le Chien du Jardinier, Les Fourberies de Scapin.*

In addition our tours (to Japan in 1960, to South America in 1961, to the USSR in 1962, to Italy, to Germany in 1963, to Canada, to the United States – third visit – in 1964, to England, to Rumania, to Czechoslovakia, to Austria, etc.) were helping to make the Théâtre de France into that 'international theatre, French language section', which we had dreamed of with such fervour for more than twenty years. The whole world recognized us, we had attained a kind of fulfilment. But it had had to be paid for dearly. Dearly enough to break anyone who was less of a 'rhinoceros' than I was.

From time to time I would receive a reminder from the Ministry that I ought to submit my future programme to my Minister. I would send a note

---

[1] Decor by Jacques Noël, as in the case of *Rhinocéros* and of *La Petite Molière.* Jacques Noël . . . a true accomplice!

in reply, and Malraux would send it back to me with the following minute:
'Agreed, next move yours!' That was all. Our alliance was perfect.

He knew how much we had had to struggle; we knew with what firmness he
was supporting us.

One day General de Gaulle set me a real facer. He wanted to be present *incog-nito* at a performance of *Le Soulier de Satin*. There was no escort. A black
Citroën drew up close to the main entrance. I was on the steps to welcome
him and Mme de Gaulle. He was in mufti. We threaded our way through the
crowd – some of them turned to look, no doubt because this gentleman seemed
to them particularly tall – and just as the people in the auditorium had recog-nized him the show began.

At the interval he came on stage to compliment the company, and at the end
he made his escape through an emergency exit before which his Citroën was
waiting for him. I can still hear him saying:

'Hurry, Yvonne!'

He was very fond of Claudel and made a pungent observation about him:
'Ce Claudel, tout de même, il a du ragoût!' ('That Claudel, when all's said,
has got some spice!')

That is what I call criticism. That is what is meant by a man 'having his
pencil point in his eye'. My thoughts return to Blaise Cendrars, who also had
spice.

As regards that third *Soulier de Satin*: nothing is harder than re-doing a
production. You need the support of a really powerful play. I have done four
of the *Soulier*. The fourth was for the Roman theatre at Orange.

A few words on the method I adopted for the third production. Encouraged
by the experiment of *Christophe Colomb* with its significant object (the sail),
I looked for some object that could act as a catalyst for the whole play. At
Bahia (Brazil) I had admired the Portuguese baroque altars in the churches:
they were the very soul of Claudel. I had observed, indeed, that the main styles
of theatre are inspired by the places in which the actors have to play. The style
of the Elizabethan theatre is based on the courtyard of an inn. The style of
the medieval 'mansions' is based on the steps before the doors of the churches.
The arrangement of a Japanese Noh play resembles the small island (peninsula,
really) I had seen at Nara: it was connected with the land by a narrow isthmus
on the left-hand side. Vilar's style for the T N P came from the big courtyard
of the Papal Palace at Avignon. The style of the Greek theatre comes from the
natural tiers of seats that are supported against a wall of rock.

And so I wondered what would be the natural place in which to act *Le
Soulier de Satin*. My choice fell upon a church altar. In the play Prouhèze
says:

Quand je m'élancerai vers le mal, que ce soit avec un pied boiteux.
La barrière que vous avez mise, quand je voudrai la franchir, que ce soit
avec une aile rognée.

29, 30 With Edwige
Feuillière in *Partage
de Midi* (The Division
of Noon) by Paul
Claudel, 1948

31–33 *Les Fourberies de Scapin (Scapin's Tricks) by Molière, 1949*

34 *Élisabeth d'Angleterre*
(Elizabeth of England)
by Ferdinand Brückner
at the Marigny, 1949.
Jean-Louis Barrault as
Philip of Spain being
congratulated by
Maurice Chevalier
after the performance

35 *Malatesta* by Henry
de Montherlant.
Marigny, 1950

36 *Lazarus* by André Obey. Marigny, 1951

37 *Bacchus* by Jean Cocteau. Marigny, 1951

◄ 38 *Le Château* (The Castle) by Franz Kafka, 1957

39 *Le Soulier de Satin* (The Satin Slipper) by Paul Claudel. Odéon Théâtre de France, 1959

40 *Numance* by Cervantes. A rehearsal

41 *Rhinocéros* by Ionesco. Odéon, Théâtre de France, 1960

42 *Le Piéton de l'Air* by Ionesco. Odéon, Théâtre de France, 1963

43, 44 *Les Paravents* (The Screens) by Jean Genet. Odéon, Théâtre de France, 1966.
(Left) Madeleine Renaud, (right) Jean-Louis Barrault

45 *Tête d'Or* by Paul Claudel, the last play by the Renaud-Barrault company at the
Odéon, Théâtre de France, 1968

46 A student meeting
inside the Odéon,
Théâtre de France
during the events of
May 1968

47, 48 *Rabelais*. Queues outside the Élysée-Montmartre Theatre, 1968; (below) a scene from the play presented at the Old Vic, 1969

49, 50 Rehearsing *Rabelais* in Paris and (below) at the Roundhouse, London, in 1971

51 Sir Laurence Olivier,
Madeleine Renaud and
Jean-Louis Barrault
outside the Royal
Court Theatre in
London, 1969

52 Jean-Louis Barrault
with scenery at the
Vincennes warehouse, 1970

53 Madeleine Renaud and Jean-Louis Barrault with the famous leather bag at Orly
airport, before flying to London, 1971

54 *Sous le vent des îles Baléares* (Part Four of *The Satin Slipper*). Jean-Louis Barrault in
the performance at the Gare d'Orsay, 1972

(When I make a rush towards evil, let it be with a limping foot.

The barrier you have placed – when I want to cross it, let it be with a clipped wing.)

Sin, being the thing one cannot help committing, demands of the sinner that he should give himself to it wholly. But at the same time the Claudelian sinner wants to encounter obstacles that may prevent him from reaching satisfaction. Passion wrestling with the guardian angel.

The altar is order. But if one breaks the altar one satisfies the disorder of passion. Therefore the altar (in the play) is made in several pieces. Sometimes the pieces are separated and the passion of disorder is given its head. Sometimes the pieces are put together again and order is reconstituted. By using the three pieces of the altar, plus two sets of steps and a revolving pedestal, we were able to embody imaginatively all the permutations of the thirty-three scenes of the *Le Soulier de Satin*.

All that remained was to add, each time, a few light props to suggest the locality.

Because continuity was now more fully respected, we were also able to put back certain scenes that had been cut in the original production, especially that of the 'Double Shadow', which Claudel had been so sorry to lose.

I had given up playing Rodrigue. Once again I felt the pain of being separated from certain characters. As with creators, who find that some of their works can separate themselves from them while others remain attached to them for life, actors have roles from which they can easily separate themselves, but others that remain stuck to their skin.

I know what Marie Bell, who had created the role of Prouhèze so splendidly, had to suffer when she was parted from it.

Our profession is a cruel one. And the more we offer it our life, the sharper is the cruelty. Cruelty and life go together.

THE 'PETITE SALLE'

As we reached the end of those years of struggle, we had come really to love the Odéon. By dint of effort and suffering it had become *our* theatre.

The Petit Marigny was much in our minds. By means of a muslin canopy we found a way of altering the volume of the Odéon auditorium quite quickly : all that was left of it was the stalls and the first circle – six hundred and fifty seats. A true 'royal' theatre. Its atmosphere was extraordinary. For certain plays that I call 'easel plays' it was ideal. It was in that format that Beckett's masterpiece, *Oh! les Beaux Jours*, had its first performance.

Roger Blin, whom I had asked to direct *Divines Paroles* by del Valle Inclán, had given Madeleine *Oh! les Beaux Jours* to read. She fell in love with it at first sight.

For three months Beckett and Roger Blin 'worked on her', like naturalists studying the life of insects. To a director, Madeleine is obedience itself : as soon as he has gained her confidence, she gives her whole self.

Oh! les Beaux Jours was first performed in Venice, then in Yugoslavia and then to inaugurate our 'Petite Salle'.

It was an event. Our new *Soulier de Satin* had just triumphed, four days earlier.

'Beckett pulverizes Claudel', said one critic. 'It is a festival of abjection', said another.

Actors have the reputation of being given to exaggeration; what then is one to say of critics? For forty years we had been hearing the same refrains. Either: 'A mountain of boredom, poor Monsieur So-and-So, something to run a mile from and never return.' Or else: 'The theatre was born last night – impossible to look at anything else!'

In fact, *Oh! les Beaux Jours* is a masterpiece. A perfect achievement of music in play form, a compact ball of knowledge of human nature. That sonata for woman almost unaccompanied enabled Madeleine to take a new turning in her art.

As a young girl she had played the ingénue parts – Cécile and Rosette.[1] As a young woman she became Jacqueline in the *Chandelier* and Araminte in *Les Fausses Confidences*. Then she took a first turning with Madame Ranevskaya in *The Cherry Orchard*. With Winnie a new turning: thanks to Beckett and Blin she was able to open for us a whole sack of humanity. And I am leaving out of account our comic Madeleine.

It is very rare for an actress to be able to change her type four times in her career. But indeed this is not, I think, exactly what happened: Madeleine has no type, really; she is the human Being, naked.

Colette, who also had 'the point of her pencil in her eye', once wrote her a letter, and I will copy out a passage from it, at the risk of offending Madeleine's modesty – but I take the responsibility:

> When you are acting, one doesn't know at first what it is in you that enchants. One tells oneself: it must be the voice. Or else the expression of the face. Perhaps also a fine arm, or the curve of the shoulder. Might it be the soul?

For all of us *Les Beaux Jours* was a red letter day. The true personality of the Théâtre de France was asserting itself. It inspired François Billetdoux to achieve one of his greatest successes with *Il Faut Passer par les Nuages*. This had its first performance in the big house. A memory without a blemish. A still living play which we keep in our present repertoire.

Marguerite Duras entrusted to us *Des Journées Entières dans les Arbres*. First performance in the small house.

THE PETIT ODÉON

The Odéon was becoming a supple instrument. We wanted to make it even more supple by adding to it a still smaller hall – a hundred and fifty seats. We

---

[1] In *Il ne Faut Jurer de Rien* and *On ne Badine pas avec l'Amour*.

had noticed a place that was serving no purpose. Thanks to that understanding man Vassas, the architect-consultant, and to advice from our friend Zerfuss, this became 'Le Petit Odéon'.

From now on we could act in places of three different sizes and at the same time remain on top of one another. Theatre is promiscuity: its buildings must be filled with such a load of humanity that one always feels there is no room. In a theatre, as soon as there is a stretch of wall that cannot be 'humanized', death infiltrates, sticks to it and freezes the plane. Stage life is a race against death.

With these three sizes of places-cum-stages, we could now play over the whole gamut.

Nathalie Sarraute inaugurated the Petit Odéon with two plays as subtle and stinging as insects: *Le Silence* and *Le Mensonge*.

In that small hall we presented Beckett, Ionesco and Pinget; also authors' first plays, such as Jean-Pierre Faye's *Hommes et Pierres* and R. L. Clot's *La Révélation*.

In the large theatres we now did both *Le Mariage de Figaro* and *Le Barbier de Séville*; I even revived *Numance*. We had re-produced Cervantes' tragedy for the Roman theatre at Orange (where we played for three seasons running, at the suggestion of M. Biasini, Gaétan Picon's colleague) [1].

Its success had been considerable and the press unanimously favourable. When *Numance*, with the same production and cast, was presented at the Théâtre de France, things were not the same at all.

While the failure of our *Julius Caesar* seems to me, alas, justified, I still find the severe treatment given to *Numance* aberrant. That evening 'they' were in a bad mood, whereas 'they' had not been at Orange. One is supposed to say: 'What does it matter?' Well, it does mattter.

Why do we work in the theatre, if not to meet human beings? Then why should someone raise a barrier between them and us? Theatre is a sorcerer's art. The so-called 'bush telegraph' – the word of mouth press – operates. If the show is a mess, the public is not deceived and gradually stays away: why throw discredit, from the start, on shows that perhaps have a chance of pleasing the public? Does anyone possess inbred knowledge in sensual matters?

Both *La Petite Molière* and the new *Numance* have in fact had their careers atrophied by the pernicious influence of critics.

The critics, for the last twenty years, bear a heavy responsibility for the disarray now prevailing in our theatres. Artists and members of audiences – from *avant-garde* extremists to immobilist conservatives – no longer know to which saints they should turn.

Jouvet, in his last years, was afraid to touch anything: he kept repeating, 'They will murder us.'

Did not *they* sadden Dullin's last years?

---

[1] Besides *Numance*, we presented there *Hamlet*, *Le Soulier de Satin* (fourth production), *The Merchant of Venice* and Molière's *Amphitryon*.

Did they not reduce Claudel to despair a few months before his death, when *L'Annonce faite à Marie* was put on at the Français?

Was not Cervantes, in his time, deflected from the theatre?

Did not Racine, for the same reason, cut short his output of plays?

In the preface to *Bérénice*, Racine, at the age of thirty-one, wrote:

> All these criticisms come from four or five unfortunate little authors, who have never been able, on their own account, to arouse the curiosity of the public. They always wait for the occasion of some successful work, in order to attack it. Not out of jealousy. For on what foundation would they be jealous? But in the hope that one will take the trouble to answer them, and that one will drag them from the obscurity in which their own works would have left them for the whole of their life.

The well-known critic Gustave Planche wrote:

> Monsieur Victor Hugo is now thirty-six years old. And we see the authority of his name getting weaker and weaker . . . growing pale.

Saint-Exupéry said:

> With what standard work do you compare your work, to be satisfied with it?

I know that it is not good to be always praised, and that some criticisms spur us on. But when all is said and done, I wonder, very sincerely, whether the overall result is positive.

People now extol only what is new, only what produces a shock, causes 'an event'. They no longer know where 'the good' is to be found. They no longer know for whom or for what they are working. The profession is bewildered, like a team of horses being pulled this way and that. Luckily desire is always reborn, the need still makes itself felt, and we go on working 'desperately'.

That is really the only way of being able to pursue one's dreams. Ever since my early days I have been aware of the richness of living 'desperately'. I still feel it. And yet on certain opening nights I have wept with rage.

On these occasions Léonard never failed to quote to me in Italian the proverb 'the dog barks but the caravan passes on'. To the life of the 'strolling players' caravan' critics are sometimes more dangerous than dogs.

Madeleine and I grew more and more eager that the Théâtre de France should become a theatrical centre open to other *animateurs*. Already we had welcomed to our theatre Marguerite Jamois and Georges Wilson. Roger Blin and Jean-Pierre Granval were often given productions to direct. Bourseiller did Kafka's *L'Amérique*. Jacques Charon and Barsacq were also invited, and, later on, Lavelli, the Italian director De Lullo, Jean-Marie Serreau, P. Chabert and Laurent Terzieff. I am keeping Maurice Béjart for later. To our minds the Théâtre de France should become a national and international home of theatre.

It was at this time that we decided to create Genet's *Les Paravents* (*The Screens*).

The director I had suggested to Genet was Roger Blin. Decor and costumes: André Acquart. Sound effects: José Berghmans who, after Boulez and Girard, had become our conductor.

I informed Gaétan Picon and André Malraux: they were in entire agreement. Not the slightest objection. The play, which takes its inspiration from the war in Algeria, is a dangerous one: it presses on a flashpoint. But it immediately takes off and is soon *an epic of Misery and Death*.

Today I still consider *Les Paravents* as one of the most important plays of twentieth-century theatre. It has the amplitude of the best works of Shakespeare. This is not the place for going into detail: a whole book could be written about *Les Paravents* and Genet's poetic art.

The row it caused is well known.

Having some feeling of what we would be risking, I had written an article in the *Cahier* that would present Genet's play to the public. Here are some extracts:

Scandal and Provocation

In art there are two ways of being a cause of scandal.

First there is the scandal that 'the Others' make about the artist, that is to say about the play which is being presented for the first time; but more often than not this play is the product of a naïve, unconscious sincerity and of a particularly original temperament.

Secondly there is the scandal premeditated by the artist himself, when he has purposely fabricated a play in order to shake other people. This second case is in fact an imposture, because he is trying to pass off as unconscious and original something that is mere calculation.

The true artist never seeks to produce scandal. Suddenly, to his great surprise, astonishment, even stupefaction, he discovers that he is 'causing scandal', when he was only obeying what was evident, what was imposed by his vision.

Neither Villon, nor Baudelaire, nor Mallarmé, nor Van Gogh (and one could mention many others) sought scandal. It was their genius that was scandalous in the eyes of 'the Others'. And yet, without deliberately choosing the ground proper to scandal, the artist does sometimes *provoke*.

Provocation, contrary to what it may seem, is different from an attack. Usually it is a riposte. A riposte that takes the form of a cry of indignation, a provoking cry.

First of all it is life, as manipulated by society and especially by the society of '*honnêtes gens*', that swarms with provocations. Phoney morality, phoney rights, bad faith, hypocrisies, impostures, calculations, phoney generosity, phoney charity, phoney sentiments, the carnival of all those characters which the others play, into which they empty themselves: the stiffness of the narrow soldier, the humiliating pity of the churchy, the blind rectitude of the law; the spider's web of order, the traps of good works, the playacting in keeping up historic memories, the masquerade with the flag, the clogging effect of phoney solidarity, etc. – the 'honnêtes gens' never stop provoking us from childhood until death.

Without meaning to seek scandal, but in the name of a certain justice (that is to say, of a certain readjustment of things, and above all because one cannot stand it any longer), one ripostes with a cry that rejects that provocation, and one sends back another.

At once there comes a stupefied reaction from the sect of the 'honnêtes gens' who, having long ago lost all awareness of their own ignominy, demand sentence and punishment in the name of order, of *their* order.

Which of the two began it? Human conduct which, in art, consists in slinging provocation in the face of those who daily and stealthily provoke us, is the more courageous, more estimable conduct, but also more exacting.

Coming from a 'righteous indignation' it can only be wholesome and ready to suffer.

Being voluptuous and sympathetic, it becomes vulnerable.

The exacerbated artist who, being beside himself, has recourse to the provocative act, is like an animal defending its young, like a human being defending his skin.

He has in fact the justification of legitimate self-defence. In that cry he is denouncing social imposture, lies and hypocrisy. It is in that defiance that the nobility of provocative art resides, for there is love and nothing but love in that defiance.

The only aim of provocation is to serve life. But if one detects in it gloating, malicious pleasure, personal taste, an inner inclination, a secret indulgence, then its nobility and legitimacy vanish, for instead of love there was only vice.

And so it seems to be the same with provocation as with scandal. There is the good kind, brought into being by naïveté or indignation, and the bad kind, inspired by calculation or vice.

In the theatre there is a feeling even more sacred than the feeling for liberty, and this is Respect for the human Being.

To safeguard a complete freedom in the field of his art without doing violence to *human respect* is, on the plane of his own human behaviour, the exacting problem of a man of the theatre.

Our human behaviour, within the dramatic art, seems therefore to be caught between two fires. The freedom to say everything, and human respect which forbids us to say anything. There is only one direction that can harmonize us with those two imperatives, and that is the perspective of *justice*. Justice which readjusts life, silences impostures, purifies the passions, sanctions excess. It is the ideal kingdom of sublimated childhood.

We are about to create Jean Genet's *Les Paravents*. It is not for us to express a personal opinion on Jean Genet.

Our role is essentially and exclusively of a theatrical order; and here the importance of Genet is uncontestable. His subject? It takes its source in the tragedy of Algeria, but it moves rapidly away from that and develops by generalizing. Genet spares neither of the two camps. He remains lucid both towards colonialism and towards neo-nationalism. It is *misery* that remains always the victim. It is on that that both sides raise the screens of egoism, vulgarity, cupidity, vanity, covetousness, filth. It is misery, always left in the lurch. . . .

The play was extremely well acted. Our superb Maria Casarès, Germaine Kerjean, Paule Aanen, Madeleine, Alric, Amidou, Cattand . . . in fact all. Blin had softened nothing. During the first ten or eleven performances there was no incident. It looked as if the whole thing would go off well. At the twelfth there was a well-concerted surprise attack: 'paras' jumping from the second balcony; fights, people hurt, blood on the stage, stink bombs, safety curtain. The steadiness, the calm, the extraordinary lucid behaviour of the majority of the audience made it possible for us to carry on and complete the performance.

This happened in April 1966. During the next thirty or so performances there were fights practically every evening. The *Occident* group (extreme right) organized processions in the streets. There were questions in the Assemblée Nationale. Malraux took our side courageously. The *Préfet de Police*, M. Papon, defended the liberty of the theatre, even if the policemen he sent to protect the public seemed to us – well, some of them – to have a 'weakness' for the demonstrators.

I decided to do another series in September: thirty more performances. I hoped these people would have calmed down. The things began again. Incendiary bombs, bags of nails, volleys of electric bulbs, pelting with plaster, pelting with rats. The public remained imperturbable.

We were never obliged to cut short a performance, we always got to the end. Thanks to the determination of the audience. People nowadays believe, because of the demonstrators, that *Les Paravents* was rejected by public opinion. The opposite is true: ninety per cent of the audience were for us, for *Les Paravents* and freedom of expression; only ten per cent did their damnedest to create such disorder that the police would be led to forbid the performance.

The government of that time, that of de Gaulle and Malraux, showed by its firmness that the theatre, under French democracy, was not subjected to censorship. Let us remember the date: 1966.

In the following year, during the World Exhibition at Montreal, my friend Laurence Olivier asked me how I had managed. He was eager to put on at the British National Theatre (Old Vic) a play which seemed likely to be turned down by the Lord Chamberlain.

I could only refer to the humanism of the men who were then governing us – de Gaulle and Malraux. Never had a national theatre had so much freedom to express itself. The repercussions of this business – there is ample evidence – were international: its effect was exemplary. Alas. It was perhaps too beautiful to last. But the Paris public had given its approval.

Since then I have thought a great deal about what should guide the conduct of a man in charge of a national theatre. A national theatre must not be the government's theatre, but the *nation's theatre*. Its output, on the political and social plane, must reflect the political and social composition of Parliament.

An example: at the time of writing this, the governmental majority is 40 per cent, the rest is divided among the opposition groups. I do not at this moment know the exact proportions, but it would seem to me just that a national theatre's output should be 40 per cent governmental in spirit, about 20 per cent Communist, 20 per cent Centrist, and for the rest extreme left or right.

National theatres that limit themselves to the government's cast of mind are totalitarian state theatres, whatever their denomination. If national theatres were only oppositional they would be usurpers.

In 1966 a citizen of the French Republic could read on our posters:

Le Soulier de Satin	Paul Claudel
Andromaque	Racine
Il Faut Passer par les Nuages	Billetdoux
Oh! les Beaux Jours	Samuel Beckett
Le Barbier de Séville	Beaumarchais
Des Journées Entières dans les Arbres	Marguerite Duras
Les Paravents	Jean Genet

Besides, Jean Genet's *Les Paravents* is not a political play. It is a humanitarian play, an anarchist cry. It is above all a poet's play.

As an answer to the many accusations to which I have had to listen, I have often told the following story:

The scene is at Villefranche-sur-Saône (near Lyons). In the fifteenth-century flamboyant Gothic church a gendarme finds, one day, close to the font, a young girl letting herself be had by a he-goat. In her pleasure she is showing the whites of her eyes. Scandal! The girl is put into a reformatory. The goat is taken back into his field. The place is exorcized with holy water. And no one has noticed that, for the last five centuries, a few metres above the place of the scandal, there has been a gargoyle representing exactly the same scene. During five hundred years no one has ever thought of destroying the carved stone. Why?

Art, in its essence, is a contesting of death, a contesting of the Pharisees of all kinds, a contesting of oneself.

Art exists because we must never stop putting ourselves in question. We must kill ourselves every evening to be born afresh every morning. Art either is revolutionary or is not.

A people's level of civilization is gauged by the proportion of liberty its government allows to the 'fine arts', to the spirit of tolerance.

I do, however, recognize – and this is why I have it in for the political strategies – that this liberty is too often exploited by opposition parties which are in fact merely other, parallel governments, busy anticipating office. When that happens, everybody falls back into the same repression, the same mediocre quality of civilization. Today no one in the world any longer *deserves* democracy. That is the disaster.

The attacks against us were cruel. Some critics went as far as denunciation. They openly called for the police. That reminded me of something:

> *Beast of the Apocalypse!*
> *Scum of humanity!*
> *As dangerous with his impiety*
> *As by the scandalousness of what he says.*
> *Neither fear of God, nor respect for Man.*
> *He slings calumny at all the orders*
> *Without distinction!*
> *A disgrace to good manners and to public decency!*

Putherbe [1], Rabelais' accuser, came to mind – and one or two others:

> *His soul is no different from the dogs and the swine.*   (Calvin)

Not to mention what Molière suffered at the time of *Tartuffe*.

From that day I longed to serve Rabelais.

On 1 January 1967, as a member of one of the 'constituted authorities', I had gone early in the morning to offer my good wishes to the President of the Republic. After the customary speeches the learned assembly moved to the buffet. Someone came over to me and said:

'*Monsieur le Président* wishes to speak to you.'

I approached de Gaulle. Half intimidated, half prepared.

'Well, Barrault, you have got yourself talked about a great deal recently.'

'Other people have talked about me, *Monsieur le Président de la République*, but it is not my doing.'

'Do you think it was worth while?'

'I am happy that you should ask me that question, *mon général*. I think, in fact, that nobody can have a better understanding of the play in question than the man who has fought against human misery, for the Resistance, against injustice and for decolonization.'

'*Dans ce cas, mon cher maître, allez vous sustenter.*' [2]

Was it a sentence of death? Was it a confidential approval? He would be a very clever man who could say. I never saw General de Gaulle again.

---

[1] Gabriel du Puy Herbault, a monk at Fontevrault, attacked Rabelais fiercely in a book called *Theotismus, sive de tollendis et expurgandis malis libris* (Paris, 1549). Rabelais nicknamed him Putherbe. See Book IV, chapter xxxii. (*Translator's note.*)

[2] 'In that case, *mon cher maître*, keep up your strength.' Or perhaps, 'fend for yourself'.

On the day of the last performance of *Les Paravents*, André Malraux was in the house. He came round afterwards to my dressing-room and confirmed to me his admiration for the play. I thanked him once more for his courageous support. He left : with him too it was my last real contact.

At about the same time – I am not good at precise dates – there must have been a certain change in the conduct of the government. Boulez quarrelled with Malraux. Gaéton Picon and his team were dismissed from their jobs, or anyhow they resigned. The thing is beyond me. What I can say is that they were no longer there and that I was sorry. Something must have been changing. What? I did not know.

The old Odéon had to recognize its original vocation – as a theatre of youth, a modern theatre, a fighting theatre. Because the Théâtre des Nations could not any longer stay at the Théâtre Sarah-Bernhardt under the direction of A.-M. Julien and his colleagues, I agreed to take charge of it.

We invited both the *avant-garde* and the principal theatre companies in the world : Bunraku, Noh, Kathakali, Germany, U S S R, Poland (the first Grotowski shows), England, the Metropolitan Opera, Strehler's productions (Italy), Julian Beck's Living Theatre; and we invited for the first time the young and dynamic international Festival of Nancy, directed by Jack Lang; etc.

The Théâtre de France plus Théâtre des Nations became a high place that was at once French and international, bringing together students and veteran companies.

An international cartel was created. A new aspect of the Théâtre des Nations took form. We all felt that it must become a theatre not just of welcome but of creations. This is what it should, today, become officially : in 1967 we were already laying the foundations for this.

I started the first research studio, which I entrusted to my great friend Peter Brook. I found a hall for him in the Gobelins factory. He and I agreed on the purpose and the subject : he would form, for the first time in the world, an international company, and would organize a show based on Shakespeare's *The Tempest*. Ariel, for instance, would be Japanese.

With the help of Claude Gallimard and of Simone Ben Mussa (who ran our *Cahiers*), we started the free Tuesdays. A young audience 'of all ages' rushed to take advantage of them.

We were well on the way towards world theatre. And yet, while our marvellous adventure was constantly reaching fresh heights, I had secret anxieties. I had begun to feel that, in that non-religious monastery, I was becoming a prior.

In 'the world of *Les Paravents*' I had been defended by some astonishing human beings. One of them, in particular, was the priest of one of the big Paris parishes. Another was a four-star general. Because of us he nearly did not get his fifth star. Luckily he did : if he had not, I should never have forgiven myself, for he was an admirable person, a true fighter. He had in fact been an officer in the Legion. I have often seen him since then, he has confided in me, and I feel that what he said applied to me : 'When I was a lieutenant,' he said, 'I was happy, I was living with my men. As a captain, as a major, it was still all right. As soon as I was promoted to colonel, I began to lose the feeling of my men. As a general, I was cut off from them and I was unhappy – they were moving away from me.'

At the same time, Léonard had left me : he had asked for the retirement to which he had a right. I was very sorry. And Marthe, my secretary, our 'daughter', had died painfully. Our family enterprise was coming to pieces in the midst of splendour.

To replace Léonard, I had asked my tutelary Ministry to second Félix Giacomoni, an official who was in love with literature, to the Théâtre de France-des-Nations; and Giacomoni – who was a man of devotion and integrity, a difficult character but beyond reproach – had readjusted the running of our company and made it like the administration of a public department. I no longer understood it at all. That branch was escaping me of its own accord.

Add to all this the more and more inextricable complications of our tax affairs and dealings with bureaucracy; I was completely lost. In that polyglot theatre, the administrative language alone was foreign to me. And yet I had always loved the administrative part of the life of a theatre.

In short, the more the Théâtre de France, joined to the Théâtre des Nations, consolidated its positions, the more isolated I felt.

As an enterprise grows, makes progress and expands, its financial means must follow suit. They were not doing so. Would we be obliged to cut down, that is to say renounce expansion, or would we continue stubbornly along the way of progress at the risk of rather serious financial difficulties?

Every year we warned our tutelary Ministries, in advance, of our growing difficulties. These warnings received no sympathy.

'Increase the amount of your takings !'

'They could not be more healthy, our average is 75 per cent. This is the maximum for a theatre running in repertory.'

'Cut down your activity !'

'That would be a pity. All the instrument asks for is to develop.'

The problem was becoming insoluble. And so there I was, alone and lost in the twists and turns of administration and finance.

In that third period of the Théâtre de France I experienced one disappointment, Henry VI; two joys, La Tentation de Saint Antoine and the Saint-Exupéry show; and one victory, the revival of Tête d'Or.

HENRY VI

I have a particular love for this work of Shakespeare's. In this youthful work he has laid down all his themes. It is a densely packed play which moves from the Middle Ages to the Renaissance. All Shakespeare is in it.

I wanted to do the same sort of work on Henry VI as I had done on Le Soulier de Satin and on the Oresteia. I adapted the three plays so as to make them into one play lasting four hours. Settings by Acquart. Costumes by Marie-Hélène Dasté. Music by Miroglio.

In spite of a few indulgences which I ought to have cut out, I was pleased with the result. I have always sinned by greediness.

I introduced entrances and exits through the auditorium. Simultaneity of scenes. The actors mingling with the audience. I was pushing still further the style to which I kept aspiring – theatre in the state of being born.

There were moments that were really well done. I felt I was confirming and forming certain ideas that were not new ones but had been pursuing me for twenty years. We were happy about the enormous effort, we were full of hope.

It is a typical Renaissance work : in the course of one evening we went from primitive medieval sorcery (the Joan of Arc sequence) to popular Elizabethan theatre (the Jack Cade sequence), then to cruel theatre (the York sequence), to debouch on the 'birth of a monster' (Richard III).

The summary of the renewal of a human cycle.

All we got was insults. The critics condemned us. Influenced by them, the public showed indifference. I was deeply hurt. Some members of the company began looking at me as in the time of L'Etat de Siège. It is still a bitter memory. Besides, I could understand to some extent the difficulties Camus and I had come up against with L'Etat de Siège; but I confess that, in the case of Henry VI, I no longer understood. I still think, today, that the show, in spite of certain points that did not come off, contained the best I am capable of doing.

One loses confidence. For, if our sensations remain the same, our desires as strong, our vision as clear, we are led to wonder whether, in spite of our efforts, our power of execution has not gone off. Not to understand is terrifying.

LA TENTATION DE SAINT ANTOINE

For a long time I had been trying to entice Maurice Béjart, whom I greatly admire, to work with us. Béjart, by way of the dance, is a great man of the theatre. I now made fresh advances to him. He said :

'Ever since my youth I have had a dream I would like to realize, but you wouldn't consent.'

'Tell me, all the same.'

'I would like to adapt Flaubert's Tentation de Saint Antoine.'

'That's perfect. I too, for the last twenty-five years. I have even made notes for it several times. Do it in our theatre.'

'Would you agree to play Antoine?'

'My God, yes; under your direction. I promise you I will work like a pupil.'

As I have said several times, I love putting myself in question all over again. And getting myself 'cleaned' by artists in whom I believe. I handed myself over to him blindly.

From the first minutes of rehearsal, my trust in him was total. Generally, when you know how to drive a car, you are not keen on being driven by someone else. Sitting beside the driver, you go through, in spite of yourself, the driver's movements – you brake, you accelerate. With Béjart those reflexes disappeared at once. Everything he felt, I felt too. And so I merely had to concentrate on my role.

With Wogensky and Martha Pan to do the settings, Germinal Casado for the costumes and Pierre Henry for the musical arrangements, Béjart did a marvellous job of work.

The success was considerable and my joy unmixed.

In my art I have experienced indignation and anger – indignation when a show that seems to me bad is praised, anger when some colleague has been before me with something good that I had not thought of : that is to say, anger against myself. In the case of Béjart, I experienced only enthusiasm and joy : he was realizing what I loved, he was advancing the theatre in the direction I desired, he was bringing me a confirmation of the thing to which I aspired. All I had to do was to be happy about it. I was. Béjart, while remaining faithful to Flaubert, managed to avoid the pitfalls inherent in the subject – managed not to let himself be carried away by an unbridled imagination into decorative profusion, but, on the contrary, by means of rigour to transpose that hallucinatory poetry into an abstract quintessence. One sentence of Flaubert's gave us the key : 'It is not the pearls that make the necklace but the thread.' Béjart contrived, simply by means of human beings making figures in space, to reel off, purely and with a most penetrating selectivity, the thread which Flaubert had unwound, in terms of writing, throughout the novel.

Saint Antoine was the *Hamlet* of my fifties. I would like to act him again.

But can one, in our day and age, live in continuity? Like people who are ill, we now only care for change.

The 1967 season was a flourishing one. Lavelli followed up Béjart's success by bringing off Seneca's *Medea* perfectly : Casarès was very fine in it. Edwige Feuillère, Madeleine, Simone Valère and Claude Dauphin had a triumph in Edward Albee's *A Delicate Balance*.

And finally, I added to my *Connaissance* collection a Saint-Exupéry.

SAINT-EXUPÉRY

That year Canada was organizing a big international exhibition called 'Terre des Hommes'. I suggested I should compose for the occasion a show on the theme of human adventure, centred on Saint-Exupéry.

It was created in Montreal, as part of the opening of the theatres in the Place des Arts in collaboration with our friends the Canadian actors; it was also designed for the Petit Odéon, where Nathalie Sarraute's two plays were still running. In point of fact we tried it out in Paris (February 1967) and made our début with it in Montreal on 1 May.

Thanks to the kindness of Air France, I was able to bring to our Canadian friends armfuls of lilies-of-the-valley: 'Le Petit Prince' gave these to them on stage, to bring them luck.

A *sign of life*. By chance I travelled from Orly to Montreal with Didier Daurat, under whom Saint-Exupéry had worked. During the flight he talked to me about Mermoz, Guillaumet and Saint-Exupéry himself. There in the aircraft, I realized how much the family of pilots had become, for us itinerant actors, a second family. That 'theatrical' adventure still vibrates in me with a surprising radioactivity. What mutual support! What communion between men!

The trajectory of a human life is comparable to the trajectory of an aeroplane. I had polarized on stage Saint- Exupéry's humanity. None of us was physically impersonating him – each kept his own personality as man and actor; but he was fluttering round us, his presence filled the space like a bond; each of us was a part of him. This problem is one that is very interesting to solve. It prepared me perfectly for the Rabelais show, on which I was still working. And, later on, for the Jarry show also.

On one side there was *Le Petit Prince*, on the other side the Berber chieftain of the *Citadelle*. In between the two, three groups:

1. The women.
2. The administration and the generals: the immobilists.
3. The pilots, the mechanics, the active.

We all contain these different facets of *man*. In the end the show went beyond the particular case of Saint-Exupéry. The real subject of the drama was the human trajectory.

THE SEVEN HORSES OF LIGHT

We will now play at imagining that trajectory as achieved by the movement of Seven Horses of Light.

One is born a child. One dies a child. In between, the child is doubled with a man. And this man has a life. And this life describes a trajectory. The duration of the flight matters little. What does matter is its density and perfection. There is the choice of the departure airstrip, the take-off, the cruising speed, the points at which to stop and refuel, the meaning of the flight, its aim, the obstacles and the final landing. A recommendation: try to make that landing when the aim is attained and not before.

A man's trajectory comprises:
– The spark of vocation.
– Initiation into the profession.
– Conversion to love for human beings.
– The creature developing.
– The individual ordeal.
– The collective ordeal.
– The reconversion of oneself. (And this is a thing that can be renewed.)

Such, it seems, are the Seven Horses of Light which draw the chariot of our life. This is not a matter of relays at posting-stages, but of an accumulation. Once the choice of the first horse has been made, the others add themselves to it and the race goes on as a simultaneous gallop.

The vocation, for instance, must spark afresh every morning till the end of our life – if not, all the rest collapses.

And if one ceases, even for a day, to identify oneself with one's profession, how can one continue converting oneself to life and to men, how feel the desire for 'what is greater than oneself'?

And if this desire gets blunted, how will one know the suffering without which one cannot reconvert oneself?

Certainly to master the gallop of Seven Horses at the same time is no small matter – unless it be very simple. . . .

The vocation

The child rubs up against life. He rubs up against his parents, his friends, lessons, books, games. Grown to be a young man he rubs up against professions, adventures, illusions, despairs, dreams. From this *friction* there suddenly springs a *spark*. He catches light : the vocation is born, and *desire* appears. This is the first horse : young, high-spirited, virginal.

The profession

The profession comes and transforms desire into Love. If not, it is a chore.

One couples with one's profession as one couples with a woman. The relations one has with it are sensual.

It is important, therefore, to identify oneself with it, melt into it, become *it*. The objectives of a profession are of secondary importance. One's profession has a value in itself.

A profession breathes.

Thanks to his profession, a man can live beyond his own life through the objects he has created, just as a man lives beyond his life through the children he has engendered.

Lastly, his profession assures a man his dignity as a man.

It is our profession that binds us to things. This second horse – profession – is the *bond*.

All men are equal in their profession. They communicate, they exchange, they share. And here comes, adding itself to desire, to the bond of the professions, *exchange* – the third horse then joins the others. It is *enthusiasm*.

Being more

Yet the consciousness of loneliness, the perverse idea of possible fall and the fear of death remain planted in us like three nails, and our fervour lives side by side with an infinite capacity for distress.

> *We men put on great airs, but we know, in the secrecy of the heart,*
> *hesitation, doubt and sorrow.*   (Saint-Exupéry)

It is to help us break out from that, it is to help us keep our heads above water, that we are animated by a kind of passion – for what is greater than ourselves. There is defiance in this, and yet its only cause is the instinct of conservation. To defy loneliness, to defy the fall, to defy death.

In spite of appearances, this feeling does not come from a taste for danger. On the contrary, it is in order to escape from fear.

Caught in events, the man is no longer frightened. Only the unknown terrifies him. So the man creates the event; and when he faces the obstacles, he transforms the world and becomes seed. From that moment, he grows.

It is not love of death, but love of life that makes him take risks.

Immobility, alone, is death.

The Promethean fire is the love of life.

To desire, to the bond and to enthusiasm there is added the horse of fire, which will lead the team.

The man's trajectory attains its apogee, the time of ordeals is approaching.

Individual ordeal

Up to now one may say that all is going well. But there is something outside us, lying in wait for us.

Too confident, we do not always pay enough attention to our own fissures. Here comes the first fall.

There we are with all four hooves in the air.

The spirit of death has entered into us, but is there not, in some corner, a small flame that goes on burning? Life has been reduced to almost nothing – and yet from our ashes fresh flames are springing. The ordeal of an extreme despair produces a reinforcement of Faith.

Despair purifies. At the crossroads of all deaths, the inner being, in a sudden shudder like those shudders that make a horse's skin quiver, has recognized the way of life. Only real, genuine suffering could trigger off this miraculous shudder. This shock which says 'perhaps', this reflex of expectation called *hope*.

Collective ordeal

Just as, to his surprise, Man in his trajectory experiences a fall, so humanity, through a kind of delirium that turns against it, experiences excess and covetousness. What maleficent influence has made humanity capsize into injustice, cupidity and hate?

Why does man pounce on man? Why do men kill each other? Why do they let themselves be caught up in the fury of domination? Starving some, torturing others? Why does a man, deep down, prefer destruction to construction?

In some it is disarray and fear.

Others take advantage of this to exploit and dominate.

Others – and they are perhaps the worst – explain. Recourse to logic, to reason, to Intelligence : men write History.

The 'elect' curse. Others, in the name of liberty, turn their backs and run away.

All music has fallen silent, and we remain cringing with fear in the middle of a heap of stones, bewildered by the wind of words from the 'preachers' and the doctors, sent astray by the licence of those who cannot adapt – those who go their way holding in each hand an individual despair.

The picture of humanity is in the end, always, the ruins of Troy, the ashes of Oradour, and over them a preacher booming away, a philosopher explaining and a tub-thumper blustering.

Where has the man gone?

And yet, if one listens carefully, there is still, in the charred chaos, a membrane that palpitates, a cell that breathes. Always that small persistent gleam. Always that shudder of life, that tremor of *charity*, which means cherishing. Everything can then begin again.

Reconversion of oneself

Reconverting, I believe, is also a financial term. Which means that it is essential to be practical, 'of the earth earthy'. When everything has been destroyed, or almost, there is nothing for it but to manage with what one has.

The suffering has warned us. Thanks to it, life has begun to vibrate in us. Life has also vibrated outside us. Even should nothing be left but the suffering, this must serve some purpose. It has served – as a reflex. It has revealed the rebirth of life.

Note that the landscape has changed. Still the heap of stones, the sermons, the speeches and the agitation. As for the man's trajectory, it is, to say the least, in poor shape. The chariot has been overturned. The horses are pulling in all directions.

What is to be done, except recover action, control and direction?

The only way of doing that is to reinvent work, morality and *what binds us to things*. The meaning, is it not, of the word religion? When one plants a tree, it begins to 'work'. There is no need to give it an advance guarantee of the advantage of its action. Having rubbed up against the soil, it is seized by the desire to suck. It is only later that it will discover the use of this suction: foliage.

Wood, they say, works. It is in this sense that one has to rediscover what 'works' in a man. First, by fervour – that is to say, by natural heat – I give. My chance is, precisely, my blind fervour – thanks to it I shall one day receive. And what I shall have received will help me to give more still.

Luckily the suffering, like a heap of dead leaves, has served as manure. It is the humus of reconversion.

The gift of oneself so as to receive, constraint for the sake of liberty, one step after another without worrying about the length of the road, in order to be able to go further. Still the lesson of the tree, which digs into the earth so as then to grow.

Then certainty arises. A certainty that is stubborn yet detached from any immediate interest.

What matters is the bond that unites us to everything. First to ourselves, then to others.

M.T.—12

The individual is a world that must be bound like a sheaf, later to be bound to other sheaves.

Things in themselves do not matter; any more than the duration of a man.

What does matter is the bond and the 'going movement', which binds.

What does matter is not so much life as the function of living. Without greed, but with warmth.

What does matter, lastly, is not the man so much as his trajectory. When the man has disappeared, there will still remain the team of horses like seven rays of light.

The *desire*. The *bond*. The *enthusiasm*.

The *fire*. The two horses of suffering – *Hope* and *Charity*. And at length the seventh, which finally takes the lead : *Desire renewed*.

TÊTE D'OR

While I was reproducing, through Saint-Exupéry, the drama of the human trajectory, I never suspected the individual and collective ordeals that were soon going to rise up in front of us. Our feeling was rather that of being led onwards by the horse of fire. The Théâtre de France had found its own level and was climbing. Harnessed to the Théâtre des Nations, it reached its peak.

Dazzling proof of this was given by a revival of *Tête d'Or*, still with Alain Cuny and Laurent Terzieff. This time, success was complete. The houses were full.

Tête d'Or had taken nine years to get itself established.[1] The season ended in April 1968 in a kind of apotheosis. Our chariot, its reins held by the 'King with the mane of gold', was being drawn along by those Seven Horses of Light, with the horse of Fire at their head.

> And the others, turning an eye towards him,
> Trot side by side with him and caress him with the bit that binds them
> ... (*Tête d'Or*.)

I did not know that, a few days later ...

To end that season with a flourish, we went again to London, for three weeks. I took with me, in my bag, 'my Rabelais', which had already reached its third version. I meant to finish it there, in the gentleness of the English spring.

PAUSE OF FRIENDSHIP: LONDON

I am particularly fond of London. Is it because of Shakespeare, because of my friends, because of the ineffaceable memories we have brought back from there each time? I love London. The movement in the streets, its mysterious quarters, its alley-like mews, the liberty-in-the-natural-state that one breathes there,

[1] What am I saying, nine years? The play had been written in 1889, which makes seventy years plus nine. That now really deserves the name *avant-garde*!

the courtesy in ordinary human relationships, its small houses, its colonnades on the scale of private life, the easy air of the passers-by, the love these people have for dogs, the trotting horses, its taxis in uniform, its buses like toys, its wooden soldiers round about Buckingham Palace, the ducks in Green Park, the smells of Covent Garden, Soho, the hippies in the King's Road, the Bond Street shops; its nights, its mists, its filtered suns, the cottages in its suburbs, the tiny gardens, the spring flowers, the enormous masses of its trees – elms, oaks and plane trees – and above all, when the sun goes down, the whole city awakening to the theatre.

In London you do not find the sort of theatre where, if the worst comes to the worst, you can go to kill time: theatre in London is a congenital collective reaction. Theatre is part of custom, and the television programmes fail to diminish the fervour of the British playgoer. In London, when night comes, theatre appears.

I wish I could have added to my life an 'English period'.

Just after the War, in 1945, Laurence Olivier came to Paris to act *Richard III* at the Français. The triumph he had is well known. He was extraordinary in the part. To me he represented the ideal of the actor: his stature, his presence, his voice, his diction, his talent, his sense of humour, his irresistible charm, his feeling for composition. We were witnessing perfection.

Between him and us there was a real meeting, at once, from the first contact.

Not long afterwards we went to London to admire him in the Old Vic Theatre Company, in *Henry IV*, *Oedipus Rex* and Sheridan's *The Critic*. There were also Gielgud, Richardson: a golden age of the British theatre.

In 1946 he came to Paris again. Why? To see *Hamlet* in French. He was working on his film. Fresh contact. Our friendship was acquiring body.

In 1948 I had the honour to perform *Hamlet* in Gide's translation at Edinburgh. Across the road a film of Laurence Olivier's was showing: *Hamlet*.

The bonds between us drew closer still.

In 1951 Vivien Leigh and Laurence Olivier, at the zenith of their career, were running that delicious theatre the St James's (wickedly destroyed, since then, by developers). They invited us to go there with our shows. *They will eat you!* they predicted to us.

Vivien and Larry formed a princely couple. Presented by them to the Londoners, we made acquaintance with one of the best theatre publics in the world: spontaneity, fundamental childhood, openness, human warmth. All of which does not prevent it from expressing its opinion frankly on occasion. One cannot be always in agreement and remain civilized. Individual taste and human respect are not incompatible – on the contrary.

I took back home a 'stool',[1] to bring luck and in memory of that first season.

After that, we paid frequent visits to our friends across the Channel. After the St James's Theatre, the Palace; then three times the charming Aldwych,

---

[1] The type of small wooden folding stool used by theatre-goers queueing outside theatres. While waiting, people are often treated to a preliminary show put on by buskers made up as clowns.

under the auspices of our friends Molly and Peter Daubeny; finally, in 1969, the Old Vic, with *Rabelais*.

I love the Garrick Club. I am sorry Paris has no similar meeting place. They say the English are gifted for commerce; what I love is their 'human commerce', in the classic sense of the term. I have never felt the easy play of democracy so strongly as in that Kingdom.

Speaking of royalty, the mountebank soul in me was both proud and touched at the chance that was given me of meeting the young Queen Elizabeth. I think it was during our second visit that I was asked to do some mime for the Royal children, Charles and Anne. They were then quite small. A place was chosen: the private house of a cousin of Her Majesty's. It was in the afternoon, at tea time. Madeleine and Pierre Bertin went with me. Thorough musician that he is, Bertin was to play the piano. Only one suggestion had been made to me: not to frighten the children. There were about fifteen in all – the others having been invited to join the Royal party.

The Queen arrived with her two. We were introduced to Her Majesty. The first minutes were full of shyness. I must say: on both sides. Was that attractive young woman, with the fine blue eyes, the fresh complexion and straight back, really the Queen of England? Within half an hour she was on the same wavelength. Anne, with her mischievous look, sat on a chair, as good as gold. Charles clung to his mother's knee.

I began: the horse, swimming, hunting, fishing, someone climbing a tree to pick a fruit and eat it, etc.

'What fruit has he eaten?' Prince Charles asked.

An apple – imaginary, of course.'

Then, for him, I ate a banana, a pear, a very ripe fruit, a very sweet fruit. Anne and Charles wanted to act the horse. I showed them how. The other children followed suit. I am not sure the parents did not. No one knows horses better than the Queen. Childhood, eternal childhood, took possession of us all.

The moment for tea came. There were two tables – one for the children, the other for the grownups. I was at the Queen's right hand – that is, all formality had been dropped. At the other table Charles was bombarding his friends with bullets made from the cake papers. Laughter and ragging were continuous. 'Charles, be quiet,' said the Queen gently. Family life was in full swing. We were talking shop. Such a fairy-tale experience can only happen to stage people. The king and his clown. I thought of Shakespeare's clowns, those great friends of his kings.

Her Majesty was gradually becoming a little girl again. By now informality was unconstrained. Her face relaxed. She regaled us with spontaneous humour. She talked to us about the actual weight of the crown of England. A heavy crown to wear. I can well believe it. She described to us the rehearsals for her Coronation, the terrors of the day itself. She rehearsed without a carpet. On the day of the ceremony the carpet had been fixed with the nap the wrong way. She thought she would never manage to drag her train. She made a great effort to move forward. Just at that moment a young girl trod on the train. Nobody saw. She pursued her triumphal advance – which all of us were following in Paris on television, as if she were our own Queen.

'Do you know why George V always learned his speeches by heart?' she said to me. 'Because he couldn't read without glasses and, when he put them on, his crown tilted.'

She laughed like a girl. Such simplicity and fresh gaiety enchanted us. My respect was transformed into respectful tenderness.

Time was going by, we had been there chatting for nearly three hours – some audience! – and the moment for our performance was drawing near. We could not say so, or go. Suddenly she cried:

'Oh! I've got to go and get ready. I too have a performance this evening. I am presiding at the Royal Navy banquet!'

We went our separate ways, each to play his part, as Shakespeare would have said. 'Kings and strolling players.'

Since then she has never missed a chance of showing her sympathy towards us. I have already told how much she appreciated *Amélie*. On another occasion she had honoured with her presence our opening performance of *Andromaque*. I was playing Oreste. Just as I came on stage, a walk-on caught his foot in my cape. I jammed on the brakes, then moved forward again.

That evening, at supper at the Embassy, she said to me, with a sly smile:

'The same thing happened to you as happened to me. Someone trod on your train.'

I call that royal memory.

During the 1957–58 season Vivien Leigh asked me to go and direct *Duel of Angels* (Giraudoux's *Pour Lucrèce*, adapted by Christopher Fry). She was to act the part Edwige Feuillère interpreted for us.

The work was fascinating. It brought me close to English actors. I love their special quality: just as French actors involuntarily have a Molière inheritance, English actors always more or less recall the courtyard of an Elizabethan inn. There is more of the human being than of make-up about them.

Vivien Leigh's face! The prettiest nose ever seen, a witty chin, an acid-drop mouth, her feline body, her cat gaze: what a 'person'! And how well we understood each other. There was only one thing that surprised me about her. She worked on her part with a hatred for her character – in this case Paola. She assailed her. She was constantly on the lookout for reasons for not loving her. This forced me to plead for Paola. She attacked her by provoking antipathy. It was only when she had exhausted all the reasons for hating her that she assumed her. In the part she was not merely a cat, she had become a panther.

When, a few years later, the radio announced her death, I could not believe that so captivating, so beautiful, so irresistible a creature – like the most diabolical of angels – could have vanished. Madeleine and I were profoundly distressed.

According to her wishes she was cremated. Her ashes were scattered in the garden of her house. The place has been sold. Nothing is left of her – nothing but the living memory which we and many others still have.

April 1968. So there we were, once more, in *our London*. Once more we were to give our performances at the Aldwych. Once more we were there under the auspices of the French ambassador Geoffroy de Courcel, and encouraged by the affectionate protection of his wife.

I came over first, to pave the way. Lecture at Oxford. Lecture on Claudel at the Institut Français. The plays we brought were : *Partage de Midi*, Billetdoux's *Il Faut Passer par les Nuages* and *Le Barbier de Séville*.

Once again the season was glorious, thanks to the warm friendliness of our London public. After performances we spent a large part of the night in hippy haunts, in Chelsea, and the 'Arts Lab' in Drury Lane. I remember particularly an astonishing place called 'Middle Earth' among Covent Garden's mountains of vegetables.

I have always been struck by the behaviour of the Prince of Wales in Shakespeare's *Henry IV*. As a young man he lives among rogues, frequents sleazy dens with his friend Falstaff, mixes with his people, makes their acquaintance, so to speak, from inside, from below. And suddenly, when he becomes king, he rejects that past life and now assumes his people from above, as sovereign.

It seems to me that every Englishman, in his attitude to himself, has that 'Prince of Wales complex'. As a student he dresses lousily, takes to low life, sows his wild oats not only freely but anarchically. He purges his rogue side – which is as likeable as that of Falstaff's likeable companions. And suddenly, growing up, he forgets all that, decides to assume himself, as king of his own kingdom. This is no repentance. It is simply change. For him the only risk is that of drying up. We French undergo a more austere education, an inheritance from the nineteenth-century bourgeoisie, which contains the danger that it may constrict our youth and make of us, when we have grown up, repressed children.

On 11 May 1968, after that fresh bath in friendship, we returned to Paris. In London, by hammering away at it, in spite of our theatre season, I had managed to complete the third version of *Rabelais*.

I had not done with England, I hope I never will have. However, as we landed at Orly, certain events were waiting for us.

May '68, collective ordeal, individual ordeal

> All men are alike in words, it is only their actions
> that show they are different.   (Molière)
>
> And who knows if your laws are sacred among the
> dead?   (Antigone to Creon)

We have now come to a flashpoint.

The so-called 'May events' still puzzle public opinion. People have had the shock, lived through the fear, imagined the reaction. They still do not know the range, the repercussions.

It is not a French affair, it is a worldwide phenomenon. In May the lightning struck in Paris, that is all. The storm, it seems to me, came from far away, and is still wandering all round the world. I have not the impression that it is over – that is the least one can say. Some time earlier, we had experienced two advance signs of it.

In the course of the 1967–68 season we had thought up, for one of our free Tuesdays, an evening devoted to beatnik poetry. My impression was that that movement was not born spontaneously, that it was the result of a continuous evolution whose origin went back to the Surrealist movement before the Second World War. I recognize my underground self in it.

The programme seemed to me well put together: certain poets had very kindly agreed to give the evening its impetus. Perhaps it would have been wiser of us not to take part ourselves. One is never really aware of the image one has in the eyes of other people.

To my rather naïve mind the Théâtre de France seemed identical with that of As I Lay Dying, and I did not feel as if I had moved away from the time when, with André Breton, we used to read pages of Brisset, and when, with Robert Desnos, we took part in automatic writing sessions. I had twice invited the Living Theatre (The Brig and Mysteries) to the Théâtre des Nations. Our relations had been excellent. We were friends and, judging from their spontaneous reaction, I felt with perfect naturalness one of them. We imagined we were admitted.

The 'young' must have seen us in a different light. I had yet to learn that what is called 'the conflict of generations' does not necessarily come from the behaviour of the older people, but from rejection by the younger. Anyhow, in that case, I had reason for hoping and being happy; l seemed to be witnessing, in the most natural way in the world, a meeting, even a uniting under the sign of shared ideas, of a common indignation, of a solidarity in contesting certain things, the age on our birth certificates being no longer important. In reality I was behaving like a child.

The house was full. The Odéon was packed to bursting. On stage there were as many heads of long hair as in the rows of seats. I had the impression that we were all gathered together for a festivity.

At zero hour the demo exploded, started – yes – by one of the actors of the Living Theatre. It was a fine mess. With the exception of the instigators, who must have been following their plan, the others, both on stage and in front, understood little of what was going on.

As regards the object of the evening, it seemed to me there was nothing wrong with it. If what we had proposed had been out of place or disagreeable, we ought to have met with either :

1. a refusal to take part, or
2. a boycott by the 'young' audience,

in which case the performance would not have taken place.

Therefore the tactics seemed to me definitely premeditated : you agree, you let the show be organized, and it becomes an occasion for provoking trouble. I discovered in this behaviour a method that was new to me – a method that could therefore only be political. We were a long way from what we set out to do.

It left me with a brackish, disagreeable impression. Our sincerity had been taken by surprise. It had in fact been held up to ridicule. The thing made me more sad than annoyed. Sincerity is always close to ridicule. Only the non-sincere are seldom ridiculous.

A few months later – to be precise, on 19 April 1968 – Jack Lang, the director of the Nancy Festival, with whom I have very friendly relations, had invited us – Alain Cuny, Laurent Terzieff, Jorris, Madeleine Vimes and me – to go and give some extracts from *Tête d'Or*. We had spontaneously accepted the fraternal invitation. I had twice invited to the Théâtre des Nations the best student companies who were performing at Nancy under the auspices of the Festival International du Théâtre Universitaire.

I always respond to what can provoke contacts, communication, exchange. It seemed to me natural and satisfactory that a whole body of youth should want to listen to the cries of rebellion uttered in the past by a young poet aged twenty-one, when these were so well interpreted by Cuny and Terzieff. Claudel's *Tête d'Or* has nothing to do with *La Vierge à Midi* (which, by the was, is a sublime poem, as perfect as a piece of Johann Sebastian Bach).

The evening had begun with a speech by Jack Lang about money and political theatre. Then I had done a lead-in, giving the history of *Tête d'Or* and introducing the extracts. All this had gone well. And then my companions did their stuff warmly and successfully.

At 22.15 the debate began. House and stage were overwhelmed by methodical provocation and violent intrusion of political agitators. Claudel was made responsible for the assassination of Martin Luther King, etc. At the end of an hour we came to blows. The hatred spread and continued in the street. At 1.30 in the morning I collapsed on my bed, overcome with depression.

For the second time I had fallen into the trap. I was left with the disagreeable impression of something which I did not understand, but which seemed to me calculated and, here again, to have come from far away – yes, I repeat, from *far away*.

In London the news of the social upheavals in Paris had reached us. We had heard of that 'mistake', the police repression in the rue Gay-Lussac on 10 May.

On 11 May we landed in Paris. Clashes all over the place. Especially in the Sorbonne quarter: 30,000 insurgent students, with the teachers on their side. The rue Gay-Lussac business had put public opinion on the side of the students.

At 16.30 I was at the Théâtre de France. It was a Saturday, and the Théâtre des Nations was in full swing. Its season had begun marvellously. The Bunraku – the famous Japanese puppet theatre – was triumphing before a full house.

Would there be a general strike on the 13th? The Paul Taylor Ballet Company (U S A) was to make its début that day.

The strike was on.

Political agitation grew. The talk was of extremist groups, of cultural revolution. Charles de Gaulle, President of the Republic, was in Rumania; the Prime Minister, Georges Pompidou, in Persia.

On Tuesday the 14th the opening performance of the Paul Taylor Ballet took place. It went off admirably. The contrast was striking. I even put on, after the performance, a reception in the 'Embassy reception' style: the swan song, as it may seem, of a way of life which perhaps will not recur.

We are passing, without realizing it, from an age of contradicting to an age of rejection.

Contradiction implies a recognition of the other side, the side one wants to contradict. Rejection systematically refuses to recognize any other side, it suppresses *a priori* the existence of the antagonist. The rejection man brooks no contradiction. The rejection man contests the very existence of the man he is rejecting.

The revolutionary fever increased. The Sorbonne and other principal universities were occupied by the students. Barricades, tear gas, trees uprooted. The police disappeared as though by enchantment.

I shall only relate facts. I remained unaware of the causes.

It was the misfortune of the Odéon to be situated at the centre of the clashes. There were rumours that the students were going to march on the Senate, the Institut, the Louvre and as far as the O R T F (French Radio and Television).

The hour of general insurrection had come.

On 15 May I heard, by telephone and by a direct report from one of our company returning from Censier,[1] that the students had decided to occupy the Odéon.

---

[1] The 'hot' sector of the University.

M.T.—12*

At my request Félix Giacomoni, my administrator, telephoned to the Ministry to find out what its orders were. The official reply from the Ministry was: 'If the students put their plan into practice, *ouvrez-leur les portes et entamez le dialogue!*' (open the doors to them and start discussion).

And indeed, what else was there to do?

It was about 17.00. I took a walk round the quarter; nothing seemed to me abnormal. The street was neither deserted nor agitated, it was natural. That, indeed, is what I find astonishing when I go back over my memory of those moments. Two hundred metres away, the atmosphere could change completely. The climate of civil wars, no doubt.[1]

Since nothing was happening, the evening's performance took place, before a full house. The Paul Taylor Ballet Company were admirable, their freshness brought something new: just right for the young audience.

The interval arrived. Still nothing.

I took another walk in the neighbouring streets; everything was still going on normally. Not a demonstrator in sight, not a policeman. It seemed to me therefore that the invasion was not for that evening; tomorrow we would see. My advisers thought the same. I decided to go home.

I was no sooner home, when Giacomoni phoned to say that 'they were there'. We had not had to open the doors. They had chosen the moment when the audience came out of the theatre. Indeed many of them had been present at the show and had stayed in the auditorium.

'Right, I'm coming!'

Madeleine wanted to come with me. So we both went.

Red and black flags. Arm bands. There were about two thousand five hundred people. M. Raison, head of the theatre section in the Ministry of Cultural Affairs, was there as an observer.

We had now to *'entamer le dialogue'*. We went on stage. There were so many people that we were afraid the boards would not hold. Under the stage in a theatre it is hollow, and I could hardly imagine what it would be like if two to three hundred people fell some twenty metres.

The row was indescribable. I began to speak. I reminded them of the international character of the Théâtre des Nations. Nobody listened. Everyone was talking at the same time. M. Raison was a few metres away from us, in the wings.

I recognized in the crowd Julian Beck from the Living Theatre and some young directors and writers who were friends of mine. In what spirit they had come there I do not know.

Out of that general confusion, what remains in my mind is this:

1. That the action of the students was not directed against either a man or a programme (this was soon stated in their first *bulletin d'occupation*).

2. That the Théâtre de France, as emblem of 'bourgeois culture', was suppressed.

---

[1] We should remember the account of the day of 14 July 1789 given by Restif de la Bretonne in *Les Nuits de Paris.*

3. That the Odéon would now be used as a political forum.

4. That no *dialogue* (discussion) was possible.

Towards four in the morning we went home.

We were given an appointment by the Minister for noon.

16 May : rue de Valois, noon, with M. Raison. In a few moments André Malraux, who must surely know all, would be able to enlighten us. 14.00. Malraux had not received us. Only his private secretary, an official of the Ministry and Jean Darcante, representing the *conseil supérieur* [1] of the Théâtre des Nations. No decision, no directive. I was astonished at the voluntary disappearance of all governmental authority. There was something there that I did not understand.

The theatre was now entirely occupied : offices, telephones, typewriters, roneo equipment, press office; dressing-rooms transformed into dormitories, into kitchens; graffiti on the walls; the velvet curtains soiled. My technicians were champing at the bit. They too had received no instructions from their Unions.

Night of the 16th and 17th. New attempt at dialogue. The atmosphere had changed. There were ringleaders. For at least an hour we were insulted, with insolent irony, by a short ginger-haired man who seemed to me to possess a certain revolutionary technique, even though the 'audition' he was giving seemed to me rather conventional in its choice of electoral gimmicks. But it was having its effect. 'Malraux, bourgeois culture, the Théâtre de France, Barrault, the whole lot has got it coming : all that is finished ! zero ! annulled ! suppressed ! killed !'

Madeleine and I, sitting on the floor side by side, asked our neighbours who the young gentleman was.

'Cohn-Bendit.'

'Ah ! . . . the famous . . . oho !'

I remembered him from two years before, when he had laid about him in defence of *Les Paravents*. My 'old' education, composed of surrealist humour, came back into my head. People were looking at us. They asked me to reply. With the same insolent irony, only using courtesy instead of insults, I did so, and concluded with :

'All right ! Barrault is dead, but there remains facing you a living creature, so what are we going to do?'

Cat-calls, bravos, whistles, general confusion.

Someone in the crowd shouted : 'After all, *Les Paravents* is not bourgeois theatre !'

'Sorry, it is reinsurance, to save bourgeois culture.'

Whistles, cat-calls, bravos.

There was evidently no way out.

---

[1] Roughly equivalent to a Board of Governors. (*Translator's note.*)

Next day, the only part of my conclusion the 'well-intentioned' newspapers printed was 'Barrault is dead'.

I was rung up: 'M. *le Ministre* is not pleased with you,' M. Raison told me. 'Don't make pronouncements.'

'If only he would break his silence, he might help me in my task.'

Within the theatre 'speech' continued to flow. Speeches of rejection and of 'spontaneous' expression. I was surprised to see how those who were rejecting the teachers were the first to wish to give lessons. On the now occupied roof, red flags, black ones and tricolours took turns in a lamentable ballet. The square outside had become a regular fairground: a man with a monkey, a man with a bear, guitarists, rubbernecks, and more or less camouflaged ambulances. Slogans all over the walls. In the basements of the theatre, Molotov cocktails, petrol bombs, grenades – preparations for a siege.

And still not a sign from the Minister. Complete silence. I understood it less and less. Nerves were growing tense.

On the side of the insurrection I could distinguish the genuine students, who were also beginning to feel disgusted, from the extremist groups, who appeared to me thoroughly organized. They relieved one another, section by section, the outgoing section moving off to get orders elsewhere; some people even said they were going abroad. But such a lot of things were being said.

There were agitators, whose business was to promote disorder constantly. There were others who had nothing in common with the students and were infiltrating.

De Gaulle had returned from Rumania and had said: '*Réforme oui, chienlit, non!*' (Reform yes, chaos, no!) [1]

The CAR (Comité d'Action Révolutionnaire) took possession of the building. I recognized among them not a few actors and actresses.

We felt we were being betrayed on all sides, and had no inclination to join up with anything. Only the students, the genuine ones, touched us. They seemed to me quite as much betrayed as we were.

I called our actors, technicians and administrative staff together. I could feel they were politically divided.

Our behaviour must now answer to three objectives:

1. To protect the building and our equipment.
2. To avoid direct confrontation, so that there might be no bloodshed.
3. To maintain our unity on the professional plane.

Four or five days went by like this, in disorder, silence and desertion. We had managed to lower the safety curtain and smash its mechanism. This cleared the stage.

Twenty-four hours after twenty-four hours the whole 'house' – actors, technicians and other staff – maintained a watch in rotation. We were protecting, as best we could, the *instrument* of our work.

---

[1] But *chienlit* can also mean bed-wetting, and the General was apt to use army language when he thought fit. (*Translator's note.*)

For nearly a week the words had been flowing nonstop: $7 \times 24 = 168$ hours of words. 'In '89 they took the Bastille, in '68 they have taken the Floor.'[1]

21 *May.* At last a message reaches us from the Ministry: we are ordered to leave the building. This time we were really scandalized: such an order! We who were defending our assets! We obeyed, nonetheless, that afternoon; but at 22.00, in an almost animal reaction, we came back to continue protecting our costumes, our props, our life's work. Who can imagine the state of mind we were in?

22 *May.* The *conseil supérieur* of the Théâtre des Nations adjourned the season. Not possible, surely? Here, indeed, was the first initiative. I was summoned to the rue Saint-Dominique, to the Arts and Letters section of the Ministry, and had to listen to this:

'The Ministry requests you to call on the E D F [Electricité de France] "on your own responsibility" to cut off the electricity and the telephone, so as to stop all communication.'

And what about bloodshed? And the building? And people being injured, even killed? On my responsibility? I refused categorically. With my usual plain speaking, and overcome with fury and indignation, I added uncontrollably:

'When there is something I have to do, I don't have it done by someone else. In Pigalle they have a name for that. I refuse, and I am scandalized.'

'Repeat that.'

'I refuse, and I am scandalized.'

Next *day,* 23 *May.* Opening *Le Figaro,* I read: 'Jean-Louis Barrault disavowed by his Minister', followed by a laconic note dictated by Malraux's private secretary.

I might at least have been told in advance.

24 *May. Le Figaro* published my reply. (I had been careful, the night before, to inform the Prime Minister in advance.) The gist of it was:

'To *Réforme, oui; chienlit, non!* I reply: *Serviteur, oui; valet, non!* What is more, I have not been a cipher.'

After which, one of two things:

– either the Ministry would have to reverse its disavowal;

– or the Ministry would dismiss me from my post.

I never imagined there could be a third thing: silence, emptiness, nothing. In short, no change.

The silence of André Malraux persisted. It was real torture for me, for I was constantly expecting that silence to be broken. Nothing of the sort.

---

[1] Witticism from someone or other.

For our part, we continued to watch over our equipment. We were no longer very clear as to who were the students, who were other elements, whether they were extreme left, extreme right or police.[1]

Something like eight to ten thousand persons per day were milling about in the corridors, dressing-rooms, auditorium, and on the roof. And the words kept drooling. Impression of hell.

The curtains were destroyed, the prop store (helmets, swords, halberds, etc.) forced and plundered.

28 May. The costume stores also broken into. People had got in after breaking the skylights and had then indulged in an orgy of destruction, of vandalism pure and simple. We found ourselves walking in a soup of costumes sixteen inches deep. Not only the costumes of the Théâtre de France, but those of our own company (let us not forget that we had generously supplied the State with the equipment of nineteen plays). In short, twenty years of work soiled, ruined, annihilated.

I confess I broke down: this time I burst into tears. I kept repeating: 'For nothing! Why? Nothing! Purposeless! Waste! Pure hate and for nothing!' That flouting of our work and that hatred manifested in so ugly a way (the whole of that soup was filled with excrement) hurt me more than all the rest.

By an instinct of self-preservation, perhaps, and in order to cling to some plank that might save me, I plunged into a fourth version of 'my' *Rabelais*.

> *Extract from my notebooks, 29 May:*
> Reread the first part aloud. This fourth version seems to me the final one. I think the style is emerging. It is only sixty-nine pages. The first was a hundred. The second was slashed and did not hold together properly. The third went back to the plan of the first but exceeded eighty-four pages. I think I have caught it now.

30 May. I gave myself the pleasure of writing the word 'End' after the second part, and I added the date.

That day de Gaulle suddenly disappeared. For a whole day nobody knew where he was. Then he reappeared.

Inside the Odéon the rot continued, systematically.

Our accounts department took refuge in the Hôtel Michelet, room 53. This enabled me to pay the actors. Some oddities about the relations between my admin and myself led me to guess that secret instructions had been given to certain persons.

In fact, I was no longer being kept informed.

As part of the Théâtre des Nations I had set up a research studio which I had entrusted to Peter Brook. We decided that this studio should go to London and should present itself in that unusual, marvellous place, the Roundhouse.

[1] On a wall, one of the graffiti said: 'Messieurs les policiers en civil, attention à la marche'. (Police in mufti, mind the step.)

In France there were now nine million strikers. The workers were keeping clear of the students, and these were disavowed, in turn, by public opinion. In high places the game, it seemed, was being played with skill. The insurrection of youth was being adroitly deformed into Trade Union claims.

At the Odéon they were still talking. There were fewer and fewer students, more and more agitators and bruisers of all sorts. I remembered this sentence of Pascal's:

> When Plato and Aristotle wrote about politics, it was as if they had to run a madhouse.

I was beginning to understand what the role of the Odéon in those historic events would prove to have been. The government, unable on 15 May to use the police because of that unfortunate night of the rue Gay-Lussac, had allowed the Odéon to be taken as one gives a bone to a dog. The Odéon had become a fixation abscess. Because of this the Académie, the Senate, the Louvre and the ORTF were spared. The police could then reappear prudently – and, very soon, as saviours.

As for the people who were now occupying the Odéon, 'they will go of their own accord,' I was told.

'What are we supposed to do?' our technicians asked, and were told, 'Restez chez vous!'

The rot was being allowed to go on. Obviously, that's one method.

Completely disgusted in the midst of the mob, the sack and the dirt – for vermin was now in evidence – I plunged into Restif de la Bretonne's *Les Nuits de Paris* and took refuge in my *Rabelais*, with the aid of Michelet.

De Gaulle had said, '*La situation est insaisissable*' (the situation is elusive). That reminded me, exactly, of the business of the Placards under François I. He, when confronted by 'the elusive', had deserted the humanists, burnt the heretics and reconciled himself with Rome and Charles V.

That, no doubt, is what de Gaulle had crossed the Rhine to do. It must be what was embarrassing Malraux. At least, this was my version. But I was no expert on politics and putrescence.

14 *June*. The CRS, wearing helmets, surrounded the Odéon and liberated it.

It seems that some '*Katangais*', who had been driven out of the Sorbonne after infiltrating there, had just taken refuge in the attics of the theatre. The police were therefore justified in 'protecting the students' against what they called *les affreux* (monsters).

When I arrived (as I did every morning), the operation was just ending. My administrator had not informed me. But indeed, there had not been very many people left in the building, in any case hardly any students. After a short ceremony presided over by the *Préfet de Police* (who seems to me to have behaved with a great deal of humanity during these events) with, just behind him, two representatives of the Affaires Culturelles (at last they were putting in an appearance), 'order' was re-established.

It made me think of nineteenth-century engravings, with 'those gentlemen' in frock coat and top hat in the midst of the uprooted paving-stones, wounded men, the *garde nationale* with fixed bayonets – and in the background a few clouds above the Paris roofs. A Gavarni or a Daumier.

A guard was posted, and 'order' withdrew, satisfied at duty accomplished. '*L'ordre-gris*'.[1]

Overcome with fierce anger, I penetrated into 'my' theatre. My tears were flowing like sweat at the sight of that defiled Odéon, empty now, a cellar of dirt, hate, filth, destruction, from which all life had disappeared. The dead emit, besides putrefaction, a peculiar smell like a kind of grey dust, the bitter taste of the mouth whose tongue and mucous membranes are now as stony as their teeth.

The stage, the auditorium, were a yawning mouth. The air one breathed was fetid. It pricked one's nose.

The Odéon had been fouled for a long time to come. My distress was greater than ever. At least, for the last month, life had swarmed there – by way of the absurd, no doubt, but there had been life.[2] Now the old Odéon, for which we had worked during nine years, made me think of a man tortured to death.

In the course of the day the actors and technicians returned. A kind of false joy took hold. I remained prostrate. There was eager discussion. Some of them felt delivered. Others looked at me askance. Only Maiène and Madeleine shared my distress.

Someone had been killed : a place that had had life.

'You think daily life will be able to start again as before? To my mind it is impossible. There has been a defilement. There has been murder.'

Feeling rose high, and I shouted : 'If Baudelaire had had the cold-bloodedness of a general, his name would have been Aupic.'[3] Some of them thought I no longer knew what I was saying.

> *From my notebooks, Saturday, 15 June.*
>
> In a month, twenty years of work destroyed, nine years of Théâtre de France annulled. My happiness, which was won by my passion, my efforts and Madeleine's marvellous support, has been settled – as you settle a bill. To whom? To Injustice! I am being treated as a 'black sheep'. I do in fact feel closer to Villon than to. . . . All this has not stopped me from going to see my secretary and correcting the stencils of the first part of *Rabelais*. Marvellous [sic] I would like to produce my *Rabelais* with a mixed company of students and professionals, and give it its first performance in the big amphitheatre of the Sorbonne. I would like from now on to devote myself only to the students, to the genuine ones who must also be very 'disenchanted'.

[1] 'Grey order.' A pun on verdigris and perhaps ordure. (*Translator's note.*)
[2] As an old lady of eighty wrote to me, quoting Victor Hugo : 'It was a fine thing badly done.'
[3] Aupic, Baudelaire's stepfather, rose to be a general and an ambassador. (*Translator's note.*)

In any case, now that a page had been turned, I hoped Malraux would at last receive me. If only for a final explanation.

No : the silence, the emptiness, the nothing continued.

Was it hate? Was it shame? After all, they are two short words that go together.

So there we were, committed to a tunnel from which we would not emerge till the end of August. Two months and a half in the mud.

In the trajectory of my life, our 'horses of light' were plunged in darkness, each with his four hooves in the air.

It was time for reconversion. But a man of the theatre is not alone, he is responsible for a human community. If I had been alone, facing that game of hide-and-seek which Malraux was imposing on me, I would have sent in my resignation. But in so doing I would have been depriving my comrades of the tools of their trade. These were not free-lance actors, they were artists attached to a house, who were devoting their lives to it and who, because of this, were not being offered engagements by other managements. To reduce them to unemployment because of events for which they were not responsible seemed to me unthinkable. Some of them, like Jean Desailly, Simone Valère, Régis Outin, and Granval, had devoted their youth to it, for the last twenty years. Others had been with us for more than ten years.

In high places they were perhaps waiting for the results of the June elections.

All the same, I could not believe that, with Malraux, it was impossible to raise the problem on a *noble plane*.

Let us pick out days :

18 *June*. I noticed, to my great surpise, that the damage was still going on, objects were still disappearing. It was, to say the least, curious.

The programme for the next season was as follows :

> 17 September. reopening, with *La Tentation de Saint Antoine*, in repertory with *The Cherry Orchard*.
> Mid-November : creation of *Rabelais*.
> December : *Le Mariage de Figaro*.
> January : a new creation – the Fourth Day of *Le Soulier de Satin* (*Sous le vent des Iles Baléares*).

I kept thinking of the company. I made fresh administrative plans. With the architects we worked out the cost of repairs. But I could feel I was being more and more thrust on one side.

> *From my notebooks:*
> 23 *June* : In the book I shall write, *Travaux et Traverses*, I shall conclude with this sentence : Our company has been murdered, it is not dead. To develop in the direction of an international existence will be the way to harvest what we have sown during more than twenty years.

24 June: When, in 1959, Malraux, moved by the homelessness of our company, asked us to create the Théâtre de France, Gaullism was humanistic and progressive. It was the Gaullism of decolonization, of nationalization, of votes for women and of Free France. During nine years we have managed to create, in the jungle of dramatic and literary art, a kind of 'reserve' from which hate was excluded.

In this way we have managed to make live side by side a fauna so varied as to include Claudel, Genet, Beckett, Molière, Ionesco, Racine, Duras, Nathalie Sarraute, directors like Blin, Béjart, Bourseiller, Lavelli, young playwrights like Billetdoux, Schéhadé, Vauthier, etc. The whole of life at liberty. It would have been possible to organize safaris.

Add to that the Théâtre des Nations, that meeting place for the highest Shakespearean traditions and those of the Far East – Noh, Kabuki, Bunraku – with the most modern experiments: Grotowski, the Living Theatre, Barba and that international research centre which I had set up, this year, with Peter Brook.

It took only the coming of some young poachers, attacking this wild life with their slings, to make the hunters recognized by the law reappear.

Moral: end of the 'reserve'. Let us get back to the forest. Alas, this time I am fifty-eight, and life will become hard. We are going to start again from scratch.

25 June: I get in touch with Jean Richard, with a view to joining up with him and using his circus for four months per year. He likes the idea.

27 June: Reading of *Rabelais* in front of my comrades in the Petit Odéon. Wrote a draft of a letter to Malraux, which I did not send.

1st July: I became aware that, on 15 May, I had felt obscurely that the Théâtre de France had had its day. When it was created, no political consideration came into it. Now, supposing it ought to be continued, there would be a political commitment on the part of whoever took responsibility for it. To remain in agreement with myself, I would be obliged to refuse.

It was really my double who said: 'Barrault is dead.' He meant, obviously, the personage, director of the Théâtre de France, not the human being.

From my notebooks:

Look for a place in which to set up a society for international production, with those who would consent to participate in it with us, in all the countries of the world. A kind of autonomous Théâtre des Nations.

3 July: Visit to the Jean Richard circus. Vendôme.
4 July: Returned to Paris.

Set up a 'house of creations' as one sets up a publishing house, with different 'collections': large format, easel format, mobile format (tours). Find a big production building: studio, costumes and settings workshop, even recordings for T V and cinema (video-cassettes).

5 July : I could hold out no longer : I took in person to the Palais-Royal, rue de Valois, a short letter which I wanted to place on Malraux's desk :

> *Monsieur le Ministre,*
>
> *J'ai l'honneur de solliciter de votre haute bienveillance la faveur d'un entretien privé, qui me permette de parler avec vous de l'avenir du Théâtre de France, de sa troupe et de son directeur. Je tiens à maintenir avec vous, sur le terrain noble, les rapports que nous avons toujours eus.*
>
> *Dans l'espoir d'une réponse favorable, veuillez agréer, Monsieur le Ministre, l'assurance de mes sentiments respectueux et dévoués.*[1]

The ushers who had known me for years, some of them from the time of Jean Zay (1937), welcomed me with great kindness. I met genuine looks.

It was 15.30. I was going out again towards the Cour de Chartres. André Malraux was just getting out of his car. I went over to him.

'*Monsieur le Ministre,* I have just left for you a note I have taken the liberty of addressing to you.'

He moved his head two or three times, looking past me, with an unpleasant smile. He remained silent, turned his back on me and disappeared. It was clear now. That was worth any number of dismissals conveyed through newspapers.

So it was practically over. And yet I still had to wait for nearly two months – in silence.

That same evening, to avoid going over and over in my head the verbal terror from the extreme left and the brutality of the extreme right, and the policy of letting things rot, and, on the 'noble plane', the history of the Théâtre de France, and the sequence of events and how tightly, in such a case, a free man finds himself hemmed in, etc. – I read in Chateaubriand, that exhibitionist of genius, a phrase which would suit Madeleine perfectly : 'A nothing upsets her, but nothing shakes her.'

She at that moment was at Villefranche-sur-Saône, making a film, *Le Diable par le Queue,* by Philippe de Broca. It was a distraction for her. It was providential. I would go from time to time and spend two or three days with her in the Beaujolais.

18 July : Lightning journey to London; objective the Roundhouse, where Peter Brook was at last presenting the results of his work for our Centre International de Recherches du Théâtre des Nations.

At Brown's Hotel, I welcomed our friend the great critic of the *Sunday Times,* Harold Hobson. He is one of the few Englishmen who love Claudel. So I had every possible prejudice in his favour. Besides, he is a sincere friend of France. He was accompanied by a young colleague on his paper. Our con-

---

[1] *Monsieur le Ministre,*

I have the honour to ask your high benevolence for the favour of a private interview, to enable me to discuss with you the future of the Théâtre de France, of its company and of its director. I am anxious to maintain with you, on the *noble plane,* the relations which we have always had.

In the hope of a favourable reply, etc.

versation took place in French – Hobson knows our language well; the young man, on the contrary, understands it imperfectly. After a few moments he departed. Hobson stayed for a long time, and we chatted like real friends.

We separated. That evening I was at a second performance of Peter Brook's, after having done some work myself with his company, demonstrating mime and breathing.

London has an extraordinary vitality. There the insurrection of youth – which is, let us not forget, of world dimensions – was being manifested in an atmosphere of emancipation, far more than of claims.

In Paris, in four weeks, we had lived through the whole of the French Revolution : from the celebrations of the Fédération in '89 to the Terror, and then to Saint-Just. In London, liberty had widened.

20 July : Return to Paris. No answer from Malraux to my letter.

End of July : I joined Madeleine in the Beaujolais, where she was still working on the film. A cure of solitude and reflection.

This period of introspection did me good. Madeleine finished her film. We decided to go and spend several days at Trouville-Deauville. I forced myself to swim the equivalent of two kilometres a day, either in the sea or in a swimming-pool. Swimming and walking are my favourite sports.

We were still there on 25 August when, at last, we received news from M. Raison, the head of the theatre section, who had been at our side on 15 May, when we tried to *'entamer le dialogue'*.

An appointment was made for 28 August at 17.30.

27 August : We attended, with Father Carré, a reading and discussion on Saint Francis of Assisi, in the theatre of the Deauville Casino.

28 August : Paris. Madeleine came with me. M. Raison simply handed us the following letter.

27 Août 1968.

Monsieur,

Au moment où vont être publiés les nouveaux statuts du Théâtre de France, je dois vous informer qu'après vos diverses déclarations, j'estime que vous ne pouvez plus continuer d'assumer la direction de ce théâtre, quelle que soit sa future vocation.

J'ai chargé le directeur du théâtre et des maisons de la Culture d'examiner les problèmes découlant de cette décision.

Veuillez agréer, etc.,

André Malraux [1]

M. Raison was genuinely upset.

---

[1] Monsieur,

At the moment when the new basis for the Théâtre de France is about to be published, I must inform you that, after your various declarations, I consider that you can no longer continue to assume the direction of that theatre, whatever its future function may be.

I have instructed the head of the theatre section and of the Maisons de la Culture to examine the problems resulting from this decision.

Veuillez agréer, etc.,

He showed us an article in the *Sunday Times*, signed by the young man who had, for a brief moment, accompanied my friend Hobson. Apparently this article had ruined everything. I read it, for I had not known of its existence. It dated from the end of July. It contained, clearly, some erroneous statements, or rather confusions. But nothing that could be considered as personal declarations of mine. The pretext, therefore, seems a bit clumsy. Malraux would have done better to send me that letter on 5 July last when he turned his back on me. We would have saved two months.

We thanked M. Raison for his kindness, for his feelings of genuine friendship, and we left.

> *Fear and servitude pervert human nature.* (Rabelais)

And so the 'events of May '68' conclude that part of our life. What makes us suffer, and always will make us suffer, is the waste, the silence, the evasion and, above all, that *contempt*, which I will not allow myself to call cowardice.

A year later, de Gaulle and Malraux were themselves climbing into the tumbril. Mere chance? Destiny according to Æschylus? What matters is to remain in agreement with oneself.

Of the Marigny period, of our tours, of the Théâtre de France period, nothing now was left to us. Twenty-two years annihilated, for the sake of whom? For the sake of what? [1]

FINAL PAUSE
BEAUTIFUL ANOMALIES

History is the depiction of all the dirty *histoires* that men do to each other. While it acquires colour by the exalted deeds of the military – the shadows being reserved for the poverty of the peoples – the charm of the picture is also sometimes heightened by beautiful anomalies. These are the moments when law and convention, when the 'screens' of the Pharisees, are by-passed by Imagination.

Monseigneur de Harlay, Archbishop of Paris, refusing to let Molière be buried in consecrated ground, is the Law. Louis XIV finding a way round so that Molière could be buried there all the same is a 'beautiful anomaly', and this one detail does him more honour than all his conquests.

Michelangelo was painting the Sistine Chapel. Julius II came to pay him a visit, and Michelangelo, disturbed, behaved as if he was not there. The Bishop in attendance said to the Pope: 'Excuse him, Holy Father, those people are boors, who know nothing but their trade!' And the Pope broke his stick on the back of his Bishop: 'You are the boor!'

'Beautiful anomaly' – there you have the Renaissance.

---

[1] That ordeal did, on the other hand, show us where our true friends were. There were many. I think especially of the dignified and firm behaviour of Roger Blin.

Rabelais being excommunicated by the Catholics and cursed by the Protestants is convention. But his managing to slip between two condemnations to the stake, thanks to the connivance of Cardinal du Bellay, is a beautiful anomaly.

André Malraux, defending in the Assemblée Nationale the epic of poverty and death written by the poet-anarchist Jean Genet, will go down to history as a 'beautiful anomaly', to be placed, later on, to the credit of a humanist government.

Those for whom beautiful anomalies make their appearance are men called Villon, Rabelais, La Fontaine, Sade, Baudelaire, Verlaine, Rimbaud, Artaud, etc.

The *poète maudit*, the Shakespearean clown and the black sheep have been created to counterbalance the insurmountable Tedium of Convention and Law.

And so the Théâtre de France period should be considered, in the history of the theatre, as a beautiful anomaly. Starting off with Claudel's *Tête d'Or* – a play of rebellion, a symbol of the thrust of youth – it ended on that same Tête d'Or hugging the Sun in his arms.

When I have no more strength I will stop. (Antigone)

So on 28 August I was dismissed from my post. One week later, on 5 September, I visited the Elysée-Montmarte and came to an immediate understanding with its director, Roger Delaporte.

On 30 September, having completed the contract of association with the Elysée-Montmarte at 15.00, I signed all the actors' contracts, two hours later, in our flat – the flat which in 1946 had seen the birth of the company. On the first of October the rehearsals of *Rabelais* began.

At the time of *Numance* I hired a studio in the building of the Théâtre des Champs-Elysées, I now hired a studio in the building of the Gaumont Cinema. As at the time of *As I Lay Dying*, I found myself once more in the same block as the Théâtre de l'Atelier. I renewed contact with the Café de la Poste where, more than thirty years before, I used to go and drink coffee with Decroux. I returned to the *Bon Bock*, in the rue Dancourt. I revisited the paths of my footsteps over the whole of the hill of Montmartre, where the smell of fried potatoes is the incense of the quarter.

The 'horses of light', on their feet again, were being carried along by *Desire Renewed*.

At the same time, on 29 September, I made an agreement, with the Ligue de l'Enseignement, for the Récamier to become our social centre and to shelter the little that was left to us.

From my notebooks:
   After *Rabelais*, I want to be able to form that international centre of theatre research, French section, which I set up last year as part of the Théâtre des Nations. This and the international cartel are the points which interest me. We will shut the house, cover the stalls with a huge

platform, and turn the place into a sanctuary of theatre research. Not every Tom, Dick and Harry shall come in. It will be a closed studio.[1]

What guide could have indicated to me all those immediate reactions, if not life itself?

NO PAUSE: RABELAIS

In my room, on the wall, I have a blackboard. At night I sometimes write a few words on it in chalk, either to note an impression, or as a peg to hang thoughts on. So, in September 1959, when I had to organize the Théâtre de France, I wrote this line from Racine (it is still there): *'Parmi les loups cruels prêts à me dévorer'* (Among the cruel wolves spoiling to feast on me). In fresh chalk, dating from 1968, there is: 'Rabelais, my father now I am fifty-eight.'

And yet, when I was at the start of my work, I had not thought of him. The longing to do a show based on Rabelais came to me, as I have said, because of *Les Paravents*. To reply to all the Putherbes, to all the *enragés*: sacroshams, creeping Jesuses, gullygutses, church vermin, mealymouths, devourers of men's substance who, with Genet as pretext, had as good as called in the police to have us banned and arrested. Just as, four centuries earlier, they did to the priest of Meudon. All the *voyeurs*, the chicken-arses, the hypocritical sanctimonious sorbonnizing right-thinkers, had made me determined to stage the arse-wiping scene.

What had at first been a mere riposte, even a schoolboy joke, quickly became a re-cognition.

Rabelais had always been, to me, a special favourite. It was like coming upon the Ancestor again.

Every time I get my teeth into him, my mouth becomes filled with such a juice, my blood receives such a fresh flow, my spinal column such a sap, that I utter 'horrific' cries of enthusiasm. He is Childhood embracing life with both arms. He is made of the very soil of France. He is at one and the same time regional, French and universal. Everything I would like to be.

In the garden of France – Touraine is that – he gave himself up to bouts of cosmic vagabondage. In the Chinon cellar, between two gulps of 'September broth', he thought of interplanetary voyages. The oracle of the divine bottle is in Cathay (North China). He is Jacques Cartier and Copernicus melted together with Gutenberg in a winegrower's temperament.

He is a tree. His roots suck the clay and dung. His trunk is stiff like a phallus. His foliage is encyclopaedic (the word is his). His flourishing reaches the sky and touches God.

He did not live withdrawn upon himself, he is turned towards the World. Given to scoffing, an eternal student, stubborn, cunning, nomadic, his temperament inclined him, for all his fidelity to traditions, to take sides with those who were fighting for new ideas.

[1] Which is what will happen this year, three years later.

And, unlike so many others, he paid cash. Caught between Roman repressive orthodoxy and the progressive fanaticism of the Protestant 'gladiators', he chose the most uncomfortable side – that of *Tolerance*.

He struggled desperately for universal reconciliation. Therefore he had to be a fugitive in order to escape torture and the stake. That was his 'navigation'.

A *divine thing, not to take and receive, but to enlarge and to give.*

He preaches exchange. He lends, he gives, he borrows. His laughter is a healing elixir against fear and loneliness, through gaiety, consolation and the relief he provides. In his soul, he is 'theatre'. And finally, he represents *the free man*.

Fais ce que voudras parce que gens sont libres. And so he is Life itself, in the biological sense. *Conservative* through his mania for knowledge and his earthy ancestry. *Revolutionary* through his scientific imagination and his passion for being more. *Prince of himself* through the freedom of his choices.

He is the man who comes nearest to the living cell which our scientists today describe with such skill. His vital ternary is total and revolves about itself perfectly.

He is a whole man. His glandular system is complete. His belly (gaster), his heart, his head and his double – who, by reflecting life and death, supplies him with humour and joy – work like a well serviced engine.

Rabelais is my oxygen. He, though I did not know it, was the one who would assure the continuity of my personal trajectory. In my unconscious search for a Father, which had made me choose a Dullin and a Claudel, it was inevitable that, one day, I should ask to be adopted by Rabelais.

Does he not contain in him that other ternary which will prove to have dictated, throughout my life, my conduct as a whole: the peasant – the Dominican – the libertarian?

And so, once again – after having been attracted only by the odd detail, by Genet, the absurd moralizers and the arse-wiping – I had begun, and continued for the last three years, to garner a seed which was fertilizing me, regenerating me, engendering me. Who could have foreseen that, three years later, this nourishment would be such a support to me? The faculty of perception in our secret radars is very mysterious, no doubt a function of the unconscious. Unless it be the *sixth sense*.

Technically, he was providing me with the elements for a new manifesto, to follow up those of 1935 (*As I Lay Dying*), 1943 (*Le Soulier de Satin*), 1946 (*Le Procès*), and 1953 (*Christophe Colomb*), etc.

Theatre in the state of being born, through language as well as through bodily expression. The style of the strolling player. Close relations between actors and spectators. The joy of the body and the joy of the spirit. The carnal faculty of touching the mysteries of life. *Breaking out of one's own circle* by an exaltation and enlargement of soul. And that ineffable feeling of primitive charity which had driven me, beginning in childhood, to rush towards *human beings*, all the human beings on earth.

The rehearsals were difficult. The Gaumont studio was not always practical. At the Elysée-Montmartre there were serious problems to be solved, among them acoustical difficulties. Whenever it rained, the glass roof made a noise like a drum. We had to cover the roof with fibreglass and at the last moment add a canopy. Our voices were worn out. We had launched ourselves into a fresh folly. Would it work out as well as the others had? This one seemed to be reaching the limits of the possible.

The style of Rabelais, being unfamiliar, threw some of our actors. Others, after the May events, were dreaming of new approaches to work, and this went against discipline. Some had contracted the virus of tyrannical Trade Unionism. But the faith of the majority won the day, and Rabelais's vigour did the rest.

The coming of Michel Polnareff galvanized our group. The presence of the dancer Valérie Camille brought joy and fantasy. Matias was making the costumes, which succeeded perfectly: no easy job. Our company was more alive than ever.

Of the Théâtre de France company, there were eighteen of us left: Maiène, Pierre Bertin, J.-P. Granval, Alric, Régis Outin, Santarelli, Gallon, etc. From the administrative and technical team: Gilles Bernard, J.-P. Mathis, Yvette (our wardrobe mistress) and Simone Ben Mussa had remained faithful to us for more than ten years. My beloved Léonard, scenting adventure, reappeared on the surface.

Authentic talents had joined us. Virlojeux, outstanding in his truthfulness and style. Audoubert, (a splendid Frère Jean des Entommeurs), J-P. Bernard, Dora Doll, Jorris and some young ones 'with a will to them'. Young girls whose bodies had wit – good actresses and irresistible dancers.

For me the only shadow was that there was no part for Madeleine. Our good 'little horse of light', the real one, was then having a triumph of her own on another Paris hill, the hill of Chaillot – in the TNP, where she created L'Amante Anglaise by Marguerite Duras.

From our first contact with the audience, we fell into a knockabout style, the style of the eternal theatre.

Friday, 13 December. Public preview. The house was full – not only were the eleven hundred seats occupied, but there were five to six hundred people standing at the back. Happy human communication, joy, insolence, youth and health won the audience. That evening we all witnessed the rebirth of our theatre.

14 December. Official first performance. When we were still at the Théâtre de France, I had planned the opening of *Rabelais* for mid-November: in fact the May events had made us only a month late.

We were helped by an excellent, encouraging press. Unquestionably we were living *an event*.

(To reveal a secret: we had scraped the bottom of every drawer to make this folly a reality, and had committed ourselves far beyond that. It was really 'all or nothing'.)

Even so, in spite of the enthusiasm of the young, the attention our ordeals had attracted, the curiosity of the public and the favourable press, it took us a good two weeks to win through.

Madeleine at the T N P and we at the Elysée-Montmartre were winning a victory, undeniably: nonetheless, financially, as regards *Rabelais*, the difficulties were all too clear – the show was expensive and the immediate results seemed to me so-so.

From my notebooks:

24 December: Double moral success for Madeleine and us. But administrative difficulties. Some of the actors want to leave us as early as February. On 27 December I shall carry out the election of three Union delegates. Bitterness. We are fighting battles on all flanks. For the last few days I have been doing the accounts. Every time I do this, I break out in a sweat. This morning, to the Bank to see where I stood. The essential is to be able to pay the actors and the State taxes.

Night of 25-26 December: This Christmas Day I was dreading has been marvellous. Enormous success. In spite of the financial difficulties, tonight I am full of hope. But what a trade ! ! !

30 December: The queue at the box office never stops. Nor does the telephone. Everyone is up to the eyes. As we are working in tiny rooms, one doesn't know where to look for a place to sit and work. It is Bohemia, a real caravan life. I am fighting an attack of 'flu. I sleep on the floor. Little time for thinking. I was forgetting to say that, after consultation with the actors, we shall do no tour, except Rome. They prefer staying at home – bourgeois characters, or employee souls. Besides, practically all of them are married, with children. What has become of the artist's life? [*sic-sic-sic*, it is there in my notebook !]

2 in the morning: Who would have told me, ten days ago, that they would be bringing extra chairs into the Elysée-Montmartre? The actors who wanted to leave have told me they were staying. Tours are coming back to the surface.

The event is confirmed. In short, this evening: it is *rosy*. [End of notebook.]

The success was complete. We played two seasons running. Who was the first to visit us? Laurence Olivier, from London. *The friend*, arrived to set the seal on our effort in the eyes of the world. He was inviting us, officially, to the British National Theatre; as in the past, in 1945, he had been invited by France to the Comédie Française.

I shall never forget this support he gave us. As usual, he received us in princely fashion. We played for two weeks. At the same time, at the Royal Court, Madeleine was giving performances of Beckett's *Oh! les Beaux Jours* and Marguerite Duras' *L'Amante Anglaise*. On both sides of the Thames the Londoners offered us the support of their warm friendship.

We moved on to Berlin, to the Akademie der Kunst. Two adjoining theatres were thrown into one by opening a partition: in this way the two stages, back to back, were made into a single one, and we were able to act as though in the round. The students demonstrated in order to get in. The security services stopped them. We got them in over the roof. 'The black sheep' were reuniting human beings across the routines of 'order'.

The life of man on earth divides into three: geographical countries, peoples and governments. Distrust these last – they often prevent you from communicating with peoples and getting to know the countries.

Rabelais, in the past, had gone to Rome three times, under the protection of Cardinal du Bellay, that humanist prelate who had the virtue of constancy. It was from one of these journeys that he imported the plane-tree into France. When my eyes light on a plane-tree, I address a thought to Rabelais. Now we gave him a fourth journey to Rome.

Thanks to my old friend the painter Balthus, who was director of the Académie de France in Rome, and to the protection afforded by His Excellency Etienne Burin des Roziers,[1] we put up in the gardens of the Villa Medici an Italian big top, under which we acted *Rabelais* for the *Premio di Roma*, with our friends the Guierreris as our management. It is one of the finest theatrical memories. During the whole week the big top never ceased to be filled, and in the course of the last day we turned away five thousand persons. For anyone who knows the Roman playgoer, with his reputation as a surfeited connoisseur, that is a unique fact. I enjoyed listening, from the terrace in the gardens of the Villa Medici, to Rabelais airing, in the city of the 'Popehawk', his libertarian and heretical reflections based on tolerance and love for Christ.

From Rome we flew, via Milan and Paris, to San Francisco and the University of California at Berkeley. Once again, it was folly. We had no subsidy from the French government. Starting with the risk of a deficit of thirty thousand dollars, we managed, thanks to success, to lose only three thousand.

On the University campus we were to perform in the Zellerbach theatre (2,500 seats), one of the few modern theatres to have kept the atmosphere of the old theatres.

On our arrival: a transport strike. With the complicity of a remarkable man, Travis Bogard, director of the theatre departments of the University of California, we went off by lorry and, also with the highly American complicity of the customs services, improvised a hold-up: in the middle of the night our stuff set off on its way to the theatre.

We did not spare ourselves. The very next day, we went on. The students, the most rejectionist in the world, were there – they had just been giving pop concerts on the campus.

We were to perform six times. After the fourth performance, tragedy. Students of Kent University had been killed by members of the National Guard.

[1] Geoffroy de Courcel and Etienne Burin des Roziers, French ambassadors and close to General de Gaulle, supported us courageously in this difficult ordeal. My gratitude to them will never be effaced.

Result: general strike. Clashes, tear gas bombs, Molotov cocktails. It was starting all over again.

The Chancellor of Berkeley closed the campus. Our last performance was going to be cancelled. Then something extraordinary happened: police and students, each from their own side, decided on a four hours' truce ... to 'allow *Rabelais* to express itself' !

We were given authorization to act. We merely had to begin on time, shorten the interval and be out before midnight.

I asked that the doors should be opened to all, and it was among four thousand students, in that place whose capacity was only two thousand five hundred, that we performed *Rabelais*. The most subtle shades met with most refined understanding. It was an unforgettable moment.

A people that can react in that way is one of the most authentic in the world. At a distance of four centuries, the student Rabelais was winning the assent of four thousand students of Berkeley, California. When the moment of the creation of the Abbey of Thélème arrived, we dressed ourselves, extempore, in Berkeley jerseys. It was a unique moment of the victory of the spirit, of the supremacy of human intelligence: the human heart was taking off like a rocket. If invited tomorrow, I would return to Berkeley as to a place of election.

Molière has given us the feeling for happy dénouements – quick and unforeseen. It shows that he is a free man.

I shall therefore stop there, on that sensation of youth, naïve perhaps, but alive with an intact faith.

I have the impression that I have shovelled the trajectories of my life on to you, higgledy-piggledy. Perhaps I ought to have respected the conventions: presented you with either a recital of anecdotes, or else a summary of my thoughts. I came to think, as I was writing, that the anecdotes would have given my experiences too superficial a tone, and that the thoughts might have appeared too austere. It was for the sake of lightness that I decided to mix the lot together.

Do we not live every day on several levels at the same time?

As I reread these extracts from my life, I notice that I weep much too much, that I do an exaggerated amount of wondering, that my resentment against the critics and the intellectuals is uselessly repetitive, and that my distrust of psychoanalysts possibly hides 'complexes' I am unaware of. This is clearly a fault. Should I not bear in mind La Fontaine's advice, when he tells us: 'One should always leave the reader with something to do'?

Well, no! I have been as restrained as I could. The truth is that I should weep much more, that I should marvel much more, I should suffer much more from meeting with obstacles that prevented me from getting close to human beings or discouraged them from responding to our appeal. As for the unconscious, it is our saviour, our juice. To spend, now and then, a night dancing is worth any amount of psychoanalysis.

That propensity to go into ecstasies or sink into despair comes from the damnable awareness which has been given to me and has made me a double person. Because of it I live and, at the same instant, am a member of life's audience.

Can I help marvelling at feeling myself live? How can I help howling with grief at the idea that this life might be taken away from us?

I am not at all sure, really, that each of us does not secretly keep in his heart a small child, one who also is conscious and doubled, who either sobs or exults. But we dare not admit it, for fear of ridicule.

> *And, so saying, cried like a cow; but all of a sudden laughed like a calf.*
> (Rabelais)

Let us conclude: please do not see in this book the work of a writer.

In producing it, in the midst of my daily tasks, I have had to 'rush to catch the post'. Please remember that, right at the beginning, I confided to you three of my principal mottoes:

'Badly, but quickly.'
'About man, by a man, for man.'
'Feel passion for it all and cling to nothing.'

To be continued...

if God, or if destiny according to Æschylus, or if Moses, or if the Buddha, or if 'the Sword and the Mirror', or if ... or if ...

or if *life*, above all, is willing.

12 October – 21 December 1971

Index

Figures in italic refer to illustrations

334